Decision Technologies for Financial Engineering

PROGRESS IN NEURAL PROCESSING

Series Advisors

Alan Murray *(University of Edinburgh)*
Lionel Tarassenko *(University of Oxford)*
Andreas S. Weigend *(Leonard N. Stern School of Business, New York University)*

Vol. 1: Neural Networks: The Statistical Mechanics Perspective
Eds. Jong-Hoon Oh, Sungzoon Cho & Chulan Kwon

Vol. 2: Neural Networks in Financial Engineering
Eds. Apostolos-Paul Refenes, Yaser Abu-Mostafa, John Moody & Andreas Weigend

Vol. 3: Parallel Implementation of Backpropagation Neural Networks on Transputers: A Study of Training Set Parallelism
by S. Saratchandran, N. Sundararajan & S.-K. Foo

Vol. 4: Analogue Imprecision in MLP Training
by Peter J. Edwards & Alan F. Murray

Vol. 5: Applications of Neural Networks in Environment, Energy, and Health
Eds. Paul E. Keller, Sherif Hashem, Lars J. Kangas & Richard T. Kouzes

Vol. 6: Neural Modeling of Brain and Cognitive Disorders
Eds. James A. Reggia, Eytan Ruppin & Rita Sloan Berndt

Vol. 8: Neural Networks: Best Practice in Europe
Eds. Bert Kappen & Stan Gielen

Progress in Neural Processing • 7

Decision Technologies for Financial Engineering

Proceedings of the Fourth International Conference on Neural Networks in the Capital Markets (NNCM '96)

Pasadena, California, USA 20–22 November 1996

Editors

Andreas S. Weigend
Leonard N. Stern School of Business, New York University

Yaser Abu-Mostafa
California Institute of Technology

A.-Paul N. Refenes
London Business School

World Scientific
Singapore • New Jersey • London • Hong Kong

Published by

World Scientific Publishing Co. Pte. Ltd.
P O Box 128, Farrer Road, Singapore 912805
USA office: Suite 1B, 1060 Main Street, River Edge, NJ 07661
UK office: 57 Shelton Street, Covent Garden, London WC2H 9HE

British Library Cataloguing-in-Publication Data
A catalogue record for this book is available from the British Library.

DECISION TECHNOLOGIES FOR FINANCIAL ENGINEERING

ISBN 981-02-3123-7
ISBN 981-02-3124-5 (pbk)

Printed in the United Kingdom.

FOREWORD

YASER S. ABU-MOSTAFA
Department of Electrical Engineering and Computer Science
California Institute of Technology 136-93
Pasadena, CA 91125, USA
yaser@cs.caltech.edu

This volume contains selected papers that were presented at the *Fourth International Conference on Neural Networks in the Capital Markets* (NNCM-96) held at the Ritz-Carlton hotel in Pasadena, California on November 21-22, 1996. NNCM is an annual, fully refereed, research meeting sponsored by the California Institute of Technology and the London Business School. It is an independent meeting with no commercial sponsorship of any kind. To reflect the broadening scope of the meeting, we will adopt the new title *Computational Finance* starting 1997.

The papers in this volume were presented by academicians and practitioners from both the neural networks side and the capital markets side. The areas of the papers include price forecasting for stocks, bonds, commodities, and foreign exchange; asset allocation and risk management; volatility analysis and pricing of derivatives; cointegration, correlation, and multivariate data analysis; credit assessment and economic forecasting; statistical methods, learning techniques, and hybrid systems.

I would like to thank the members of the organizing committee for their efforts in refereeing the papers, and especially Andreas Weigend for his efforts in editing this volume. We hope that this publication will help establish the fast-growing field of computational finance beyond the reach of NNCM itself.

Yaser S. Abu-Mostafa, Chair, NNCM-96

INTRODUCING THE VOLUME: DECISION TECHNOLOGIES FOR FINANCIAL ENGINEERING

ANDREAS S. WEIGEND
Department of Information Systems
Leonard N. Stern School of Business, New York University
44 West Fourth Street, MEC 9-74, New York, NY 10012, USA
aweigend@stern.nyu.edu
www.stern.nyu.edu/~aweigend

YASER S. ABU-MOSTAFA
Department of Electrical Engineering and Computer Science
Caltech 136-93, Pasadena, CA 91125, USA
yaser@cs.caltech.edu

A.-PAUL N. REFENES
Department of Decision Science
London Business School
Regents Park, London, NW1 4SA, UK
prefenes@lbs.ac.uk

This volume contains a subset of the papers that were presented at the *Fourth International Conference on Neural Networks in the Capital Markets* (NNCM-96). The papers presented at the conference had been fully refereed by three reviewers. The papers presented here are a subset of the conference papers, selected by the editors of this volume after the conference, in order to ensure the highest level of quality. By reducing the number of papers, each paper could be more detailed, in comparison to the proceedings of NNCM-95.[a]

This volume is organized into four parts:

- Decision technologies (including trading systems and execution issues);
- Risk management;
- Statistical learning for financial problems;
- Foreign exchange trading and analysis.

[a] *Neural Networks in Financial Engineering* (Proceedings of the *Third International Conference on Neural Networks in the Capital Markets*, NNCM-95), edited by A.-P. N. Refenes, Y. Abu-Mostafa, J. Moody and A. Weigend. World Scientific, Singapore, 1996.

1 DECISION TECHNOLOGIES

The ten papers in Part 1 all address issues that go beyond simple predictions towards making decisions and formulating trading strategies. **Choey and Weigend** introduce a nonlinear neural network that learns to optimizes the Sharpe ratio (risk-adjusted excess returns of a strategy, expressed in units of its standard deviation) and back-test its performance on the German equity index DAX (Deutscher Aktien Index). **Moody and Wu** describe a trading and portfolio system that uses reinforcement learning and takes transaction costs, market risk, and taxes into account. **Bengio** also optimizes financial utility and shows results on a portfolio of stocks traded on the Toronto Stock Exchange. **Kil and Shin** propose a hybrid approach that includes hidden Markov models, genetic algorithms and neural networks and apply this approach to trading S&P500 futures. **Mahfoud, Mani and Reigel** combine neural networks and genetic algorithms to help solve the problem of stock selection and apply it to active portfolio management. **Atiya** uses neural networks to design time-variable stop losses and profit objectives, and illustrates their performance on 200 companies on the New York Stock Exchange. **Baram** introduces a soft classifier that allows for indecision when the information is insufficient to make a trade, and compares its performance to nearest neighbor methods on ten stocks. **Szeto, Chan and Cheung** present a new tool, based on simulated annealing, in comparison to CART (Classification and Regression Trees) on equity indices from the United States, Hong Kong, Korea and Thailand. **Gutjahr** describes a live future trading system at the DTB (Deutsche Terminbörse Frankfurt) that is based on a mixture model. Part 1 concludes with a paper by **Levitt** that describes a decision support system aimed at day traders and presents results on six months of high-frequency foreign exchange data.

2 RISK MANAGEMENT

Part 2 consists of six papers pertaining to the areas of market risk, credit risk and transaction risk. **Magdon-Ismail and Abu-Mostafa** show that a maximum likelihood framework leads to a systematic under-prediction of risk and compute a correction factor that depends on the sample size. **Pedersen** carefully evaluates neural networks for financial diagnosis of bankruptcy prediction, bond rating, and loan decisions. **Bassi and Hernandez** explore different network architectures including a mixture of experts for credit risk scoring, and present results based on a real-world example of a major bank.

Cottrell et. al. use a Monte Carlo on a Kohonen map to generate long-term scenarios, difficult in the original RiskMetrics framework introduced by J. P. Morgan. **Klenin** outlines a probabilistic approach for risk analysis of timed price forecasts, and uses it on a portfolio of 34 stocks. In the last paper of Part 2, **Skurikhin and Surkan** apply Bayesian neural networks to bond rating.

3 STATISTICAL LEARNING FOR FINANCIAL PROBLEMS

Part 3 presents ten papers that apply new ideas from areas such as machine learning, computational statistics, and applied mathematics to problems in finance. The methods range from hybrid models and portfolios of models to stochastic differential geometry and cumulant-based approaches. The applications include option pricing, interest rates term structure, and time series forecasting, both on daily and on intra-day (tick-by-tick) data. In addition, note the emergence of papers that address the important area of testing procedures for neural network model identification and specification.

Addressing the modified Black model's biases of moneyness and of time to maturity, **Lajbcygier and Flitman** compare non-parametric techniques for option pricing and report that neural networks outperform projection pursuit and kernel regression. **Bolland and Burgess** exploit volatility mispricing based on discrepancies between implied and actual market volatility, and find that using both multivariate data and non-linear techniques significantly improves the accuracy of the predictions. For bond futures, **Connor, Bolland and Lajbcygier** track movements of the interest rates term structure on a tick-by-tick basis, showing how less frequently observed elements can be inferred from the more heavily traded parts of the term structure. **Taranenko and Barnes** use stochastic differential geometry to derive equations for the evolution of the term structure of interest rates that incorporate the Heath-Jarrow-Morton model and provides self-consistency and completeness. **Refenes, Zapranis and Utans** present a framework for specification tests for model identification and input selection. **Zapranis, Utans and Refenes** apply this framework to asset allocation and show the presence of nonlinear relationships between the economic variables and asset class returns. **Burgess** addresses the problem of model selection by combining a portfolio of complementary models and applies this approach to a set of daily European equity indices. **Zimmermann and Weigend** focus on predicting dynamic variables (such as derivatives and curvatures on different time scales) that can be combined to give predictions based on different information sets, and show on the

DAX index that the learning behavior of such a network is more stable and less prone to overfitting than standard approaches. **Deco, Neuneier and Schürmann** present a new approach to the problem of non-stationary time series by selecting segments of the data using a non-parametric cumulant based statistical approach. **Mason and Badii** propose a short-term/long-term functional decomposition to account for different dynamics on different time scales.

4 FOREIGN EXCHANGE TRADING AND ANALYSIS

The last part consists of six papers that analyze and predict currency exchange rates. **Lawrence, Giles and Tsoi** approach the old problem of predicting the sign of tomorrow's return from a new perspective by using a symbolic representation from a self-organizing map, and show the improvement on the benchmark set of five daily currencies. **Moody and Wu** analyze high-frequency data with state space models assuming random walks, random trends, and fractional Brownian motion. **Utans, Holt and Refenes** apply principal component analysis to hourly exchange rates and claim that the principal components reveal the main factors driving the market. **Anders, Hann and Nakaheizadeh** investigate the amount of nonlinearities contained in daily USD/DEM data. **Leung, Cheung and Xu** exploit the fact that foreign exchange quotes are quantized for predictive regression models. The last paper, by **de la Maza**, describes a simulation of market participants (small speculators, large speculators, hedgers, central banks, and bid/ask traders) defined by several attributes (information set, model set, algorithm set, constraint set, utility function) and shows that the behavior of the simulated currency market resembles the European currency market.

The Appendix summarizes the post-NNCM-96 workshop on teaching. That workshop provided a forum for participants to share their experiences and ideas on teaching the subjects of this conference and other computer intensive data analysis methods that are relevant for solving problems in finance. The volume concludes with an author index and a keyword index.

Andreas S. Weigend — NEW YORK UNIVERSITY STERN Leonard N. Stern School of Business
Yaser S. Abu-Mostafa — California Institute of Technology 1891
A.-Paul N. Refenes — London Business School

Organizing Committee of NNCM '96

Dr. Y. S. Abu-Mostafa, Chairman *(Caltech)*
Dr. A. Atiya *(Cairo University)*
Dr. N. Biggs *(London School of Economics)*
Dr. D. Bunn *(London Business School)*
Dr. M. Jabri *(Sydney University)*
Dr. B. LeBaron *(University of Wisconsin, Madison)*
Dr. A. Lo *(MIT Sloan School)*
Dr. I. Matsuba *(Chiba University)*
Dr. J. Moody *(Oregon Graduate Institute)*
Dr. C. Pedreira *(Catholic Univ. PUC-Rio de Janeiro)*
Dr. A-P. N. Refenes *(London Business School)*
Dr. M. Steiner *(Universitaet Augsburg)*
Dr. A. Timmermann *(UC San Diego)*
Dr. A. S. Weigend *(Stern School of Business, New York University)*
Dr. H. White *(UC San Diego)*
Dr. L. Xu *(Chinese University of Hong Kong)*

CONTENTS

APPENDIX

Part 1
Decision Technologies

NONLINEAR TRADING MODELS THROUGH SHARPE RATIO MAXIMIZATION

MARK CHOEY
Advanced Technology Group
Siemens Nixdorf Information Systems, Inc.,
200 Wheeler Road
Burlington, MA 01803
choey@ix.netcom.com

ANDREAS S. WEIGEND
Department of Information Systems
Leonard N. Stern School of Business, New York University
44 West Fourth Street, MEC 9-74
New York, NY 10012
aweigend@stern.nyu.edu
www.stern.nyu.edu/~aweigend

While many trading strategies are based on price prediction, traders in financial markets are typically interested in risk-adjusted performance such as the Sharpe Ratio, rather than price predictions themselves. This paper introduces an approach which generates a nonlinear strategy that explicitly maximizes the Sharpe Ratio. It is expressed as a neural network model whose output is the position size between a risky and a risk-free asset. The iterative parameter update rules are derived and compared to alternative approaches. The resulting trading strategy is evaluated and analyzed on both computer-generated data and real world data (DAX, the daily German equity index). Trading based on Sharpe Ratio maximization compares favorably to both profit optimization and probability matching (through cross-entropy optimization). The results show that the goal of optimizing out-of-sample risk-adjusted profit can be achieved with this nonlinear approach.

1 Introduction

1.1 Risk-adjusted Performance

A trader ideally would like to have very high profit (return on investment) with very low risk (variability of return). However, there is a fundamental relationship between profit and risk: the higher the expected profit, the greater the risk and similarly, the lower the expected profit, the lower the risk. This paper focuses on the tradeoff between profit and risk (as opposed to profit or risk alone). One way of representing this tradeoff is to combine profit and risk by taking the expected profit and dividing by the risk measure. This single quantity is called the *reward-to-risk* ratio or *risk-adjusted* performance. There are several risk-adjusted measures based on different notions of risk.

Examples are the *Sharpe Ratio* (the focus of this paper), the *Jensen Alpha*, and the *Treynor Ratio* (Hammer, 1991).

1.2 The Sharpe Ratio

The Sharpe Ratio (SR) takes the mean of the excess profit or excess return and divides it by the standard deviation of the excess return (Sharpe, 1970; Sharpe, 1994). The excess return is defined as the rate of return on an asset minus the return available on a baseline asset. The baseline asset is typically a short-term risk-free asset such as the three-month U.S. Treasury Bill. SR expresses the excess return in units of its standard deviation as

$$\mathrm{SR} = \frac{\text{average excess return}}{\text{standard deviation of excess return}} \quad . \tag{1}$$

One important implication of using only the first and second moments of the excess returns is that positive returns and negative returns are treated identically—large positive and negative returns of the same magnitude have the same effect on the risk measure.

SR scales as $\sqrt{T}$ with the time period over which it is measured, where T is the number of periods SR is calculated over. It is common to *annualize* SR which allows for the fair comparison of different training strategies even if the time scales of the strategies are not comparable.

2 Trading Strategy based on the Sharpe Ratio

Traditionally, SR is used to *evaluate* the performance of a trading strategy. In technical trading, strategies are often optimized by minimizing the sum-squared error (SSE) (or a more robust measure such as log(cosh(.)), Zimmermann & Weigend (1997)) of point predictions, and subsequently evaluated with SR or other risk-adjusted measures. Optimizing SSE while evaluating on SR will often lead to results with an optimal out-of-sample SSE, but a sub-optimal SR. A recent example of such a mismatch between the function used in training and the ultimate goal is the paper by Pi & Rögnvaldsson (1996). Here, a network is trained to predict a price, but evaluated on the SR which includes an ad-hoc translation of the price prediction to a trading strategy.

Here we take SR seriously and do not try to predict prices, instead *directly* use SR as our objective function. We assume that there are two asset classes, risky and risk-free, and on period i, the optimal position size or *allocation* for the risky asset is selected to maximize the SR. The allocation, α, takes on continuous values between $[-1, 1]$. If α is positive, a *long* position is taken, and if α is negative, a *short* position is taken. A short position means that the risky asset is borrowed by the trader and sold to an investor with the hope that the asset will fall in price, allowing the trader to repay the borrowed asset at a lower price and make a profit. If $\alpha = 0.5$, 50% of available cash are used to purchase (take a long position) the risky asset; if $\alpha = -0.5$, 50% of the total cash reserves are set aside as collateral for the short position.

3 Architecture

The trading strategy is implemented by using a neural network with multiple inputs, multiple hidden units, and one output. The inputs depend on the problem and are explained below in the specific examples (see Section 6 and 7). The hidden units are tanh sigmoids allowing re–representation of the inputs for the task. The output is also a (-1,1) tanh unit; its activation value, α_i, represents the allocation on day i.

4 Objective Functions

This section discusses the iterative weight updates for the SR objective function and compares it to alternative objectives, focusing on the comparison to the updates for profit maximization. For clarity, we derive the update rule for a single weight, w, to the output unit. As usual, hidden layers require the chain rule for their weight updates, see e.g. Rumelhart *et al.* (1996). The output of the network is the allocation, α_i, for period i.

4.1 Update rule for SR Maximization

For simplicity of language, we assume that we have daily data. Define p_i to be the price of the asset on day i, and x_i to be the *relative price returns* on day i

$$x_i = \ln(p_i) - \ln(p_{i-1}) \approx \frac{p_i - p_{i-1}}{p_i} \quad . \tag{2}$$

Additionally, define the asset *returns* (that includes the position size α_i) to be

$$\xi_i = \alpha_i x_i \quad . \tag{3}$$

The asset return is equal to the position size multiplied by the relative price return of the risky asset on day i. The average daily return, μ, is given by

$$\mu = \frac{1}{N} \sum_{i=1}^{N} \xi_i \tag{4}$$

and the average daily excess return, μ_e, is

$$\mu_e = \mu - k \tag{5}$$

where k is the daily risk-free rate of return and is assumed to be constant over time. The standard deviation of the excess return is given by

$$\sigma = \left\{ \frac{1}{N} \sum_{i=1}^{N} (\xi_i - \mu_e)^2 \right\}^{1/2} . \tag{6}$$

Now, the annualized SR is defined as

$$\mathrm{SR}_T = \sqrt{T}\, \frac{\mu_e}{\sigma} \tag{7}$$

T is the number of trading days per year and we assume that $T = 253$.

To update the weight with gradient ascent, we now need to calculate the gradient by taking the partial derivative of the annualized SR [a] with respect to the weight, w

$$\frac{\partial \mathrm{SR}_T}{\partial w} = \frac{\sqrt{T}}{\sigma^2} \left(\sigma \frac{\partial \mu_e}{\partial w} - \mu_e \frac{\partial \sigma}{\partial w} \right) . \tag{8}$$

Next, we take the partial derivative of μ_e

$$\frac{\partial \mu_e}{\partial w} = \frac{\partial \mu}{\partial w} = \frac{1}{N} \sum_{i=1}^{N} x_i \frac{\partial \alpha_i}{\partial w} \tag{9}$$

where

$$\frac{\partial \alpha_i}{\partial w} = \frac{\partial \alpha_i}{\partial \gamma_i} \frac{\partial \gamma_i}{\partial w} . \tag{10}$$

γ is the "net-input" to the output unit (i.e., the network input multiplied by w) and

$$\frac{\partial \alpha_i}{\partial \gamma_i} = 1 - \alpha_i^2 \tag{11}$$

$$\frac{\partial \alpha_i}{\partial w} = (1 - \alpha_i^2)\gamma_i \tag{12}$$

since $\partial \gamma_i / \partial w = \gamma_i$. The partial derivative of σ with respect to w can be calculated by taking the partial derivative of the variance of the excess returns,

[a] Note that in this case taking the partial derivative of $\log(\mathrm{SR}) = \log(\mu_e) - \log(\sigma)$ is mathematically not possible since μ_e can be negative.

σ^2, and using the relation $\partial\sigma/\partial w = (1/2\sigma)(\partial\sigma^2/\partial w)$ to arrive at $\partial\sigma/\partial w$. Taking the partial derivative of σ^2 we get

$$\frac{\partial\sigma^2}{\partial w} = \frac{2}{N}\left[\sum_{i=1}^{N}(\xi_i - \mu_e)\left(x_i\frac{\partial\alpha_i}{\partial w} - \frac{\partial\mu_e}{\partial w}\right)\right]$$

$$= \frac{2}{N}\left[\sum_{i=1}^{N}\xi_i x_i\frac{\partial\alpha_i}{\partial w} - \sum_{i=1}^{N}\xi_i\frac{\partial\mu_e}{\partial w} - \sum_{i=1}^{N}\mu_e x_i\frac{\partial\alpha_i}{\partial w} + \sum_{i=1}^{N}\mu_e\frac{\partial\mu_e}{\partial w}\right] \quad . \tag{13}$$

From Eq. 9, the last two terms cancel

$$\frac{\partial\sigma^2}{\partial w} = \frac{2}{N}\left[\sum_{i=1}^{N}\xi_i\left(x_i\frac{\partial\alpha_i}{\partial w} - \frac{1}{N}\sum_{j=1}^{N}x_j\frac{\partial\alpha_j}{\partial w}\right)\right] \quad , \tag{14}$$

arriving at $\partial\sigma/\partial w$

$$\frac{\partial\sigma}{\partial w} = \frac{1}{\sigma N}\left[\sum_{i=1}^{N}\xi_i\left(x_i\frac{\partial\alpha_i}{\partial w} - \frac{1}{N}\sum_{j=1}^{N}x_j\frac{\partial\alpha_j}{\partial w}\right)\right] \quad . \tag{15}$$

Substituting $\partial\sigma/\partial w$ (Eq. 15) and $\partial\mu_e/\partial w$ (Eq. 9) into $\partial\mathrm{SR}_T/\partial w$ (Eq. 8)

$$\frac{\partial\mathrm{SR}_T}{\partial w} = \frac{\sqrt{T}}{\sigma N}\left[\sum_{i=1}^{N}x_i\frac{\partial\alpha_i}{\partial w} - \frac{\mu_e}{\sigma^2}\sum_{i=1}^{N}\xi_i x_i\frac{\partial\alpha_i}{\partial w} + \frac{\mu_e}{N\sigma^2}\sum_{i=1}^{N}\xi_i\sum_{j=1}^{N}x_j\frac{\partial\alpha_j}{\partial w}\right] \quad . \tag{16}$$

Interchanging the order of summation on the right side and factoring out $x_i\partial\alpha_i/\partial w$, we get

$$\frac{\partial\mathrm{SR}_T}{\partial w} = \frac{\sqrt{T}}{\sigma N}\sum_{i=1}^{N}\left[1 - \frac{\mu_e}{\sigma^2}\left(\xi_i - \frac{1}{N}\sum_{j=1}^{N}\xi_j\right)\right]x_i\frac{\partial\alpha_i}{\partial w} \quad . \tag{17}$$

With $\mu = \frac{1}{N}\sum_{j=1}^{N}\xi_j$ (Eq. 4) and $\mu = \mu_e + k$ we can define

$$\kappa_i = \frac{\sqrt{T}}{\sigma}\left[1 - \frac{\mu_e}{\sigma}\frac{(\xi_i - (\mu_e + k))}{\sigma}\right] \tag{18}$$

and the SR update rule can be written in its final form as

$$\frac{\partial\mathrm{SR}_T}{\partial w} = \frac{1}{N}\sum_{i=1}^{N}\kappa_i x_i\frac{\partial\alpha_i}{\partial w} \quad . \tag{19}$$

4.2 Comparison to Other Objectives

There are several objective functions we could use to train the network including: SSE, typically used for prediction; cross-entropy, which gives the probability of x_i being positive or negative; and profit, which maximizes the return of the trading strategy.

SSE is given by

$$\sum_{i=1}^{N}(y_i - x_i)^2 \tag{20}$$

where y_i is the prediction and x_i is the price return for day i. SSE is fundamentally different from SR because SSE only tries to minimize prediction errors using pattern-by-pattern supervised learning. A trading strategy based on SSE optimization does not necessarily lead to an optimal SR.

Cross-entropy is given by

$$-\sum_{i=1}^{N}[d_i \ln y_i + (1 - d_i)\ln(1 - y_i)] \tag{21}$$

where $d_i \in \{0, 1\}$. Equation 21 is the familiar cross-entropy of two classes (Buntine & Weigend, 1991; Rumelhart *et al.*, 1996). In order to create a trading strategy, we substitute $\frac{1}{2}(1 + t_i)$ for d_i and $\frac{1}{2}(1 + \alpha_i)$ for y_i and obtain

$$-\sum_{i=1}^{N}\left[\frac{1 + t_i}{2}\ln\frac{1 + \alpha_i}{2} + \frac{1 - t_i}{2}\ln\frac{1 - \alpha_i}{2}\right] \tag{22}$$

where $t_i = \text{sign}(x_i)$ is the target class (i.e., positive or negative price return) and α_i becomes the allocation. Cross-entropy is used as objective function when the goal is to obain the probability of an event (e.g., of the return being positive). It falls into the class of pattern-by-pattern supervised learning. It does not take risk into account.

The objective based on profit maximization we call the *profit objective* is measured by the average daily return, μ (Eq. 4). Like SSE and cross-entropy, the profit objective does not explicitly consider risk. Its update rule is the partial derivative of μ (Eq. 9, repeated here)

$$\frac{\partial \mu}{\partial w} = \frac{1}{N}\sum_{i=1}^{N} x_i \frac{\partial \alpha_i}{\partial w} \quad . \tag{23}$$

Comparing the SR update rule (Eq. 19) and the profit objective update rule (Eq. 23), we notice that they are identical with the exception of κ_i. For this reason, we call κ the *profit objective weight.*

The profit objective weight, κ_i (Eq. 18), controls (on a daily basis) the network's emphasis between maximizing profit and minimizing risk. This is completely determined by sign(κ_i): a positive κ_i causes all of the weights to be modified in the same direction (not the same magnitude) as if training on the profit objective. Conversely, a negative κ_i causes all of the weights to be modified in the opposite direction. Note that the two update rules modify the weights identically if $\kappa_i = 1$.

Analyzing Eq. 18, we can see when the SR update rule maximizes profit and when it minimizes risk. The SR update rule maximizes profit (i.e., κ_i is positive) when the inequality,

$$\frac{\mu_e}{\sigma} \frac{(\xi_i - (\mu_e + k))}{\sigma} < 1 \quad , \tag{24}$$

is satisfied and minimizes risk when it is not satisfied. Eq. 24 consists of two factors: the daily SR (μ_e/σ) and a quantity similar to a test statistic, $(\xi_i - (\mu_e + k))/\sigma$. Focusing on the case when $\mu_e/\sigma > 0$, the SR update rule maximizes profit for day i when:

1. an individual pattern is below the average profit ($\xi_i < \mu$) or

2. the return on day i does not deviate from the average profit by more than $(\xi_i - (\mu_e + k))/\sigma < (\mu_e/\sigma)^{-1}$.

The interpretation of the first point is that while overall, the trading strategy is outperforming the risk-free asset (since $\mu_e/\sigma > 0$), the individual return, ξ_i, is below the average profit, μ. For this pattern, the SR update rule will move in a direction, by adjusting the weights, that will increase ξ_i (i.e., increasing profit) which brings the return closer to μ. Conversely, if ξ_i is above μ, the SR update rule moves in a direction that decreases ξ_i (i.e., decreasing profit, but also decreasing risk). This has the effect of drawing the individual patterns towards μ, forcing the daily returns to be as consistent as possible which, in general, also decreases σ.

The second point is responsible for the continuous increase of μ during the training process. Assuming the daily SR to be 1, ($\mu_e/\sigma = 1$), if the deviation of ξ_i from μ is within one σ, the SR update rule will increase ξ_i (because Eq. 24 will be satisfied). If the deviation is not within one σ, the SR update rule decreases ξ_i. The effect is to increase those ξ_i that are close to μ and to decrease those ξ_i not close to μ. The degree of closeness is determined by $(\mu_e/\sigma)^{-1}$. The larger the SR, the closer ξ_i needs to be to μ in order to satisfy the inequality (Eq. 24).

5 Search

Gradient ascent is performed on the SR to update the network parameters. The SR objective function is a *global* (requires all patterns to compute SR) cost function, but the updates are made *locally* or on a per-pattern basis. Therefore, for the optimal calculation of $\partial \mathrm{SR}_T/\partial w$, we recompute $\{\alpha_i\}$, μ_e, and σ after each pattern since $\{\alpha_i\}$ changes with every update. Thus, μ_e and σ also change every update.

The search procedure used is summarized in the following steps:

1. Calculate the set of allocations, $\{\alpha_i\}$, in response to all patterns by making a feed-forward pass through the network.
2. Calculate μ_e and σ (Eq. 5 and Eq. 6 respectively) using all patterns.
3. Choose a pattern i at random and calculate ξ_i (Eq. 3).
4. Calculate $\partial \mathrm{SR}_T/\partial w$ (Eq. 19) using μ_e, σ, and ξ_i.
5. Update the network weights (Eq. 25).
6. Repeat using the next pattern.

The weights are updated with

$$w = w + \eta \Delta w \tag{25}$$

where

$$\Delta w = \frac{\partial \mathrm{SR}_T}{\partial w} = \kappa_i x_i (1 - \alpha_i^2) \gamma_i \quad . \tag{26}$$

During the course of training we expect σ to typically decrease since we are maximizing the SR. However, in revisiting Eq. 18, we see that the $1/\sigma$ term outside of the brackets contributes to *increasing* the size of Δw as training progresses. This has an effect that is opposite to that of simulated annealing. One variation we tried was to remove this term, which helps to stabilize the magnitude of weight changes as learning progresses.

The computational cost of the weight updates can be reduced by using block-mode training which accumulates gradients for a block of patterns *before* updating the weights. Additionally, rather than computing μ_e and σ for all the patterns, (i.e., after feed-forward passes through the entire training set to produce $\{\alpha_i\}$), a stochastic approximation of μ_e and σ can be employed.

6 Computer-generated Data Experiments

The trading strategy's two key variables are the price return, x, and the allocation, α. The network only has control of the variable α. It is interesting to see the optimal value of α if given *perfect* knowledge of x (i.e., the future values of x are known exactly). The optimal α in this experiment should give us the *best possible* SR we could ever obtain since we have a perfect estimate of the price return for tomorrow, i.e., the data is *noise-free*. The noise-free price return data is our first computer-generated data experiment.

In real-world situations however, we do not have perfect knowledge of x, we can only expect to have an estimate of x that includes error bars or confidence intervals of that estimate. In this more realistic scenario, the framework of determining the expected value (m_i) and the standard deviation (s_i) of a target price return (Nix & Weigend, 1995) could be utilized to provide the network with two separate inputs. The problem is then broken down into two stages: the first is predicting m_i and s_i, and the second is determining α_i based on the predicted m_i and s_i. In this case, what are the values of α as a function of m_i and s_i? Intuitively, the best SR achievable cannot be as large as the value obtained in the noise-free experiment and we would expect α to decrease as s_i increases. The noisy price return data is our second experiment.

The two computer-generated data experiments will help us answer two fundamental questions: 1) the theoretical allocation and 2) the relationship of the allocation and the noise level in the data.

In order to generate the price return data for each day i, we draw x_i from a Gaussian random variable with parameters $\mu = m_i$ and $\sigma = s_i$ where m_i and s_i are themselves drawn from random variables. The mean on day i, m_i, is drawn from a random variable that is uniformly distributed over $(-\sqrt{3}, \sqrt{3})$ for both experiments. The standard deviation on day i, s_i, is set to 0 for the first experiment and is drawn from a random variable uniformly distributed over $(0, 2\sqrt{3})$ for the second experiment.

For both experiments, a 10-tanh hidden unit feed-forward network is trained on three different objective functions: SR, profit, and cross-entropy, and evaluated on four measures: SR, annual profit, annual standard deviation, and cross-entropy. This gives 12 combinations to analyze. 2000 "price returns" are generated and split into four even sets of 500 points for the training set and for each of the three test sets.

6.1 Noise-free data

Fig. 1 shows the training curves for the training and test sets vs. iterations (an iteration is defined as a weight update of a *single* pattern). The training curves

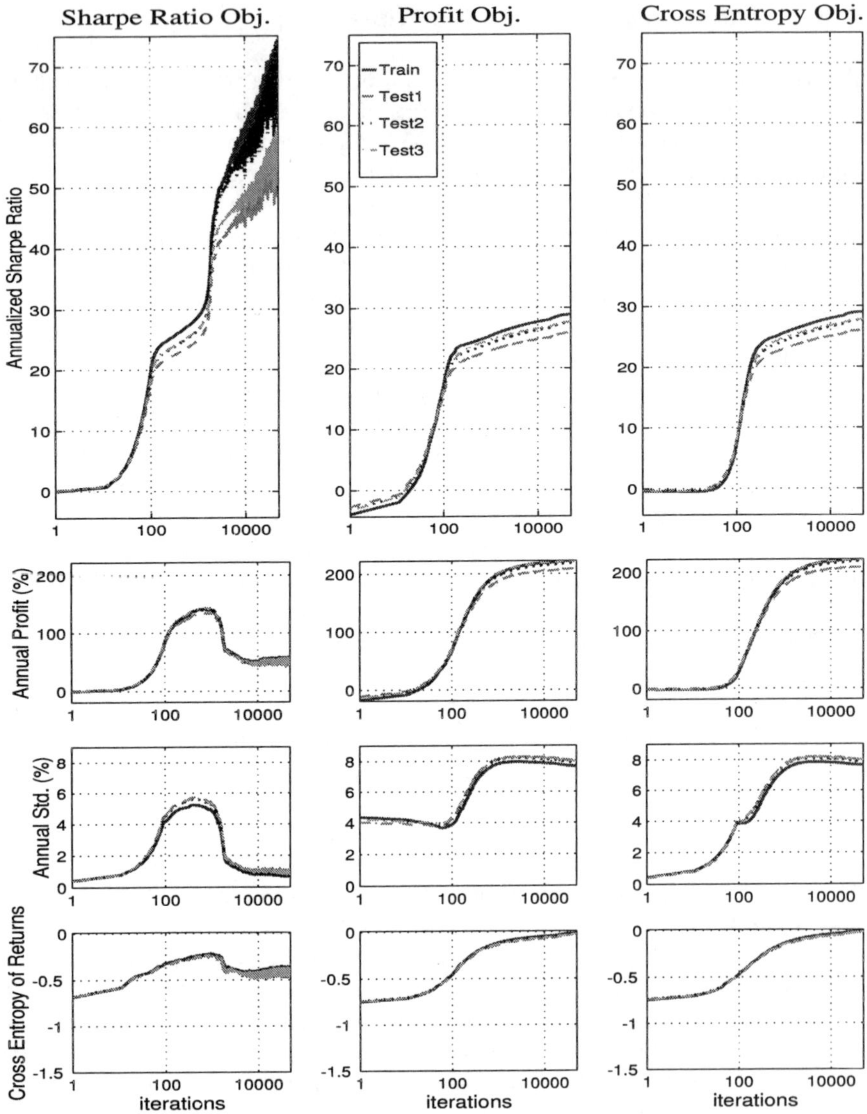

Figure 1: Training curves for the noise-free experiment. Each column of plots show results of *training* on each objective while each row of plots show the *evaluation* of each objective. The SR objective has a much lower annual profit as well as standard deviation (risk-reward tradeoff). In this experiment, the profit and cross-entropy objectives have similar training curves because the optimal α which maximizes their respective objectives are identical.

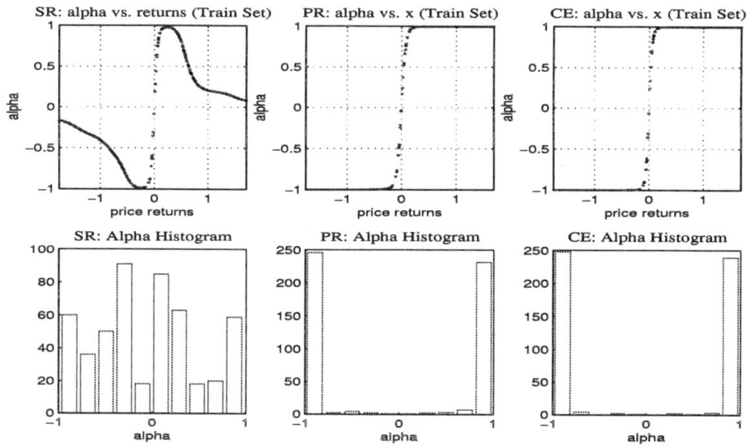

Figure 2: Noise-free data experiment: scatter plots of α vs. x and histograms of α for all objective functions. The top three plots from left to right are the plots for α vs. the price returns, x, for the SR, profit, and cross-entropy objectives while the bottom row of plots are the corresponding histograms of α. The top left plot shows that for the SR objective, abs(α) is a decreasing function of abs(x). The profit and cross-entropy have identical α vs. x plots because of the noise-free data.

for the SR objective are averaged over 10 patterns for better presentation in the plots. The training curves show that the SR objective's SR increases steadily, while its annual profit and standard deviation fluctuates. The profit and cross-entropy objectives' final values for all four evaluation measures are almost identical. Note that for the profit and cross-entropy objectives, the annual profit and annual standard deviation are much higher than the SR's corresponding values. This illustrates the SR objective's inclination to tradeoff large profit for smaller risk. Additionally, note that the cross-entropy obtains its maximum towards the end of training.

Inspection of each of the plots of α with respect to x in Fig. 2 provides insight into the theoretical allocations of each of the objectives when the data is noise-free. The top row of scatter plots shows α plotted versus the price returns x for each of the objective functions and the bottom row of plots shows the histogram of α for each of the objective functions.

For the profit objective, it is no surprise that the optimal $\alpha_i = \text{sign}(x_i)$, because the way to make the most profit is by taking full positions (long or short) based on the sign of x_i. Likewise, for the cross-entropy objective, optimal $\alpha_i = \text{sign}(x_i)$, because cross-entropy maximization implies finding the probability x_i is positive or negative. Since the data is noise-free, the probability is always 1.0 and therefore the α_i equals sign(x_i).

However, for the SR objective, the result is not straight-forward:

- For $x > 0$, α is a decreasing function of x towards 0.
- For $x < 0$, α is an increasing function of x towards 0.

Therefore, the optimal abs(α) decreases as an increasing function of abs(x). This relationship can be seen because the standard deviation is symmetrical: it is indifferent to the sign of the return and reveals one of the intrinsic weaknesses of SR as a performance measure (Sharpe, 1970).

6.2 Noisy Data

In the second experiment, s_i is no longer constant, but now drawn randomly, for each pattern, from a uniform distribution $(0, 2\sqrt{3})$. Both m_i and s_i are given to the network as inputs. How do the values of the respective objective functions compare to the first experiment, and how does α vary with respect to m_i and s_i? Fig. 3 shows the training curves vs. iterations for the second experiment. Similar shapes in the training curves can be observed, however the levels of all objective function values are significantly reduced, attributable to the increased noise level in the price returns.

The top row of scatter plots in Fig. 4 shows α plotted versus x for each of the objective functions, while the bottom row shows the histogram of α for each of the objective functions. The noise in the data smears the solid shapes exhibited in the plots of α vs. x for all of the objectives when compared to their theoretical counterparts in the noise-free experiment. However, the SR objective still has the tendency to take on moderate position sizes compared to the other objectives and is indicative of its risk-minimization behavior. Although the histogram of the profit objective α is still relatively binary, it is now not strictly a function of sign(x), which is caused by the noisy estimates. Although not as extreme as the profit objective, the cross-entropy objective takes larger position sizes relative to the SR objective.

Fig. 5 is a surface and contour plot of the SR objective's optimal α vs. m and s. The trend of increasing s is clear: abs(α) decreases towards 0, indicating that the best action is to take very small positions in the risky asset if s_i is relatively large (i.e., the estimate of x is noisy).

Summarizing the two experiments with computer-generated data, the SR objective performs well at adjusting its position sizes to avoid risk when compared to the other objectives because it is encouraged to decrease α during periods of large abs(x) and large noise levels. For the noise-free case, α decreases as abs(x) increases: profit is sacrificed for lower σ. For the noisy case,

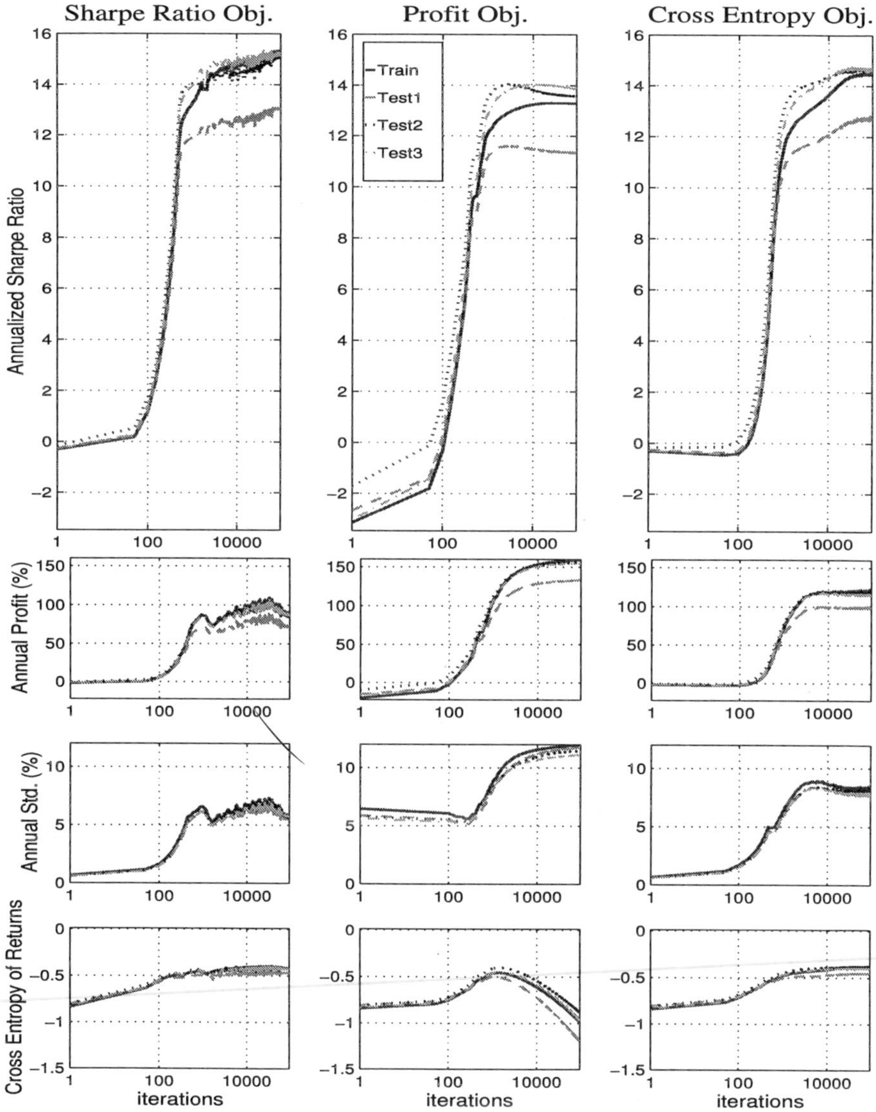

Figure 3: Training curves for the noisy computer generated data. Each column of plots shows results of *training* on each objective while each row of plots shows the *evaluation* of each objective. The SR objective has a higher SR than the profit objective and slightly higher than cross-entropy on all test sets at the end of training. As in the noise-free experiment, the SR objective has the lowest annual profit and standard deviation while the profit objective has the highest annual profit and standard deviation. One iteration denotes the presentation of a single pattern.

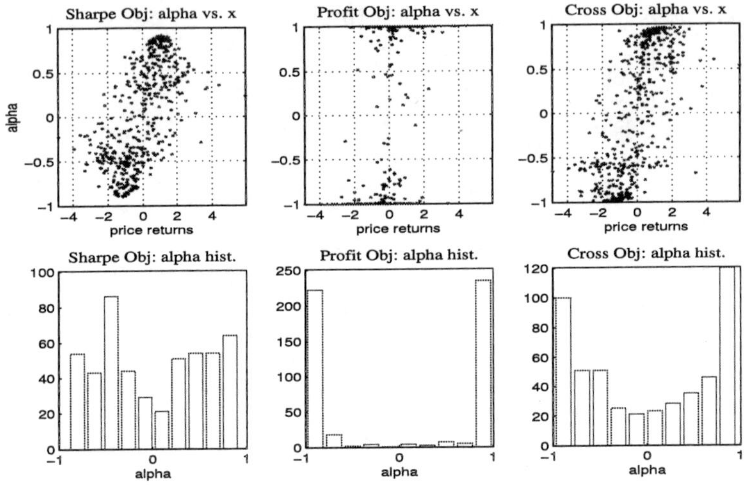

Figure 4: Noisy data experiment: α as a function of x and histograms of α for all objective functions. The top three scatter plots from left to right are the respective optimal α plotted vs. the price returns, x, for the SR, profit, and cross-entropy objectives. The bottom row of plots are the corresponding histograms. All plots of α vs. x have gone through significant changes and have become much more blurred when compared to the noise-free experiment. In the histograms, note that the profit and cross-entropy objectives still have the tendency to take binary position sizes as opposed to the SR objective which takes smaller position sizes to minimize risk.

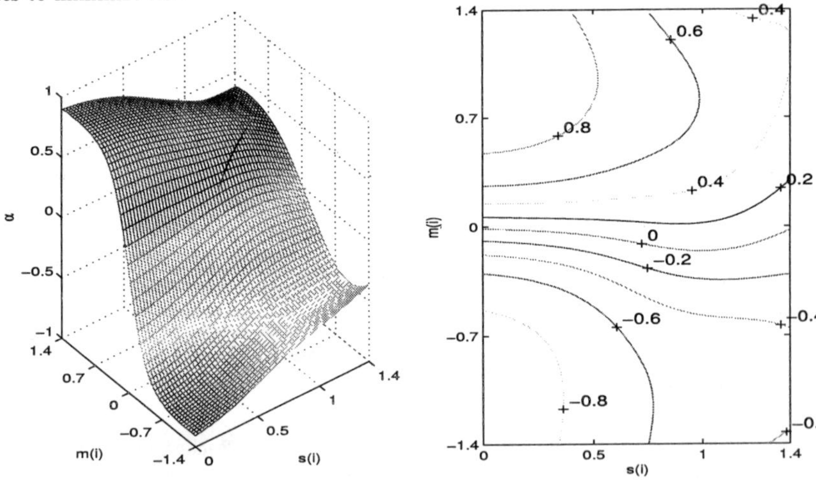

Figure 5: Noisy data experiment surface and contour plot of the SR's optimal α vs. m_i and s_i, the mean and standard deviation of the price returns, x_i. The main feature of the surface plot on the left is that for increasing s_i, abs(α) decreases: the more uncertain the estimate of x, the smaller the position size.

α decreases with increasing noise level: uncertainty in the value of x results in a decreasing position size.

7 Applications to German Stock Index Trading

As an application of our trading strategy to real world data, we use the German Stock Index DAX (Deutscher Aktien Index) from January 14, 1986 through June 29, 1996. Table 7 summarizes how the entire data set is split into a training and three test sets. Test set 2 is used as a tuning or cross-validation set to determine the point during training where the network starts to overfit on the training set.

Set	*Dates*	*Length*
Training set	November 29, 1988 to August 29, 1994	1500 days
Test set 1	December 15, 1987 to November 28, 1988	250 days
Test set 2 (tuning)	August 30, 1994 to August 14, 1995	250 days
Test set 3	August 15, 1995 to July 29, 1996	250 days

Table 2: Partitioning of the DAX data into a training set and three test sets. The dates and size of the data sets are given. Test set 2 is used as the tuning set.

We use 19 inputs: 5 inputs derived from the DAX Indicator index (30 stock index), 3 inputs derived from the DAX Composite (100-200 stocks), 2 inputs derived from the Morgan Stanley German Price Index, 2 inputs from the Dow-Jones Industrial Average, 2 inputs from the U.S. Dollar/Deutsche-Mark exchange rate, 1 input each for the 30-Year U.S. Bond, the price difference of Gold, the price difference of the Nikkei-225 index, and 2 inputs from the Morgan Stanley European Price Index. All networks have 15 tanh hidden units. We train networks with three objective functions: SR, profit, and cross-entropy. The networks are evaluated on four: SR, annual profit, annual standard deviation, and cross-entropy.

Fig. 6 shows the training curves for all objective functions. The three panels in the top row show the annualized SR for all objectives. The bottom set of nine plots shows the annual relative profit in percent, annual relative standard deviation in percent, and cross-entropy values for all objectives. The plots show that the SR objective overfits on the SR at around iteration 40,000. The SR objective is more prone to overfitting when compared to the other objectives.[b]

[b]The phenomenon that overfitting is particularly strong on the quantity that is optimized has been noted in other contexts before, e.g., Weigend (1994) discusses this in a classification context, and Weigend *et al.* (1995) give the example of a regression mixture model.

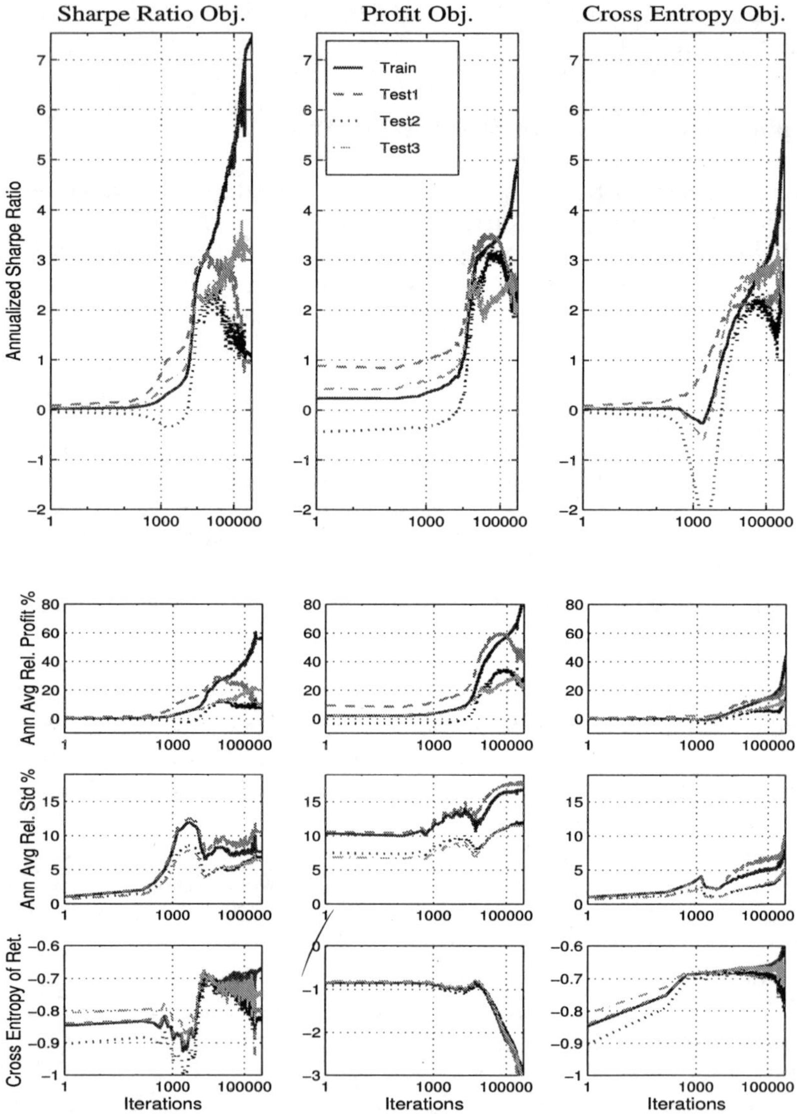

Figure 6: DAX training curves: each column of plots show results of *training* on each objective while each row of plots show the *evaluation* of each objective. The three objectives obtain fairly high SR's on test sets, but all achieve it differently. The SR objective has moderate profit and standard deviation while the profit objective has higher profit as well as standard deviation. The cross-entropy objective has the smallest profit and standard deviation of the three objectives.

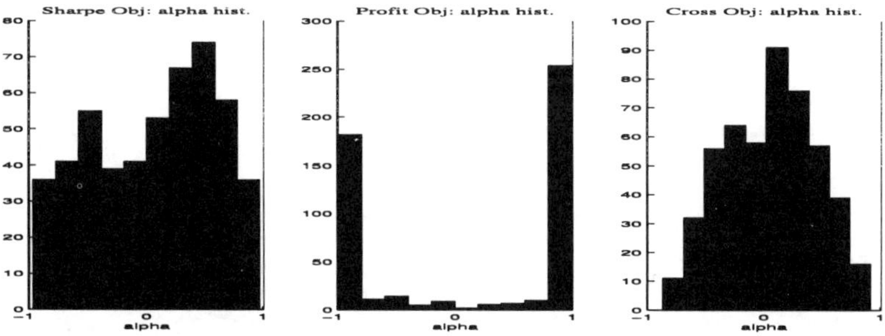

Figure 7: DAX histograms of α for all objective functions. The SR objective has the tendency to position sizes that are more evenly distributed compared to the profit and cross-entropy objectives. The profit objective for the most part takes full positions sizes which has as a result large profit as well as a large standard deviation of returns. The cross-entropy objective takes small position sizes which is indicative of the noisy data.

The SR of the test sets for all three objectives is similar, but achieved in different ways. The SR objective has a moderate profit and moderate standard deviation. The profit objective has the highest profit and highest standard deviation. Finally, the cross-entropy has the lowest profit and lowest standard deviation.

Fig. 7 illustrates the distribution of position sizes for each objective function. When compared to the profit objective, the SR objective takes moderate positions, which shows the effects risk minimization has on the position size. The cross-entropy objective has the tendency to take small position sizes which results in small profit and standard deviation.

Fig. 8 shows the profit and loss curves of all objective functions along with the simple buy-and-hold strategy. We use the network at iteration 40,000 for the SR objective, 192,000 for the profit objective, and 40,000 for the cross-entropy objective. The stopping points were determined by monitoring the validation set of their respective objectives. The plot shows that the SR objective obtains moderate profit when compared to the other two objectives which is as expected. Clearly, the profit objective should have the highest profit. However, the profit objective pays for high profit with the highest standard deviation. Not surprisingly, the SR objective achieves moderate profit and modest standard deviation while the cross-entropy has the lowest profit and standard deviation.

The profit and loss curves were computed without transaction costs. In trading, however, transactions costs can play an important role. With the common assumption of proportionality to the absolute value of the change in

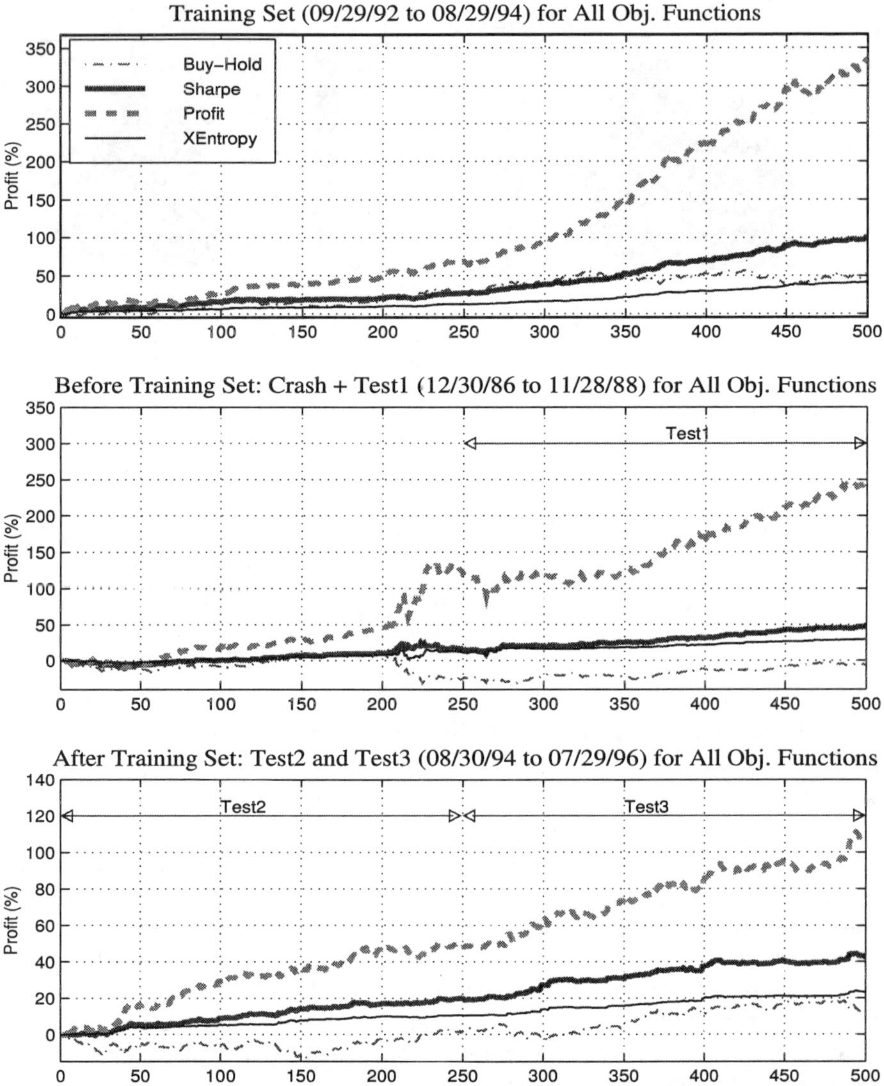

Figure 8: DAX P&L curves for the training and three test sets with dates as given in the plot titles. The network was evaluated at the overfitting point which was determined by test set 2. The center panel includes the US stock market crash of 1987 as the first 250 points for the profit evaluation. As expected, the profit objective does well in profit while the SR objective has moderate profit and the cross-entropy has very little profit above the simple buy-and-hold strategy.

position size, i.e.,

$$\text{transaction cost} \propto \sum_{i=2}^{N} |\alpha_i - \alpha_{i-1}| \quad , \tag{27}$$

we find that the strategy generated by training on profit has significantly higher transaction costs than the strategy generated by training on SR, while the transaction costs for the network trained on cross-entropy is somewhat smaller:

$$\text{transaction cost (profit)} \approx 1.8 * \text{transaction cost (SR)} \tag{28}$$

$$\text{transaction cost (cross-entropy)} \approx 0.8 * \text{transaction cost (SR)} \quad . \tag{29}$$

Revisiting Fig. 8, this will mean that the dashed line (profit) gets pulled down about 1.8 times as much as the thick solid line (SR). The thin solid line (cross-entropy) will be pulled down about 80 per cent as much. Only the dash-dotted line (buy-and-hold) remains unchanged, since there are no transactions.

8 Conclusion

We have presented a method for SR maximization using an iterative update rule and developed a trading strategy based on this method. The trading strategy is based on taking positions between two asset classes: risky and risk-free. We implemented an iterative update (gradient ascent) for a neural network architecture and tested the method on computer-generated and real-world data. The computer-generated data for the noise-free experiment shows how SR may not be an ideal risk-adjusted measure. The computer-generated data for the noisy experiment gives insight into how α is optimized in the presence of noise. The real-world data application to German Stock Index trading shows good results for the SR objective when compared to both the profit objective and cross-entropy, in terms of annual profit as well as standard deviation of returns. The technique of SR optimization is shown to be a feasible approach to explicitly consider both profit (average excess return) and risk (standard deviation of excess return) in a trading strategy. However, using standard deviation as the risk measure has the necessary limitation that positive returns are penalized. This problem can be addressed by using an asymmetrical risk-measure such as semideviation (Markowitz, 1962; Harlow, 1991) in trading applications.

Acknowledgments

We wish to thank Alan Yamamura for discussions in 1994, Jaewoo Kang for his contributions to the initial stages of this work in 1995 and Michelle Hsu, Tom McCabe, Ralph Neuneier, Shanming Shi, and Hans Georg Zimmermann.

References

Buntine, W. L. and A. S. Weigend. 1991. Bayesian back-propagation. *Complex Systems* **5**, 603–643.

Hammer, D. A. 1991. *Dynamic Asset Allocation: Strategies for the Stock, Bond, and Money Markets.* John Wiley and Sons, New York.

Harlow, W. V. 1991. Asset allocation in a downside-risk framework. *Financial Analysts Journal* **47**, 28–40.

Markowitz, H. M. 1962. *Portfolio Selection: Efficient Diversification of Investments.* John Wiley and Sons, New York.

Nix, D. A. and A. S. Weigend. 1995. Learning local error bars for nonlinear regression. In *Advances in Neural Information Processing Systems 7 (NIPS*94)*, G. Tesauro, D. S. Touretzky and T. K. Leen (eds), pp. 488–496. MIT Press, Cambridge, MA.

Pi, H. and T. S. Rögnvaldsson. 1996. A neural network approach to futures trading. In *Neural Networks in Financial Engineering (Proceedings of NNCM'95, London)*, A.-P. N. Refenes, Y. Abu-Mostafa, J. Moody and A. Weigend (eds), pp. 17–25. World Scientific.

Rumelhart, D. E., R. Durbin, R. Golden and Y. Chauvin. 1996. Backpropagation: The basic theory. In *Mathematical Perspectives on Neural Networks*, P. Smolensky, M. C. Mozer and D. E. Rumelhart (eds), pp. 533–566. Lawrence Erlbaum Associates, Hillsdale, NJ.

Sharpe, W. F. 1970. *Portfolio Theory and Capital Markets.* McGraw-Hill Book Company, New York.

Sharpe, W. F. 1994. The Sharpe Ratio. *The Journal of Portfolio Management* **21**(1), 49.

Weigend, A. S. 1994. On overfitting and the effective number of hidden units. In *Proceedings of the 1993 Connectionist Models Summer School*, M. C. Mozer, P. Smolensky, D. S. Touretzky, J. L. Elman and A. S. Weigend (eds), pp. 335–342, Hillsdale, NJ. Lawrence Erlbaum Associates.

Weigend, A. S., M. Mangeas and A. N. Srivastava. 1995. Nonlinear gated experts for time series: Discovering regimes and avoiding overfitting. *International Journal of Neural Systems* **6**, 373–399.

Zimmermann, H. G. and A. S. Weigend. 1997. Representing dynamical systems in feed-forward networks: A six layer architecture. In *Decision Technologies for Financial Engineering: Proceedings of the Fourth International Conference on Neural Networks in the Capital Markets (NNCM-96)*, A. S. Weigend, Y. Abu-Mostafa and A.-P. N. Refenes (eds), Singapore. World Scientific.

OPTIMIZATION OF TRADING SYSTEMS AND PORTFOLIOS

JOHN MOODY, LIZHONG WU
Nonlinear Prediction Systems
P.O. Box 681, University Station, Portland, OR 97207
also at:
Oregon Graduate Institute, Computer Science Dept.,
Portland, OR 97291-1000

We propose to train trading systems and portfolios by optimizing objective functions that directly measure trading and investment performance. Rather than basing a trading system on forecasts or training via a supervised learning algorithm using labelled trading data, we train our systems using recurrent reinforcement learning algorithms. The objective functions that we consider as evaluation functions for reinforcement learning are profit or wealth, economic utility, the Sharpe ratio, and our proposed *Differential Sharpe Ratio*. The trading and portfolio management systems require prior decisions as input in order to properly take into account the effects of transactions costs, market impact, and taxes. This temporal dependence on system state requires the use of reinforcement versions of standard recurrent learning algorithms. We present empirical results in controlled experiments that demonstrate the efficacy of some of our methods. We find that maximizing the differential Sharpe ratio yields more consistent results than maximizing profits, and that both methods outperform a trading system based on forecasts that minimize MSE.

1 Introduction: Objective Functions and Reinforcement Learning for Trading

Many trading systems are optimized using supervised learning, either using labelled trading data or by generating trading signals from price forecasts. Optimizing forecasts typically involves minimizing squared error, while the investor's or trader's ultimate goal is to maximize profits, economic utility or risk-adjusted return. Minimizing forecast error thus corresponds to optimizing an intermediate quantity that is not the ultimate objective of the system and may lead to suboptimal performance. Directly training a system using data labelled with desired trades avoids this intermediate step. The data can be labelled either by an "expert" or by an algorithm designed to constructed an optimal labelling.

Training on labelled data is a two-step procedure. The algorithm for labelling the data attempts to solve the *temporal credit assignment* problem, while subsequently training the system on the labelled data attempts to solve the *structural credit assignment* problem.[a] A system can be optimized to solve

[a] This terminology was proposed in (Sutton, 1988).

both problems simultaneously using *reinforcement learning.* We will adopt this approach here. In reinforcement learning, target outputs are not provided. Rather, the system takes actions (makes trades), receives feedback on its performance (an evaluation signal), and then adjusts its internal parameters to increase its future rewards.

A solution of the structural credit assignment problem (training the system parameters) will generally require using a *recurrent* learning algorithm. Trading system profits depend upon sequences of interdependent decisions, and are thus path-dependent. Optimal trading decisions when the effects of transactions costs, market impact, and taxes[b] are included require knowledge of the current system state. Including information related to past decisions in the inputs to a trading system results in a *recurrent* decision system.[c] The proper optimization of a recurrent, path-dependent decision system is quite different from the simple supervised optimization techniques used for direct forecasts or for labelled trading data.

The reinforcement learning analogs of recurrent learning algorithms required to train our proposed systems include both off-line (batch) training algorithms like back propagation through time or on-line (adaptive) algorithms like real time recurrent learning or dynamic backpropagation.

2 Structure and Optimization of Traders

2.1 *Single Asset with Discrete Position Size*

In this section, we consider trading objective functions for trading systems that trade a single security with price series z_t. The trader is assumed to take only long, neutral, or short positions $F_t \in \{-1, 0, 1\}$ of constant magnitude. A conservative strategy for stock or bond investments might be restricted to $F_t \in \{0, 1\}$, while a simplified reversal trading strategy could have no neutral state $F_t \in \{-1, 1\}$. The constant magnitude assumption can be easily relaxed to enable better risk control. (This will be discussed later.) The position F_t is established or maintained at the end of each time interval t, and is reassessed at the end of period $t + 1$. A trade is thus possible at the end of each time period, although nonzero trading costs will discourage excessive trading.

---

[b]For brevity, we omit further discussion of market impact and tax effects.

[c]Here, recurrence refers to the nature of the algorithms required to optimize the system. For example, optimizing a feed forward NAR(p) model for one-step-ahead prediction does not require a recurrent learning algorithm, while optimizing the same NAR(p) model to perform iterated predictions *does*. The fact that a forecast or decision is made by a feedforward, non-recurrent network does not mean that optimizing it correctly can be done with a standard, non-recurrent training procedure.

In order to properly incorporate the effects of transactions costs, market impact, and taxes in a trader's decision making, the trader must have internal state information and must therefore be recurrent. An example of a single asset trading system that could take into account transactions costs and market impact would be one with the following decision function:

$$F_t = F(\theta_t; F_{t-1}, I_t) \quad \text{with} \quad I_t = \{z_t, z_{t-1}, z_{t-2}, \ldots; y_t, y_{t-1}, y_{t-2}, \ldots\} \qquad (1)$$

where θ_t denotes the (learned) system parameters at time t and I_t denotes the information set at time t, which includes present and past values of the price series z_t and an arbitrary number of other external variables denoted y_t. More general decision functions could include the current trade's profit / loss (for capturing capital gains tax effects), past positions F_{t-s} and past profits and losses (in analogy with the moving average components of $ARIMA$ models), and other factors.

2.2 Optimizing Profit and Wealth

Trading systems can be optimized by maximizing objective functions $U()$ such as profit, wealth, utility functions of wealth, or performance ratios like the Sharpe ratio. Sharpe ratios will be discussed in section 5. The simplest and most natural objective function for a risk-insensitive trader is profit. We consider two cases: additive and multiplicative. The transactions cost rate (per share, per contract, or per dollar amount, depending on context) is denoted δ.

Additive profits are appropriate to consider if each trade is for a fixed number of shares or contracts of security z_t. This is often the case, for example, when trading small futures accounts or when trading standard US$ FX contracts in dollar-denominated foreign currencies. With the definitions $r_t = z_t - z_{t-1}$ and $r_t^f = z_t^f - z_{t-1}^f$ for the price returns of a risky (traded) asset and a risk-free asset (like T-Bills) respectively, the additive profit accumulated over T time periods with trading position size $\mu > 0$ is then defined as:

$$P_T = \sum_{t=1}^{T} R_t = \mu \sum_{t=1}^{T} \left\{ r_t^f + F_{t-1}(r_t - r_t^f) - \delta |F_t - F_{t-1}| \right\} \qquad (2)$$

with $P_0 = 0$ and typically $F_T = F_0 = 0$. We have implicitly defined the return for the trade completed at time t as R_t. Note that the transaction costs for switching between short to long positions are twice those for switching between neutral and long/short positions. Equation (2) holds for continuous quantities also. The wealth is defined as $W_T = W_0 + P_T$.

Multiplicative profits are appropriate when a fixed fraction of accumulated wealth $\nu > 0$ is invested in each long or short trade. Here, $r_t =$

$(z_t/z_{t-1} - 1)$ and $r_t^f = (z_t^f/z_{t-1}^f - 1)$. If no short sales are allowed and the leverage factor is set fixed at $\nu = 1$, the wealth at time T is:

$$\begin{aligned} W_T &= W_0 \prod_{t=1}^{T} \{1 + R_t\} \\ &= W_0 \prod_{t=1}^{T} \left\{1 + (1 - F_{t-1})r_t^f + F_{t-1}r_t\right\} \{1 - \delta|F_t - F_{t-1}|\} \ , \end{aligned} \tag{3}$$

where R_t is the return realized for the period ending at time t. In this case, the profit is $P_T = W_T - W_0$. If short sales or leverage $\nu \neq 1$ are allowed, then the correct expression depends in detail on the timing of the sequence of trades. For brevity, we omit the discussion for this case.

3 Structure and Optimization of Portfolios

3.1 Portfolios: Continuous Quantities of Multiple Assets

When the risk-free rate of return r_t^f is included in single risky-asset trading models above, one actually has a simple two asset portfolio. For trading multiple assets in general (typically including a risk-free instrument), a multiple output trading system is required. Denoting a set of m markets with price series $\{\{z_t^a\} : a = 1, \ldots, m\}$, the market return r_t^a for price series z_t^a for the period ending at time t is defined as $((z_t^a/z_{t-1}^a) - 1)$. Defining portfolio weights of the ath asset as $F^a()$, a trader that takes only long positions must have portfolio weights that satisfy:

$$F^a \geq 0 \quad \text{and} \quad \sum_{a=1}^{m} F^a = 1 \ . \tag{4}$$

With these constraints, standard Markowitz mean-variance portfolio optimization is a quadratic programming problem. However, when optimizing the parameters of a nonlinear trading system, portfolio optimization becomes a nonlinear programming problem.

One approach to imposing the constraints on the portfolio weights (4) without requiring that a constrained optimization be performed is to use a trading system that has softmax outputs:

$$F^a() = \frac{\exp[f^a()]}{\sum_{b=1}^{m} \exp[f^b()]} \quad \text{for} \quad a = 1, \ldots, m \ . \tag{5}$$

Here, the $f^a()$ could be linear or more complex functions of the inputs, such as a two layer network with linear outputs. Such a trading system can be optimized using unconstrained optimization methods. Denoting the set of raw and normalized outputs collectively as $\mathbf{f}()$ and $\mathbf{F}()$ respectively, a recursive trader will have structure $\mathbf{F}_t = \text{softmax}\{\mathbf{f}_t(\theta_{t-1}, \mathbf{F}_{t-1}, I_t)\}$.

3.2 Profit and Wealth for Portfolios

When multiple assets are considered, the effective portfolio weightings change with each time step due to price movements. Thus, maintaining constant or desired portfolio weights requires that adjustments in positions be made at each time step. The wealth after T periods for a portfolio trading system is

$$\begin{aligned} W_T &= W_0 \prod_{t=1}^{T} \{1 + R_t\} \\ &= W_0 \prod_{t=1}^{T} \left\{ \left(\sum_{a=1}^{m} F_{t-1}^a \frac{z_t^a}{z_{t-1}^a} \right) \left(1 - \delta \sum_{a=1}^{m} |F_t^a - \tilde{F}_t^a| \right) \right\} , \end{aligned} \tag{6}$$

where $\tilde{F}_t^a$ is the effective portfolio weight of asset a before readjusting, defined as

$$\tilde{F}_t^a = \frac{F_{t-1}^a (z_t^a / z_{t-1}^a)}{\sum_{b=1}^{m} F_{t-1}^b (z_t^b / z_{t-1}^b)} , \tag{7}$$

and we have defined the trading returns R_t implicitly. In (6), the first factor in the curly brackets is the increase in wealth over the time interval t prior to rebalancing to achieve to newly specified weights F_t^a. The second factor is the reduction in wealth due to the rebalancing costs. The profit after T periods is $P_T = W_T - W_0$.

4 Optimizing Economic Utility

The optimization of profit and wealth described above assumes that investors are insensitive to risk. However, most investors are more sensitive to losses than to gains, and are therefore willing to sacrifice some potential gains in order to have less risk of loss. There is also an intrinsic asymmetry between percentage losses and gains: a 25% loss must be followed by 33% gain in order to break even. Utility functions of wealth $U(W)$ can capture various kinds of risk/reward preferences.

In 1738, Daniel Bernoulli proposed the logarithmic utility $U(W_t) = \log W_t$ (see Bernoulli (1954)). A more general class of utility functions that capture varying degrees of risk sensitivity are the power law utilities:

$$\begin{aligned} U_\gamma(W_t) &= W_t^\gamma/\gamma \quad \text{for } \gamma \neq 0 \\ U_0(W_t) &= \log W_t \quad \text{for } \gamma = 0 \ . \end{aligned} \tag{8}$$

These utility functions have constant relative risk aversion, defined as

$$\mathcal{R}(W) = -\frac{d \log U'(W)}{d \log W} = 1 - \gamma \ . \tag{9}$$

The case $\gamma = 1$ is risk-neutral, and $U_1(W)$ corresponds to absolute wealth or profit (equation 2), while utilities with $\gamma > 1$ describe risk-seeking or "thrill-seeking" behavior. Most investors have risk-averse utility functions ($\gamma < 1$), with smaller values of γ corresponding to greater sensitivity to loss. The limit $\gamma \mapsto -\infty$ corresponds to absolute risk aversion.

The sensitivity to risk on a per time period or per trade basis can be seen by considering a second order Taylor expansion of the contribution of R_t to $U_\gamma(W_T)$:

$$\begin{aligned} U_\gamma(1+R_t) &\approx \frac{1}{\gamma} + R_t + \frac{\gamma-1}{2} R_t^2 \quad \text{for} \quad \gamma \neq 0 \\ U_\gamma(1+R_t) &\approx 0 + R_t - \frac{1}{2} R_t^2 \quad \text{for} \quad \gamma = 0 \end{aligned} \tag{10}$$

Taking the expectation value of $U_\gamma(1 + R_t)$, and defining risk to be $E(R_t^2)$, we see that for $\gamma > 1$, risk is positively-weighted, while for $\gamma < 1$, risk is negatively-weighted.

5 The Sharpe Ratio and the *Differential* Sharpe Ratio

5.1 Optimizing the Sharpe Ratio

The Sharpe ratio is a measure of risk-adjusted return (Sharpe, 1966; Sharpe, 1994). Denoting as before the trading system returns for period t (including transactions costs) as R_t, the Sharpe ratio is defined to be

$$S_T = \frac{\text{Average}(R_t)}{\text{Standard Deviation}(R_t)} \tag{11}$$

where the average and standard deviation are estimated over returns for periods $t = \{1, \ldots, T\}$. A trading system can be trained to maximize the Sharpe

Ratio as follows. First, we define the Sharpe ratio for n returns R_i in terms of estimates of the first and second moments of the returns distributions:

$$S_n = \frac{A_n}{K_n(B_n - A_n^2)^{1/2}} \tag{12}$$

with

$$A_n = \frac{1}{n}\sum_{i=1}^{n} R_i \quad B_n = \frac{1}{n}\sum_{i=1}^{n} R_i^2 \quad K_n = \left(\frac{n}{n-1}\right)^{1/2} . \tag{13}$$

The normalizing factor K_n is required for an unbiased estimate of the standard deviation, but is not relevant for optimization. The derivative with respect to the system parameters (using scalar notation for θ, even though it's generally a vector) is:

$$\begin{aligned} \frac{dS_n(\theta)}{d\theta} &= \sum_{i=1}^{n}\left\{\frac{dS}{dA_n}\frac{dA_n}{dR_i} + \frac{dS}{dB_n}\frac{dB_n}{dR_i}\right\}\left\{\frac{dR_i}{dF_i}\frac{dF_i}{d\theta} + \frac{dR_i}{dF_{i-1}}\frac{dF_{i-1}}{d\theta}\right\} \\ &= \frac{1}{n}\sum_{i=1}^{n}\left\{\frac{B_n - A_n R_i}{K_n(B_n - A_n^2)^{3/2}}\right\}\left\{\frac{dR_i}{dF_i}\frac{dF_i}{d\theta} + \frac{dR_i}{dF_{i-1}}\frac{dF_{i-1}}{d\theta}\right\} . \end{aligned} \tag{14}$$

The above expression as written with scalar F_i applies to the traders of a single risky asset described in section 2, but can be trivially generalized to the vector case for portfolios, as described in section 3.

The system can be optimized in batch mode by repeatedly computing the value of S_n on forward passes through the data and adjusting the trading system parameters by using gradient descent (with learning rate ρ)

$$\Delta\theta = \rho\frac{dS_n(\theta)}{d\theta} \tag{15}$$

or some other optimization method. A simple incremental optimization might consider only the term in (14) dependent on the last realized return R_n. Note that the quantities $dF_i/d\theta$ are *total derivatives* that depend upon the entire sequence of previous trades. To correctly compute and optimize these total derivatives requires that a recurrent algorithm like BPTT, RTRL, or dynamic backpropagation be used.

5.2 Running and Moving Sharpe Ratios

In order to facilitate on-line learning, an incremental Sharpe ratio is required. First, we define a *running Sharpe ratio* by making use of recursive estimates of the first and second moments of the returns distributions:

$$A_n = \frac{1}{n}R_n + \frac{n-1}{n}A_{n-1} \quad \text{and} \quad B_n = \frac{1}{n}R_n^2 + \frac{n-1}{n}B_{n-1} \tag{16}$$

with $A_0 = B_0 = 0$. Next, we extend this definition to an *exponential moving average Sharpe ratio* on time scale η^{-1} by making use of moving average estimates of the first and second moments of the returns distributions:

$$S_\eta(t) = \frac{A_\eta(t)}{K_\eta(B_\eta(t) - A_\eta^2(t))^{1/2}} \tag{17}$$

with

$$\begin{aligned} A_\eta(t) &= \eta R_t + (1-\eta)A_\eta(t-1) \\ B_\eta(t) &= \eta R_t^2 + (1-\eta)B_\eta(t-1) \\ K_\eta &= \left(\frac{1-\eta/2}{1-\eta}\right)^{1/2} \end{aligned} \tag{18}$$

initialized with $A_\eta(0) = B_\eta(0) = 0$. In (17), the normalization factor K_η is required for an unbiased estimate of the moving standard deviation. For purposes of trading system optimization, however, this constant factor can be ignored.

5.3 Differential *Sharpe Ratios for On-Line Optimization*

While both the running and moving Sharpe ratios can be used to optimize trading systems in batch or off-line mode, proper on-line learning requires that we compute the influence on the Sharpe ratio of the return at time t. With the running or moving Sharpe ratios defined above, we can derive *Differential Sharpe Ratios* for on-line optimization of trading system performance. It is advantageous to use on-line performance measures to (1) speed the convergence of the learning process (since parameter updates can be done *during* each forward pass through the training data), and (2) to adapt to changing market conditions during live trading. Using simplified notation, the update equations for the exponential moving estimates can be rewritten

$$\begin{aligned} A_t &= A_{t-1} + \eta\Delta A_t = A_{t-1} + \eta(R_t - A_{t-1}) \\ B_t &= B_{t-1} + \eta\Delta B_t = B_{t-1} + \eta(R_t^2 - B_{t-1}) \ , \end{aligned} \tag{19}$$

where we have implicitly defined the update quantities ΔA_t and ΔB_t. Treating A_{t-1}, B_{t-1}, and K_η as numerical constants, note that η in the update equations

(19) controls the magnitude of the influence of the return R_t on the Sharpe ratio S_t. Taking $\eta \mapsto 0$ turns off the updating, and making η positive turns it on.

With this in mind, we can obtain a *differential* Sharpe ratio by expanding (17) to first order in η:[d]

$$S_t \approx S_{t-1} + \eta \frac{dS_t}{d\eta}|_{\eta=0} + O(\eta^2) \ . \tag{20}$$

Noting that only the first order term in this expansion depends upon the return R_t at time t (through ΔA_t and ΔB_t), we define the *Differential Sharpe Ratio* as:

$$D_t \equiv \frac{dS_t}{d\eta} = \frac{B_{t-1}\Delta A_t - \frac{1}{2}A_{t-1}\Delta B_t}{(B_{t-1} - A_{t-1}^2)^{3/2}} \ . \tag{21}$$

The influences of risk and return on the differential Sharpe ratio are readily apparent. The first term in the numerator is positive if R_t exceeds the moving average A_{t-1}, while the second term is negative if R_t^2 exceeds the moving average B_{t-1}. Assuming that $A_{t-1} > 0$, the largest possible improvement in D_t occurs when

$$R_t^* = B_{t-1}/A_{t-1} \ . \tag{22}$$

Thus, the Sharpe ratio actually penalizes returns larger than R_t^*.

The Sharpe ratio is not a standard economic utility function, since it's value depends not just on current wealth (or current changes in wealth), but also on past performance. This can be seen by comparing the numerator of the differential Sharpe ratio (21)

$$-\frac{1}{2}A_{t-1}B_{t-1} + B_{t-1}R_t - \frac{1}{2}A_{t-1}R_t^2 \tag{23}$$

with (10). In a sense, the Sharpe ratio is an adaptive utility function, since the relative weightings of risk and return depend on past performance as measured by A_t and B_t.

Note that a second expression for a differential Sharpe ratio can be obtained by expanding S_t of equation (17) in a Taylor series about $R_t = A_{t-1}$ to second order in ΔA_t, and expressing the coefficients in terms of information available at time $t-1$. The result is:

$$S_t \approx \frac{1}{(1-\eta)^{1/2}} \left\{ S_{t-1} + \frac{\eta}{K_\eta} D_t + O((\Delta A_t)^3) \right\}$$

[d] Again, we treat A_{t-1}, B_{t-1}, and K_η as constants. As a technical point, differentiation of K_η with respect to η can be avoided by considering an expansion with terms $K_\eta^{-1} d^m (K_\eta S_t)/d\eta^m$.

$$D_t \equiv \frac{(B_{t-1} - A_{t-1}^2)\Delta A_t - \frac{1}{2}A_{t-1}(\Delta A_t)^2}{(B_{t-1} - A_{t-1}^2)^{3/2}} \; . \tag{24}$$

The numerators of (21) and (24) differ only by a constant. As for (21), this expression too is maximized when $R_t^* = B_{t-1}/A_{t-1}$. Whether optimizing a trading system with (21) or (24), the relevant derivatives have the same simple form:

$$\frac{dD_t}{dR_t} = \frac{B_{t-1} - A_{t-1}R_t}{(B_{t-1} - A_{t-1}^2)^{3/2}} \; . \tag{25}$$

6 Empirical Results

We have tested techniques for optimizing both profit and the Sharpe ratio in a variety of settings. In this section, we present results for optimizing three simple trading systems using data generated for an artificial market. The systems are short/long trading systems with recurrent state similar to that described in section 2. Two of the systems are trained via reinforcement learning and RTRL to maximize the differential Sharpe ratio (21) or profit. These two systems are compared to a third trading system built on a forecasting system that minimizes forecast MSE.

In our simulations, we find that maximizing the differential Sharpe ratio yields more consistent results than maximizing profits, and that both methods outperform the trading system based on forecasts.

6.1 Data

We generated a log price series as a random walk with autoregressive trend process. The two parameter model is thus:

$$p(t) = p(t-1) + \beta(t-1) + k * \delta(t) \tag{26}$$

$$\beta(t) = \alpha * \beta(t-1) + \gamma(t) \; , \tag{27}$$

where α and k are constants, and $\delta(t)$ and $\gamma(t)$ are normal random deviates with zero mean and unit variance. We defined the artificial price series as

$$z(t) = \exp\left(\frac{p(t)}{R}\right) \tag{28}$$

where R is a scale defined as the range of $p(t)$: $\max(p(t)) - \min(p(t))$ over a simulation with 10,000 samples.[e] In our current simulation, we set $\alpha = 0.9$ and

[e]This is slightly more than the number of hours in a year (8760), so the series could be thought of as representing hourly prices in a 24 hour artificial market. Alternatively, a series

$k = 3$. The artificial price series are trending on short time scales and have a high level of noise. An example of the artificial price series is shown in the top panel of Figure 1.

6.2 Simulated Trading Results

Figure 1 shows results for a single simulation of an artificial market as described above. The trading system is initialized randomly at the beginning, and adapted using real-time recurrent learning to optimize the differential Sharpe ratio (21). The transactions costs are fixed at a half percent during the whole real-time learning and trading process. Transient effects of the initial learning while trading process can be seen in the first 2000 time steps of figure 1.

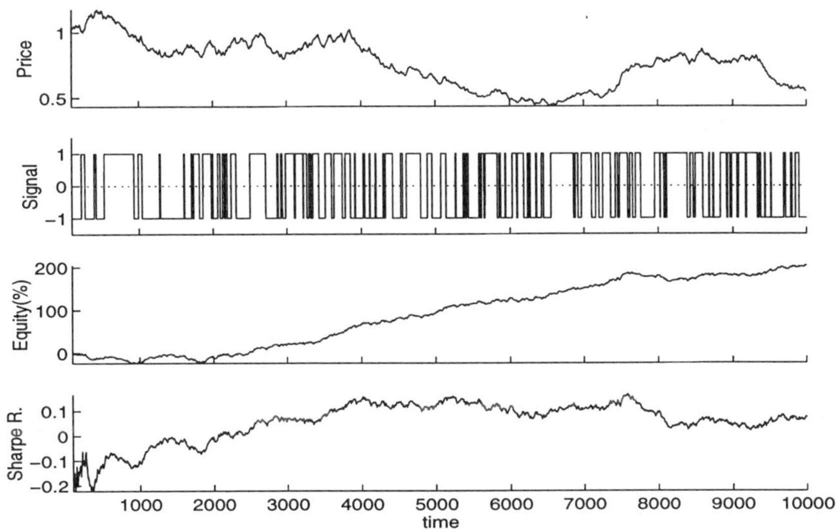

Figure 1: Artificial prices (top panel), trading signals (second panel), cumulative sums of profits (third panel) and the differential Sharpe ratio with $\eta = 0.01$ (bottom panel). (Note that the values of the Sharpe ratio are not annualized.) The system performs poorly while learning from scratch during the first 2000 time periods, but its performance remains good thereafter.

Figure 2 compares three kinds of trading systems. "Max.SR" maximizes the differential Sharpe ratio, "Max.Profit" maximizes the cumulative profit,

---

of this length could represent slightly less than five years of hourly data in a market that trades about 40 hours per week.

and "Min.MSE" minimizes the mean-squared forecast error. In this comparison, the transaction costs are set to 0.5%. As shown, the "Max.SR" and "Max.Profit" trading systems significantly out-perform the "Min.MSE" systems. "Max.SR" achieves slightly better mean return than "Max.Profit" and is substantially more consistent in its performance over 100 such trials.

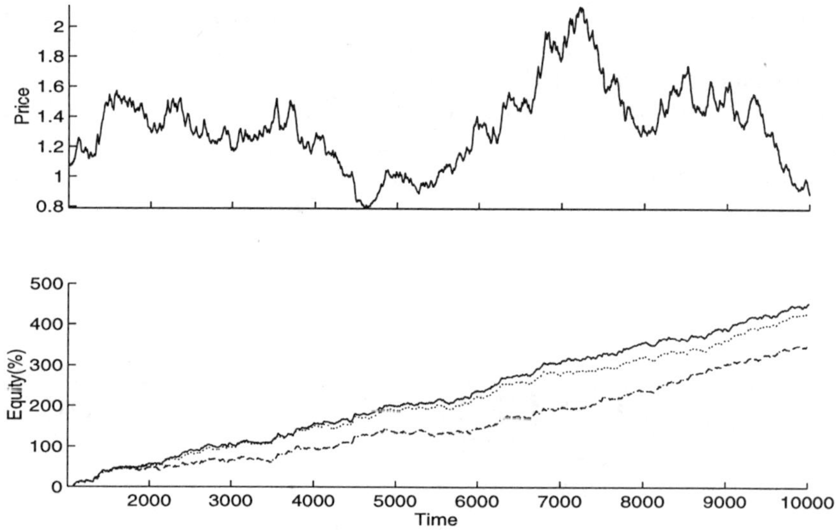

Figure 2: Comparison of the cumulative profits of three trading systems for 9,000 time steps out of sample. The transaction cost is 0.5%. The price series is plotted in the upper panel. The lower panel shows the cumulative sum of median profits over 10 different trials. The solid curve is for the "Max.SR" system, the dotted curve is for the "Max.Profit" system, and the dashed curve is for the "Min.MSE" system.

7 Conclusions and Extensions

Our empirical results to date verify the efficacy of training trading systems via reinforcement learning to maximize profits and the Sharpe Ratio. The results also demonstrate the effectiveness of on-line optimization using our proposed *Differential Sharpe Ratio*. In addition, we have proposed to maximize economic utility functions, such as the Bernoulli and power law utilities. Extensions to the methods presented here include maximizing other economic utility functions and maximizing other performance ratios that use different definitions of risk. These include the Sterling ratio (that uses maximum drawdown) and measures based on the *semi-variance* (Markowitz, 1959) and the *second lower partial moment* (SLPM) (White, 1996). Our ongoing empirical work includes refining, testing, and comparing such methods for optimizing both trading systems and portfolios on both simulated and real data series. Using simulated data for which we have a good understanding enables extensive controlled experiments.

This paper is a slightly revised version of Moody & Wu (1996). A more detailed treatment of this work and additional empirical results are presented in Moody & Wu (1997). Related work includes that of Timmermann & Pesaran (1995), Neuneier (1996), Kang *et al.* (1996), Bengio (1996), and White (1996).

Acknowledgements

We gratefully acknowledge support for this work from Nonlinear Prediction Systems and from DARPA under contract DAAH01-96-C-R026.

References

Bengio, Y. 1996. Training a neural network with a financial criterion rather than a prediction criterion. NNCM*96 Conference Record.

Bernoulli, D. Jan 1954. Exposition of a new theory on the measurement of risk. *Econometrica* **32**, 23–26.

Kang, J., M. Choey and A. Weigend. 1996. Nonlinear trading models and asset allocation based on sharpe ratio. NNCM*96 Conference Record.

Markowitz, H. 1959. *Portfolio Selection: Efficient Diversification of Investments.* New York: Wiley.

Moody, J. and L. Wu. 1996. Optimization of trading systems and portfolios. NNCM*96 Conference Record.

Moody, J. and L. Wu. 1997. Optimization of trading systems and portfolios. *Journal of Forecasting* . To Appear.

Neuneier, R. 1996. Optimal asset allocation using adaptive dynamic programming. In *Advances in Neural Information Processing Systems 8*, D. Touretzky, M. Mozer and M. Hasselmo (eds). MIT Press.

Sharpe, W. F. Jan 1966. Mutual fund performance. *Journal of Business* , 119–138.

Sharpe, W. F. Fall 1994. The sharpe ratio - properly used, it can improve investment management. *The Journal of Portfolio Management* , 49–58.

Sutton, R. S. 1988. Learning to predict by the methods of temporal differences. *Machine Learning* **3**, 9–44.

Timmermann, A. and H. Pesaran. 1995. Predictability of stock returns: Robustness and economic significance. *Journal of Finance* **50**, 1201–1228.

White, H. 1996. Personal communication. Unpublished.

TRAINING A NEURAL NETWORK WITH A FINANCIAL CRITERION RATHER THAN A PREDICTION CRITERION

YOSHUA BENGIO
Dept. IRO, Université de Montréal,
Montréal, Qc, Canada, H3C 3J7
and CIRANO, Montréal, Qc, Canada

A common approach to quantitative decision taking with financial time-series is to train a model using a prediction criterion (e.g., squared error). We find on a portfolio selection problem that better results can be obtained when the model is directly trained in order to optimize the financial criterion of interest, with a differentiable decision module.

1 Introduction

Most applications of learning algorithms to financial time-series are based on predicting the value (either discrete or continuous) of output (dependent) variables given input (independent) variables. For example, the parameters of a multi-layer neural network are tuned in order to minimize a squared error loss. However, in many of these applications, the *ultimate goal* is not to make good predictions, but rather to use these often noisy predictions in order to *take some decisions*. In fact, the performance of these systems is sometimes measured in terms of financial profitability and risk criteria, after some heuristic decision taking rule has been applied to the trained model's outputs.

Because of the limited amount of training data, and because financial time-series are often very noisy, we argue here that better results can be obtained by *choosing the model parameters in order to directly maximize the financial criterion of interest.* What we mean by *training criterion* in this paper is a scalar function of the training data and the model parameters. This scalar function is minimized (or maximized) with an optimization algorithm (such as gradient descent) by varying the parameters. Previous theoretical and experimental work has already shown the advantages of optimizing a criterion that is closer to the real objective of learning (e.g., for classification tasks (Hampshire & Waibel, 1990), or (Driancourt *et al.*, 1991), and multi-module systems (Bottou & Gallinari, 1991; Bengio, 1996a)). In particular, it has been proven (Hampshire & Kumar, 1992) for classification tasks that a strategy that separates the learning of a model of the data and the decision-taking rule is less optimal than one based on training the model with respect to the decision surfaces, which may be determined by a *discriminant function* associated to each class (e.g., one output of a neural network for each class). In (Bengio, 1997), we show why two modules in sequence (such as M_1, for prediction, and M_2, for decisions, in Figure 1) can be more optimally trained with respect to a financial criterion C that depends directly on the output of M_2 by training them jointly with respect to C, rather than independently training M_1 to minimize a prediction error over some horizon to be decided. In the area of financial decisions, it has already been shown (Leitch & Tanner, 1991) in cases of interest rate forecasting that profit and forecast accuracy are not significantly correlated. In this paper, we push this idea further by estimating the parameters of a neural network predictor in such a way as to maximize the utility of the decisions taken on the basis of those predictions. With this procedure, we find that better financial utility is obtained than when the parameters are estimated in order to minimize forecasting errors.

In section 2, we present a particular cost function for optimizing the profits of a portfolio, *while taking into account losses due to transaction costs.* It should be noted that including transactions in the cost function makes it non-linear (and not quadratic) with respect to the trading decisions. When the decisions are taken in a way that depends on the current asset allocation (to minimize transactions), all the decisions during a trading sequence become dependent of each other. In section 3 we present a particular decision taking, i.e., trading, strategy, and a *differentiable* version of it, which can be used in the direct optimization of the model parameters with respect to the financial criterion. In section 4, we describe a series of experiments which compare the direct optimization approach with the prediction approach.

2 A Training Criterion for Portfolio Management

In this paper, we consider the practical example of choosing a discrete sequence of portfolio weights in order to maximize profits, while taking into account losses due to transactions. We will simplify the representation of time by assuming a discrete series of events, at time indices $t = 1, 2, \ldots, T$. We assume that some decision strategy yields, at each time step t, the portfolio weights $w_t = (w_{t,0}, w_{t,1}, \ldots, w_{t,n})$, for $n+1$ weights. In the experiments, we will apply this model to managing n stocks as well as a *cash* asset (which may earn short-term interest). We will assume that each transaction (buy or sell) of an amount v of asset i costs $c_i|v|$. This may be used to take into account the effect of differences in liquidity of the different assets. In the experiments, in the case of cash, the transaction cost is zero, whereas in the case of stocks, it is 1%, i.e., the overall cost of buying and later selling back a stock is about 2% of its value. A more realistic cost function should take into account the non-linear effects of the amount that is sold or bought: transaction fees may be

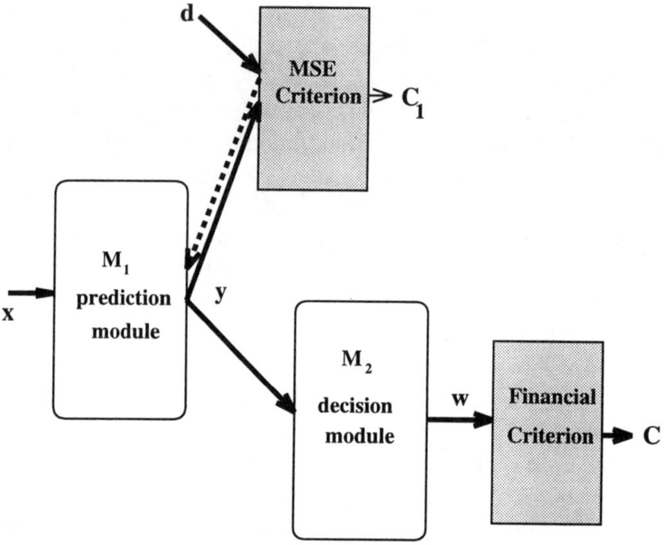

Figure 1: Task decomposition: a prediction module (M_1) with input x and output y, and a decision module (M_2) with output w. In the case of separate optimization, an intermediate criterion (e.g., mean squared error) is used to train M_1 (with desired outputs d). In the case of joint optimization of the decision module and the prediction module, gradients with respect to the financial criterion are back-propagated through both modules (dotted lines).

proportionally higher for small transactions, transactions may only be allowed with a certain granularity, and slippage losses due to low relative liquidity may be considerably worse for large transactions.

The training criterion is a function of the whole sequence of portfolio weights. At each time step t, we decompose the change in value of the assets in two categories: the return due to the changes in prices (and revenues from dividends), R_t, and the losses due to transactions, L_t. The overall return ratio is the product of R_t and L_t over all the time steps $t = 1, 2, \ldots, T$:

$$\text{overall return ratio} = \prod_t R_t L_t \tag{1}$$

This is the ratio of the final wealth to the initial wealth. Instead of maximizing this quantity, in this paper we maximize its logarithm (noting that the logarithm is a monotonic function):

$$C \stackrel{\text{def}}{=} \sum_t (\log R_t + \log L_t) \tag{2}$$

The yearly percent return is then given by $(e^{CP/T} - 1) \times 100\%$, where P is the number of time steps per year (12, in the experiments), and T is the number of time steps (number of months, in the experiments) over which the sum is taken. The return R_t due to price changes and dividends from time t to time $t+1$ is defined in terms of the portfolio weights $w_{t,i}$ and the multiplicative returns of each stock $r_{t,i}$,

$$r_{t,i} \stackrel{\text{def}}{=} \text{value}_{t+1,i}/\text{value}_{t,i}, \tag{3}$$

where $\text{value}_{t,i}$ represents the value of asset i at time t, assuming no transaction takes place: $r_{t,i}$ represents the relative change in value of asset i in the period t to $t+1$. Let $a_{t,i}$ be the actual worth of the ith asset at time t in the portfolio, and let a_t be the combined value of all the assets at time t. Since the portfolio is weighted with weights $w_{t,i}$, we have

$$a_{t,i} \stackrel{\text{def}}{=} a_t w_{t,i} \tag{4}$$

and

$$a_t = \sum_i a_{t,i} = \sum_i a_t w_{t,i} \tag{5}$$

Because of the change in value of each one of the assets, their value becomes

$$a'_{t,i} \stackrel{\text{def}}{=} r_{t,i} a_{t,i}. \tag{6}$$

Therefore the total worth becomes

$$a'_t = \sum_i a'_{t,i} = \sum_i r_{t,i} a_{t,i} = a_t \sum_i r_{t,i} w_{t,i} \tag{7}$$

so the combined worth has increased by the ratio

$$R_t \stackrel{\text{def}}{=} \frac{a'_t}{a_t} \tag{8}$$

i.e.,

$$R_t = \sum_i w_{t,i} r_{t,i}. \tag{9}$$

After this change in asset value, the portfolio weights have changed as follows (since the different assets have different returns):

$$w'_{i,t} \stackrel{\text{def}}{=} \frac{a'_{t,i}}{a'_t} = \frac{w_{t,i} r_{t,i}}{R_t}. \tag{10}$$

At time $t+1$, we want to change the proportions of the assets to the new portfolio weights w_{t+1}, i.e, the worth of asset i will go from $a'_t w'_{t,i}$ to $a'_t w_{t+1,i}$. We then have to incur for each asset a transaction loss, which is assumed simply proportional to the amount of the transaction, with a proportional cost c_i for asset i. These losses include both transaction fees and slippage. This criterion could easily be generalized to take into account the fact that the slippage costs may vary with time (depending on the volume of offer and demand) and may also depend non-linearly on the actual amount of the transactions. After transaction losses, the worth at time $t+1$ becomes

$$\begin{aligned} a_{t+1} &= a'_t - \sum_i c_i |a'_t w_{t+1,i} - a'_t w'_{t,i}| \\ &= a'_t (1 - \sum_i c_i |w_{t+1,i} - w'_{t,i}|). \end{aligned} \tag{11}$$

The loss L_t due to transactions at time t is defined as the ratio

$$L_t \stackrel{\text{def}}{=} \frac{a_t}{a'_{t-1}}. \tag{12}$$

Therefore

$$L_t = 1 - \sum_i c_i |w_{t,i} - w'_{t-1,i}|. \tag{13}$$

To summarize, the overall profit criterion can be written as follows:

$$\begin{aligned} C = \sum_t \; & \log(\sum_i r_{t,i} w_{t,i}) + \\ & \log(1 - \sum_i c_i |w_{t,i} - \frac{w_{t-1,i} r_{t-1,i}}{\sum_i w_{t-1,i} r_{t-1,i}}|) \end{aligned} \tag{14}$$

At each time step, a trading module computes w_t, from w'_{t-1} and from the predictor output y_t. To backpropagate gradients with respect to the cost function through the trader from the above equation, one computes $\frac{\partial C}{\partial w_{t,i}}$, when given $\frac{\partial C}{\partial w'_t}$. The trading module can then compute $\frac{\partial C}{\partial w'_{t-1}}$ from $\frac{\partial C}{\partial w_t}$, and this process is iterated backwards in time. At each time step, the trading module also computes $\frac{\partial C}{\partial y_t}$ from $\frac{\partial C}{\partial w_t}$.

To conclude this section, it should be noted that the introduction of transaction losses in the training criterion makes it non-linear in the decisions (whereas the profit term is linear in the decisions). Note that it is not even differentiable everywhere (but it is differentiable almost everywhere, which is enough for gradient descent optimization). Furthermore, when the decision at time t is taken in function of the previous decision (to avoid unnecessary transactions), all the decisions are coupled together, i.e., the cost function can't be separated as a sum of independent terms associated to the network output at each time step. For this reason, an algorithm such as back-propagation through time has to be used to compute the gradients of the cost function.

3 The Trading Modules

We could directly train a module producing in output the portfolio weights $w_{t,i}$, but in this paper we use some financial a-priori knowledge in order to modularize this task in two subtasks:

1. with a "prediction" module (e.g., M_1 in figure 1), compute a "desirability" value $y_{t,i}$ for each asset on the basis of the current inputs,

2. with a *trading module*, allocate capital among the given set of assets (i.e., compute the weights $w_{t,i}$), on the basis of y_t and $w'_{t-1,i}$ (this is done with the decision module M_2 in figure 1).

In this section, we will describe two such trading modules, both based on the same a-priori knowledge. The first one is not differentiable and it has hand-tuned parameters, whereas the second one is differentiable and it has parameters learned by gradient ascent on the financial criterion C. The a-priori knowledge we have used in designing this trader can be summarized as follows:

- We mostly want to have in our portfolio those assets that are desirable according to the predictor (high $y_{t,i}$).

- More risky assets (e.g., stocks) should have a higher expected return than less risky assets (e.g., cash) to be worth keeping in the portfolio.

- The outputs of the predictor are very noisy and unreliable.

- We want our portfolio to be as diversified as possible, i.e., it is better to have two assets of similar expected returns than to invest all our capital in one that is slightly better.

- We want to minimize the amount of the transactions.

In order to produce the portfolio weights w_t, at each time step, the trading module takes as input the vectors y_t (predictor output) and w'_{t-1} (previous weights, after changes in value due to multiplicative returns r_{t-1}). Here we are assuming that the assets $0 \ldots n-1$ are stocks, and asset n represents cash (earning short-term interests). The portfolio weights $w_{t,i}$ are non-negative and sum to 1.

Our first experiments were done with a neural network trained to minimize the squared error between the predicted and actual asset returns. Based on advice from financial specialists, we designed the trading algorithm described in figure 2.

Statement 1 in figure 2 is to minimize transactions. Statement 2 assigns a discrete quality (`good`, `neutral`, or `bad`) to each stock in function of how the predicted return compares to the average predicted return and to the return of cash. Statement 3 computes the current total weight of `bad` stocks that are currently owned, and should therefore be sold. Statement 4 uses that money to buy the `good` stocks (if any), distributing the available money uniformly among the stocks (or if no stock is `good` increase the proportion of cash in the portfolio).

In the experiments, the parameters c_0, c_1, c_2, b_0, b_1, b_2, τ were chosen using basic judgment and a few trial and error experiments on the first training period. However, it is difficult to numerically optimize these parameters because of the discrete nature of the decisions taken. Furthermore, the predictor module might not give out numbers that are optimal for the trader module. This has motivated the differentiable trading module described in figure 3.

Statement 1 of figure 3 defines two quantities ("goodness" and "badness"), to compare each asset with the other assets, indicating respectively a willingness to buy and a willingness to sell. Statement 2 computes the amount to sell based on the weighted sum of "badness" indices. Statement 3a then computes a quantity δ_t that compares the sum of the goodness and badness indices. Statement 3b uses that quantity to compute the change in cash (using a different formula depending on wether δ_t is positive or negative). Statement 3c uses that change in cash to compute the amount available for buying more stocks (or the amount of stocks that should be sold). Statement 4 computes the new proportions for each stock, by allocating the amount available to buy new stocks according to the relative goodness of each stock.

There are 9 parameters, $\theta_2 = \{ c_0, c_1, b_0, b_1, a_0, a_1, s_0, s_1, \tau \}$, five of which have a similar interpretation as in the hard trader. However, since we can compute the gradient of the training criterion with respect to these parameters, their value can be learned from the data. From the algorithmic definition of the function $w_t(w'_{t-1}, y_t, \theta_2)$ one can easily write down the equations for $\frac{\partial C}{\partial y_{t,i}}$, $\frac{\partial C}{\partial w'_{t-1,i}}$ and $\frac{\partial C}{\partial \theta_2}$, when given the gradients $\frac{\partial C}{\partial w_{t,j}}$, using the chain rule.

1. By default, initialize $w_{t,i} \leftarrow w'_{t,i}$ for all $i = 0 \ldots n$.
2. Assign a $\text{quality}_{t,i}$ (equal to **good**, **neutral**, or **bad**) to each stock ($i = 0 \ldots n-1$):
   (a) Compute the average desirability $\bar{y_t} \leftarrow \frac{1}{n}\sum_{i=0}^{n-1} y_{t,i}$.
   (b) Let $\text{rank}_{t,i}$ be the rank of $y_{t,i}$ in the set $\{y_{t,0}, \ldots, y_{t,n-1}\}$.
   (c) **If** $y_{t,i} > c_0\bar{y_t}$ and $y_{t,i} > c_1 y_{t,n}$ and $\text{rank}_{t,i} > c_2$
   Then
   $\text{quality}_{t,i} \leftarrow$ **good**,
   Else,
   If $y_{t,i} < b_0\bar{y_t}$ or $y_{t,i} < b_1 y_{t,n}$ or $\text{rank}_{t,i} < b_2$
   Then, $\text{quality}_{t,i} \leftarrow$ **bad**,
   Else, $\text{quality}_{t,i} \leftarrow$ **neutral**.
3. Compute the total weight of **bad** stocks that should be sold:
   (a) Initialize $k_t \leftarrow 0$
   (b) **For** $i = 0 \ldots n-1$
   - **If** $\text{quality}_{t,i} =$ **bad** and $w'_{t-1,i} > 0$ (i.e., already owned), **Then**
     (SELL a fraction of the amount owned)
     $k_t \leftarrow k_t + \tau w'_{t-1,i}$
     $w_{t,i} \leftarrow w'_{t-1,i} - \tau w'_{t-1,i}$
4. **If** $k_t > 0$ **Then** (either distribute that money among **good** stocks, or keep it in cash):
   (a) Let $s_t \leftarrow$ number of **good** stocks *not owned*.
   (b) **If** $s_t > 0$
   Then
   - (also use some cash to buy **good** stocks)
     $k_t \leftarrow k_t + \tau w'_{t-1,n}$
     $w_{t,n} \leftarrow w'_{t-1,n}(1-\tau)$
   - **For** all **good** stocks not owned, BUY: $w_{t,i} \leftarrow k_t/s_t$.

   Else (i.e., no **good** stocks were not already owned)
   - Let $s'_t \leftarrow$ number of **good** stocks,
   - **If** $s'_t > 0$
     Then For all the **good** stocks, BUY: $w_{t,i} \leftarrow w'_{t-1,i} + k_t/s'_t$
     Else (put the money in cash) $w_{t,n} \leftarrow w'_{t-1,n} + k_t$.

Figure 2: Algorithm for the "hard" trading module.

4 Experiments

We have performed experiments in order to study the difference between training only a prediction module with the Mean Squared Error (MSE) and training

1. (Assign a goodness value $g_{t,i}$ and a badness value $b_{t,i}$ between 0 and 1 for each stock)
   - (Compute the average desirability) $\bar{y_t} \leftarrow \frac{1}{n}\sum_{i=0}^{n-1} y_{t,i}$.
   - (goodness) $g_{t,i} \leftarrow \text{sigmoid}(s_0(y_{t,i} - \max(c_0\bar{y_t}, c_1 y_{t,n})))$
   - (badness) $b_{t,i} \leftarrow \text{sigmoid}(s_1(\min(b_0\bar{y_t}, b_1 y_{t,n}) - y_{t,i}))$
2. (Compute the amount to "sell", to be offset later by an amount to "buy")
   $k_t \leftarrow \sum_{i=0}^{n-1} \text{sigmoid}(\tau) b_{t,i} w'_{t-1}, i$
3. (Compute the change in cash)
   (a) $\delta_t \leftarrow \tanh(a_0 + a_1 \sum_{i=0}^{n-1}(b_{t,i} - g_{t,i}))$
   (b) **If** $\delta_t > 0$ (more bad than good, increase cash)
   Then $w_{t,n} \leftarrow w'_{t-1,n} + \delta_t k_t$
   Else (more good than bad, reduce cash)
   $w_{t,n} \leftarrow -w'_{t-1,n}\delta_t$
   (c) So the amount available to buy is:
   $a_t \leftarrow k_t - (w_{t,n} - w'_{t-1,n})$
4. (Compute amount to "buy", offset by previous "sell", and compute the new weights $w_{t,i}$ on the stocks)
   (a) $s_t \leftarrow \sum_{i=0}^{n-1} g_{t,i}$ (a normalization factor)
   (b) $w_{t,i} \leftarrow w'_{t-1,i}(1 - \text{sigmoide}(\tau) b_{t,i}) + \frac{g_{t,i}}{s_t} a_t$

Figure 3: Algorithm for the "soft" (differentiable) trading module.

both the prediction and decision modules to maximize the financial criterion defined in section 2 (equation 14).

4.1 Experimental Setup

The task is one of managing a portfolio of 35 Canadian stocks, as well as allocate funds between those stocks and a cash asset ($n = 35$ in the above sections, the number of assets is $n + 1 = 36$). The 35 companies are major companies of the Toronto Stock Exchange (most of them in the TSE35 Index). The data is monthly and spans 10 years, from December 1984 to February 1995 (123 months). We have selected 5 input features (x_t is 5-dimensional), 2 of which represent macro-economic variables which are known to influence the business cycle, and 3 of which are micro-economic variables representing the profitability of the company and previous price changes of the stock.

We used ordinary fully connected multi-layered neural networks with a single hidden layer, trained by gradient descent. The same network was used for all 35 stocks, with a single output $y_{t,i}$ at each month t for stock i. Preliminary experiments with the network architecture suggested that using approximately 3 hidden units yielded better results than using no hidden layer or many more hidden units. Better results might be obtained by considering different sectors of the market (different types of companies) separately, but for the experiments reported here, we used a single neural network for all the stocks. When using a different model for each stock and sharing some of the parameters, significantly better results were obtained (using the same training strategy) on that data (Ghosn & Bengio, 1997). Here, the parameters of the network are therefore shared across time and across the 35 stocks. The 36th output (for desirability of cash) was obtained from the current short-term interest rates (which are also used for the multiplicative return of cash, $r_{t,n}$).

To take into account the non-stationarity of the financial and economic time-series, and estimate performance over a variety of economic situations, multiple training experiments were performed on different training windows, each time testing on the following 18 months. For each of the 10 training trials (with different initial weights), 4 training experiments were performed on different training windows (of respectively 33, 51, 69 and 87 months), each time using the following 18 months for early-stopping validation and the remaining 18 months for testing and estimating generalization. The overall return was computed for the whole test period (72 months, 03/89–02/95). Training lasted between 10 and 200 iterations of the training set, with early stopping based on the performance on the validation set.

A buy-and-hold *benchmark* was used to compare the results with a conservative policy. For this benchmark, the initial portfolio is distributed equally among all the stocks (and no cash). Then there are no transactions. The returns for the benchmark are computed in the same way as for the neural network (except that there are no transactions). The *excess return* is defined as the difference between the overall return obtained by a network and that of the buy-and-hold benchmark.

4.2 Results

In the first series of experiments, the neural network was trained with a mean squared error criterion in order to predict the return of each stock over a horizon of three months. We used the "hard decision trader" described in figure 2 in order to measure the financial profitability of the system. We quickly realized that although the mean squared error was gradually improving during training, the profits made sometimes increased, sometimes decreased. This

Table 1: Comparative results: network trained with Mean Squared Error to predict future return vs network trained with financial criterion (to directly maximize return). Averages and standard deviations are over 10 trials. The test set represents 6 years, 03/89-02/95.

	Avg. Excess Return on Training Sets	(Standard Deviation)	Avg. **Excess Return** on Test Sets	(Standard Deviation)
Net Trained with MSE Criterion	8.9%	(2.4%)	**2.9%**	(1.2%)
Net Trained with Financial Criterion	19.9%	(2.6%)	**7.4%**	(1.6%)

actually suggested that we were not optimizing the "right" criterion.

This problem can be visualized by looking at scatter plots of the profit versus prediction mean squared error (Bengio, 1997; Bengio, 1996b). Although there is a tendency for returns to be larger for smaller MSE, many different values of return can be obtained for the same MSE. This constitutes an additional (and undesirable) source of *variance* in the generalization performance. Instead, when training the neural network with the financial criterion, the corresponding scatter plots of excess return against training criterion would put all the points on a single exponential curve, since the excess return is maximized by the training procedure.

For the second series of experiments, we created the "soft" version of the trader described in figure 3, and trained the parameters of the trader as well as the neural network in order to maximize the financial criterion defined in section 2 (which is equivalent to maximizing the overall excess return). A series of 10 training experiments (with different initial parameters) were performed (each with four training, validation and test periods) to compare the two approaches. Table 1 summarizes the results. During the whole 6-year test period (March 89 - February 95), the benchmark yielded returns of 6.8%, whereas the network trained with the prediction criterion and the one trained with the financial criterion yielded in average returns of 9.7% and 14.2% respectively (i.e, 2.9% and 7.4% in excess of the benchmark, respectively). The direct optimization approach, which uses a specialized financial criterion clearly yields better performance on this task, both on the training and test data.

The experiments were then replicated using artificially generated returns, and similar results were observed. The artificially generated returns were obtained from an artificial neural network with 10 hidden units (i.e., more than the 3 units used in the prediction module), and with additive noise on the return. Again we observed that decreases in mean squared error of the predictor were not significantly correlated with increases in excess return. When training with respect to the financial criterion instead, the average excess return on the test period increased from 4.6% to 6.9%. As in the experiments with real data, the financial performance on the training data was even more significantly superior when using the financial criterion (corroborating the hypothesis that as far as the financial criterion is concerned, the direct optimization approach offers more capacity than the indirect optimization approach).

5 Conclusion

We consider decision-taking problems on financial time-series with learning algorithms. Theoretical arguments suggest that directly optimizing the financial criterion of interest should yield better performance, according to that same criterion, than optimizing an intermediate prediction criterion such as the often used mean squared error. However, this requires defining a differentiable decision module, and we have introduced a "soft" trading module for this purpose. Another theoretical advantage of such a decision module is that its parameters may be optimized numerically from the training data.

The inadequacy of the mean squared error criterion was suggested to us by the poor correlation between its value and the value of the financial criterion, both on training and test data, confirming previous observations (Leitch & Tanner, 1991).

We have shown with a portfolio management experiment on 35 Canadian stocks with 10 years of data that the more direct approach of choosing the parameters of the model in order to optimize the financial criterion of interest yields better profits than the indirect prediction approach.

In general, for other applications, one should carefully look at the ultimate goals of the system. Sometimes, as in our example, one can design a differentiable cost and decision policy, and obtain better results by optimizing the parameters with respect to an objective that is closer to the ultimate goal of the trained system.

Acknowledgements

The author would like to thank S. Gauthier and F. Gingras for their prior work on data preprocessing, E. Couture and J. Ghosn, for their useful comments, as well as, the NSERC, FCAR, IRIS Canadian funding agencies for support.

We would also like to thank André Chabot from Boulton-Tremblay Inc. for the economic data series used in these experiments.

References

Bengio, Y. 1996. *Neural Networks for Speech and Sequence Recognition.* International Thompson Computer Press, London, UK.

Bengio, Y. 1996. Using a financial training criterion rather than a prediction criterion. Technical Report #1019, Dept. Informatique et Recherche Operationnelle, Universite de Montreal.

Bengio, Y. 1997. Using a financial training criterion rather than a prediction criterion. *to appear in the International Journal of Neural Systems* .

Bottou, L. and P. Gallinari. 1991. A framework for the cooperation of learning algorithms. In *Advances in Neural Information Processing Systems 3*, R. P. Lippman, R. Moody and D. S. Touretzky (eds), pp. 781–788, Denver, CO.

Driancourt, X., L. Bottou and P. Gallinari. 1991. Learning vector quantization, multi-layer perceptron and dynamic programming: Comparison and cooperation. In *International Joint Conference on Neural Networks*, vol. 2, pp. 815–819.

Ghosn, J. and Y. Bengio. 1997. Multi-task learning for stock selection. In *Advances in Neural Information Processing Systems 9*, vol. 9, Cambridge, MA. MIT Press.

Hampshire, J. B. and B. V. K. V. Kumar. 1992. Shooting craps in search of an optimal strategy for training connectionist pattern classifiers. In *Advances in Neural Information Processing Systems*, J. Moody, S. Hanson and R. Lippmann (eds), vol. 4, pp. 1125–1132, Denver, CO. Morgan Kaufmann.

Hampshire, J. B. and A. H. Waibel. June 1990. A novel objective function for improved phoneme recognition using time-delay neural networks. *IEEE Transactions of Neural Networks* **1**(2), 216–228.

Leitch, G. and J. Tanner. 1991. Economic forecast evaluation: Profits versus the conventional error measures. *The American Economic Review* , 580–590.

A Hybrid Classification Approach to Predicting Mean and Volatility of Stock and FX Data and Performance Quantification Using an Optimality Score

David H. Kil and Frances B. Shin
School of Management
Arizona State University West
6932 W. Via Montoya Dr.
Glendale, AZ 85310, U.S.A.
(602) 925-7436
(602) 925-6988 (fax)
{kild, shinf}@master.tds-az.lmco.com

In financial data analysis, we are confronted with two fundamental issues—a forecasting model's ability to capture all the useful information present in input data efficiently and simultaneous estimation of mean and volatility to maximize an investor's utility function—provided that input data contain useful information. In this paper, we explore the concepts of sufficient statistics, class separability, and data compression to quantify the extent to which a classifier approximates the Bayes classifier. We further investigate how hidden Markov models, genetic algorithms, and artificial neural networks can be combined to address the two issues. The key ingredient in our hybrid classification approach is judicious reduction of model parameters for both improved prediction performance and computational tractability. We illustrate the effectiveness of this hybrid approach with S&P 500 and foreign exchange (FX) rate prediction.

1 Introduction

In parameter estimation, the Cramer–Rao lower bound (CRLB) provides the best achievable estimation accuracy and an estimator that attains the CRLB is called an *efficient* estimator. In pattern recognition, we typically implement a number of classifiers and select the one that provides the best performance. Unfortunately, this heuristic approach does not address the degree of optimality or efficiency of the selected classifier in comparison with the Bayes classifier, which provides the theoretical upper bound on classification performance. Economically, it is of great importance to know the performance upper bounds so that we can generate realistic performance-versus-cost curves for various problems.

Just as important is the prediction of mean and volatility since an investor's indifference curve is a function of both expected return (measured in mean) and risk (measured in variance or volatility) (Mansfield, 1996). In this paper, we attempt to address the following question: given T_o observation points, predict the expected return and variance[a] associated with data points that lie between $T_o + T_p$ and $T_o + T_p + T_{pd}$, where T_p and T_{pd} refer to the prediction length and prediction duration, respectively.

This paper is organized as follows. We first explore the concepts of sufficient statistics, data compression, and class discrimination to quantify the extent to which a classifier approximates the Bayes classifier. We explain the classification CRLB algorithm with two examples—a theoretical model and S&P 500 price data. We then proceed to the hybrid modeling approach, where various models are combined in a synergistic manner for robust mean and volatility prediction. We apply the hybrid algorithm to S&P 500 and FX market data.

2 Classification CRLB Estimation

In this section, we explore how we can quantify classification CRLB. We first describe the underlying concepts of data compression, sufficient statistics, and class separability. We then proceed to the CRLB algorithm description.

2.1 Sufficient Statistics and Class Separability

Let us make a suite of measurements y that can be described by the probability function $p_\theta(y)$, where θ parameterizes $p(y)$ and $p_\theta(y) = p(y|\theta)$. If $z = f(y)$, where the dimension of z is smaller than that of y and $p_\theta(y|z) = p(y|z)$, then we say that z captures all the useful information in y. Furthermore, z is more memory-efficient than y since $f(\cdot)$ compresses y into a sufficient statistic (Scharf, 1991).

Sufficient statistics are closely related to class separability. In general, optimality score J is measured by

$$J = \frac{1}{N_y} \int_{\Omega} \mathrm{CS}\left[p_{\theta_1}(y), \cdots, p_{\theta_{N_c}}(y)\right] dy, \qquad (1)$$

where N_y is the dimension of y, Ω is the overlapped region[b] in z projected onto y, and $\mathrm{CS}(\cdot)$ is a class separability function that measures the degree of feature space overlap between classes. $\mathrm{CS}(\cdot)$ encompasses multimodal overlap measure, divergence, and Bhattacharyya distance (Kil & Shin, 1996a). In essence, a classifier performs the $f(\cdot)$ operation. Therefore, θ is equivalent to class label[c] while y and z denote an input feature vector and a classification

[a] After a differencer.

[b] Between two classes.

[c] That is, market moving up (up class) or down (down class).

LLR score, respectively. In short, the degree of sufficient statistics can be measured by class separability in the multidimensional feature space Ω.

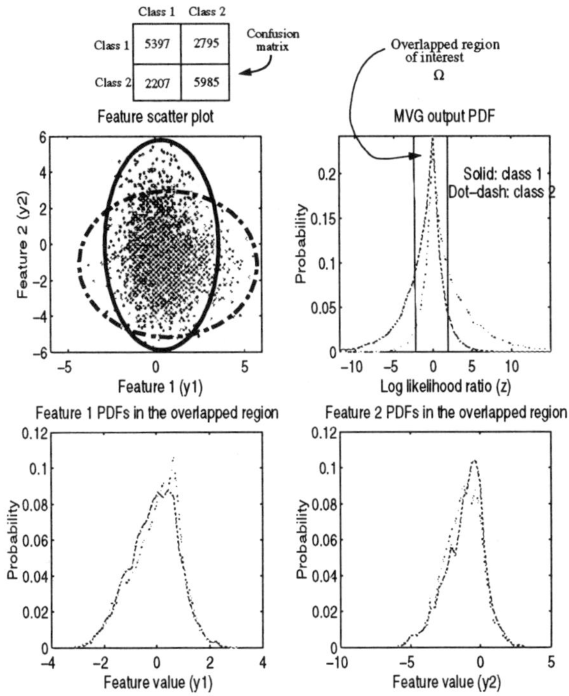

Figure 1: The property of the Bayes classifier—similar class-conditional PDFs in Ω. In this case, $J = 0.035$.

This concept can be reinforced with an interesting two-class, two-feature problem as shown in Figure 1. For this problem, the two class-conditional PDFs—$p_{\theta_1}(y)$ and $p_{\theta_2}(y)$—are both normal with different covariance matrices and mean vectors. Naturally, the multivariate Gaussian classifier (MVG) that assumes that class-conditional PDFs are normal is the Bayes classifier. For a two-class problem, MVG computes the log likelihood ratio (LLR) by performing the following operation:

$$\mathrm{LLR} = (y - \mu_{\theta_1})^t R_{\theta_1}^{-1} (y - \mu_{\theta_1}) - (y - \mu_{\theta_2})^t R_{\theta_2}^{-1} (y - \mu_{\theta_2}), \tag{2}$$

where θ_i, R_i, and μ_i represent the ith class, covariance matrix of the ith class, and mean vector of the ith class, respectively.

In order to measure the extent to which MVG captures useful information present in the two input features, the following class separability function is used:

$$\mathrm{CS} = |p_{\theta_1}(y|z_\Omega) - p_{\theta_2}(y|z_\Omega)|, \tag{3}$$

where z_Ω is the region in z with high class overlap. As expected, CS ≈ 0 when $p_{\theta_1}(y|z_\Omega) \approx p_{\theta_2}(y|z_\Omega)$. The areas in z with relatively little class overlap are excluded since prediction errors in those regions are minimal. That is, we zero in on the area with most prediction errors to investigate the extent to which prediction performance can be further improved.

Based on numerous experiments with a number of known and unknown class-conditional PDFs, J of less than 0.0375 implies that a classifier is in essence the Bayes classifier. That is, the correct classification performance of around 69.5% in this case cannot be further improved by changing the classifier architecture. Instead, we should concentrate on gathering additional input data to improve the information content. Applying different class separability measures yields similar outcomes for J.

2.2 *Classification CRLB Estimation Algorithm*

In this subsection, we provide a set of procedures to compute the classification CRLB.

1. Rank order features and find the minimum classification dimension.

2. Decorrelate input features using the orthogonality criterion via the singular value decomposition (SVD) of a feature covariance matrix (Golub & Loan, 1989). This step allows us to compute sufficient statistics using marginal densities. Advantages of working with marginal densities are computational tractability and mitigation of the curse of dimensionality in estimating sufficient statistics.

3. Compute classification LLR scores for test feature vectors.

4. Generate the LLR PDF curves at the classifier output. Identify regions of overlap Ω between the two classes.

5. Find and compute marginal PDFs of the test feature vectors that fall into the regions of overlap.

6. Calculate the class separability (CS) score. If $p_{\theta_1}(y|z_\Omega) = p_{\theta_2}(y|z_\Omega) = \cdots = p_{\theta_{N_c}}(y|z_\Omega)$, then the classifier transforms y into a sufficient statistic and we no longer need to investigate additional classifier architecture.

7. Integrate CS along y derived from Ω for each feature and compute the average score J as shown in equation 1.

2.3 S&P 500 Data Analysis Results

Features are derived from the following data base provided by Telechart 2000:

- raw S&P 500 price data (9/18/86 to 10/17/95, once-per-day sample rate),
- advance and decline line,
- % of stocks above 200-day moving average,
- % of stocks above 40-day moving average,
- the ratio of the number of stocks breaking their 4-week high share prices to the number of stocks that fall below 4-week low prices,[d]
- the ratio of 52-week high to 52-week low, and
- cumulative volume index.

We randomly partition the data into separate training and test subsets for cross-validation. For this analysis, we use the observation (T_o) and prediction (T_p) durations of 32 and 64 days, respectively (Kil & Shin, 1996b).

Figure 2 illustrates a two-class (i.e., market doing better or worse than inflation plus commission) problem. The compressed feature scatter plots exhibit highly multimodal characteristics with large class overlap.

We now apply the same set of procedures described in Section 2.2. Since both class-conditional PDFs are highly multimodal and non-Gaussian, MVG is not an optimal classifier for this problem. Figure 3 shows that $p_{\theta_{\mathrm{up}}}(y|z_\Omega) \neq p_{\theta_{\mathrm{down}}}(y|z_\Omega)$ for MVG.

Now we explore a different classifier architecture. The adaptive clustering probabilistic neural network (ACPNN) embodies all the good qualities of k-nearest neighbor (kNN), learning vector quantizer (LVQ), probabilistic neural network (PNN), maximum likelihood PNN (Streit, 1990), and scale-space clustering (Wong & Posner, 1993). ACPNN combines scale-space clustering with a Gaussian mixture model to estimate class-conditional PDFs in a computationally efficient, yet robust manner. Instead of finding the right number of clusters using computationally expensive *free fractional energy*, we initially overestimate the number of clusters and set the threshold on the minimum

[d]Or simply the ratio of 4-week high to 4-week low.

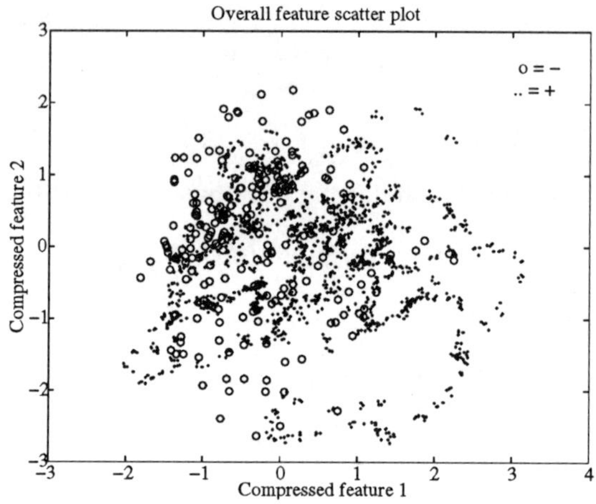

Figure 2: Actual compressed feature distribution.

Mahalanobis distance between any two clusters. Next, we perform a single-step cluster merging operation to reduce the number of clusters followed by estimation of parameters (mean vector and covariance matrix) associated with each merged cluster. The parameter estimation step can be replaced with an iterative expectation–maximization algorithm similar to the parameter refinement step in hidden Markov models (HMM) and LVQ. We compute the LLR score as follows:

$$d(j) = \operatorname*{Min}_{1\leq n\leq M_j} (y-\mu_n^j)^t(R_n^j)^{-1}(y-\mu_n^j), \tag{4}$$

$$j_y = \operatorname*{arg\,min}_{1\leq j\leq N_c} d(j), \tag{5}$$

$$\mathrm{LLR}_{ij} = d(i) - d(j), \tag{6}$$

where M_j is the number of clusters for the jth class.

As shown on Figure 4, ACPNN provides near optimal performance with J of 0.0266 in comparison to 0.1153 for MVG. The score of 0 for J indicates a perfect match between the two class-conditional densities. As mentioned in Section 3.1, J of less than 0.0375 implies that the classifier is near optimal and that little performance improvement can be realized by changing a classifier architecture. That is, $J < 0.0375$ implies that the classifier is in essence the Bayes classifier that provides the theoretical upper bound on classification performance. On the other hand, $J \gg 0.0375$ implies that classifier archi-

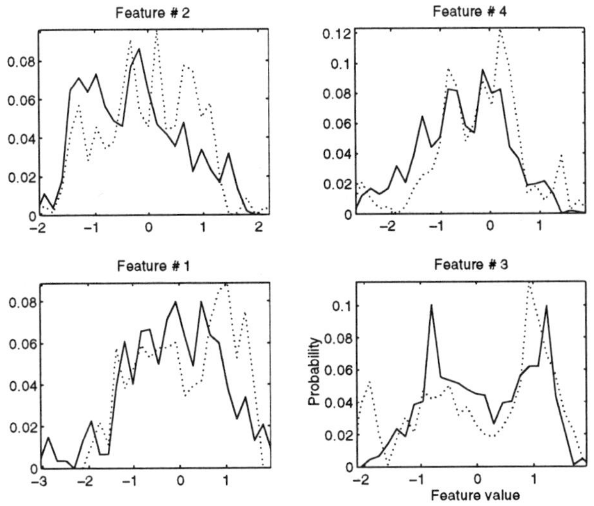

Figure 3: It is quite apparent that the two class-conditional probability functions for MVG are not identical. This implies that there is some room for improvement by changing the classifier structure.

tecture can be improved to extract additional discriminatory information for more accurate prediction performance.

For comparison, ACPNN and MVG yield correct prediction performances of 89.2 and 65.7%, respectively. As expected, J is negatively correlated with the prediction performance. When J is small, the only way to improve prediction performance further is to fuse and optimize more features derived from additional data sources, such as M2 money supply, daily federal funds rate, daily market yield on long-term U.S. government securities, and so on (Kil & Shin, 1997). The major benefit of additional data sources is that they tend to provide useful, and hopefully orthogonal information for forecasting.

3 Hybrid Classification Approach

A key requirement in efficient and accurate forecasting of dynamic market conditions is construction of a minimal-state model that captures all the useful information or sufficient statistics from raw data. That is, it is crucial that the model incorporate market dynamics in an efficient manner. In this section, we explore a symbiotic use of (1) low-dimensional data projection stemming from nonlinear and linear signal modeling, (2) an hidden Markov model (HMM),

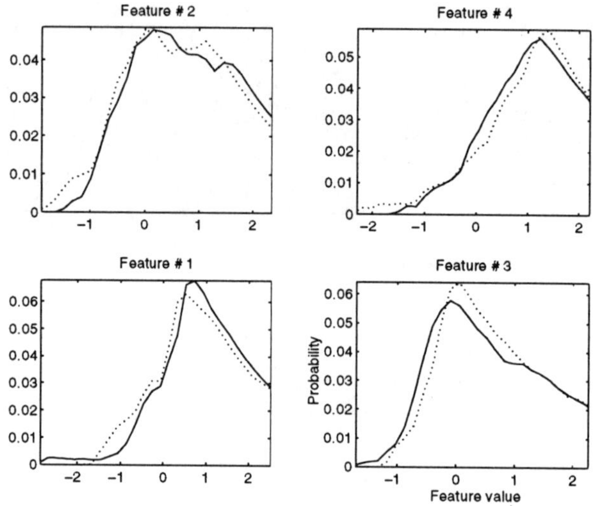

Figure 4: ACPNN yields nearly identical class-conditional probability functions, implying that it captures nearly all the useful information in the input feature data.

(3) a genetic algorithm (GA), and (4) an artificial neural network (ANN) in robust mean and volatility forecasting. Figure 5 shows the flowchart of our approach and defines the following prediction terms: T_o, T_p, and T_{pd}.

3.1 Signal Analysis & Feature Extraction

We take advantage of low-dimensional transformation spaces and HMMs to capture static and dynamic properties of time-series data for improved signal-to-noise ratio (SNR) and robustness (Shin & Kil, 1996). We explore the following four projection spaces for signal characterization:

1. *Compressed phase map:* We capture dynamical properties of time-series data with the time-embedded phase map. Such a representation is popular in modeling chaotic systems for noise reduction and weak-signal recovery (Myers & etal., 1992). In general, the phase map is constructed by time-embedding the raw time-domain data:

$$X = [x_0 \; x_1 \; \cdots \; x_{K-1}], \tag{7}$$

where $x_n = [x(n) \; x(n+1) \; \cdots \; x(n+N-1)]^t$. We perform the principal component analysis on R_x $(= XX^t)$ to reduce the dimension of the phase

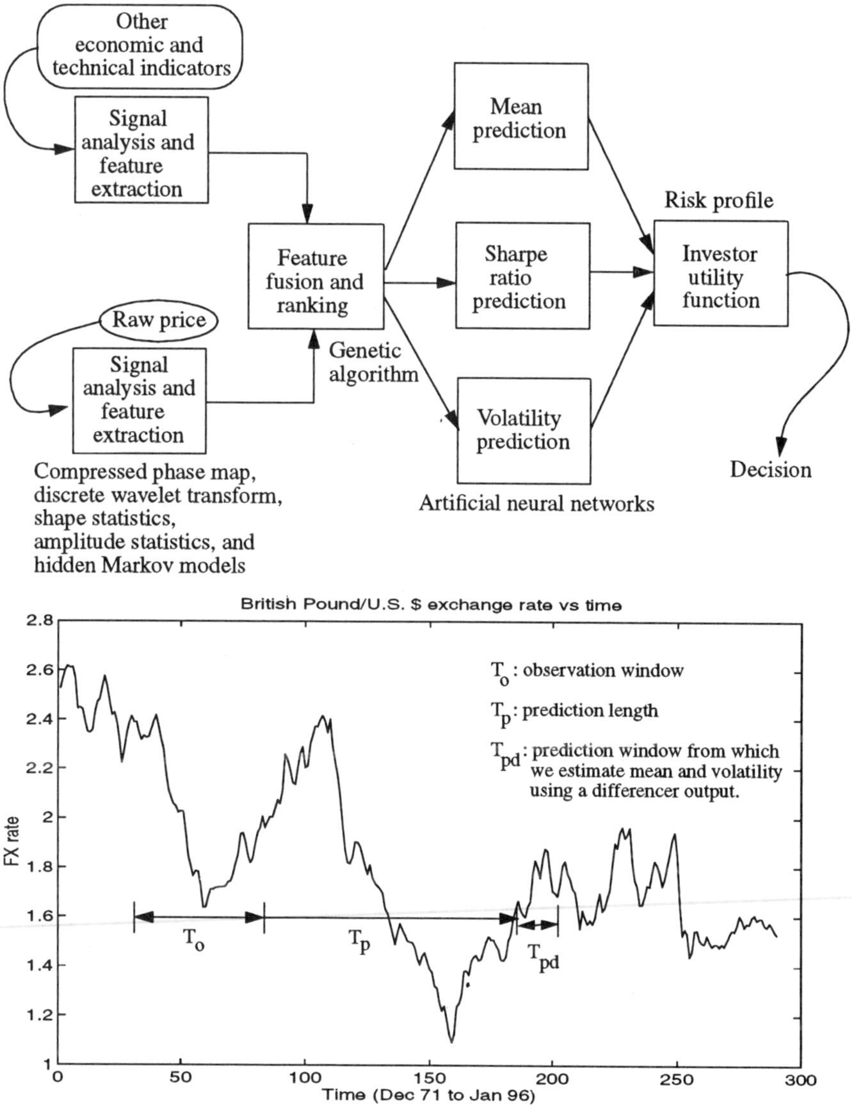

Figure 5: Our approach to mean and volatility prediction.

map. That is, the compressed phase-map coefficients constitute a feature set from this projection space.

2. *Discrete Wavelet transform (DWT):* We apply DWT to capture multiresolution spectral properties of time-series data. From each hierarchical subband, we estimate mean and variance to characterize cyclical behaviors of local price and economic data.

3. *Shape and amplitude statistics:* We calculate mean, standard deviation, skewness, and kurtosis associated with shape and amplitude of local observation data of length T_o. This projection space allows us to compactly express the local population distribution.

4. *Ergodic Hidden Markov Model:* Contrary to the popular use of an HMM as a recognizer in speech recognition, we use an ergodic HMM as a preprocessor that reports transitory characteristics of observation data. We initially estimate the HMM parameters—initial state occupancy probabilities, state transition probabilities, and observation probabilities—via vector quantization (VQ) and counting, and refine them later with the segmental k-means (SKM) algorithm (Kil & Shin, 1996a). We extract state transition and obervation likelihood score sequences associated with each observation sequence during testing.

In summary, we extract a total of 305 features for later feature optimization with a genetic algorithm. For this case, T_o, T_p, and T_{pd} are equal to 32, 64, and 10 trading days, respectively.

3.2 Genetic Algorithm—Feature Ranking

GA combines both stochastic and combinatorial optimization methods to efficiently search a multidimensional feature space for feature optimization and dimension reduction. Bala and *et al.* describe an approach that integrates GA and tree structures to efficiently determine an optimal feature subset for robust pattern recognition (Bala & etal., 1995). This approach with the exception of mutation is conceptually similar to a branch-and-bound algorithm for feature subset selection. Our objective is to find the most efficient feature-space representation. This step allows us to reduce the classification dimension from 305 to 8.

3.3 Prediction with Artificial Neural Networks

ANNs transform the reduced feature vector space to an output decision space to facilitate decision making. Since each classifier performs input-to-output mapping differently, it is imperative that we select the right classifier architecture that minimizes model mismatch errors. That is, we would like to use a classifier that achieves sufficient statistics from the original feature space.

3.4 Real-Data Analysis Results

Besides the database described in Section 2.3, we used the following additional data to evaluate our hybrid algorithm:

- dollars trade-weighted exchange index averages of daily figures (TWEX),
- the ratio of 26-week high to 26-week low,
- daily federal funds rate,
- daily market yield on long-term U.S.
- government securities,
- M1 money supply, and
- M2 money supply.

From the 305 initial feature candidates, we selected the top 8 features using the genetic algorithm. In order to simplify our analysis, we coarsely quantized the output into two levels—better or worse than average. We used a training fraction of 0.6 for random partitioning while that for front-and-back partitioning[e] varied from 0.6 to 0.8. Figures 6 and 7 display prediction performances of S&P 500 price and TWEX rate data, respectively, as a function of classifier architecture, feature dimension, and data partitioning.

Prediction performance is averaged over eight cross-validated runs with random partitioning. Since most features are generally multimodal and non-Gaussian, it seems intuitive that MVG is suboptimal. That is, MVG tends to suffer from model mismatch. On the contrary, ACPNN estimates class-conditional PDFs using multiple Gaussian clusters and provides excellent prediction performance. This example illustrates the importance of matching the classifier topology to the underlying feature distribution.

It is quite interesting that although ACPNN clearly outperforms MVG on randomly partitioned data sets, the performance gap between the two classifiers narrows or even reverses the trend for front-and-back partitioning. With random partitioning, the degree of data mismatch between training and test sets is expected to be low. That is, there is less probability of encountering

[e]The first $X\%$ for training and the next $Y\%$ for testing, where $X + Y = 100$.

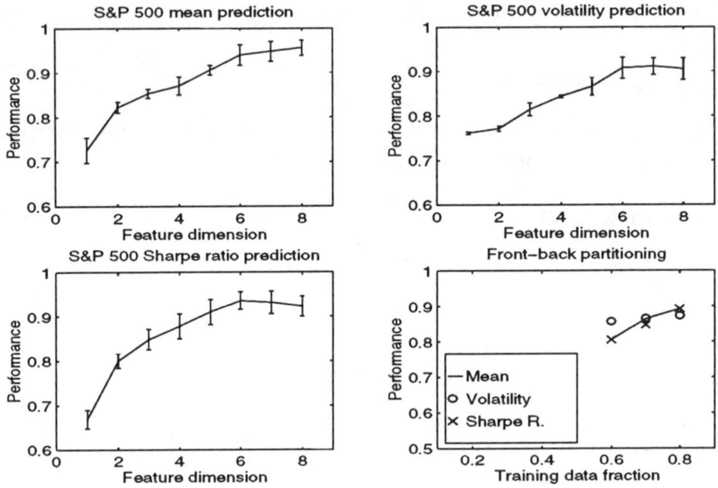

(a) ACPNN forecasting performance—random and front-back partitioning

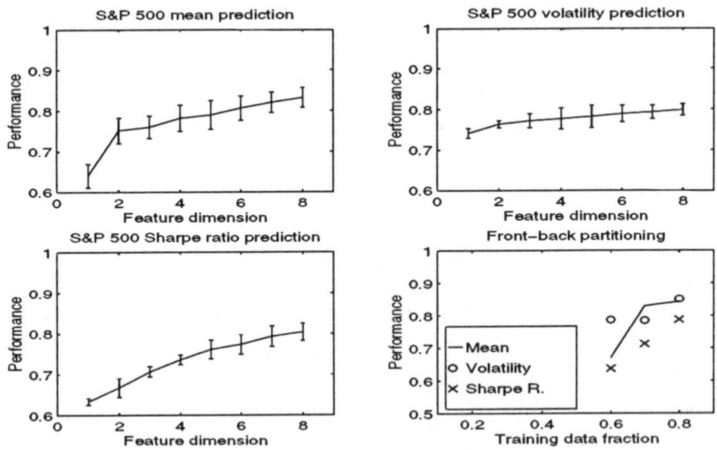

(b) MVG forecasting performance.

Figure 6: S&P 500 price mean and volatility prediction performance summary. Error bars are derived from 8 randomly partitioned and separate training and test data sets.

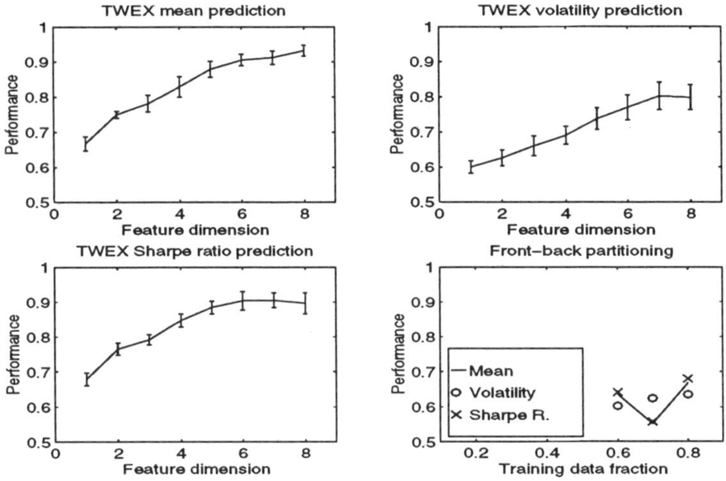

(a) ACPNN TWEX forecasting performance

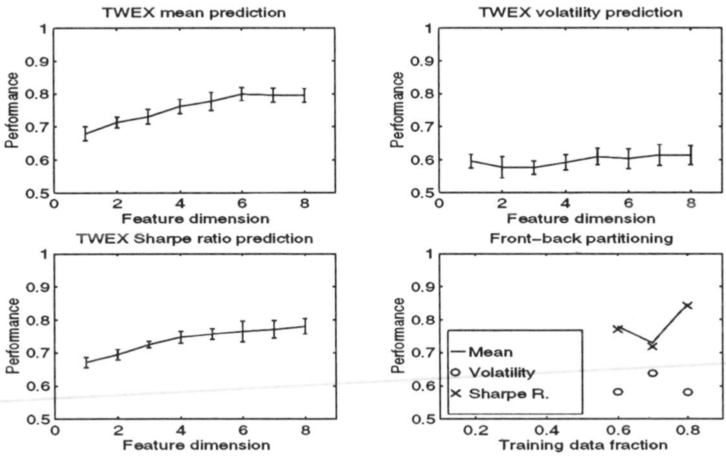

(b) MVG forecasting performance

Figure 7: TWEX rate mean and volatility prediction performance summary. In general, volatility prediction is more difficult than mean prediction. In the front-and-back partitioning case (especially with training fraction of 0.6), MVG outperforms ACPNN!

new, unexpected patterns in the test set, which makes random partitioning ideal for establishing performance upper bounds. In this case, injecting extra degrees of freedom to a classifier model (ACPNN has more parameters than MVG) pays off, especially when feature PDFs are complex—multimodal and non-Gaussian with nonlinear class boundaries.

However, the same strategy can backfire when there exists a relatively high degree of data mismatch[f] between training and test sets. In such a case, using a simpler model can sometimes yield more robust prediction performance. The TWEX case with a relatively low training fraction (0.6) is such an example. Figure 8 shows three-dimensional joint class-conditional PDFs for both training and test sets with a training fraction of 0.6. The two sets of PDF plots exhibit some amount of mismatch between training and test data sets as evidenced by the two somewhat different class-conditional PDFs. It is interesting to note that MVG outperforms ACPNN by 14% for this data set (77.85% to 63.56%). The reason is that although each class-conditional density in the training set is not exactly normal, MVG generalizes it to a normal density. On the other hand, ACPNN faithfully constructs each class-conditional PDF using multiple clusters. While more accurate, ACPNN makes itself vulnerable to data mismatch. Therefore, model selection requires a careful trade-off between actual class-conditional PDF derived from training data and the extent of data mismatch.

4 Conclusion

In this paper, we presented a classification CRLB algorithm and a hybrid classification approach to mean and volatility prediction. A central tenet in our approach is selection of a minimal-state model that achieves sufficient statistics through low-dimensional projection-space investigation, feature fusion, GA-based feature-dimension reduction, and ANN-based decision mapping. Since our good-feature distribution is quite complex, ACPNN provides much better mapping and less model mismatch than MVG for randomly partitioned data sets, illustrating the importance of a flexible classifier architecture. However, for front-and-back partitioning with substantial data mismatch between training and testing, a simpler model can sometimes provide more robust prediction performance These results clearly point to the importance of a careful trade-off between performance and robustness. In short, we advocate a hybrid approach that combines the best attributes of various algorithms in a synergistic manner to extract the maximum amount of useful information present in raw data. Our

[f] On the contrary, model mismatch refers to a forecasting model's inadequacy in approximating the actual class-conditional PDF.

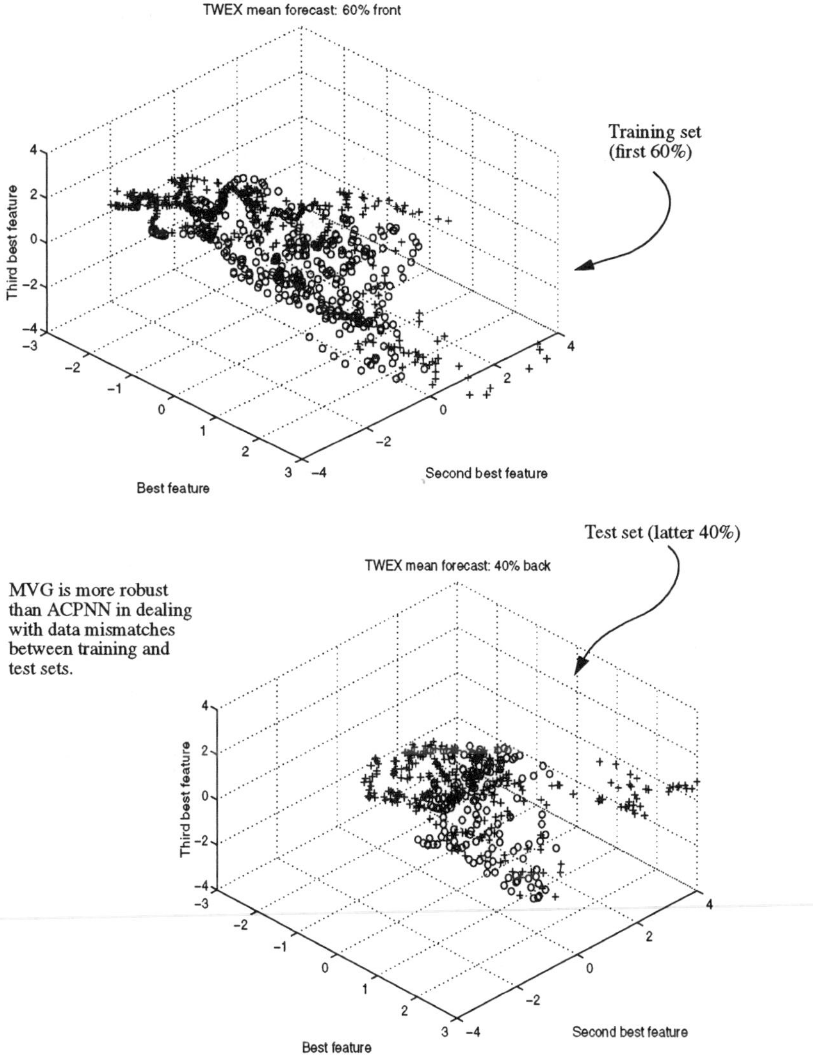

Figure 8: In some instances, MVG can be more robust than ACPNN in dealing with data set mismatches. This points to the importance of understanding the impacts of both model and data mismatches on forecasting performance.

future effort will focus on investigating the feasibility of situationally adaptive classifier architecture that adapts its structure to changing market conditions in a timely manner. We will also explore the utility of fusing features from corporate financial statements.

5 Acknowledgment

We thank Prof. Blake LeBaron of the University of Wisconsin for pointing out the Federal Reserve Bank of St. Louis web site for economic database, which we ftped to support our data analysis.

References

Bala, J. and et al. 1995. Hybrid learning using genetic algorithms and decision trees for pattern classification. *Proc. IJCAI Conference* .

Golub, H. and C. V. Loan. 1989. *Matrix Computations.* Johns Hopkins.

Kil, D. and F. Shin. 1997. A hybrid approach to modeling and forecasting mean and volatility of stock prices and fx rates with a combination of genetic algorithms, hidden markov models, and artificial neural networks. *Proc. of NNCM'96* .

Kil, D. and F. Shin. 1996a. *Pattern Recognition and Prediction with Applications to Signal Characterization.* AIP Press.

Kil, D. and F. Shin. 1996b. Stock price prediction using an integrated pattern recognition paradigm. In *Neural Networks in Financial Engineering (Proceedings of NNCM'95, London)*, A.-P. N. Refenes, Y. Abu-Mostafa, J. Moody and A. Weigend (eds), pp. 270–283. World Scientific.

Mansfield, E. 1996. *Managerial Economics.* W.W. Norton & Company.

Myers, C. and et al. 1992. Modeling chaotic systems with hidden markov models. *Proc. ICASSP-92* .

Scharf, L. 1991. *Statistical Signal Processing.* Addison-Wesley.

Shin, F. and D. Kil. 1996. Full-spectrum signal processing using a classify-before-detect paradigm. *J. Acoust. Soc. Am.* **99**(4), 2188–2197.

Streit, R. L. 1990. A neural network for optimum neyman-pearson classification. *Proc. Int. Joint Conf. Neural Networks* **1**, 685–690.

Wong, Y. and E. Posner. 1993. A new clustering algorithm applicable to multispectral and polarimetric sar images. *IEEE Trans. Geosci. Remote Sensing* **31**(3), 634–644.

NONLINEAR VERSUS LINEAR TECHNIQUES FOR SELECTING INDIVIDUAL STOCKS

SAM MAHFOUD
GANESH MANI
SUSAN REIGEL
Advanced Investment Technology
311 Park Place Blvd., Suite 250
Clearwater, FL 34619, USA
E-mail: {sam, ganesh, susan}@ait-tech.com

Neural networks and genetic algorithms, two nonlinear artificial-intelligence-based forecasting methods, are applied to the task of predicting the relative returns of individual stocks. The nonlinear methods are compared to each other and to a linear method, least-squares linear regression, that is applied to the same task. The experiments consist of running each algorithm on 293 stocks at 12 historical time points, uniformly spread over a three year period. Additional analysis simulates the effects of forecast combination and portfolio optimization, and attributes performance primarily to stock-specific forecasting skill.

1 Introduction

Selecting stocks for inclusion in a portfolio is a challenging task. Human investment managers fall into two broad camps: passive and active. The goal of the passive or indexing camp is to select stocks in an index and weight them according to their respective weights in the index, thus tracking the performance of the index as closely as possible. The goal of active management is to construct portfolios that outperform an underlying index or other benchmark. Typically, this is done by overweighting stocks that are expected to outperform the underlying benchmark and underweighting or short-selling stocks that are expected to underperform.

Like other active managers, we believe that it is possible to distinguish, statistically speaking, stocks that will outperform and underperform an index. Large amounts of data – both fundamental and technical – are available for each stock. The key to superior stock selection appears to be the ability to decide which data items are relevant and what their relationship is to future stock prices. Active managers have grown in number, and many of them make the arguably reasonable assumptions that all people do not react similarly to publicly available data, and that everybody does not react at the same speed. These assumptions open up the possibility that one can beat the consensus by performing better or more efficient analysis, using advanced computer and mathematical tools as well as time-series modeling techniques (e.g., Farmer and Sidorowich, 1988; Weigend and Gershenfeld, 1994; White, 1994).

Neural networks (NNs), genetic algorithms (GAs), and, in general, nonlinear artificial intelligence (AI) techniques are promising forecasting methods for the active management of stock portfolios (Freedman, 1995). While traditional forecasting techniques such as regression typically assume a linear relationship between past data and future performance, nonlinear techniques allow that relationship to be nonlinear. The manager who employs nonlinear AI techniques generally assumes that most existing linear relationships have already been discovered and exploited by others; the manager hence uses nonlinear algorithms to seek out relationships that might be invisible to linear prediction techniques.

2 The neural network system

Neural networks (Hertz, Krogh, and Palmer, 1991) are micro-modular computing models that are loosely inspired by the human brain. A neural network is best thought of as a group of interlinked processing units, where each processor computes a weighted sum of the data coming from other processors. Each processor then outputs a single number, a nonlinear function of the weighted sum. A popular type of NN is a *feedforward* network, where processing units are arranged by layers, and where each layer is connected to the next. A learning algorithm called *backpropagation* (Rumelhart, Hinton, and Williams, 1986) adjusts the weights on each link based on gradient descent. Learning takes place by changing the weights based upon the difference between the NN's actual output and its expected or target output. Many iterations – often up to several hundred *epochs* – are required before satisfactory convergence is obtained. An epoch is one pass through the entire training data set.

Neural networks have the advantage of being somewhat robust to noise in the data (as opposed to algorithms such as decision trees [Mooney, Shavlik, Towell, and Gove, 1989]). The *black-box* nature of NNs, on the other hand, makes it hard to explain the relationships that the trained network encodes.

The NNs that we employ are part of the AXON system that is described more fully in another paper (Mani, Quah, Mahfoud, and Barr, 1995). Our NNs are feedforward, with one hidden layer of nodes. They train via backpropagation. Our NNs (as well as the other techniques studied in this paper) perform stock-specific modeling: they assume that each stock has its own unique performance footprint.

3 The genetic algorithm system

Genetic algorithms (Goldberg, 1989; Holland, 1992) are general-purpose problem-solving techniques that operate analogous to evolution. GAs iteratively manipulate a *population* of candidate *solutions*. Solutions are ranked or rated according to their quality or *fitness*. Each iteration is called a *generation*. In traditional GAs, a generation consists of the population undergoing *selection*, *crossover*, and *mutation* operations. Basically, selection duplicates better solutions and discards worse solutions; crossover is a binary operator that mixes components from differing solutions; and mutation is a unary operator that alters solutions.

Many components are necessary to the design of a GA-based forecasting system. We briefly highlight some of the major components below. Our GA-based system is described more fully in other papers (Mahfoud and Mani, 1995, 1996). Other GA-based systems for forecasting include Packard's (1990) and de la Maza's (1989).

Our system optimizes populations of classification rules. When the GA has finished running, the population contains a set of rules that functions much like the rule base of an expert system. That is, when new data is input to that set of rules, certain rules are triggered, and some rule outputs a prediction.

As the GA runs, a niching method (Mahfoud, 1995) ensures that the population maintains a diverse, cooperative set of rules. Each rule's fitness is negatively correlated with the frequency and magnitude of its prediction errors, taken over some quantity of data in a training database. In situations where the GA is unclear on which prediction to make, it has the option of outputting no prediction at all.

4 Experiments

We conduct a set of experiments with the intent of demonstrating two hypotheses. The first hypothesis is that nonlinear AI techniques such as neural networks and genetic algorithms are able to identify stocks that will outperform the market, as well as stocks that will underperform the market. The second hypothesis is that nonlinear AI techniques are more proficient at the above task than are linear techniques such as regression.

We utilize a set of 16 proprietary factors, derived from both fundamental data (such as company earnings) and technical data (such as prices), for each experiment. We choose 12 dates on which to make predictions, during the three years, 1992-1994, maximally separated (three-month intervals). We choose 293 stocks, based upon data availability, on which to run algorithms for each date. The stocks represent many industries, are highly liquid, and are mostly LargeCap stocks. For each experiment (running a particular algorithm on a particular stock on a particular date), we make a single prediction – the future 12-week relative return. Our benchmark index is the equally-weighted S&P 500. The relative return for a given stock is defined as the stock's return over a 12-week period, minus the index's return over the same 12-week period.

Performance measures are computed as a function of predicted relative returns and actual relative returns. Specifically, our performance measures group forecasts according to their magnitudes, and compute the average actual relative return for each group of forecasts.

Neural networks and genetic algorithms run for each stock on each date, yielding a total of 3516 NN and 3516 GA experiments. Ordinary least-squares linear regression also runs on the same data, for a total of 3516 regression experiments. All algorithms run on identical data.

5 Results

Figure 1 shows performances on each date for the three algorithms. (The top graph is for the NN; the middle graph, for the GA; and the bottom graph, for linear regression.) On each date, the graphs display the actual relative returns for two groups of forecasts, averaged over the number of stocks in each group. The first group of forecasts (labeled "Buy") is the top quintile of all positive forecasts for each date. The second group (labeled "Sell") is the bottom quintile of all negative forecasts for each date. Higher performance numbers in the Buy group are better than lower ones; the opposite is true for the Sell group.

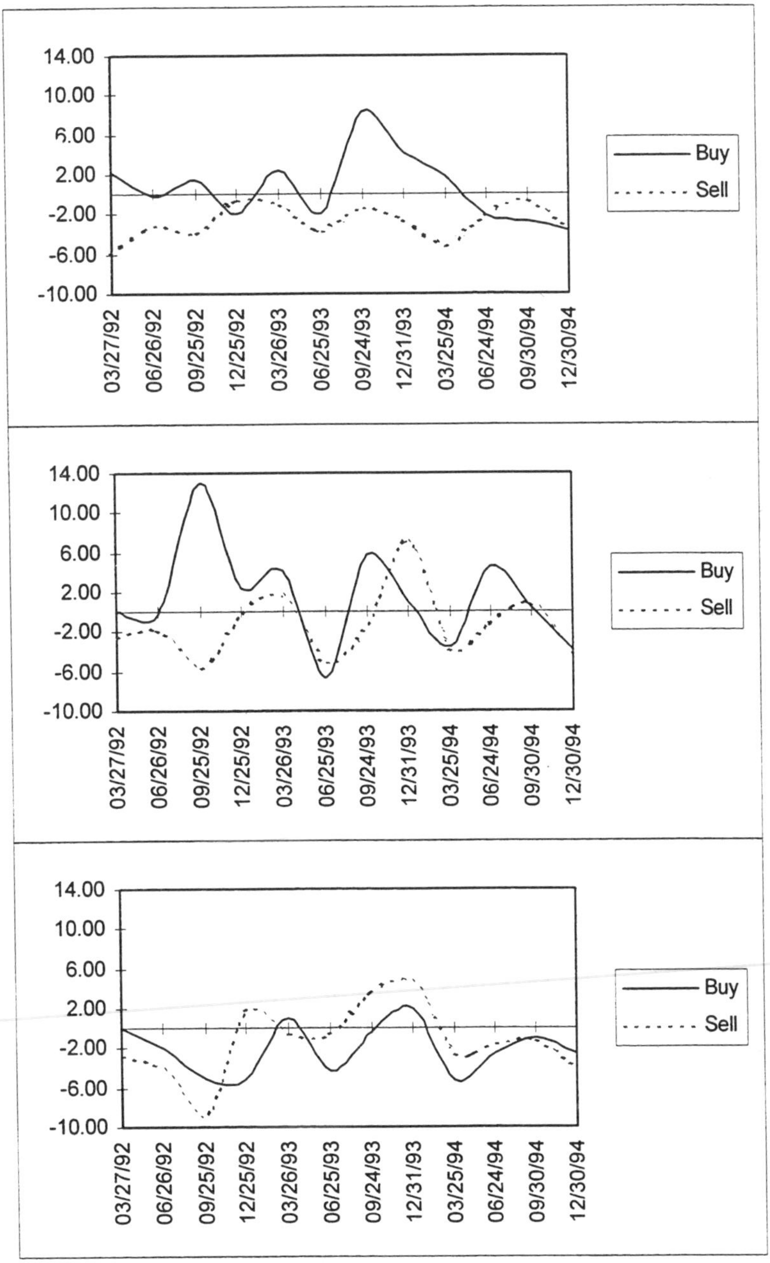

Fig. 1: Average actual relative returns are shown for the highest-magnitude forecasts. The top graph is for the NN; the middle graph, the GA; and the bottom, regression.

Subtracting the performance of the Sell group from that of the Buy group for each date yields a performance measure we call *spread*. The higher the spread, the more skillful the model. Note that spread is an index-independent performance measure – no matter what index is used as a benchmark, the spread remains the same.

We compute the average spread across all 12 dates. The NNs have an average spread of 3.40%; the GAs, 2.78%; linear regression, –0.77%. Results for the NNs and the GAs are statistically significant at the 95% confidence level. That is, with greater than 95% probability, the average spread for the NNs is greater than zero; the same holds for the GAs.

Since linear regression has a negative spread, we can reject any notion that it displays skill. However, we can test its utility as a contrary indicator (that would consistently output poor predictions). At the 95% confidence level, the spread for linear regression is not significantly less than zero. Therefore, we must conclude that linear regression is not skillful, even in a contrary sense.

Overall, linear regression underperforms both the NNs and the GAs. This underperformance is statistically significant at the 95% confidence level. While the GAs have a lower spread than the NNs, the difference between NN and GA spreads is not statistically significant at the 95% confidence level.

6 Forecast combination

In the experiments, two different forecasting techniques, the NNs and the GAs, produce good results. This observation brings up the question of how a combined approach would fare. By combining the NN and GA forecasts into a single nonlinear forecast, one might hope to achieve a synergistic effect, analogous to having multiple human experts perform identical tasks and pool their results afterward. Moreover, if the experts are fairly independent, one might have greater confidence in their results should they reach similar conclusions.

We start out with the premise that using a combination of two skillful forecasting methods (in our case, NNs and GAs) is beneficial, particularly if the forecasting methods are relatively independent. We measure independence using the correlation between the NN and GA forecasts. If the correlation is either positive or negative and fairly close to zero, then independence is high. If the correlation is close to one, then independence is low.

The correlation between the NN and GA forecasts, across all 3516 experiments (and hence across all 12 time periods), is 0.28. The lowest correlation for any single time period is 0.17, while the highest is 0.38. Therefore, the two forecasting methods are fairly independent.

Our combination technique strives to form combined Buy and Sell groups that are similar in size to the Buy and Sell groups for the individual methods. Our technique also tries to keep the NN and GA Buy and Sell groups fairly well represented in the combined Buy and Sell groups. Therefore, we combine forecasts after binning. The combined Buy group is the union of the NN and GA Buy groups, minus stocks that appear in either the NN or the GA Sell group. The combined Sell group is, likewise, the union of the NN and GA Sell groups, minus stocks that appear in either the NN or the GA Buy group.

Other combination methods are possible, such as averaging either raw or scaled forecasts, or taking the intersections of bins. In practice, these or more sophisticated methods that explicitly factor in the correlation between NNs and GAs (instantaneous or over some trailing window), may yield equivalent or better results (Grinold and Kahn, 1994). In fact, a prior study (Mahfoud & Mani, 1996) that combined forecasts using bin intersection produced combined performances significantly higher than those for either the NN or the GA, in isolation.

Figure 2 shows the performance of the combined forecasts on each date. The combined forecasts have an average spread of 3.02%, which is roughly midway between the average spread for the NNs and the average spread for the GAs.

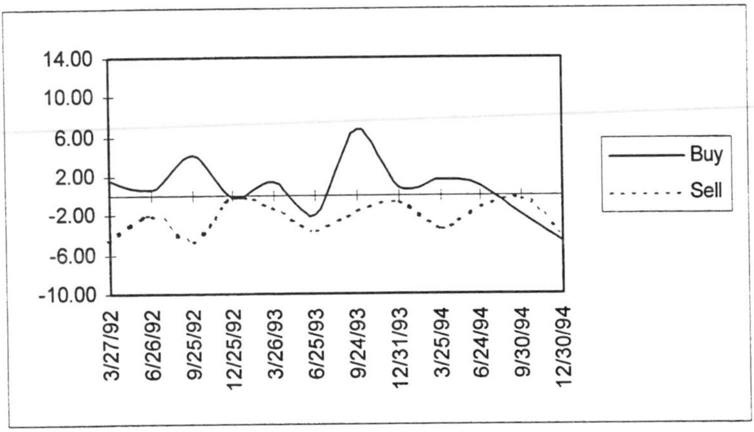

Fig. 2: Average actual relative returns are shown for the highest-magnitude, combined NN and GA forecasts.

Figure 3 shows theoretical cumulative returns, over the three-year experimental time frame, for a long-short portfolio that utilizes the combined forecasts and that realizes the full profit potential inherent in the spreads. The average annualized return is 12.41% for the spreads, with an annualized standard deviation of 6.68%. This works out to a Sharpe ratio of 1.33, factoring in an average annual risk-free return of 3.54%. (The Sharpe ratio is computed by dividing the risk premium for the portfolio – the difference between the portfolio return and the risk-free rate of return – by its standard deviation. It measures the risk premium earned per unit of risk exposure.)

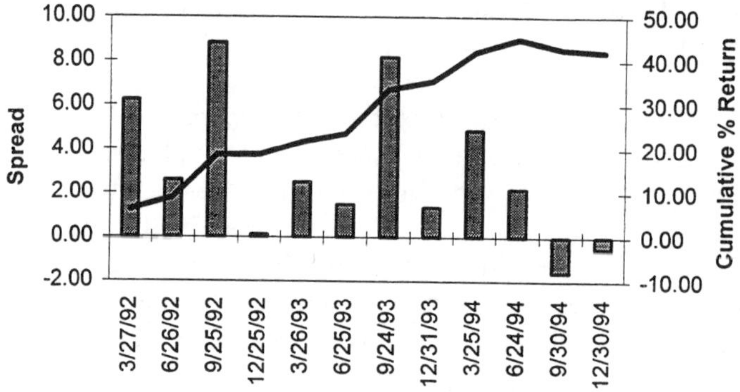

Fig. 3: Theoretical cumulative returns are shown for the combined NN and GA forecasts.

7 Portfolio optimization

A realistic portfolio would not hold equally weighted positions. Typically, portfolios optimize towards a benchmark (in our case an equally weighted S&P 500) while targeting specific risk constraints. Let us apply a minimal set of constraints to the Buy and Sell groups of the combined forecasts. These constraints are a position size ranging from 0% to 6%, a beta close to 1.0, and a constant risk multiplier that limits total risk. We keep the same stocks in the Buy and Sell lists as before optimization, but use optimization to decide on the size of each stock's position.

Returns from the optimized bins are less variable because of the portfolio constraints. The average spread for the optimized bins is 2.10% with a standard deviation of 2.40%, versus an average spread for the equally weighted bins of 3.02% with a standard deviation of 3.34%. The optimized bins have less risk (the average beta is 1.00 for the optimized Buy group and 1.01 for the optimized Sell group), but the trade-off is less return.

Performance attribution analysis of the optimized Buy and Sell groups shows that returns are primarily due to specific-stock selection, rather than other sources of risk such as beta, style biases (value versus growth), capitalization biases, or industry exposures. This confirms that the nonlinear systems are doing what they were designed to do – select individual stocks.

Additional simulation would be necessary to draw more firm conclusions about how a live portfolio would have performed during the three-year time period. Additional return can potentially be generated by letting the optimization process dip into bins other than those labeled Buy and Sell. Additional return might also be generated by updating the forecasts and the resulting portfolios more often than once a quarter. On the negative side, transaction costs, including market impact, must be factored in. Current holdings are also a major consideration in any optimization.

8 Discussion and conclusion

The two nonlinear methods tested, neural networks and genetic algorithms, demonstrate significant forecasting skill in identifying stocks that will both outperform and underperform the market. This skill is primarily due to individual stock selection as opposed to taking on various risks. The linear method, linear regression, does not demonstrate forecasting skill.

In our set of experiments, nonlinear methods have significantly greater forecasting skill than linear methods. The skill of one nonlinear method is not significantly higher than the skill of the other.

One possible reason for linear regression's poor performance is its current popularity. Because linear patterns are relatively easy to find and because so many managers are finding them, it is exceedingly difficult for one linear-based manager to gain an advantage over another. That brings up a parallel issue for nonlinear technologies. What is the implication of a much larger number of managers using nonlinear technologies? We feel that rather than the advantages disappearing, the rewards will go to whoever has the best nonlinear technologies.

Data is a major consideration as well. Whoever has better data and designs better transformations will ultimately make better predictions.

One might ask whether we might obtain different results by utilizing data other than the inputs and output of this study; perhaps linear regression's performance would improve. While a better set of data could no doubt be designed for linear regression, no attempt was made to optimize the data factors of this study for any particular algorithm. Performing such optimization is an interesting extension of this research that we are currently pursuing.

One reason for linear regression's popularity is that its straightforward mapping between input and output values is easily understood by human users. It is worth noting that genetic algorithms also offer this advantage. GAs, in fact, have the flexibility of being able to operate upon a variety of user-comprehensible solution structures, such as the rule sets we employ. We are currently examining the possibility of exploiting the explanation capabilities of these rule sets.

Combining nonlinear forecasts appears to be a promising way of either boosting or stabilizing performance. However, additional research is necessary to examine the various methods of combination.

Optimizing a portfolio of forecasts can control risk, typically by trading off some return. Simulating portfolio optimization methods is another promising area for additional research.

9 Acknowledgments

The authors thank Dean Barr, K.K. Quah, Doug Case, and Kevin Jacobs – members of the Advanced Investment Technology research team – for their contributions to this research.

10 References

Farmer, J. D., and Sidorowich, J. J., 1988, Can new approaches to nonlinear modeling improve economic forecasts?, in *The economy as an evolving complex system: SFI studies in the sciences of complexity*, edited by P. W. Anderson, K. J. Arrow, and D. Pines (Redwood City, CA: Addison-Wesley).

Freedman, R. S. (Ed.), 1995, *Proceedings of the Third International Conference on Artificial Intelligence Applications on Wall Street*, (Gaithersburg, MD: Software Engineering Press).

Goldberg, D. E., 1989, *Genetic algorithms in search, optimization, and machine learning* (Reading, MA: Addison-Wesley).

Grinold, R., and Kahn, R., 1994, Refining and combining investment information, in *Spring 1994 BARRA Newsletter*, 5-11.

Hertz, J., Krogh, A., and Palmer, R. G., 1991, *Introduction to the theory of neural computation* (Redwood City, CA: Addison-Wesley).

Holland, J. H., 1992, *Adaptation in natural and artificial systems* (Cambridge, MA: MIT Press).

Mahfoud, S. W., 1995, Niching methods for genetic algorithms (Doctoral dissertation, University of Illinois at Urbana-Champaign), *Dissertation Abstracts International* **56**(9), 4987B (University Microfilms No. 9543663).

Mahfoud, S., and Mani, G., 1995, Genetic algorithms for predicting individual stock performance, in *Proceedings of the Third International Conference on Artificial Intelligence Applications on Wall Street*, 72-78.

Mahfoud, S., and Mani, G., 1996, Financial forecasting using genetic algorithms, *Applied Artificial Intelligence* **10**, 543-565.

Mani, G., Quah, K. K., Mahfoud, S., and Barr, D., 1995, An analysis of neural-network forecasts from a large-scale, real-world stock selection system, in *Proceedings of the IEEE/IAFE 1995 Conference on Computational Intelligence for Financial Engineering (CIFEr)*, 174-181.

de la Maza, M., 1989, A SEAGUL visits the race track, in *Proceedings of the Third International Conference on Genetic Algorithms*, 208-212.

Mooney, R., Shavlik, J. W., Towell, G., and Gove, A., 1989, An experimental comparison of symbolic and connectionist learning algorithms, in *Proceedings of the Eleventh International Joint Conference on Artificial Intelligence.*

Packard, N. H., 1990, A genetic learning algorithm for the analysis of complex data, *Complex Systems* **4**(5), 543-572.

Rumelhart, D. E., Hinton, G. E., and Williams, R. J., 1986, Learning internal representations by error propagation, in *Parallel distributed processing: Explorations in the microstructure of cognition: Volume I: Foundations*, edited by D. E. Rumelhart and J. L. McClelland (Cambridge: MIT Press), 318-362.

Weigend, A. S., and Gershenfeld, N. A. (Eds.), 1994, Time series prediction: Forecasting the future and understanding the past, in *Proceedings Volume XV, Santa Fe Institute Studies in the Sciences of Complexity* (Reading, MA: Addison-Wesley).

White, H., 1994, Using artificial neural networks to develop trading systems for the S&P 500 index futures, presented at the *Second International Workshop on Neural Networks in the Capital Markets*, Pasadena, CA.

DESIGN OF TIME-VARIABLE STOP LOSSES AND PROFIT OBJECTIVES USING NEURAL NETWORKS

AMIR ATIYA
Dept. of Electrical Engineering
Caltech 136-93
Pasadena, CA 91125
amir@work.caltech.edu

Stop losses and profit objectives are important components in many trading strategies, and are used to limit losses and secure achieved profits. An investor, who buys an asset or a security at a particular price, decides that if the price drops beyond a certain level, called a stop loss, then the investor sells the security in an attempt to avoid further losses. On the other hand, if the price appreciates beyond a certain level (profit objective), the investor sells the security to secure the achieved profit, for fear that the security has become overpriced and might fall in price. In this study we propose time variable stop losses and profit objectives. Their values are not constant, but vary in the course of trade. We design a method to obtain optimal stop loss and profit objective curves, using multilayer neural networks. The method is tested on the stock market.

Keywords: Neural networks, backpropagation, trading system, stop loss, profit objective, portfolio.

1 Introduction

Stop losses and profit objectives are a major component of investment and trading strategies. They determine the timing to exit a trade, or terminate an investment, and are therefore utilized by most investors. An investor, who buys an asset or a security at a particular price, decides that if the price drops beyond a certain level (called a stop loss or a stop), then the investor sells the security in an attempt to avoid further losses. On the other hand, if the price appreciates beyond a certain level (profit objective), the investor decides that the security has become overpriced and therefore he sells the security. How far should the investor place his stop and profit objective is one of the major decisions confronting him, and is almost as important in the impact on the profit as the price forecast and the decision when to buy the security.

In Atiya (1995) we have analyzed the role of stops and profit objectives. We have derived optimal values for them, based on a certain stochastic market model. We have proved that for markets exhibiting a trending behovior, it is best to choose tight stops and wide profit objectives (with the profit objectives becoming wider for higher transaction costs). For markets exhibiting a mean reverting behavior (a market where the prices tend to oscillate in a narrow range), it is best to have tight profit objectives and somewhat wider stops (increasing with the increase of transaction costs). In this paper we further analyze the role of stops and profit objectives. Unlike [1], we propose here time-variable stops and profit objectives. This means that they are not constant in the course of the trade (or investment) duration, but vary according to how far away in the trade we have proceeded. Having variable stops and profit objectives is an additional parameter, that can help in improving further the performance of the trading system. The argument in favor of variable stops and profit objectives is that it is often worth to have a stop and profit objective that is progressively tightened in the course of trade, as this system will avoid getting stuck with a security that is staying almost constant, and therefore generating little or no profit for the length of time we hold it. Some market participants use variable stops and profit objectives, that are proportional to the volatility of the market. Others reevaluate the the stops and profit objectives periodically in the course of trade, mostly based on qualitative estimates. Our approach here is quantitative and different, and we assume the stops and profit objectives vary only as a function of how far in the trade we have proceeded. We will develop a method to design these variable stops and profit objectives, using multilayer networks. This method is explained in the next section.

2 The Model:

Let the start of a trade be at time $t = 0$ (assume it is a buy trade, i.e. we bought the security at time $t = 0$). Let the price of the security be $x'(t)$, and let the stop and the profit objective be respectively $s'(t)$ and $p'(t)$. We assume $s'(t) \leq x'(0)$ and $p'(t) \geq x'(0)$ ($x(0)$ represents the buy price). We assume that $s'(t)$ and $p'(t)$ are predetermined. They do not vary from trade to trade, and cannot be adjusted or changed in the course of a trade. Let us normalize everything as follows: from trade to trade, and cannot be adjusted or changed in the course of a trade. Let us normalize everything as follows:

$$x(t) = \frac{x'(t) - x'(0)}{x'(0)}, \tag{1}$$

$$s(t) = \frac{s'(t) - x'(0)}{x'(0)}, \tag{2}$$

$$p(t) = \frac{p'(t) - x'(0)}{x'(0)}, \tag{3}$$

where now the new price signal will start at zero level, and the level at time t represents the relative appreciation or depreciation of the asset, relative to the buy price. If in the course of the trade, the price has gone up, until it hit the profit objective curve $p(t)$, then we terminate the trade and achieve a profit equal to the value at the intersection point. On the other hand, if the price signal has gone down and hit the stop curve first, then we exit the trade with a loss equivalent to the intersection value.

The objective is to design two neural networks, one for the stop and the other for the profit objective. We use a one-input/one-output neural network for each. The input for the first neural network is the time t, and the output is $s(t)$. For the second neural network the input is t, and the output is $p(t)$:

$$s(t) = -g\Big(\sum_{i=1}^{H} v_i^{(s)} g(u_i^{(s)} t + u_{i0}^{(s)}) + v_0^{(s)}\Big) \tag{4}$$

$$p(t) = g\Big(\sum_{i=1}^{H} v_i^{(p)} g(u_i^{(p)} t + u_{i0}^{(p)}) + v_0^{(p)}\Big) \tag{5}$$

where g is the regular sigmoid function: $g(x) = 1/(1 + \exp(-x))$. Let us arrange all the weights $v_i^{(s)}$, $u_i^{(s)}$, $u_{i0}^{(s)}$, associated with the stop network in one long vector $\mathbf{w}^{(s)}$, and those associated with the profit objective network: $v_i^{(p)}$, $u_i^{(p)}$, $u_{i0}^{(p)}$, into vector $\mathbf{w}^{(p)}$. For abbreviation, the stop and profit objective can be put in the following general forms:

$$s(t) = G_s(\mathbf{w}^{(s)}, t), \tag{6}$$

$$p(t) = G_p(\mathbf{w}^{(p)}, t). \tag{7}$$

Investors are interested not only in achieving a high profit, but also a high profit in a short period of time. Rather than using merely the average profit as our objective function, we will use the average profit per time in the market (or an equivalent measure would be the annualized profit):

$$J = \frac{\text{Average profit per trade}}{\text{Average trade duration}}.$$

Let the training set consist of a number of trades with profits $P_1, ..., P_N$, and with trade durations: $T_1, ..., T_N$. Then,

$$J = \frac{\sum_{i=1}^{N} P_i}{\sum_{i=1}^{N} T_i}. \tag{8}$$

Let $x_i(t)$ be the (normalized) price signal associated with trade i, where t represent the continuous time variable.

Then, T_i is given by the intersection of $s(t)$ with $x_i(t)$, or the intersection of $p(t)$ with $x_i(t)$, whichever occurs first. Let U_s be the set of trades that hit the stop first, and U_p be the set of trades that hit the objective first. Let U_r be the set of remaining trades, that is the trades that neither hit the stop, nor the profit objective, and therefore stay until the maximum allowable length (say T).

We start with an initial weight configuration, and adjust the weights iteratively, by ascending on the objective function (8). Thus,

$$\Delta \mathbf{w}^{(s)} = \eta \frac{\partial J}{\partial \mathbf{w}^{(s)}}, \tag{9}$$

$$\Delta \mathbf{w}^{(p)} = \eta \frac{\partial J}{\partial \mathbf{w}^{(p)}}, \tag{10}$$

where η is the learning rate. Let C be the transaction costs per trade. The objective function can be expressed as:

$$J = \frac{\sum_{i \in U_s} G_s(\mathbf{w}^{(s)}, T_i) + \sum_{i \in U_p} G_p(\mathbf{w}^{(p)}, T_i) + \sum_{i \in U_r} x_i(T) - NC}{\sum_{i=1}^{N} T_i}, \tag{11}$$

where NC represents the transaction costs for the N trades. In order to obtain the gradient of J w.r.t. the weights $\mathbf{w}^{(p)}$ and $\mathbf{w}^{(s)}$, we have to pay attention to the fact that T_i and $G_p(\mathbf{w}^{(p)}, T_i)$ (or $G_s(\mathbf{w}^{(s)}, T_i)$) represent the coordinates of the intersection of $x_i(t)$ and the profit objective curve $p(t)$ (or the stop loss curve $s(t)$). A small change in $\mathbf{w}^{(p)}$ (or $\mathbf{w}^{(s)}$) will change T_i, as well as $G_p(\mathbf{w}^{(p)}, T_i)$ (or $G_s(\mathbf{w}^{(s)}, T_i)$). The derivative of T_i, $G_p(\mathbf{w}^{(p)}, T_i)$, and $G_s(\mathbf{w}^{(s)}, T_i)$ w.r.t. the weights can be obtained graphically (see Appendix for the details of the derivation of the gradient). The final update equation becomes:

$$\Delta \mathbf{w}^{(s)} = \frac{\eta}{\sum_{i=1}^{N} T_i} \left[\sum_{i \in U_s} \frac{\frac{\partial G_s}{\partial \mathbf{w}^{(s)}} \frac{\partial x_i}{\partial t}}{\frac{\partial x_i}{\partial t} - \frac{\partial G_s}{\partial t}} - J \sum_{i \in U_s} \frac{\frac{\partial G_s}{\partial \mathbf{w}^{(s)}}}{\frac{\partial x_i}{\partial t} - \frac{\partial G_s}{\partial t}} \right], \tag{12}$$

$$\Delta \mathbf{w}^{(p)} = \frac{\eta}{\sum_{i=1}^{N} T_i} \left[\sum_{i \in U_p} \frac{\frac{\partial G_p}{\partial \mathbf{w}^{(p)}} \frac{\partial x_i}{\partial t}}{\frac{\partial x_i}{\partial t} - \frac{\partial G_p}{\partial t}} - J \sum_{i \in U_p} \frac{\frac{\partial G_p}{\partial \mathbf{w}^{(p)}}}{\frac{\partial x_i}{\partial t} - \frac{\partial G_p}{\partial t}} \right], \tag{13}$$

The gradient vectors $\frac{\partial G_s}{\partial \mathbf{w}^{(s)}}$, $\frac{\partial G_p}{\partial \mathbf{w}^{(p)}}$, $\frac{\partial G_s}{\partial t}$, and $\frac{\partial G_p}{\partial t}$ can be obtained by a backpropagation like scheme (except that we are not backpropagating the error derivative, but the output derivative). The time derivative of the price signal, $\frac{\partial x_i}{\partial t}$, can be obtained by a finite difference approximation. The iterations are performed until the objective function is maximized. We note that it is desirable to start with fairly tight initial choices of $s(t)$ and $p(t)$, so that all price signals have intersections, otherwise they will not have an effect in the training process. We note also that there can be abrupt changes in J from one iteration to the next, if one price signal suddenly stops intersecting with $s(t)$ or $p(t)$, or vice versa. This happens if that price signal was nearly tangent to $s(t)$ or $p(t)$. Therefore it is preferrable to keep track and save the maximum of J and the corresponding weights in the course of the iterations.

3 Implementation Results:

We have tested the new method on the stock market. We have considered 200 companies from the New York Stock Exchange. The companies chosen are the first 200 companies in alphabetical order, as a way to avoid any selection bias. We partition the stocks into 100 companies for training, and 100 companies for testing. The buy signal is taken from Neurosoft Inc.'s proprietary trading system, which has been developed based on the same training set of 100 companies used here (no parameters are tuned on any other stocks). The period considered is from July 1989 till October 1994, a period during which the general stock market was not getting extraordinary returns. The S&P 500 index rose only from about 328 to 468 during this period, i.e. about 42.7% (about 7.9% per year).

We used a 3-hidden node network for each of the profit objective and stop loss networks. Training is performed for 60 iterations using a learning rate of 0.01. We use the same stop loss $s(t)$ and the same profit objective $p(t)$ for all stocks, otherwise we would have many neural networks, and definitely an overparametrized trading system. The results for the profit objectives is that it was about constant (in the course of the trade) at 9% above the buy price. On the other hand, the stop loss varied in the course of the trade. It started at about 5% below buy price, and kept tightening, until it reached 3.7%, and stayed constant on that level. This result is consistent with the results of Atiya (1995). Since stocks tend to exhibit a trending rather than mean reverting behavior, profit objectives have to be wider than stop losses. Also the fact that stop losses tighten in the course of trade is consistent with the arguments in the introduction, that one would more readily like to terminate trades that stay for a longer time without producing much profit.

After training the networks, the system is tested on the testing data corresponding to the 100 testing stocks. A crude portfolio is created out of the resulting trading signals. We assume a 100,000$ starting investment capital. A commission of 25$ per trade is taken into account. No pyramiding or reinvestment of profits is performed. At the end of the testing period, the portfolio equity was up to about 281,700$. The generated profit was about 181.7% (about 33.7% per year). One can see that the profit is significantly larger than the general market appreciation.

Appendix:

Let us make a small change in the weight vector, from $\mathbf{w}^{(p)}$ to $\mathbf{w}^{(p)} + \Delta\mathbf{w}^{(p)}$. The objective function becomes

$$J = \left[\sum_{i\in U_s} G_s(\mathbf{w}^{(s)}, T_i) + \sum_{i\in U_p} G_p(\mathbf{w}^{(p)} + \Delta\mathbf{w}^{(p)}, T_i + \Delta T_i) + \sum_{i\in U_r} x_i(T) - NC\right] / \sum_{i=1}^{N} (T_i + \Delta T_i) \tag{14}$$

where

$$\Delta T_i = T_i\big|_{\mathbf{w}^{(p)}+\Delta\mathbf{w}^{(p)}} - T_i\big|_{\mathbf{w}^{(p)}}. \tag{15}$$

Also, let

$$\Delta G_p(\mathbf{w}^{(p)}, T_i) = G_p(\mathbf{w}^{(p)} + \Delta\mathbf{w}^{(p)}, T_i + \Delta T_i) - G_p(\mathbf{w}^{(p)}, T_i). \tag{16}$$

Now consider the two quantities ΔT_i and ΔG_p. Figure 1 shows graphically these variables. Ignoring second order terms and beyond, one can see from the figure that

$$\frac{\partial x_i}{\partial t}\Delta T_i - \frac{\partial G_p}{\partial t}\Delta T_i = \frac{\partial G_p}{\partial \mathbf{w}^{(p)}}^T \Delta\mathbf{w}^{(p)}. \tag{17}$$

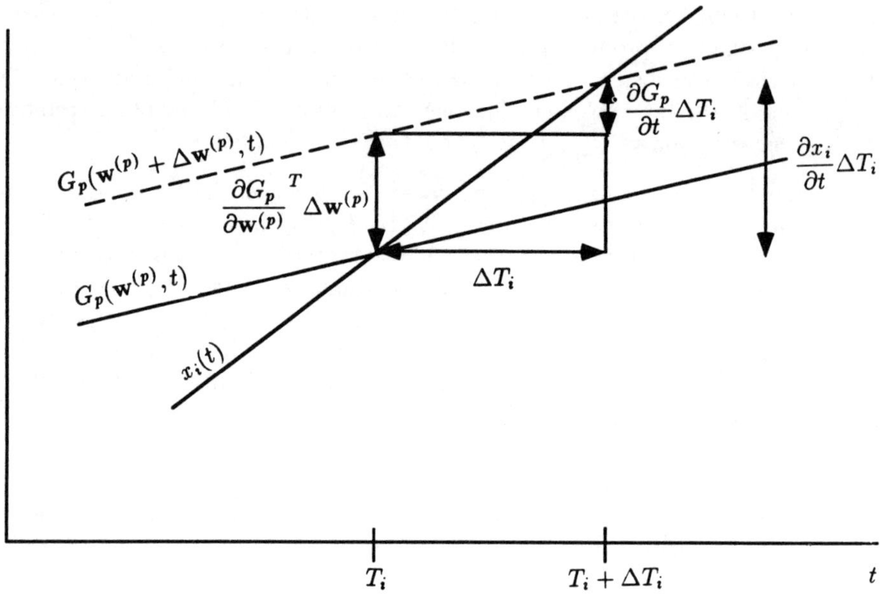

Figure 1: A graphical illustration of the effect of changing the weights on T_i and G_p.

Therefore,

$$\Delta T_i = \frac{\frac{\partial G_p}{\partial \mathbf{w}^{(p)}}^T \Delta\mathbf{w}^{(p)}}{\frac{\partial x_i}{\partial t} - \frac{\partial G_p}{\partial t}}. \tag{18}$$

Also, using the figure and using Eq. (16),

$$\Delta G_p(\mathbf{w}^{(p)}, T_i) = \frac{\partial x_i}{\partial t}\Delta T_i = \frac{\frac{\partial G_p}{\partial \mathbf{w}^{(p)}}^T \Delta\mathbf{w}^{(p)} \frac{\partial x_i}{\partial t}}{\frac{\partial x_i}{\partial t} - \frac{\partial G_p}{\partial t}}. \tag{19}$$

Using Taylor series expansion on (14), and retaining only first order terms, we get

$$J\big|_{\mathbf{w}^{(p)}+\Delta\mathbf{w}^{(p)}} = J\big|_{\mathbf{w}^{(p)}} + \frac{1}{\sum_{i=1}^{N} T_i}\Big[\sum_{i\in U_p} \Delta G_p(\mathbf{w}^{(p)}, T_i) - J\sum_{i\in U_p} \Delta T_i\Big]. \tag{20}$$

Substituting from (18) and (19) into (20), we get:

$$J\big|_{\mathbf{w}^{(p)}+\Delta\mathbf{w}^{(p)}} = J\big|_{\mathbf{w}^{(p)}} + \frac{\Delta\mathbf{w}^{(p)T}}{\sum_{i=1}^{N} T_i}\left[\sum_{i\in U_p} \frac{\frac{\partial G_p}{\partial \mathbf{w}^{(p)}}\frac{\partial x_i}{\partial t}}{\frac{\partial x_i}{\partial t} - \frac{\partial G_p}{\partial t}} - J\sum_{i\in U_p} \frac{\frac{\partial G_p}{\partial \mathbf{w}^{(p)}}}{\frac{\partial x_i}{\partial t} - \frac{\partial G_p}{\partial t}}\right], \tag{21}$$

It follows that the steepest ascent rule will be

$$\Delta\mathbf{w}^{(p)} = \frac{\eta}{\sum_{i=1}^{N} T_i}\left[\sum_{i\in U_p} \frac{\frac{\partial G_p}{\partial \mathbf{w}^{(p)}}\frac{\partial x_i}{\partial t}}{\frac{\partial x_i}{\partial t} - \frac{\partial G_p}{\partial t}} - J\sum_{i\in U_p} \frac{\frac{\partial G_p}{\partial \mathbf{w}^{(p)}}}{\frac{\partial x_i}{\partial t} - \frac{\partial G_p}{\partial t}}\right], \tag{22}$$

where η denotes the learning rate. Similarly, with the stop loss we obtain:

$$\Delta\mathbf{w}^{(s)} = \frac{\eta}{\sum_{i=1}^{N} T_i}\left[\sum_{i\in U_s} \frac{\frac{\partial G_s}{\partial \mathbf{w}^{(s)}}\frac{\partial x_i}{\partial t}}{\frac{\partial x_i}{\partial t} - \frac{\partial G_s}{\partial t}} - J\sum_{i\in U_s} \frac{\frac{\partial G_s}{\partial \mathbf{w}^{(s)}}}{\frac{\partial x_i}{\partial t} - \frac{\partial G_s}{\partial t}}\right]. \tag{23}$$

Reference

Atiya, A. 1995. An analysis of stops and profit objectives in trading systems, *Neural Networks in Financial Engineering: Proc. Third Internat. Conf. on Neural Networks in the Capital Markets*, World Scientific Publ., London, England, pp.588-596.

SOFT PREDICTION OF STOCK BEHAVIOR

YORAM BARAM*
Department of Computer Science
Technion, Israel Institute of Technology
Haifa 32000, Israel.

Abstract

A "soft" classifier allows for indecision with respect to objects which are insufficiently or ambiguously supported by the data. We show that, under a certain condition on the indecision rate, a soft classifier can produce a higher benefit than a firm classifier, which assigns each object to a class, regardless of the data structure. Soft classifiers based on multi–linear and spherical separation are investigated. Their performances in predicting stock behavior are compared to that achieved by the nearest neighbor method.

1 Introduction

In stock trading, it is often sensible to refrain from any action, particularly when the data is insufficient or ambiguous. In this paper, we propose a decision making method, based on pattern classification, which allows for indecision. Such classification, which we call "soft", stands in contrast to "firm" classification, as performed by the nearest neighbor method (e.g., Cover and Hart, 1967), which assigns each object to a class, regardless of the data structure. The training set will be covered by local separators, each isolating a point of a given class from all the points of the competing class. In particular, multi–linear and spherical local separators are considered. A reduced subset of the local separators that covers the entire set of labeled points corresponding to a class defines a separator. Soft classification will be performed by a combination of the two separators. A domain of indecision is created between the two sets of class labeled points, and, when spherical local separators are used, at regions where there is no data. The indecision domain distinguishes the proposed approach from others, which, by and large, seek separation surfaces between the classes (e.g., Rosenblatt, 1958,

*Presently a Senior Research Associate of the National Research Council at the NASA Ames Research Center, Moffett Field, CA 94035, on sabbatical leave from the Technion. baram@cs.technion.ac.il

Baum, 1988, Fukunaga, 1990). We propose an economically motivated *benefit* function for a classifier as the difference between the probabilities of success and failure. Employing the respective benefit functions, the advantage of soft classification over firm classification is shown to depend on the rate of indecision. The proposed method is applied to the stock trading problem, and the performances of the soft classifiers are compared to that of the nearest neighbor method.

2 The Benefit of Soft Classification

Consider a finite set of points $X = \{x^{(i)}, i = 1, \ldots, N\}$ in some subset of R^n, the real space of dimension n. Suppose that each point of X is assigned to one of two classes, and let the corresponding subsets of X, having N_1 and N_2 points, respectively, be denoted X_1 and X_2. We shall say that the two sets are labeled L_1 and L_2, respectively. It is desired to divide R^n into labeled regions, so that new, unlabeled points can be assigned to one of the two classes.

We define a *local separator* of a point x of X_1 with respect to X_2 as a convex set, $s(x|2)$, which contains x and no point of X_2. A *separator family* is defined as a rule that produces local separators for class–labeled points. We define a *separator* $S(1|2)$ of X_1 with respect to X_2 as a set that includes X_1 and excludes X_2.

Given a separator family, the union of local separators $s(x^{(i)}|2)$ of the points $x^{(i)}$, $i = 1 \ldots, N_1$, of X_1 with respect to X_2,

$$S(1|2) = \cup_{x^{(i)} \in X_1} s(x^{(i)}|2) \tag{1}$$

is a separator of X_1 with respect to X_2. It consists of N_1 local separators.

Let $X_{1,c}$ be a subset of X_1. The set

$$S_c(1|2) = \cup_{x^{(i)} \in X_{1,c}} s(x^{(i)}|2) \tag{2}$$

will be called a *consistent* separator of X_1 with respect to X_2 if it contains all the points of X_1. The set $X_{1,c}$ will then be called a *consistent subset* with respect to the given separator family.

Consider the following solution to the classification problem:
Extend the class assignment of each of the labeled points to a local separator of a given family. Maximize the volume of each of the local separators without including in it any point of the competing class. The union of the maximal–volume (or, simply, *maximal*) local separators of labeled points corresponding to the same class defines a separator for these points. The intersection of the two separators defines a conflict and will be called a *domain of ambiguity of the first kind.* A region uncovered by either separator will be called a *domain of ambiguity of the second kind.* The union of the domains of ambiguity will be designated the *domain of indecision.* The remainders of the two separators,

excluding their intersection, define the conflict–free domains assigned to the two classes.

The resulting "soft" classifier rules out hard conflicts, where labeled points of one class are included in the separator of the other. Yet, it allows for indecision in areas which are either claimed by both separators or claimed by neither.

Let the true class be denoted y (with possible values, e.g., y=1 or y=2) and let the classification outcome be denoted $\hat{y}$. Let the probabilities of decision and indecision by the soft classifier be denoted P_d and P_{id}, respectively (of course, $P_{id} = 1 - P_d$), and let the probabilities of correct and incorrect decisions by the firm and the soft classifiers be denoted $P_{\text{firm}}\{\hat{y} = y\}$, $P_{\text{firm}}\{\hat{y} \neq y\}$, $P_{\text{soft}}\{\hat{y} = y\}$ and $P_{\text{soft}}\{\hat{y} \neq y\}$, respectively. Finally, let the joint probabilities of a decision being made by the soft classifier and the correctness or incorrectness of the decision be denoted, respectively, $P_{\text{soft}}\{d, \hat{y} = y\}$ and $P_{\text{soft}}\{d, \hat{y} \neq y\}$ and let the corresponding conditional probabilities be denoted $P_{\text{soft}}\{\hat{y} = y \mid d\}$ and $P_{\text{soft}}\{\hat{y} \neq y \mid d\}$, respectively.

We define the *benefit* of using the firm classifier as the difference between the probability that a point is classified correctly by the classifier and the probability that it is misclassified:

$$B_{\text{firm}} = P_{\text{firm}}\{\hat{y} = y\} - P_{\text{firm}}\{\hat{y} \neq y\} = 2P_{\text{firm}}\{\hat{y} = y\} - 1. \tag{3}$$

This definition is motivated by economic consideration: the profit produced by an investment will be, on average, proportional to the benefit function. This will become more evident in a later section, were we consider the problem of stock trading.

For a soft classifier, we similarly define the benefit as the difference between the probability of a correct classification and that of an incorrect one (which, in an economic context, assumes that indecision has no cost, other than the possible loss of profit). Now, however, these probabilities are for the joint events that a classification is made, and that the outcome is correct or incorrect, respectively:

$$\begin{aligned} B_{\text{soft}} &= P_{\text{soft}}\{d, \hat{y} = y\} - P_{\text{soft}}\{d, \hat{y} \neq y\} \\ &= [P_{\text{soft}}\{\hat{y} = y \mid d\} - P_{\text{soft}}\{\hat{y} \neq y \mid d\}]P_d \\ &= [2P_{\text{soft}}\{\hat{y} = y \mid d\} - 1]P_d \end{aligned} \tag{4}$$

Soft classification will be more beneficial than firm classification if

$$B_{\text{soft}} > B_{\text{firm}}$$

which may be written as

$$P_{id} < 1 - \frac{P_{\text{firm}}\{\hat{y} = y\} - 0.5}{P_{\text{soft}}\{\hat{y} = y \mid d\} - 0.5} \tag{5}$$

For the latter to be a useful condition, it is necessary that $P_{\text{firm}}\{\hat{y} = y\} > 0.5$, $P_{\text{soft}}\{\hat{y} = y \mid d\} > 0.5$ and

$$P_{\text{soft}}\{\hat{y} = y \mid d\} > P_{\text{firm}}\{\hat{y} = y\} \tag{6}$$

Condition (6) will be normally satisfied, since points of the same class can be expected to be denser under the corresponding separator than in the indecision domain. In other words, the error ratio produced by the soft classifier on the decided cases can be expected to be smaller than the error ratio produced by the firm classifier, which decides on all the cases. The satisfaction of condition (5) would depend on the geometry of the data. It will be satisfied for certain cases, and will not be satisfied for others. This will be numerically demonstrated for the stock trading problem.

3 Soft Classification by Multi–Linear Separators

A Multi–Linear Local Separator (MLLS) of a point x of X_1 with respect to X_2 is generated by the following algorithm:
Algorithm MLLS: Let $\tilde{X}_2 = X_2$. Find the point of $\tilde{X}_2$ nearest to x. Place a hyperplane perpendicular to the line segment connecting the two points at the midpoint. Let the new $\tilde{X}_2$ be the set of points of the old $\tilde{X}_2$ which are on the side of the hyperplane which includes x. Repeat the procedure while $\tilde{X}_2$ is non–empty.

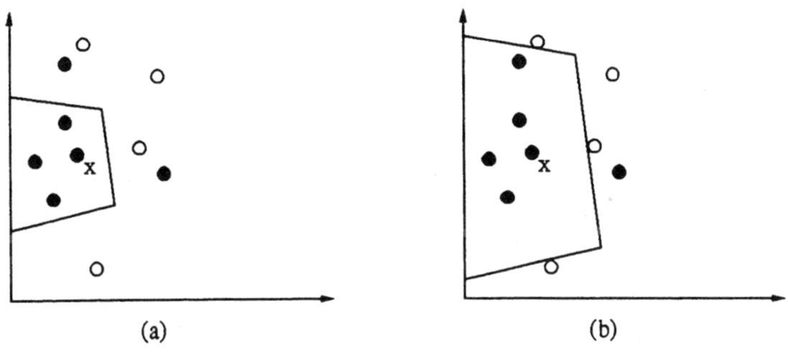

Figure 1: Separating x by (a) a multi–linear local separator (b) a maximal multi–linear local separator.

The local multi–linear separator is the intersection of the half–planes on the sides of the hyperplanes found in step 2) which include x. It is illustrated by Fig. 1(a). The local multi–linear separator of a point of X_2 with respect to the set X_1 can be found in a similar manner.
The union of the multi–linear local separators of the points $x^{(i)}$, $i = 1 \ldots, N_1$, of X_1 with respect to X_2, is a separator of X_1 with respect to X_2. It consists of N_1 local separators. A reduced separator, consisting, generally, of less local separators, is generated by the following Multi–Linear Classifier (MLC) design

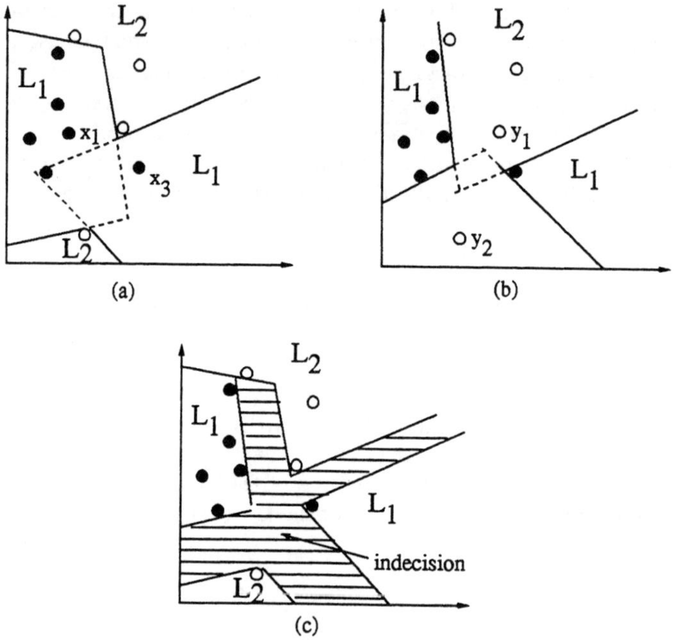

Figure 2: (a) The maximal local separators of x_1 and x_3 and the associated separator of X_1 with respect to X_2. (b) The maximal local separators of y_1 and y_2 and the associated separator of X_2 with respect to X_1. (c) The decision and indecision domains for soft classification.

algorithm, which is written in terms of $S(1|2)$, but is applicable to $S(2|1)$, with an obvious change of variable.

Algorithm MLC: Let $\tilde{X}_1 = X_1$ Select an arbitrary point of $\tilde{X}_1$. Find its multi–linear local separator with respect to X_2, employing MLS. Let the new $\tilde{X}_1$ be the set of points of the old $\tilde{X}_1$ which are outside the separator. Repeat the procedure while $\tilde{X}_1$ is non–empty. The separator is the union of the local separators.

The Maximal Multi–Linear Local Separator (MMLLS) of a point x of X_1 with respect to X_2 is generated as follows:

Algorithm MMLLS: Same as algorithm MLLS, but instead of placing the perpendicular hyperplane at the middle of the line segment connecting the two points, place it at the end of the line segment corresponding to the point of $\tilde{X}_2$. The maximal multi–linear local separator of a point $x \in X_1$ with respect to X_2 is illustrated by Fig. 1(b).

The union of a set of maximal local separators of points of X_1 with respect to X_2, which covers the whole of X_1, will constitute a separator, $\mathbf{S}(1|2)$, for X_1 with respect to X_2. Similarly, the union of a set of maximal local separators of points of X_2 with respect to X_1, which covers the whole of X_2, will form a separator, $\mathbf{S}(2|1)$, for X_1 with respect to X_2. Both separators will be used in solving the soft classification problem. Fig. 2(a) shows the two maximal multi–linear local separators of the points x_1 and x_3 that make up a separator for X_1 with respect to X_2. Fig. 2(b) shows the maximal multi–linear local separators of the points y_1 and y_2 that make up a separator for X_2 with respect to X_1. The intersection of these two separators, shown in Fig. 2(c), represents the domain of indecision.

The multi–linear soft classifier is found, then, by performing Algorithm MLC twice, once for finding $\mathbf{S}(1|2)$ and once for finding $\mathbf{S}(2|1)$, employing, in both cases, Algorithm MMLLS, instead of Algorithm MLLS, for finding the local separators of the relevant points.

4 Soft classification by Spherical Separation

Spherical local separators offer an attractive alternative to multi–linear local separators in the construction of a separator for a finite set. The memory and computation requirements reduce considerably because the specification of each spherical local separator requires a small number of parameters (only the center location and the radius), and because the construction of the separators for the class–labeled sets requires only the computation of distances between points and comparisons of such distances. Since spheres are inherently bounded, the class assignment of a labeled point is not extended very far into regions without data. This contrasts multi–linear separation (of both the minimum distance and the simplified version), which extends the class assignments of the labeled points indefinitely into unpopulated regions. Consequently, in spherical separation, there will be regions of the input space that will not be covered by the two separators. Separator intersections will be called domains of *ambiguity of the first kind*, and uncovered regions will be called domains of *ambiguity of the second kind*. Only points that fall outside these two domains will be classified.

The maximal local spherical separator of x is defined by the open sphere centered at x, whose radius $r(x|2)$ is the distance between x and the point of X_2 nearest to x. Denoting by $s(x,r)$ the sphere of radius r in R^n centered at x, the maximal local separator is then $s_M(x|2) = s(x, r(x|2))$. A maximal local spherical separator is illustrated by Fig. 3.

A separator construction algorithm employing maximal local spherical separators is described as follows:

Algorithm SSP: Let $\tilde{X}_1 = X_1$. For an arbitrary point x of $\tilde{X}_1$, find the minimal distance $r(x|2)$ to the points of X_2. This defines a maximal spherical separator for x with respect to X_2, centered at x and having a radius $r(x|2)$.

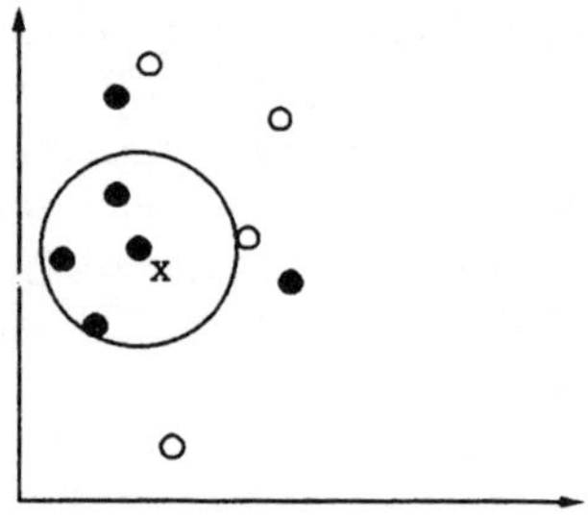

Figure 3: The maximal local spherical separator of the point x.

Eliminate from $\tilde{X}_1$ all the points whose distances from x are smaller than $r(x|2)$. Denote the remaining set $\tilde{X}_1$. Repeat the procedure while $\tilde{X}_1$ is non–empty. The union of the maximal local spherical separators is a separator for X_1 with respect to X_2. Such separators and the associated indecision domains are illustrated in Fig. 3.

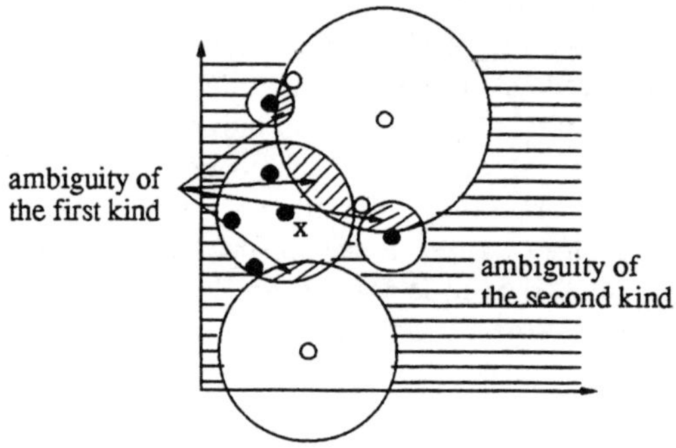

Figure 4: Spherical separation and ambiguity domains

The classifier size may be reduced by selecting for the consistent subset the point whose sphere has the maximal volume of the remaining spheres. We have the following algorithm:

Algorithm SSPR: Let $\tilde{X}_1 = X_1$. For each of the points $x^{(i)}$ of $\tilde{X}_1$, find the minimal distance to the points of X_2. Call it $r(x^{(i)}|2)$. Select the point $x^{(i)}$ for which $r(x^{(i)}|2) \geq r(x^{(j)}|2)$, $j \neq i$, for the consistent subset. Eliminate from $\tilde{X}_1$ all the points whose distances from $x^{(i)}$ are smaller than $r(x^{(i)}|2)$. Denote the remaining set $\tilde{X}_1$. Repeat the procedure while $\tilde{X}_1$ is non–empty. The union of the maximal local spherical separators is a separator for X_1 with respect to X_2.

5 Soft Prediction of Stock Behavior

Given a sequence of k daily trading ("close") values of a stock, it is desired to predict whether the next day will show an increase or a decrease with respect to the last day in the sequence. An initial value of $k = 3$ is selected, but it is increased if there are ambiguities (different predictions for the same inputs) in the training data. We call k the *minimal unambiguous tap*. Records for ten different stocks, each containing, on average, 1260 daily values were used. They are displayed in Fig. 5. About 60 percent of the data were used for training and the rest for testing.

Let the prediction success rate of a firm classifier, such as the nearest neighbor classifier, be denoted f and that of a soft classifier for the decided cases s. For a given trade, let the gain or loss per unit invested be denoted q, and the rate of indecision of the soft classifier ir. Suppose that, employing the firm classifier, a stock is traded once every day (say, at the "close" value), and that, employing the soft classifier, it is traded on a given day only if a trade is decided by the classifier (that is, the input does not fall in the indecision domain). The expected profit for M days per unit invested is $2(f - 0.5)qM$ for the firm classifier and $2(s - 0.5)q(1 - ir)M$ for the soft classifier (these values disregard possible commission and slippage costs). The soft classifier will be preferred over the firm one if the latter quantity is greater than the former, that is, if

$$ir < 1 - \frac{f - 0.5}{s - 0.5} \tag{7}$$

which is the sample representation of condition (5) for the stock trading problem.

Results for the soft multi–linear and spherical classifiers, applied to the stock data, are presented in Fig. 6. The performance of the nearest neighbor method is shown for comparison. The indecision rates and the success rates in the decided cases are then specified along with a benefit sign. A positive benefit represents a satisfaction of condition (7), with ir, f and s replaced by the corresponding sample values given in the table. This indicates a higher profit in applying the soft classifier over the application of the nearest neighbor classifier. A negative benefit indicates that a higher profit is produced by the nearest neighbor classifier. It can be seen that the indecision rates of the spherical classifier are considerably lower than those of the multi–linear classifier. Yet, the number of stocks for which soft classification is beneficial is the same (two) for the two soft classifiers. For three of the stocks (xaldnf, xdssi and xelrnf) soft classification has produced better results than firm classification, and for the remaining seven stocks firm classification has produced better results. It should be noted that the run–time of the soft classifiers was considerably shorter than that of the nearest neighbor classifier, and the run–time of the spherical classifier was considerably shorter than that for the multi–linear classifier. It is not immediately evident from observing the time histories of the different stocks, given in Fig. 5, what makes a process more suitable for soft prediction

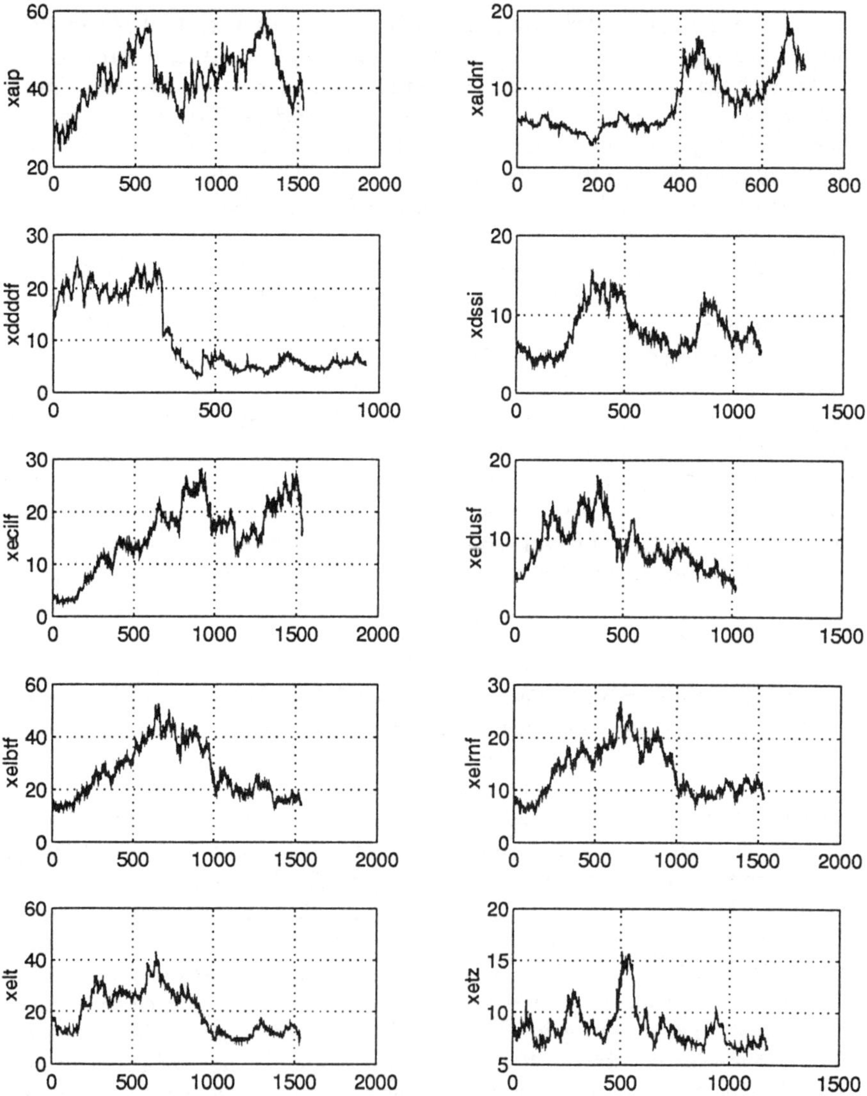

Figure 5: Daily "close" values of ten stocks

	NN	Multi-Linear			Spherical		
		indecision	success	benefit	indecision	success	benefit
xaip	61.4%	97.8%	82.0%	-	48.4%	70.1%	-
xaldnf	51.7%	60.3%	57.2%	+	74.6%	51.3%	-
xddddf	52.0%	100%	0%	-	44.3%	53.3%	-
xdssi	48.3%	91.9%	54.8%	+	43.6%	52.6%	+
xecilf	53.0%	93.7%	54.6%	-	47.6%	48.8%	-
xedusf	80.7%	75.6%	64.4%	-	30.6%	89.9%	-
xelbtf	53.7%	70.0%	56.4	-	42.2%	50.1%	-
xetz	66.0%	92.6%	72.8%	-	43.8%	68.6%	-
xelrnf	51.5%	100%	0%	-	39.2%	56.0%	+
xelt	85.6%	39.4%	76.8%	-	32.9%	93.0%	-

Figure 6: Performance summary for "soft" classifiers in predicting rise and fall in stock values.

than for firm prediction. Yet, a clue may be found in the value of k – the minimum unambiguous tap. Out of the three stocks that have the minimal value of $k = 5$, two produce a higher benefit by the soft classifiers than by the firm nearest neighbor method. Since k represents the input dimension, and since higher-dimensional data can be expected to be more highly separable than lower dimensional data (vectors belonging to different classes being significantly different from each other), a firm classifier can be expected to perform better on high dimensional data. On the other hand, low dimensional data, which can be expected to be less separable (similar vectors belonging to different classes), is more suitable for soft classification. The main lesson to be learned from these results is that the classification approach (firm or soft) and the specific classifier should be individually matched to each of the stocks in order to maximize profits.

6 Conclusion

A notion of "soft" classification has been introduced and algorithms for its implementation have been presented and analyzed. A criterion for the utility of such classification has been presented and its application in stock trading has been demonstrated.

Acknowledgment

The author thanks Dr. Amir Atiya of Cairo University for providing the stock data used in the examples and for valuable discussions of the corresponding results.

References

Baum, E. B. (1988), "On the Capabilities of Multilayer Perceptrons," J. Complexity, Vol. 4, pp. 193–215.

Cover, T. M. and Hart, P. E. (1967), "Nearest Neighbor Pattern Classification," IEEE Trans. on Information Theory, Vol. IT–13, No. 1, pp. 21–27.

Fukunaga, K. (1990), "Introduction to Statistical Pattern Recognition," Academic Press, San Diego.

Rosenblatt, F. (1958), "The Perceptron: A Probabilistic Model for Information Storage and Organization in the Brain," Psychological Review, Vol. 65, pp. 386–408.

Application of genetic algorithms in stock market prediction

K.Y. Szeto, Kin On Chan, and Kin Hong Cheung
Hong Kong Telecom Institute of Information Technology,
and
Department of Physics,
The Hong Kong University of Science and Technology,
Clear Water Bay, Kowloon, Hong Kong
Email: PHSZETO@USTHK.UST.HK

Abstract

A new technique using simulated annealing on the strength profile of the rules in classification tool based on genetic algorithm is developed. This new tool has been tested on time series for forecasting large fluctuations with superior performance compared to random guess predictor, CART, and unannealed genetic algorithm for the stock market index of US, HongKong, Korea, and Thailand as well as model data with long and short memory.

1 Introduction

Genetic Algorithm as a classifier has found applications in many areas in science and engineering(Holland, 1975; Goldberg, 1989). By representing the past sequence of data in a time series as a message unit, genetic algorithm can also be used for forecasting. In this short paper, we introduce a simple encoding scheme to preprocess a time series, so that the action unit of the classifier will be interpreted as a predictor.

The input of a time series is put into two classes: large fluctuation (class 1) and small fluctuation (class 0). The fluctuation of the input $\{X'(t)\}$ is computed as the fractional change in each interval,

$$y(t) = \frac{X'(t) - X'(t-1)}{X'(t-1)}. \tag{1}$$

If the absolute value of $|y(t)| \leq 0.01$, we give a new data $X(t) = 0$, and for $|y(t)| > 0.01$, we set $X(t) = 1$. The value 0.01 is an estimate of the execution cost. This encoding scheme generates a binary sequence of data $\{X(t)\}$. The sequence $\{X(t)\}$ is divided into two parts: training set and test set. The training set consists of M strings of length equal to 60 bits, together with the known action unit of the strings. For example, if a string $s = x_{i+1}x_{i+2}....x_{i+60}$ corresponds to the time series sequence $X(t = i+1), X(t = i+2), ..., X(t = i+60)$, then the action unit for s is $X(t = i + 61)$. The string s is the message unit, here chosen to have the dimension 60, corresponding to financial data in a period of two months. This is only for illustration purpose. A detailed analysis of the lag structure on major stock market indices can be made using maximum entropy method(Cheung *et al.*, 1996).

In additional to real time series, we also generate controlled time series with long and short memory using the whitening transformation(Fukunaga, 1990). Specifically, we want to generate a sequence of data with the a covariance matrix $\Sigma = (C_{ij})$, which is a Toeplitz matrix(Chan & Strang, 1989). We consider two cases of Σ. For the long memory case, we have a power law decay for the elements in Σ:

$$C_{1n} = (n-1)^{-\alpha}, \qquad n = 2, 3, ... \tag{2}$$

For the short memory case, we have an exponential decay for the elements in Σ:

$$C_{1n} = e^{-(n-1)/R}, \qquad n = 2, 3, ... \tag{3}$$

The exponent α and constant R are parameters characterizing the range of memory. Tests of forecasting tools based on these controlled data sets provide some insights into the dependence of their performance on the memory structure of the time series. Such a model analysis can be linked to the lag structure analysis of real-world time series(Cheung *et al.*, 1996) to select the correct tool of prediction.

2 Rules of Classification

To set up the rules for classification, we follow the statistics of each bit in the M examples in the training set. If a particular position k in the bit string has a probability p_1 to take the value 1, and p_0 to take the value 0, then the corresponding k position in the rule will also choose the value 1 and 0 with these probabilities obtained from the statistics of the training set. This is a simple center of gravity method for choosing the bit value in the rules, without concerns to the correlation between the various bits in the examples. To cope with memory factors, we introduce later a Lee metric(Lee, 1958) to describe the correlation by correcting the probabilities p_1 and p_0 by a weight function $W(k)$. This weight function can be modelled after the autocorrelation function obtained from the training set, or by some other known forms. Moreover, in order to have some generalizing power for our rules, we introduce the *don't care* ($\star$) bit which has the property that it can match any bit from the message unit. We introduce a distribution function F for these *don't care* bits. The weight $W(k)$ has a close relation with the distribution function F of don't care. In this paper, we use an exponential form for F and W:

$$W(t) = C_w e^{t/R_w}, \qquad F(t) = C_f e^{-t/R_f} \tag{4}$$

with boundary conditions that

$$W(1) = \ 0.01 \qquad F(1) = 0.99, \tag{5}$$
$$W(60) = \ 0.99 \qquad F(60) = 0.01. \tag{6}$$

Here R_w and R_f are the characteristic times while C_w and C_f are the normalization factors. These forms for F and W are better than the uniform case, as intuitively we expect that there should be more *don't care* bits far from the date of prediction, and less likely to have a *don't care* bit near the date of prediction. We have also tried other forms of W and F, and the details will be published elsewhere.

After setting up the initial population of rules, we have many strings corresponding to each class of action units. Lets consider a particular class, say, the class corresponding to large fluctuations (action unit=1). Each string i consists on 60 bits with C_{ik} being the bit value of the k-position. Note that C_{ik} can be 1, 0 or $\star$. Similarly, an input can be described by a string with bit value S_{jk} of the k-position in the j-th message. We compare a given rule (i) with an example (j) by computing the error distance

$$d_{ij} = \sum_{k=1}^{60} |C_{ik} - S_{jk}| \times W(k). \tag{7}$$

The meaning of the *don't care* bit is that $|C_{ik} - S_{jk}| = 0$ whenever $C_{ik} = \star$. This set of error distances form the basis for the computation of fitness of the rules. We also have tried other metric and a comparison will be reported in a separated article.

3 Fitness of Rules

To avoid the problem of early domination of certain rules, we introduce a new method for controlling the strength (or fitness) profile of the rules. We first calculate the error distance d_{ji} with rule (i) for a given example (j) in the training set. If the average value for this set of $\{d_{ji}\}$ is $\langle d_j \rangle$ over all the rules, then there are four cases for each training example:

(1): $d_{ji} < \langle d_j \rangle$ and the action unit of the rule $\neq$ the action unit of the example,
(2): $d_{ji} < \langle d_j \rangle$ and the action unit of the rule $=$ the action unit of the example,
(3): $d_{ji} > \langle d_j \rangle$ and the action unit of the rule $\neq$ the action unit of the example,
(4): $d_{ji} > \langle d_j \rangle$ and the action unit of the rule $=$ the action unit of the example.

For cases (1) and (2), the configuration of the rule is similar to the example (j) compared to other rules. But for case (1), the action unit of the rule is different from the example (j). Hence this rule is considered bad and its strength should be reduced. For case (2), the action unit of the rule matches the example (j) and its strength should be enhanced. For cases (3) and (4), the configuration of the rule is more different from the example (j) compared to other rules. But for case (3), the action unit of the rule is different from the example (j). This rule is still considered good since it says that the rule far from the example should give a different prediction. Its strength should be enhanced. For case (4), the action unit of the rule matches with the example (j), and its strength should be reduced.

4 Selection of Rules

The next important ingredient in our classifier is the algorithm for rules selection. First of all, we calculate the minimum value S_{min} and the average value S_{ave} of the strength of the rules. The histogram of the rules will now be shifted using the transform function $T(S_i)$ for each rule (i),

$$T(S_i) = \frac{(S_i - S_{min})}{(S_{ave} - S_{min})}. \tag{8}$$

Here $S_{ave} = \frac{1}{N_R}\sum_{i=1}^{N_R} S_i$ and N_R is the number of rules. This transformation T just shifts the profile for the strength of the rule so that $T(S_{min}) = 0$. Note that with this shifting of the strength profile, those rules in the histogram that are weak are close to zero fitness, while strong rules have strength close to the maximum fitness. This shifting therefore emphasis the difference between strong rules and weak ones.

To determine whether a rule is selected or eliminated in the next generation, we use Monte Carlo method. If we choose a random number $0 < \rho < 1$ and compare it with the Boltzmann weight

$$\pi(i) \equiv \frac{e^{-T(S_i)}}{\sum_i e^{-T(S_i)}}. \tag{9}$$

If $\rho > \pi(i)$, then the rule survives. Thus, the shifting transformation T ensures that rules with large strength should have more chance to be extracted, survive and repoduce. On the other hand, it also allows rules with small strength to have a finite probability to be extracted. By means of the shift function $T(S)$, we can prevent early convergence.

5 Annealed Genetic Algorithm

The next modification for our algorithm is to apply annealing to the strength profile. This is a systematic method of controlling the selection criterion on the rules by massaging the fitness profile. Instead of using the simple shift transformation, $T(S)$, we introduce a new transform $G_K(S)$ which has the property that it is a monotonic increasing function of the strength S, and that there is a tuning parameter K to control the center of mass of the profile. This parameter K is the tunable parameter to perform annealing. In the following discussion, we assume $0 < S_{min} \leq S_{ave} \leq S_{max}$, which can always be maintained by a suitable annealing schedule with rules initially all having identical strength $S_i = 1.0$ with a large K. There are four regimes of K that we use,

Regime 1: $0 < K < 1$
Regime 2: $1 < K < \bar{K} \equiv S_{ave}/S_{min}$
Regime 3: $\bar{K} < K < K^{\star} \equiv S_{max}/S_{min}$
Regime 4: $K^{\star} < K$

The transformed profile is given by

$$G_K(S_i) = \sigma \frac{S_i - KS_{min}}{S_{ave} - KS_{min}}. \tag{10}$$

Here $\sigma = 1$ for regime 1 and 2 and $\sigma = -1$ for regime 3 and 4. Note that $G_K(S)$ is a monotonic increasing function of S with $G_{K=1}(S) = T(S)$. The range of strength, or the gap $\Delta(K)$ defined as max$G_K(S)$ - min$G_K(S)$ is given by

$$\Delta(K) = \sigma \frac{S_{max} - S_{min}}{S_{ave} - KS_{min}} \tag{11}$$

Note that in regime 1, $G_K(S) > 0$, in regime 4 $G_K(S) < 0$, but in regime 2 and 3, $G_K(S_{min}) < 0$ and $G_K(S_{max}) > 0$. Thus, if one wants a random search initially, one should start in regime 4, with a large value of K. The gap $\Delta(K)$ will be small, so that there is very little difference in the selection (survival) probability $1 - \pi(K, i)$ with

$$\pi(K,i) \equiv \frac{e^{-G_K(S_i)}}{\sum_i e^{-G_K(S_i)}}. \tag{12}$$

As K decreases from regime 4 to regime 3, $\bar{K} < K < K^\star$, the values of $G_K(S)$ can become positive, implying that for rules with these S, $\pi(K,i)$ will be relatively smaller than rules with S such that $G_K(S)$ is negative. This means that the survival probability of the rules with high strength S will be considerably larger than those with small strength. Thus, in regime 3, selection of rules is much more sensitive on strength than in regime 4. The sensitivity of selection on strength is controlled by the parameter K.

For initial evolution of rules, the desire to have a random search on the configuration space of the rules is normal as early convergence should be avoided. Thus, we will start out with a large K in regime 4. After some generations, we will then decrease K and select rules based more sensitively on strength. A schedule of K used can be designed for a particular application, so that after several cycle of the tuning of K, we have a good set of rules that have some generalizing power. In our training of rules, we fix our annealing schedule for K.

6 Results

In order to make a systematic comparison of our modified genetic algorithm, we tested the classifier by two sets of data, one is long range correlation and the other is short range correlation which are generated by inverse whitening transformation(Fukunaga, 1990). We compare four methods:

Method(1): Random guess(Shlesinger & J.West, 1984);
Method(2): CART(Breiman, 1984);
Method(3): Monte-Carlo;
Method(4): Annealed Genetic Algorithm.

Our performance evaluation is based on two ratios: I_0 and I_1,

$$I_0 = \frac{N_{c0}}{N_0}, \qquad I_1 = \frac{N_{c1}}{N_1} \tag{13}$$

Here N_0 is the total number of guess made by the predictor on the outcome being a small fluctuation. N_{c0} is the number of correct predictions among the N_0 guess. Similarly, N_{c1} is the number of correct predictions among the N_1 guess made by the predictor on the outcome being a large fluctuation. A perfect predictor will have $I_0 = I_1 = 1.0$, implying that if the predictor says that the outcome is a large fluctuation, it will be large, and if it says that it is small, it will be small. Note that this need not be the best as the number N_0 and N_1 are also important. For example, a perfect predictor may have $I_1 = 1$, but it only make one guess, ($N_1 = 1$), over a large test set of data. Our training program will run on the training set till I_0 and I_1 are saturated and no foreseeable improvement in expected by further training. The rules are then applied on the test set. Thus the meaningful measures of the predictor are N_{c0}, N_{c1}, N_0 and N_1 on the test set. For the random guess, if the training set has a probability $P_0(P_1)$ of small(large) fluctuation, then the same probability will be applied on the test set. Therefore, if a particular method of prediction yields $I_0 > P_0$ and $I_1 > P_1$, then we have a better predictor.

We have trained and tested the above four methods on long range correlation data and short range correlation data, (Table 1,2) as well as the stock market index of US, Hong Kong, Korea, and Thailand. The results shown in Table (3-6) indicate that annealed genetic algorithm has better performance in the testing set over random guess, Monte-Carlo, and CART. The training time for the last three methods are different, but the application time of the rules on the test set is the same. For annealed genetic algorthm, the computation time for 3000 genetic operations is 2410 minutes using HP7(J200) computer.

Table 1: The performance for the rule in long range correlation data

Method study	I_o in train set	I_1 in train set	I_o in test set	I_1 in test set
Method (1)	0.636	0.354	0.887	0.113
Method (2)	0.886	0.834	0.921	0.411
Method (3)	0.832	0.761	0.900	0.555
Method (4)	0.884	0.820	0.930	0.600

Table 2: The performance for the rule in short range correlation data

Method study	I_o in train set	I_1 in train set	I_o in test set	I_1 in test set
Method (1)	0.752	0.248	0.715	0.285
Method (2)	0.794	0.725	0.725	0.555
Method (3)	0.780	0.600	0.745	0.550
Method (4)	0.850	0.725	0.830	0.560

Table 3: The performance for the rule in USA stock market data

Method study	I_o in train set	I_1 in train set	I_o in test set	I_1 in test set
Method (1)	0.765	0.235	0.862	0.138
Method (2)	0.804	0.782	0.864	0.182
Method (3)	0.770	0.300	0.860	0.200
Method (4)	0.780	0.420	0.870	0.280

Table 4: The performance for the rule in Hong Kong stock market data

Method study	I_o in train set	I_1 in train set	I_o in test set	I_1 in test set
Method (1)	0.789	0.211	0.759	0.241
Method (2)	0.812	0.726	0.763	0.333
Method (3)	0.805	0.480	0.765	0.350
Method (4)	0.815	0.500	0.770	0.360

7 Conclusion

Our new annealed genetic algorithm is shown to be better than random guess, Monte-Carlo, and CART, for controlled data with long and short memory, and most stock market indices. The superior performance over random guess and Monte-Carlo is expected as the annealing process provide a more thorough search of good rules. As to CART, with pruning, the comparison may imply that the time correlation in stock market plays a crucial role in the good performance of genetic algorithm, where the idea of Lee metric is used to simulate the real autocorrelation function.

Table 5: The performance for the rule in Korea stock market data

Method study	I_o in train set	I_1 in train set	I_o in test set	I_1 in test set
Method (1)	0.811	0.189	0.864	0.136
Method (2)	0.830	0.871	0.864	0.200
Method (3)	0.821	0.425	0.870	0.400
Method (4)	0.825	0.440	0.875	0.450

Table 6: The performance for the rule in Thailand stock market data

Method study	I_o in train set	I_1 in train set	I_o in test set	I_1 in test set
Method (1)	0.724	0.276	0.952	0.048
Method (2)	0.805	0.756	0.950	0.000
Method (3)	0.750	0.585	0.952	0.000
Method (4)	0.780	0.600	0.952	0.050

8 Acknowledgments

K.Y. Szeto thanks the support of the Hong Kong Telecom Institute of Information Technology, HKUST.

References

Breiman, L. 1984. *Classification and regression trees.* Pacific Grove, Calif. : Wadsworth and Books, Cole Advanced Books and Software.

Chan, R. H. and G. Strang. Jan 1989. *SIAM Journal of Scientific and Statistical Computing* **10**(1), 104.

Cheung, K., K. Szeto and K. Tam. 1996. Identifying time series lag structure for developing intelligent forecasting systems: A maximum entropy approach. *International Journal of Computational Intelligence and Organization* **1**(1), 94.

Fukunaga, K. 1990. *Introduction To Statistical Pattern Recognition.* Academic Press Ltd.

Goldberg, D. 1989. *Genetic Algorithms in Search, Optimization, and Machine Learning.* Addison-Wesley.

Holland, J. 1975. *Adaptation in Natural and Artificial Systems.* Ann Arbor, MI: University of Michigan Press.

Lee, C. 1958. Some properties of nonbinary error-correcting codes. *IEEE Trans. Inform. Theory IT4:77-82, Math. Rev.* **22**, 13353.

Shlesinger, M. F. and B. J.West. 1984. *Random walks and their applications in the physical and biological sciences.* New York: American Institute of Physics.

IMPROVING NEURAL PREDICTION SYSTEMS BY BUILDING INDEPENDENT COMMITTEES

Steffen Gutjahr
University of Karlsruhe
Institute of Logic, Complexity and Deduction Systems
Germany

This article shows a statistical technique for combining neural networks to form a committee. Is can be shown theoretically that the independence of the neural networks can help to improve the performance in comparison to a single neural network. Independence is achieved in a practical way by discriminating the neural networks using different input vectors. We develop a trading strategy to further improve the whole system by integrating take-profit and stop-loss rules. As an example we make daily forecasts of the 'Bundfuture' traded at the DTB (Deutsche Terminbörse) in Frankfurt . Since September 1996 the whole system is successfully used as a real time application.

1 Introduction

It is common in practice to train a variety of neural networks and to select the best, on the basis of the performance of an unseen validation set. This selection criteria has the disadvantage that the network which had best performance on the validation set might not be the one on a new test set. Especially in time series prediction this generalization problem occurs due to the noise in the data and the non-stationarity of the underlying time series. Additionally, all the afford involved in training the remaining networks is wasted.

To overcome these problems we combine neural networks together to form a committee. In this way we avoid breakdowns of one single neural network by compensating this behaviour by the other members of the committee.

The mayor feature that makes the aggregation of prediction systems difficult is the high correlation or dependence that typically occurs among the neural networks. In the following we discuss the need for having independent neural networks and the way of searching for them.

2 Independent Committee

Independence is a statistical concept which can be interpreted by saying that the decision making process of one network is not influenced by any other network and vice versa. To show the effect of independence let us assume that we have an infinity number of neural networks which make correct predictions with probability $p > 0.5$, where the target is the sign of the difference of tomorrow's price over today's price. The committee decides by majority. In the case of total dependence, where we have equal networks the prediction performance does not change, hence the hit rate is $100 \cdot p$ %. But if we have independent networks (independence in the mathematical sense) the hit rate of the committee increases to 100%. This is a direct consequence of the strong law of large numbers, (1). A similar result is shown in (2).

In practice it is not possible to create an infinite number of independent networks and consequently the increase of the hit rate is much smaller. However, by constructing good networks which are as independent as possible, the effect of increasing the hit rate can be realized.

2.1 Construction of Independent Networks

In the following we present a possible strategie for constructing independent networks to forecast economic time series. The aim is to discriminate the underlying market by using different input vectors. This means that every network considers the market in a different way and makes his decision in regard to this special view. To determine the different inputs we create four segments of potentially discriminative inputs.

1. **Charts:** We group all indicators concerning the events of the last week of the series itself, like the differences $\log x_t - log x_{t-1}$ [a] or yesterday's number of trades. This group reflects the information of the market which is converted instantaneously.

2. **Statistics:** This group represents the long time history of (x_t), e.g. skewness and kurtosis measures, volatility or long time moving averages. In contrast to class 1 we consider here the general behaviour of the market.

3. **Psychology:** We collect the more psychological aspects of the market. We consider the important buying or selling signals e.g. the golden cross which reflects the movement of a long time moving averages and a short time moving average. Other indicators of this class take also today's high and today's low into account. This so called high-low-close-stochastics, e.g. ADX (Additional Directional Movement Index) are often used by human traders, see (5). For a further discussion see also (3).

4. **Fundamentals:** The last group describes the information from other markets. In contrast to the above groups, the choice of the fundamental

---

[a] (x_t) is the underlying time series

data is highly dependent from the underlying time series. The representation is the difference of today's price over yesterday's price.

After building a variety of indicators of the different input classes we create the input vector of the neural networks by considering all the possible $2^4 - 1 = 15$ subsets of the four input classes. In this way we get 15 different input vectors to train 15 neural nets. For example one neural network receives the information of group 1 and therefore makes predictions by considering the market in the nearer past whereas a input vector of class 1 and class 4 additionally takes the behaviour of the other markets into account.

One might say that in this special case the second network always makes better predictions because of the bigger input vector but this is not true. Because of the non-stationarity of the time series the important features change over time so sometimes the fundamental information is important and sometimes not. But information of the input vector which is not relevant for the target leads to worse performance.

3 The Prediction System

The final step to create the networks is straightforward. We train and test networks where the corresponding input vector is selected as above. For the final committee we only take 5 out the 15 prediction systems because of two reasons. First of all some of the trained networks do not work, i.e. the hit rate is not significantly better than 50 %. Those neural networks are no further considered. Secondly, despite the fact that they all have different inputs some of the neural networks are highly correlated, i.e. the correlation coefficient is higher than 0.6. In this case we take only the better one. Finally we get 5 neural networks where the correlation coefficient is between 0.3 and 0.6.

As expected the neural networks are positively correlated. But in general the correlation between two networks having the same inputs is much stronger. By simply dividing the whole input space into different subspaces we reduce the dependence between networks and this improves the performance significantly as we will see afterwards.

The system consists of fully connected feed-forward networks with one hidden layer and tanh activation functions. The input dimensions lie between 13 and 23 and we use RPROP as training algorithm, see (4). The target is the sign of the difference of tomorrow's price over today's price. Every single neural network makes a simple up or down decision by looking at the sign of the output. Finally the committee decides by majority. Figure 1 shows the whole prediction system.

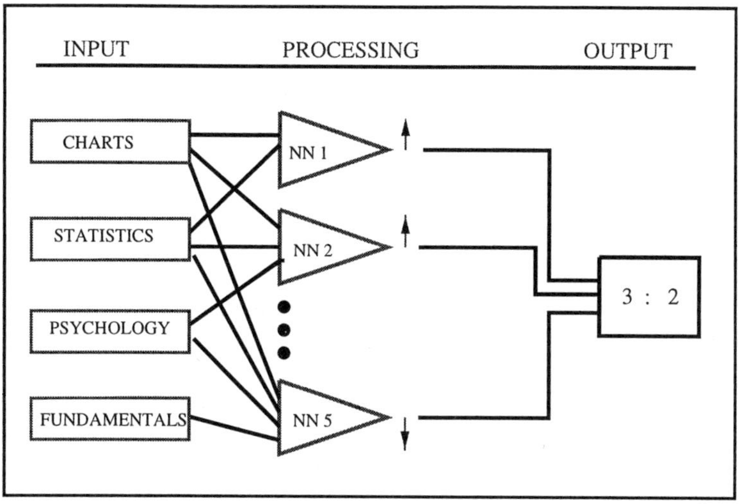

Figure 1: Presentation of the whole prediction system. We use 5 neural networks which see different aspects of the market. Every network makes a decision and the final result is calculated by majority.

4 Example: Future Price Prediction

4.1 Specification of Task

We now demonstrate the proposed method by making daily predictions of the so-called 'Bundfuture' which is the most important future traded at the DTB in Frankfurt, Germany. We used data from November 1, 1990 through July 31, 1996. We took the data up to July 31, 1993 for training and the validation set was generated from August 1, 1993 to July 31, 1994. The remaining 492 trading days formed the test period.

4.2 Results

Table 1 shows the hit rates on the training set and on the test set. We can see that in both periods the performance of the committee is better than the best neural network. The hit rate of the committee is 1.5 to 3 % better than the hit rates of the single neural networks. Compared with the 50 % hit rate of the random walk this is an enhancement of 20 to 40 %. The five neural networks show stable results, i.e. the performance on the test set and on the training set are equally good.

hit rate [%]	NN1	NN2	NN3	NN4	NN5	committee
training set	55.47	55.42	56.66	55.88	54.49	57.89
test set	54.81	56.63	55.64	55.05	55.64	58.07

Table 1: Hit rate on the training set and on the test set of the single neural networks and of the committee

4.3 Trading System

Another popular performance measure is the cumulative profit. Especially in real time applications it is interesting to see if it is possible to earn money with the prediction system or not. We trade every day depending only on the decision of the buying or selling signal of the committee. The daily profit is simply $+/-(x_{t+1}-x_t)$ depending on the correctness of the forecast. The time series is denoted in ticks $*100$ where one tick has a value of 25 DM. Figure 2 shows the cumulative profit on the test set of the five networks and of the committee.

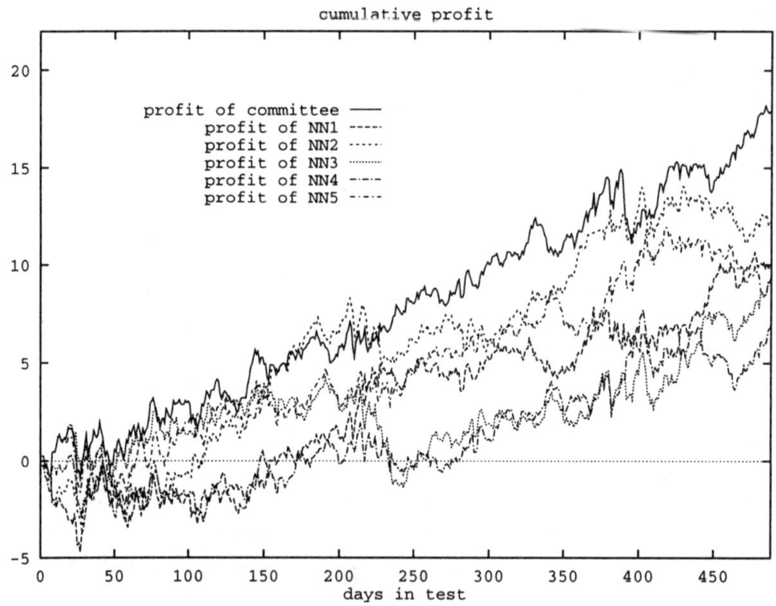

Figure 2: cumulative profit on the test set of the single neural networks and of the committee (without transaction costs)

Figure 2 shows clearly that the cumulative profit of the committee is almost all the time higher than cumulative profit of the other neural networks. By applying the committee one can get a profit of 1802 ticks. This is an enhancement compared to the single neural networks of almost 100 %. This proves that our approach works.

There is another interesting aspect which can be see by figure 2. After 400 trading days the power function of neural network 2 (NN2) is slightly above the power function of the committee. Therefore one might say that there is no difference either you take NN2 or the committee. But after 450 trading days the profit function of NN2 decreases whereas the committee still makes profit. Responsible for the profit of the last 50 days are NN3 and NN4 which had been not to successful in the past. This demonstrates the idea of the independent committee.

Another important aspect when it comes to real time applications is the use of trading strategies like stop-loss or take-profit rules. They are often used by human traders in order to reduce their risk.

The stop-loss rule is a possibility to limit the loss to a certain amount. If during the next day the time series goes into the unexpected direction the position will be closed and one realizes the loss. The take-profit rule in contrast takes the profit if the time series goes into the expected direction. For a further explanation see figure 3.

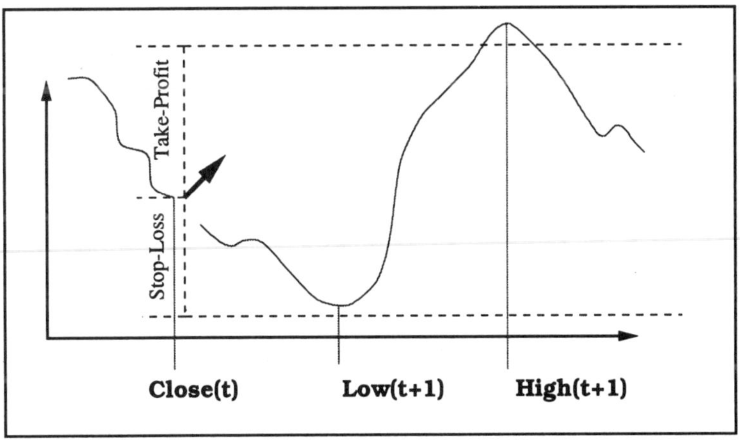

Figure 3: Explanation of stop-loss and take-profit rules. At time t the committee predicts that the time series will increase. Consequently the take-profit range is compared with the high of the next day and the stop-loss is compared with the low.

cumulative profit [ticks *100]	committee	with stop-loss	with take-profit
test set	18.02	20.26	20.91

Table 2: Cumulative profit on the test set by using stop-loss or take-profit rules.

By using one of those strategies presented above we can further improve the performance of the whole system. By using the trading rules the profit is about 10 % better. Table 2 shows the cumulative profit on the test set. In the simulations it was not possible to use stop-loss and take-profit in parallel simply because it is not known which one should be set first. The stop-loss respective take-profit is only compared with the daily high and low. However in the real time applications they can be used both.

5 Conclusion

We presented a prediction system that makes daily forecasting of the 'Bund-future' traded in Frankfurt. This system is actually used in a real time application from a german bank. It consists of a committee of 5 neural networks. The networks see different aspects of the same market and therefore get independent decisions. In this way one can construct a prediction system that is better than the best neural network itself.

By separating the whole input space into different subspaces one can reduce the dependence among the neural networks in a very comfortable way because you do not have to fit any parameters. Secondly, by reducing the input dimension the number of weights and biases reduces automatically. This makes the optimization process easier and helps to avoid overfitting.

References

[1] Terrence L. Fine: Theories of Probability, Academic Press 1973, pp. 95 - 97.

[2] Christopher M. Bishop: Neural Networks for Pattern Recognition, Clarendon Press 1995, pp. 364 - 369.

[3] Lars Tvede: Psychologie des Börsenhandels, Gabler 1991.

[4] M. Riedmiller & H. Braun: A direct adaptive method for faster backpropagation learning: The RPROP algorithm in: H. Ruspini, ed., Proc.

[5] T. Hartle: The Average Directional Movement Index (ADX) in: Technical Analysis of Stocks & Commodities

MARKET-TIME AND SHORT-TERM FORECASTING OF FOREIGN EXCHANGE RATES

MARC E. LEVITT

High Frequency Finance Inc.
1083 Robbia Drive, Sunnyvale, CA 94087, USA
E-mail: marcl@highfrequency.com
http://www.highfrequency.com

This paper presents the work of *High Frequency Finance* in the field of real-time foreign exchange rate prediction. The work is based on two main techniques – transforming the raw time series by the application of Market-Time principles and the use of nonlinear forecasting techniques on this transformed time series. Results show statistically significant predictability is possible. This predictability is used as the basis of a decision support system under construction for traders and treasury professionals.

1 Introduction

Forecasting foreign exchange rates is an extremely difficult task and most previous studies have shown little or no success in doing this. Recently, this has been changing in both academia and industry. The ability to account for hetroscedasticity by numerous models has helped, but still the ability to produce economically useful predictions is not easy. This paper presents the main features of one model being developed to predict foreign exchange rates. The three enabling technologies that allow FX rate prediction to be feasible are: high frequency data, nonlinear time transformations, and nonlinear statistical prediction techniques. These combine to allow the building of a time series model that works over short-term horizons with statistically significant results. These techniques are under development as part of a new generation of decision support systems for traders by *High Frequency Finance* (*HFF*). The economic significance of these predictions is left up to how traders and treasury professionals incorporate this information into their trading strategies.

In Section 2 the data used in this work is briefly discussed. In section 3 Market-Time is presented which is the nonlinear time transformation of the data. Section 4 presents the nonlinear prediction technique used which is heavily influenced from the field of nonlinear dynamics. Forecasting results are presented in Section 5 and results from a simple trading system are presented in Section 6. Conclusions are discussed in Section 7.

2 FX Rate Data and Properties

2.1 Data

The database of currency quotes used by *HFF* in its' modeling work consists of numerous sources including future exchanges, banks, brokers, and composite pages provided by data vendors such as Reuters, Telerate, and Knight-Ridder. Three primary sources of quotes, also referred to as ticks in this work, are used in our spot FX analysis:

- A major anonymous bank's every quote. This data is usually what the institution then sends out over Reuters, Telerate, etc..
- Every quote by a major FX broker. Like the bank above this quote is sent out to numerous composite pages provided by data vendors.
- Every quote provided to a composite page with about 120 large contributors.

The average tick frequency of these data sources differ for a given instrument on a given day. For example, the average number of bids for Wednesday averaged over a one month period for the three sources in the DEM/USD market are: bank - 700, broker - 400, composite - 7000. An entry for each data set consists of a date, time to the nearest second, and bid/ask price. While for some of the data it is known that the time stamps may not be accurate to the second, the timed order of the quotes is correct to the minute. For all data, prices are quoted prices and not trading prices. Finally, before any analysis was performed on the data a filter was used to remove any spurious data which was usually do to improper key entry. For example, a bad quote in the CHF/USD rate took on the values 2.33/1.35 - where in fact the 2.33 was a keying error with the real value most likely being 1.33/1.35 on the bid/ask. The data used for all analysis in this paper comes from the composite page, although the other sources do not change the results in any meaningful way.

2.2 Definitions and properties

We now introduce the notations and definitions used for the rest of the paper. Most follow after Muller *et. al.* (1990). The logarithmic price $x(t_j)$ at a given time t_j at which the price was recorded at is defined as

$$x(t_j) = \ln p_{bid}(t_j)$$

This quantity will also be referred to as the price. The change in price, also called the return, is given by

$$r(t_i) \equiv r(\Delta t, t_i) = x(t_i) - x(t_i - \Delta t)$$

which is calculated from the difference in two succeeding prices over a fixed time interval, Δt. The volatility is defined as a sum of absolute returns over a period

$$v(t_i) \equiv v(\Delta t, S; t_i) = \sum_{k=1}^{N} |r(t_i)|$$

where the sampling period, S, is made up of $N\Delta t$ subsamples. Other definitions of volatility could be used, including the more common one of the standard deviation of a series, without changing the results in a meaningful way.

It is well known that the FX market shows strong seasonal effects caused by the hour of the day and day of the week (Muller 1990). This can be seen in both the volatility and the quote activity in the series. Figure 1 and Figure 2 show both the intra-week seasonalities in the volatility and tick frequency. The regular patterns are due to many factors including locations of the major FX trading centers and culture of each market. This seasonality can and does effect the ability to predict the market and must be accounted for in any prediction or trading scheme. This is the purpose of the Market-Time transformation described next.

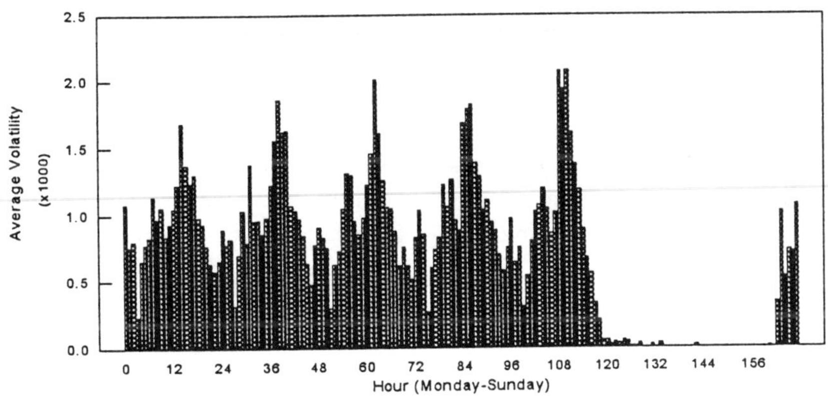

Figure 1: Weekly average volatility per hour for the DEM/USD exchange rate. Hour 0 is from 00:00:00 through 00:59:59 GMT Monday.

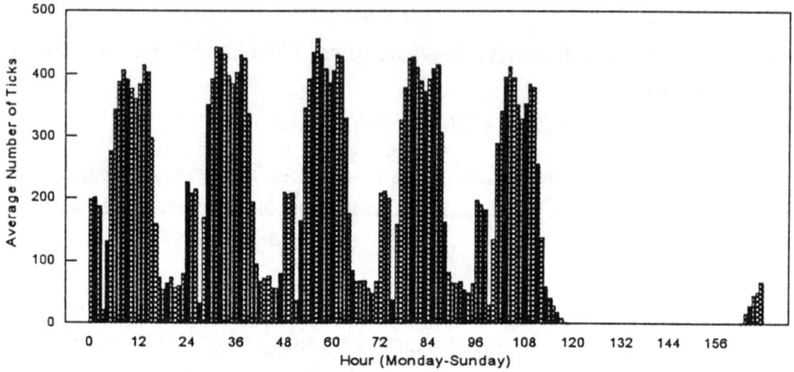

Figure 2: Weekly average quote activity per hour for the DEM/USD exchange rate. Hour 0 is from 00:00:00 through 00:59:59 GMT Monday.

3 Market-Time

Traditional and commonly used forecasting models assume equally spaced data on a physical time scale. But as we can see from the intra-week analysis there are certain times of day or the week that are more important than others. This leads to three distinct time scales for financial time series:

- $\phi - time$: Physical time (p-time) where a minute is a minute 24 hours a day seven days a week.
- $\beta - time$: Business time where a minute is a minute during normal business hours and days. This is the time scale most people are use to dealing with for time series and technical analysis with equally spaced data.
- $\mu - time$: Market-Time (m-time) where a minute depends on what the market or instrument is doing.

Market-Time lets the actual traded instrument determine what a minute is, allowing the time scale, measured in physical time, to expand and contract based on market activity. A forecasting model will update itself more when activity is high and less when it is low. This expansion and contraction allows techniques to adapt to the market by adapting the *data* fed into them, making linear methods in $\mu - time$ actually nonlinear in physical time since the mapping form physical time to Market-Time is typically nonlinear. This idea in not new, and has been proposed by numerous authors going back to Mandelbrot and Taylor (1967), Clark (1973), and more recently has been used by Dacorogna *et. al.* (1993) and Ghysels and Jasiak (1995).

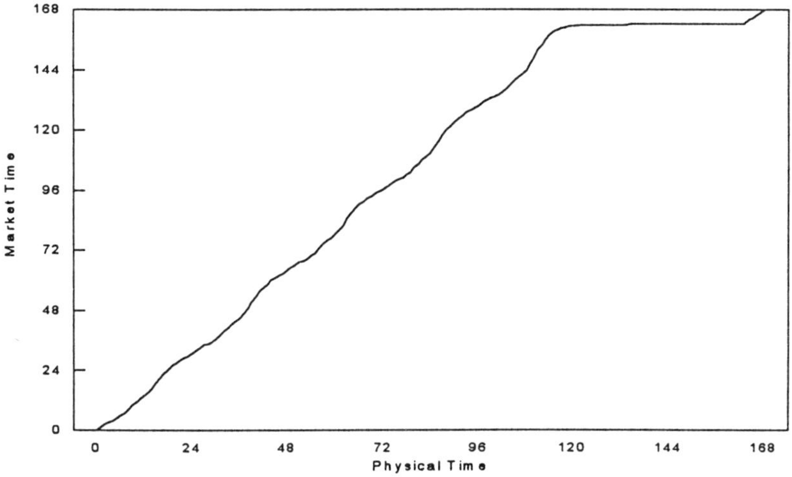

Figure 3: Mapping from Market-Time as determined by the volatility measure of activity to physical time for the USD/DEM exchange rate over a one week period.

To map from $\phi - time$ to $\mu - time$ we enlarge the active periods and shorten the less active periods. Volatility and other proprietary measures, based on price, are used as the definition of activity for this transformation. The mapping works on a one week, 168 hour, cycle where 168 hours in $\phi - time$ is equivalent to 168 hours in $\mu - time$. Mapping between the two times is done via interpolating a local neighborhood fit of the cumulative activity. Figure 3 and Figure 4 show mappings from $\phi - time$ to $\mu - time$ for a one week period. In Figure 3 the mapping is based on volatility as described. Figure 4 shows a mapping based on tick frequency, this is presented for illustration only. While there is an overall similarity between the two, differences do exist. Tick-time is not the same as volatility based Market-Time. The correlation of physical time movement in the two figures is only about 0.75. This is most pronounced "Sunday night" GMT when Asia is starting its trading week after the weekend. The number of quotes is low compared to the volatility. This is a structural issue and does not effect the impact of the price data in those quotes.

When mapping between the two time domains tick or quote volumes are not included in the Market-Time activity measure since they are heavily data source/feed dependent. With volatility based measures we only need a few "important" quoters to develop a proper forecasting model. This allows us to be less data feed dependent in developing the models. It does not matter that the

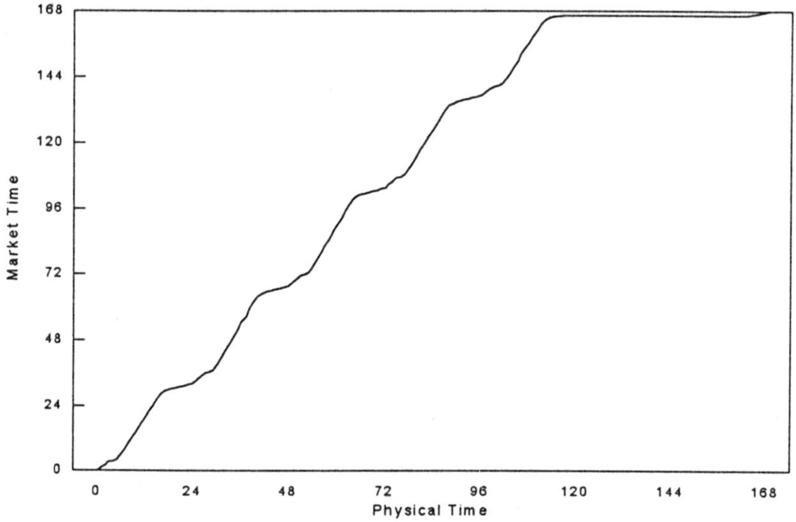

Figure 4: Mapping from Market-Time as determined by quote frequency measure of activity to physical time, also called tick-time.

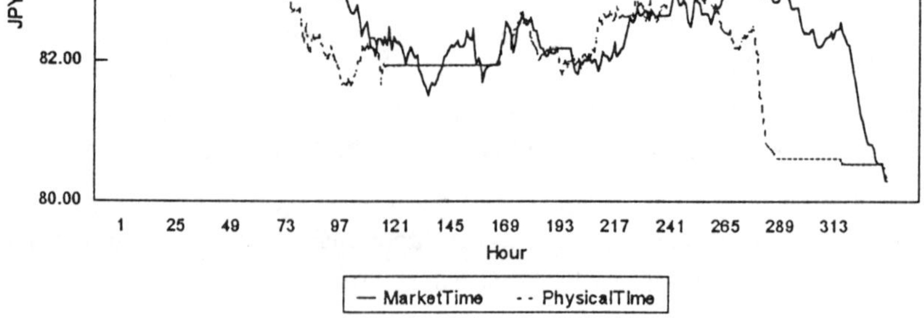

Figure 5: Market-Time and the physical time series for the JPY/DEM cross rate over a two week period.

broker's data is almost 1/20th the density of the composite page as long as they participate in the market in a meaningful way 24 hours a day. With both the structural and data feed issues the volatility based activity measure is better than tick based measures for determining market time. To illustrate the difference between physical time and Market-Time scales a graph of the hourly JPY/DEM series is presented in Figure 5. From the graph it can be seen that the Market-Time based series unveils more structure then the physical time series.

To further reduce any dependencies and modeling errors a $\phi - time$ to $\mu - time$ model is produced for each instrument forecasted, i.e. DEM/USD, GBP/USD, CHF/USD, etc. The correlation between the physical time movement these different mappings ranges from 0.7 to 0.9 depending on the two rates examined.

4 Forecasting

Once a time series has been converted to Market-Time, predictable structure that was not evident in the physical time series becomes more evident. To predict this structure techniques from nonlinear dynamics are used. Specifically, state space embedding and nearest neighbor prediction are used (Farmer 1987).

For a scalar time series $x_i = x_1, x_2, x_3, \ldots, x_n$ state space embedding creates a vectors by taking time based delays of the series x_i and creating a vector of dimension m

$$\mathbf{X}_i = (x_i, x_{i-\tau}, x_{i-2\tau}, \ldots, x_{i-(m-1)\tau})$$

Given an input vector we find the K nearest neighbors (KNN),$X_j, j = 1..K$, to it over a stored sample of input/output pairs. The nearest neighbors are determined by a distance function that can take on many forms but is usually Euclidean distance in the m-dimensional input space. Using the K neighbors an affine model of the form

$$x_{i+\tau} = \alpha_0 + \sum_{n=1}^{m} \alpha_n x_{i-(n-1)\tau}$$

is fitted. This fitted model is then used to forecast the new point, y_t. Once the new point is predicted it must be converted back to physical time. A complete flow of the forecasting procedure is given in Figure 6. Note all operations are done in $\mu - time$ except the first and last. In the actual *HFF* system the embedding is done on an multivariate series that consists of returns, price, and their transforms.

While the above discussion made use of a Euclidean distance measure to find the K nearest neighbors and a local linear fit for prediction many variations of the

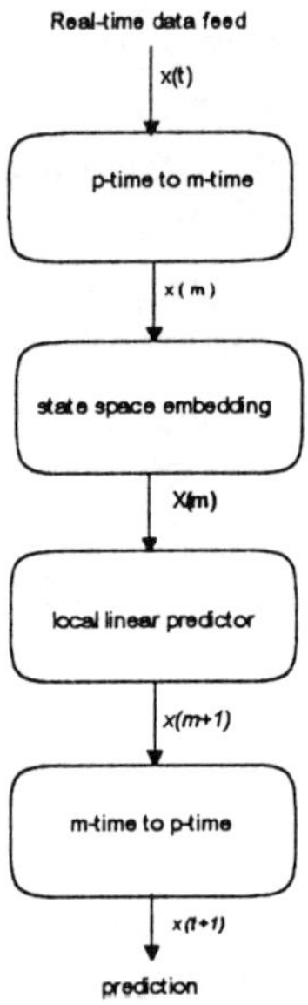

Figure 6: Overview of forecasting system.

technique do exist using different distance measures and prediction techniques for the local area (Levitt 1995).

5 Forecasting Results

Results for predicting three different exchange rates are presented covering the 6 month time period from April 1993 through September 1993. To measure the success of the forecasting procedure two different quantities are examined. The first measure is the ability to forecast the correct of sign of the market movement. This is very important to a trader since direction is usually more important then the magnitude of a move. The measure is given by

$$D = \frac{\sum_{i=1}^{n} a_i}{\sum_{i=1}^{n} b_i}$$

where

$$a_i = \begin{cases} 1 & y_t \times x_t > 0 \\ 0 & otherwise \end{cases}$$

and

$$b_i = \begin{matrix} 1 & y_t \times x_t \neq 0 \\ 0 & otherwise \end{matrix}$$

and y_t is the predicted return and x_t is the actual return. The standard deviation for D assuming a random walk is

$$\sigma_D \approx \frac{1}{2\sqrt{n}}$$

where n is the number of tests, i.e. predictions. To show better than random prediction rates one must forecast at $50\% + X\sigma_D$ where X determines the level of significance of the test, i.e. 1.96 for 5%.

The second measure is Theil's coefficient of inequality for a random walk defined as

$$T_r = \frac{\sqrt{\Sigma(y_t - x_t)^2}}{\sqrt{\Sigma(x_t - x_{t-1})^2}}$$

where a value of $T_r < 1$ implies one is doing better than the trivial random walk prediction of returns.

The effectiveness of the models for three FX rates over two different time horizons are presented in Table 1. For all rates $T_r < 1$ and many predictions are significant at the 5% level for directional quality.

6 Trading System Results

To further demonstrate the power of Market-Time a simple trading model was developed and evaluated on both m-time and p-time FX series. This is

Table 1: Results for predicting three different FX rate over two different time horizons. All directional qualities are above 50% and all Theil's coefficients are less than 1.

FX Rate	Horizon	Directional Quality	T_r
JPY/USD	1	57.0%	0.82
	2	53.5%	0.89
DEM/USD	1	55.4%	0.72
	2	54.2%	0.76
JPY/DEM	1	59.5%	0.76
	2	52.1%	0.93

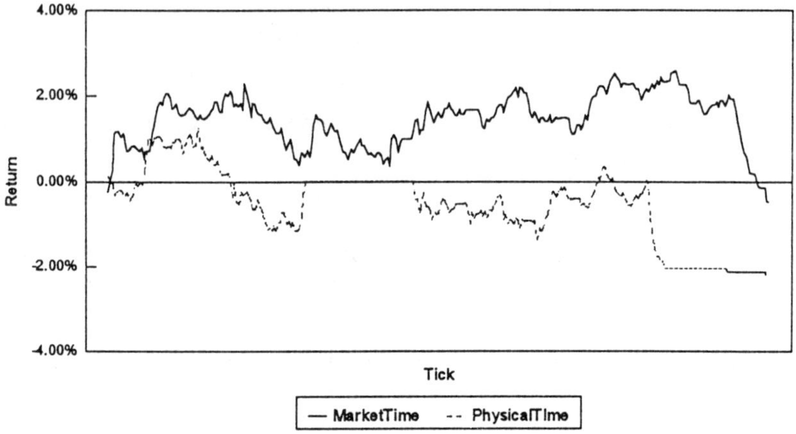

Figure 7: Hourly marked-to-market equity curve for a simple trading system on both the Market-Time based series and the physical time series over a two week period for the JPY/DEM cross rate.

presented for illustration purposes only since the system is so simple as not to be tradable in its current form. Table 2 presents the return statistics, maximum drawdown, and Sharpe ratio over a two week period for both the USD/DEM and JPY/DEM rates. The Sharpe ratio is based on hourly returns. As evidenced by the results a system based on Market-Time data performs better then the same system based on physical time data for both raw and risk adjusted results. Figure 7 presents an hourly equity curve for the trading system on the two series for the JPY/DEM rate over a two week period. While neither system is profitable it is clear that a system based on Market-Time has a better chance then the same system using physical time to be profitable.

The need to model each FX series with its own Market-Time transformation is demonstrated by the results in Table 3. In this table two versions of Market-Time are used to model the JPY/DEM exchange rate. The first model is correct Market-Time based on the actual series as outlined previously. The second model is based on the DEM/USD exchange rate derived Market-Time (similar results are obtained when using JPY/USD rate). As shown in the table the use of the correct Market-Time transformation is critical to achieving peak performance, where the correct series outperform the incorrect series in all performance statistics.

Table 2: Results for a simple trading system working on both physical-time and Market-Time based FX series. The results are for an two week period using the exact same FX-rates and each series has the same number of bars in them.

Trading System	Return %	Maximum Drawdown	Sharpe Ratio
JPY/USD Physical Time	2.5%	2.3%	0.29
JPY/USD Market-Time	3.7%	1.5%	0.51
DEM/USD Physical Time	1.7%	4%	0.08
DEM/USD Market-Time	2.6%	4%	0.12

Table 3: Results for the simple trading system with correctly and incorrectly specified Market-Time. Correct Market-Time is developed from the actual JPY/DEM series while incorrect Market-Time is developed from the DEM/USD series.

Trading System	Return %	Maximum Drawdown	Sharpe Ratio
JPY/DEM Correct MT	1.96%	1.93%	0.25
JPY/DEM Incorrect MT	0.67%	2.96%	0.02

7 Conclusion

This paper demonstrated that statistically significant forecasting of foreign exchange rates can be accomplished. This is not an easy task and a key component to accomplishing this is the concept of Market-Time. This nonlinear time transformation processes the time series into a form where nonparametric forecasting techniques give good results. The further usefulness of Market-Time over physical time was demonstrated with a simple trading system. This work is an initial step toward building a real-time decision support system for traders and treasury professionals.

8 References

Clark, P.K., 1973, *A subordinated stochastic process model with finite variance for speculative prices*, Econometrica, 41, 135-155.

Dacorogna M.M., Muller U.A., Nagler R.J., . Olsen R.B, and Pictet O.V., 1993, *A geographical model for the daily and weekly seasonal volatility in the FX market*, Journal of International Money and Finance, 12, 413-438.

Farmer J.D., and Sidorowich J.J., 1987, *Predicting chaotic time series*, Physical Review Letters, 59, 8, 845.

Ghysels E., and Jasiak J., 1995, *Trading patterns, time deformation and stochastic volatility in foreign exchange markets,* First International Conference on High Frequency Data in Finance.

Levitt M.E., *Machine learning for foreign exchange trading*, 1995, in Neural Networks in the Capital Markets, P. Refenes ed., John Wiley & Sons.

Muller U.A., Dacorogna M.M., Olsen R.B., Pictet O.V., Schwarz M., and Morgenegg C, 1990, *Statistical study of foreign exchange rates, empirical evidence of a price change scaling law, and intraday analysis*, Journal of Banking and Finance, 14, 1189-1208.

Part 2
Risk Management

SYSTEMATIC UNDERPREDICTION OF VOLATILITY IN MAXIMUM LIKELIHOOD METHODS

M. MAGDON-ISMAIL, Y.S. ABU-MOSTAFA
Caltech 136-93, Pasadena,
CA 91125, USA

In forecasting a financial time series, the mean prediction can be validated by direct comparison with the value of the series. However, the volatility or variance can only be validated by indirect means such as the likelihood function. Systematic errors in volatility prediction have an 'economic value' since volatility is a tradable quantity (e.g., in options and other derivatives) in addition to being a risk measure. We analyze the fidelity of the likelihood function as a means of training (in sample) and validating (out of sample) a volatility model. We report several cases where the likelihood function leads to an erroneous model. We correct for this error by scaling the volatility prediction using a predetermined factor that depends on the number of data points.

Keywords: Validation, Volatility Prediction, Maximum Likelihood

1 Introduction

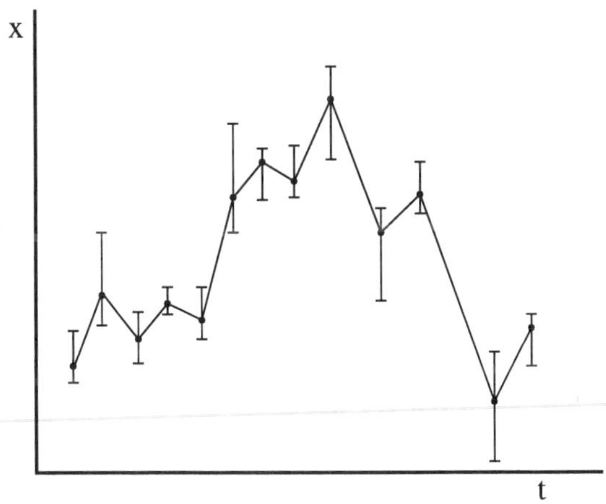

Figure 1.

Consider the time series depicted in Fig 1. Each point $x(t)$ is drawn from a distribution whose mean is $\mu(t)$ and variance is $\sigma^2(t)$. While we can only observe $x(t)$, we wish to learn about the mean $\mu(t)$ and the volatility $\tilde{\sigma}(t)$ (a normalized version of $\sigma(t)$). An accurate prediction of the mean tells us about the expected behavior of the time series. An accurate prediction of the volatility is also important, especially in the case of a financial time series. Typically, volatility prediction is used as an explicit measure of risk in static hedging, portfolio selection and margining problems. It serves to place an error bar on the predicted value.

The question arises as to how one can judge various models that are predicting a non-explicit parameter like the variance. The variance falls into the class of non-explicit parameters because, on drawing a random variable from its distribution, no direct information on the variance is conveyed. If we have more than one drawing from the distribution then some direct information does exist on the variance but we would like to consider time series with time-varying distributions, so we only get one drawing from each distribution. As a result, one has to somehow infer information on the variance, and here lies the difficulty with variance prediction. We discuss how this can be done using maximum likelihood, and we take the special case of gaussian noise to illustrate our points.

The most striking result in this paper is that, for any finite number of data points, it is more likely than not that we will pick the worse of two specific models if we use the likelihood function to compare them. It turns out that maximum likelihood will lead to an *underestimation* of the volatility, even when the mean is predicted perfectly. This naturally leads to the question "can we correct for the systematic underestimation?". This allows us to choose from a class of models and then correct for the bias in the method of selection.

Volatility factors into a number of equations in finance. Black and Scholes (1973) derived option pricing models for which the expected future volatility is an important input. Kat (1993) has shown that more accurate volatility prediction will improve the replication efficiency of delta hedging strategies using Black–Scholes hedge ratios, even if the volatility is not constant. Crouchy (1995) shows that for path independent options, the option value depends only on the average volatility while the hedge ratio itself depends on the path of future volatility. The sensitivity of the hedge ratio to short term volatility (we are interested in time-varying volatility) is more of a problem for short term options than long term options. Nonetheless this sensitivity exists and so one would like to have an accurate estimate of the volatility.

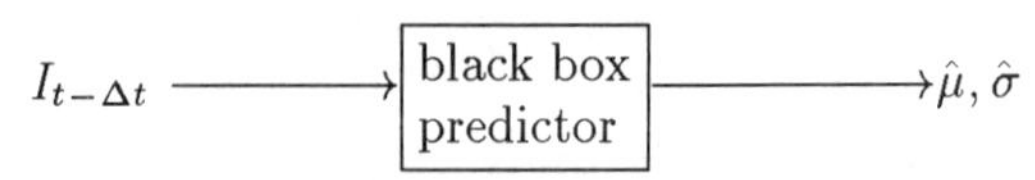

Figure 2.

We consider models that predict the mean and variance at time t as in Fig. 2. A variety of techniques exist for predicting variance or volatility. One can use the option prices to compute 'implied' volatilities, such as those derived from the Black-Scholes pricing equations. Another alternative is a multifactor model. Usually combinations of such models work best, but these models all include some constancy in the volatility. Schewert (1989) tests for the constancy of the volatility and strongly rejects this hypothesis. Thus one would like to have models that reasonably account for changing volatility. One can modify the Black-Scholes equations if the volatility is some known function of time by replacing the actual volatility by the average over the remaining life of the option. Autoregressive Conditional Heteroscedasticity (ARCH) type models introduced by Engle(1982) stipulate the conditional variance as a function of past innovations. Generalizations of this are GARCH (Bollerslev, 1986) and EGARCH (Nelson, 1991) where the conditional variance is a function of past innovations and variances. Hull (1987) has tried models that have stochastic parts to them.

One would like to have a reliable method for choosing between volatility models. Our goal is the selection of the optimal model given a number of models. Training can be viewed as a generalization of this where one chooses from a *class* of models (e.g., neural networks with a given architecture). We will evaluate maximum likelihood as a selection criterion between models.

2 Defining the Volatility

2.1 Variability versus Volatility

It is important to distinguish how "jagged" or "choppy" a time series is from the volatility. One might more accurately refer to the former as the variability. At any given time, if the mean value is known, the tendency of the actual value at that time to wander about this mean value is related to the volatility. In the case where the mean and the variance are constant, the variability will reflect the volatility. We are more concerned with time varying variance so this distinction should be made. A measure of this tendency for the actual outcome to be scattered about the mean is the variance of the value at time t.

2.2 Correspondence with the Black-Scholes Volatility Models

In modeling the time variation of a stock price, Black-Scholes assume an Ito Process (Ito, 1951) of the form $\Delta S = \tilde{\mu} S \Delta t + \tilde{\sigma} S \epsilon \sqrt{\Delta t}$. $\epsilon \sim N(0,1)$, S is the instrument price and $\tilde{\sigma}$ is defined as the volatility and is the standard deviation of the proportional change in the stock price in unit time. It is this $\tilde{\sigma}$ that enters into the calculation of the hedge ratios, option prices, etc. Hence, in the Black-Scholes model we can identify the volatility as

$$\tilde{\sigma} = \frac{\sigma}{S_{t-\Delta t}\sqrt{\Delta t}} \tag{1}$$

So to calculate option prices, hedge ratios, etc., according to the Black-Scholes prescription, it suffices to know σ^2, the variance. With this consideration in mind, we now restrict our analysis to the prediction of variance.

3 Setting Up the Problem of Variance Estimation

3.1 Basic Setup

We will consider the case of noisy time series, financial series being a special case. The problem is set up in the following way. Given the history of information (including the full history of values of the time series), there exists some conditional probability distribution for the next value. We label the time series variable x, then

$$f(x_t \mid I_{t-\Delta t}) = \begin{array}{l}\text{probability density function for } x_t,\\ \text{the value of the series at time t}\end{array} \tag{2}$$

where $I_{t-\Delta t}$ is the information available at time $t - \Delta t$. Usually, $I_{t-\Delta t}$ is taken as the past few values of the variable x. We will focus on the first two moments of f, $\mu(I_{t-\Delta t})$ and $\sigma(I_{t-\Delta t})$. A model consists of a "black box" that takes as input $I_{t-\Delta t}$ and outputs $\{\hat{\mu}^t, \hat{\sigma}^t\}$, predictions of the mean and variance for time t (Fig 2). A collection of models consists of a set of such pairs of functions $\{\hat{\mu}_i^t, \hat{\sigma}_i^t\}_{i=1}^M$. The index i refers to which model we are talking about. In this paper, we are not concerned with exactly what goes into the black box of Fig 2. All we know is that we are given a set of models (e.g., GARCH, Neural Networks,...) that take the input $I_{t-\Delta t}$ and provide estimates of the mean and variance as output.

3.2 Choosing Between the Models

In order to choose between the models, one requires some 'validation' data. Our goal is to predict the mean μ and the variance σ^2. Unfortunately one does not usually have access to the actual values of the mean and variance. All one usually has are data points $(\{d_\alpha\}_{\alpha=1}^n)$ drawn from the distributions $f(x_t \mid I_{t-\Delta t}^\alpha)$. Based on the data, one has to construct an error measure that evaluates the estimates $\hat{\mu}$ and $\hat{\sigma}$ without knowing the actual μ and σ. One then evaluates this error measure for each model and picks the model that minimizes the error. The question now arises as to what kind of error measure to take.

3.3 Using Maximum Likelihood to Choose Between Models

If we know the functional dependence of $f(x_t \mid I_{t-\Delta t})$ on the parameters that we are trying to predict, we can evaluate the likelihood that the data occurred under the assumption that model i is correct. We will assume that the data have been drawn independently and that f is gaussian. In particular, Black-Scholes models satisfy our gaussian assumption on f. A similar analysis could be done for any other assumption on f. The likelihood that the data occurred under a particular model i is given by

$$l(\vec{d} \mid \text{model } i) = \prod_{\alpha=1}^{n} \frac{1}{\sqrt{2\pi\hat{\sigma}_{\alpha}^{i\ 2}}} e^{-\frac{(d_\alpha - \hat{\mu}_{\alpha}^{i})^2}{2\hat{\sigma}_{\alpha}^{i\ 2}}} \tag{3}$$

Maximizing the likelihood, or equivalently maximizing the Log(*likelihood*) is the criterion that we will use to differentiate between the models. As an example, consider the training of Neural Networks to predict the variance using maximum likelihood as the objective function to optimize (Weigend, 1995). In this case, the models i correspond to all the functions that the Neural Network can implement and we are choosing one of them using maximum likelihood as the criterion.

4 Analysis of the Maximum Likelihood Scheme

4.1 Expected Value of the Likelihood and Log(likelihood)

Consider the likelihood function as a function of the data d_α. Thus it is itself a random variable, for which the distribution is known given the distribution of the data point d_α. One can calculate 'the expectation of $l(d_\alpha)$'=$\langle l_i \rangle$ and 'the expectation of $\log(l(d_\alpha))$'=$\langle \log l_i \rangle$ for model i. For simplicity in notation, we will drop the α index.

$$\begin{aligned}
\log\langle l_i \rangle &= -\frac{1}{2}\left[\frac{(\mu - \hat{\mu}_i)^2}{\sigma^2 + \hat{\sigma}_i^2} + \log(\sigma^2 + \hat{\sigma}_i^2) + \log 2\pi\right] \\
\langle \log l_i \rangle &= -\frac{1}{2}\left[\frac{(\mu - \hat{\mu}_i)^2 + \sigma^2}{\hat{\sigma}_i^2} + \log(\hat{\sigma}_i^2) + \log 2\pi\right]
\end{aligned} \tag{4}$$

$\langle l_i \rangle$ is maximized when the predicted mean and variance are equal to the true mean and variance. So if we expect the observed value of the Log(*likelihood*) to be close to its expected value, which will be true with enough data points, then it seems reasonable to maximize the Log(*likelihood*) in order to predict $\{\hat{\mu}, \hat{\sigma}\}$.

The expectation of the likelihood itself is not maximized at the correct values. Its maximum is when $\hat{\sigma} \to 0$. This rules out likelihood itself as a comparator because its expected behavior is not desirable. To investigate this issue further we define what it means for a model to be 'better' than another. Suppose we have two models, model 1 and model 2 with $| \hat{\mu}_1 - \mu | > | \hat{\mu}_2 - \mu |$ and $| \hat{\sigma}_1 - \sigma | > | \hat{\sigma}_2 - \sigma |$. We will then say that model 1 is worse than model 2.

If model 1 is worse than model 2 then its expected Log(*likelihood*) should also be worse. Unfortunately one can find common situations where this is not the case. This becomes evident from Fig. 3.

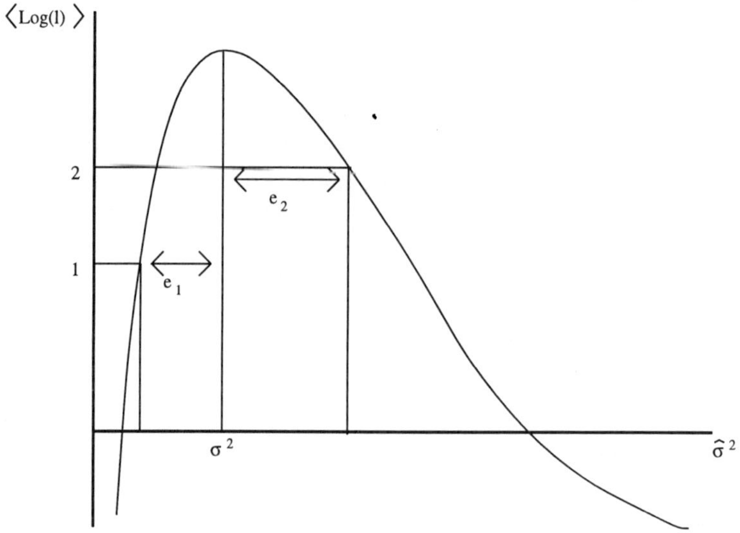

Figure 3. Plot of $\langle \log l_i \rangle$ as a function of $\hat{\sigma}_i^2$. The curve is not symmetric about the true variance. In the figure is shown how model 2 has a higher expected likelihood despite having a higher prediction error $(e_2 > e_1)$

Thus we see that even log(*likelihood*) can lead to an expected worse choice. However, note thattraining (say neural networks) by maximizing log(*likelihood*) (Weigend,1995) using small perturbations will select 'better' models on the average. Note that by initially choosing a model with lower log(*likelihood*), training could be faster owing to the asymmetry of the curve about the actual variance. If the neural network cannot implement the maximum of the curve then training may stop at a worse value than is necessary, owing to this asymmetry.

4.2 Probability of Choosing the Wrong Model

Suppose that you have two models, model 1 worse than model 2 as described above. One can ask whether it is possible that model 1 will be picked more often than model 2. This is distinct from the analysis of the expected value because it is possible for the expected value to be greater for model 1 despite the fact that the probability that model 1's Log(*likelihood*) is higher is very small. In this case one might still be content because most of the time one will be choosing the better model even though its expected Log(*likelihood*) is lower. Unfortunately, we show that this too is not the case.

We ask the question: Is it possible that one might pick a 'worse' model (in the sense described in the previous section) more often than one might pick a 'better' model? To answer this question we will compare a 'worse' model with the ground truth model. We shall see that this will lead to some striking results.

Set up the problem in the following way. We have n data points $\{I_{t-\Delta t}, d_\alpha\}$ where each of the d_α have been drawn from a (possibly *different*) distribution $\sim N(\mu_\alpha, \sigma_\alpha)$. We will consider the case where $\hat{\mu}^i_\alpha = \mu_\alpha$ (perfect prediction of the mean), while the variances predicted by the models are given by $\hat{\sigma}^i_\alpha = \lambda^i_\alpha \sigma_\alpha$, $\lambda^i_\alpha \geq 0$ thus the models are parametrized by λ^i_α,$\alpha = 1, \ldots, n$. The likelihood of model i with parameters $\vec{\lambda}_i$ is

$$l(\vec{d} \mid \vec{\lambda}_i) = \prod_\alpha N_{d_\alpha}(\mu_\alpha, \lambda^i_\alpha \sigma_\alpha) \tag{5}$$

We are going to compare the two models $\{\lambda_\alpha = 1\}$, the perfect model, and $\{\lambda_\alpha\}$. We seek the probability $(P_{\vec{\lambda}})$ that $l_{\vec{\lambda}} \geq l_{\vec{1}}$ where $l_{\vec{1}}$ is the likelihood of the ground truth model and $l_{\vec{\lambda}}$ is the likelihood of model $\vec{\lambda}$.

Now treat the data outcome $\vec{d}$ as a random variable $\vec{x}$. Then this likelihood itself is a random variable, depending on the parameter $\vec{\lambda}$, so we can ask the question: what is the probability that the random variable with parameter $\vec{\lambda}$ is greater than the random variable with parameter $\vec{\lambda} = \vec{1}$, i.e., we are asking for the frequency with which the 'worse' model is chosen over the *actual* model. For the case $\vec{\lambda} = \lambda\vec{1}$, the result is shown in Appendix A. For λ slightly less than 1, P_λ is greater than $\frac{1}{2}$. This means that a worse model will be chosen over the actual model more than $\frac{1}{2}$ the time. *This holds for any number of data points.* The smallest value that λ can be with $P_\lambda \geq \frac{1}{2}$ ($\lambda_{min}(n)$) is tabulated for various n in table 1.

n	$\lambda_{min}(n)$	$P_{max}(n)$	$\langle\frac{1}{\lambda}\rangle=\alpha_{correc}$
1	0.4937	0.6831	∞
2	0.7072	0.6321	1.7725
5	0.8729	0.5842	1.1894
10	0.9349	0.5594	1.0837
20	0.9670	0.5422	1.0397
50	0.9866	0.5268	1.0153
100	0.9934	0.5186	1.0076
500	0.9986	0.5088	1.0015
1000	0.9993	0.5059	1.0008

Table 1: Showing the results for the analysis of the probability that model $\vec{\lambda}$ is chosen more often than the actual model.For $\lambda_{min}(n) \leq \lambda \leq 1$, $P_\lambda \geq \frac{1}{2}$. $\langle\frac{1}{\lambda}\rangle$ is the expected correction factor α_{correc} for the new prediction given the maximum likelihood model prediction ($\hat{\sigma} \to \alpha_{correc}\hat{\sigma}$). $P_{max}(n)$ is the maximum value that P_λ can take and occurs for $\lambda \to 1^-$

Referring to table 1, we note that for n=100, a model with a 0.7% error in the prediction of σ will be chosen more often than the actual model. This is a fairly significant error when dealing with a tradable quantity.

5 Correcting for the Maximum Likelihood Prediction Error

Up to now we have diagnosed some problems with the maximum likelihood scheme. We now try to tackle the problem of compensating for this error using our understanding of how it fails. The models that are more probable than the actual model are models which underestimate the variance (assuming the mean is predicted perfectly). One expects that the model chosen using maximum likelihood will have a systematic bias for predicting a variance lower than the actual variance. Suppose that we have a model that is predicting $\hat{\sigma} = \lambda\sigma$ on the average. We would like to correct our prediction arrived at using maximum likelihood methods by multiplying our prediction by some correction factor to get a better prediction.

$$\hat{\sigma} \to \alpha_{correc}\hat{\sigma} \tag{6}$$

In order to calculate α_{correc} we need the probability distribution for obtaining a particular model with parameter λ. The method of compensating will depend on the the exact method that was used to arrive at the model. Here we will consider the case that seems appropriate to neural networks that are trained on the data using maximum likelihood. The general philosophy will become apparent.

5.1 Probability Distribution Over λ

We have the class of models that are parametrised by λ. Training proceeds in the following way. Start with a random λ and perturb λ a little toward the higher range and toward the lower range. So we are dealing with the three λ's $\{\lambda - \frac{d\lambda}{2}, \lambda, \lambda + \frac{d\lambda}{2}\}$. Now using the data we compare the likelihood of these three models and choose the model that produces the highest likelihood. We continue the process until no change in λ results. In actuality the learning proceeds not by varying λ but by varying the parameters of the model (in the case of neural networks, these are the weights). One might question why the model's λ should be the same for all the possible inputs. This will not be the case in general, but we are asking what the correction factor is *on the average*. To calculate this we look at the probability distribution that we end up with a model with a certain λ (for which the correction factor is $\frac{1}{\lambda}$).

What is the probability that we stop at the value λ? We consider the region $[\lambda, \lambda+d\lambda]$ and derive the probability density over λ, which we can use to calculate various desired properties like expectations. The detailed derivation of this probability density is lengthy. The final result is given in Appendix B, eq. 1. We are interested in $\langle\frac{1}{\lambda}\rangle$, the expected correction factor shown in Appendix B eq. 2. Values of the correction factor for various values of n are given in table 1. Note that for $n = 100$ the correction is about 0.8% which is not trivial.

We summarize the correction method, assuming that the models are predicting the mean well: Train the models using maximum likelihood and arrive at a model to be used for future predictions. Now given a new test input, obtain this model's prediction and correct by the correction factor described above.

5.2 Example: Training Neural Networks Using maximum Likelihood

In this example the model is a neural network with 131 weights that are involved in the training of the model to predict σ (Weigend, 1995). The input variable which we have called $I_{t-\Delta t}$ is $x \in [0, \pi]$. The mean $\mu(x)$ and variance

$\sigma^2(x)$ are functions of x and the model is a mapping $x \rightarrow \begin{bmatrix} \hat{\mu}(x) \\ \hat{\sigma}^2(x) \end{bmatrix}$. The network was trained on n examples by altering the weight in the direction that increased the likelihood that the data occurred under the model. The final network arrived at is used as the final model. It is to this network that we wish to apply the correction factor. A question arises as to what the effective number of data points (n_{eff}) is. Each parameter can be regarded as being trained on some of the data points. So n_{eff} should be approximately proportional to the number of examples, $n_{eff} \sim \gamma n$. Using this relationship we can get a theoretical prediction to compare with the experimental value. The results are summarized in table 2 [a]

n	$\langle\lambda\rangle$		$\langle\frac{1}{\lambda}\rangle = \alpha_{correc}$	
	expt.	theory	expt	theory
50	0.68±0.18	0.56±0.07	1.25±0.18	1.98±0.58
100	0.66±0.04	0.70±0.07	1.24±0.03	1.27±0.12
150	0.67±0.05	0.77±0.06	1.22±0.04	1.16±0.06
300	0.88±0.14	0.86±0.04	1.07±0.09	1.07±0.02
500	0.92±0.05	0.91±0.03	1.04±0.03	1.04±0.01

Table 2: Comparison of the theoretical results that are predicted from the induced probability distribution over λ with the experimentally obtained values for learning the variance with a neural network. The theoretical predictions were obtained by assuming a proportional relationship between n_{eff} and n, fitting γ to the data using the expected theoretical form. For $\langle\lambda\rangle$, γ was 0.006±0.002 and for$\langle\frac{1}{\lambda}\rangle$, γ was 0.044±0.014. It is interesting to compare $\frac{1}{\gamma}$ to the number of weights=N_w. $\frac{1}{N_w} = 0.008$.

The agreement between the theoretical values and the experimental values seems convincing especially as the number of data points increases. Also note that the variance in the experimental values is relatively small implying that the network has indeed settled on a model with almost a constant parameter

[a] We thank Zehra Cataltepe of the Learning Systems Group at Caltech for use of the results from her experiments in verifying the method of Weigend(1995). $\langle\alpha_{correc}\rangle$ was computed from the results only where σ was larger than a threshold because where σ is small, the behaviour is erratic. The mean as expected was learned well, so we can apply the analysis above where we assumed the mean was being predicted exactly.

of λ. How one would calculate n_{eff} for a general class of models with a given learning algorithm is not yet obvious. In our discussion we have assumed that the class of models is good enough to implement the various models with parameter λ. Exactly how we search through this space and how the models are parametrized are expected to affect n_{eff}.

6 Conclusions

It seems appropriate to summarize the path that we have followed in this paper. We started out by setting up a framework for comparing between models. In this framework, we used maximum likelihood to compare between models and we found that this leads to choosing wrong models. The results of the maximum likelihood analysis can be summarized by the picture in Fig. 4 .

	IN SAMPLE	OUT OF SAMPLE
FINITE DATA	Choosing the model that maximizes the likelihood will yield a model that systematically predicts lower variance, even if the mean is predicted well.	Probability of choosing the wrong model is $> \frac{1}{2}$ for some 'worse' models.
EXPECTED VALUE	NOT APPLICABLE	Possible to find models 1,2 with model 1 worse than 2 but $\langle \log l_1 \rangle > \langle \log l_2 \rangle$.

Figure 4: Diagram depicting what could go wrong with the Maximum likelihood scheme in the 3 possible cases.

When the mean is predicted well, we attempt to correct for the systematic underprediction of the variance by multiplying by a correction factor, α_{correc}. We find that this correction factor is economically significant even for a large number of data points. In this way we are able to choose a model from a class of models that were trained on different data, and then improve that model using the correction factor. Unfortunately this will not work when the mean is not being predicted well. In this case, the variance will tend to be over predicted to compensate for the bias. Thus one would like to have a way to predict the variance without having to predict the mean. This is a direction open for future work as is the question of combining models that have been trained on different data. It is necessary, however, to have a "good" way to compare models before one even starts to think about combining models.

Acknowledgments

We would like to thank Dr. Amir Atiya, Joseph Sill and Zehra Cataltepe for helpful discussion.

Appendix A

Treat the data outcome $\vec{d}$ as a random variable $\vec{x}$. Then the likelihood itself is a random variable, depending on the parameter $\vec{\lambda}$. We seek the probability that this random variable with parameter $\vec{\lambda}$ is greater than the random variable with parameter $\vec{\lambda} = \vec{1}$, i.e., we are asking for the frequency with which the 'worse' model is chosen over the *actual* model. This probability is given by

$$P_{\vec{\lambda}} = \text{Prob}[l_{\vec{\lambda}} \geq l_{\vec{1}}] = \int_{\{l_{\vec{\lambda}} \geq l_{\vec{1}}\}} d^n x \, l(\vec{x} \mid \vec{\lambda} = \vec{1}) \qquad (A-1)$$

With some manipulation one finally gets for $\vec{\lambda} = \lambda\vec{1}$ and n even

$$P_\lambda = 1 - e^{-\beta n} \sum_{k=0}^{\frac{n}{2}-1} \frac{(\beta n)^k}{k!} \qquad (A-2)$$

where $\beta = \frac{\lambda^2 \log \lambda}{\lambda^2 - 1}$ and $0 < \lambda < 1$.

Appendix B

By infinitessimally changing the λ parameter one eventually ends up at a model that maximizes the likelihood. The probability that this results in a model with parameter λ is (after lengthy calculation)

$$P(\lambda)d\lambda = \frac{n^{\frac{n}{2}} e^{-n\frac{\lambda^2}{2}}}{\Gamma(\frac{n}{2})} \left(\frac{\lambda^2}{2}\right)^{\frac{n}{2}-1} \lambda d\lambda \qquad (B-1)$$

The expected correction factor can now be calculated

$$\alpha_{correc} = \left\langle \frac{1}{\lambda} \right\rangle = \sqrt{\left(\frac{n}{2}\right)} \frac{\Gamma(\frac{n-1}{2})}{\Gamma(\frac{n}{2})} \qquad (B-2)$$

References

Black, F. and Scholes, M.S. 1973, The Pricing of Options and Corporate Liabilities. *Journal of Political Economy* **3**, 637-654.

Bollerslev, T. 1986, Generalized Autoregressive Conditional Heteroscedasticity. *Journal of Econometrics* **31**, 307-327.

Crouhy,M. and Galai,D. 1995, Hedging With a Volatility Term Structure. *The Journal of Derivatives* **Spring**, 45-52.

Engle, R.F. 1982, Autoregressive Conditional Heteroscedasticity with Estimates of the Variance of U.K. Inflation. *Econometrica* **50**, 987-1008.

French, K.R., Schwert, G.W. and Stambaugh, R.F. 1987, Expected Stock Returns and Volatility. *Journal of Financial Economics* **19**, 3-29.

Hull, John C., *Options, Futures and other Derivative Securities* 2nd *Ed.*, Englewood Cliffs, New Jersey: Prentice Hall, 1993.

Hull, J. and White, A. 1987, The Pricing of Options on Assets with Stochastic Volatilities. *Journal of Finance* **2**, 281-300.

Ito, K. 1951, On Stochastic Differential Equations. *Memoirs, American Mathematical Society* **4**, 1-51.

Kat,H.M.,'Replicating Ordinary Call Options: A Stochastic Simulation Study', Presented at the 13th AMEX Options and Derivatives Colloquium, New York (1993).

Nelson, D.B. 1991, Conditional Heteroscedasticity in Asset Returns: A New Approach. *Econometrica* **59**, 347-370.

Poterba, J. and Summers, L. 1986, The Persistence of Volatility and Stock Market Fluctuations. *American Economic Review* **76**, 1142-1151.

Schwert, G.W. 1989, Why Does Stock Market Volatility Change Over Time. *Journal of Finance* **44**, 1115-1153.

Shiller, Robert J., *Market Volatility*, Cambridge, Massachusetts: The MIT Press, 1993.

Weigend, A.S., Nix, D.A. 1995. Learning Local Error Bars for Nonlinear Regression. In *Advances in Neural Information Processing Systems (NIPS): Proceedings of NIPS'94*, Tesauro G., Touretzky D., Leen T. (eds), 489-496. Morgan Kauffman.

VALIDATING A CONNECTIONIST MODEL OF FINANCIAL DIAGNOSIS

PER E. PEDERSEN
Department of Economics and Business Administration
Agder College
Grooseveien 36
4890 Grimstad, Norway
E-mail: Per.Pedersen@hia.no
http://ulke.grm.hia.no/~perpe

Several studies have demonstrated a superiority of neural networks as models for financial diagnosis. It has been proposed that the ability of these models to represent intermediate abstractions is a main reason for their superior performance. It has also been proposed that the represented intermediate abstractions resemble the diagnostic concepts used by skilled diagnosticians, and thus, that they have cognitive relevance. In this paper, we investigate these propositions applying an experimental methodology to obtain valid data sets of financial diagnoses. A multilayered perceptron model is developed and validated using cross validated performance measures and analyses of error term distributions and internal representations. The hidden units of the connectionist model represent intermediate abstractions explaining the model's superior performance, but the cognitive relevance of these intermediate abstractions is not obvious.

1 Introduction

Financial diagnosis is the classification task performed when a subject makes a judgment of the financial situation of the firm based upon information from the financial statement (Methlie, 1987). This task is performed in several contexts, such as bankruptcy prediction, going concern judgment and loan decision contexts. The diagnosis task constitutes an important basis for prediction and judgment in all these contexts and has many similarities across the different contexts.

Several authors have proposed that neural networks outperform traditional statistical techniques in predicting the environmental outcome of these contexts (e.g., Tam, 1991; Tam & Kiang, 1992; Wilson & Sharda, 1994; Yoon et al., 1993). Some researchers have argued that the superior performance of the neural network models can be explained by their ability to represent intermediate features or abstractions of relevance to the task (e.g., Raghupathi et al., 1991; Srivastava, 1993). Some researchers have also proposed that these abstractions resemble those used by skilled diagnosticians (e.g., Berry & Trigueiros, 1993; Surkan & Singleton, 1990; Singleton

& Surkan, 1995). Thus, three propositions have been made regarding the properties of neural networks as predictive models for financial diagnosis. First, performance of these models are better than comparable benchmarks of traditional models. Second, the ability to represent and utilize intermediate abstractions are the main reason for this superior performance. Third, these abstractions have what we will term "cognitive relevance". Internal representations are considered to have cognitive relevance if they resemble intermediate abstractions, such as strategies, heuristics, rules, variables, concepts, prototypes or classes, previously documented to be relevant in either prescriptive or behavioral theory of financial diagnosis.

As referred above, the first proposition has been tested and confirmed by several researchers in predictive studies, but the last two propositions have received less attention. There may be several reasons for this lack of attention. First, testing these propositions implies a shift in focus from prediction to knowledge description and cognition. Second, what is considered relevant intermediate abstractions in these task contexts is not clear (Jones, 1987, p. 136), so that validation is difficult. Third, it has not been established if knowledge of the intermediate abstractions used by diagnosticians will improve the predictions of a model, since the predictive ability of diagnosticians in these task contexts is much debated (e.g., Libby, 1975; Casey, 1980, Chalos, 1985; but see Hopwood et al. 1994). Finally, the interest in analyzing internal representations found in early neural network studies (e.g., Gorman & Sejnowski 1988; Hanson & Burr, 1990) have been displaced by focus on testing predictive ability and introducing new models and algorithms. Despite these reasons, propositions on neural network models' internal representations should not go unattended.

2 Theory and model

The financial diagnosis task has been studied with different approaches. Traditional studies in accounting and finance have taken a predictive approach, and have used a wide variety of statistical and other models to predict the environmental outcome in different contexts of the financial diagnosis task (see e.g., Altman et al., 1981). Neural network models add a new technique to the "toolbox" of these researchers. Behavioral studies in accounting and finance have taken one of two different approaches. Judgment modeling studies have used models similar to those used in the predictive approach when modeling human diagnosticians' judgments of the outcomes in different task contexts of financial diagnosis, (e.g., Libby, 1975; Casey, 1980, Chalos, 1985). Cognitive studies are either experimental or descriptive in orientation. Experimental cognitive studies use cognitive theory to predict the effect on diagnosticians judgments of manipulating independent variables, such as information content and form. Consequently, the result of these studies is knowledge of how general cognitive theory applies to the financial diagnosis task. Descriptive cognitive studies follow the information processing theory tradition of Newell and Simon (1972) and apply protocol analysis to the verbal utterances of human diagnosticians during diagnosis. A main result of these studies is the formulation of productions implemented as rules in expert systems (e.g., Bouwman et al., 1987; Biggs et al., 1993).

All these approaches have contributed to the identification of diagnostic knowledge and intermediate abstractions relevant to the financial diagnosis task. Typically, these abstractions are formalized in diagnostic concepts. Table 1 shows an overview of some of the most widely applied diagnostic concepts used in different financial diagnosis task contexts.

Table 1. Diagnostic concepts in selected studies of financial diagnosis.

Concepts: / Studies:	Leverage	Profitability	Liquidity	Debt coverage	Asset balance	Cash position	Size	Interest coverage	Capital turnover	Task context[1]
Libby, 1975		X	X		X	X				BP
Abdel-khalik & El-Sheshai 1980			X	X						BP
Chalos, 1985	X	X	X		X	X				BP
Simnett & Trotman, 1989	X	X	X	X	X			X		BP
Kida, 1980	X	X	X			X			X	G
Hopwood et al., 1994	X	X	X		X	X	X			G
Rodgers, 1991	X	X	X							L
Altman, 1968	X	X			X				X	BP
Ohlson, 1980	X	X	X	X	X		X			BP
Frydman et. al, 1985	X			X	X	X		X		BP
Zavgren & Friedman, 1988	X	X	X			X			X	BP
Mutchler, 1985	X	X	X	X						G
Srinvasan & Kim, 1987	X	X	X				X			L
Kaplan & Urwitz, 1979	X	X		X			X	X		B
Ziebart & Reiter, 1992	X	X					X	X		B

If we accept the importance of intermediate abstractions in the financial diagnosis task, a model of the task can be suggested. Instead of a simple classification model in which a diagnosis is given directly from an evaluation of the stimulus dimensions of the financial statement, a somewhat more complex classification model is suggested. The next step in adding complexity to a classification model is by introducing intermediate abstractions, often termed abstract stimulus dimensions (Smith & Medin, 1981). These intermediate abstractions are formed by evaluating or transforming the original stimulus dimensions of the financial diagnosis. Often it is assumed that several original stimulus dimensions of the financial statement can be

[1] BP = Bankruptcy prediction, B = Bond rating, G = Going concern judgement and L= Loan decision.

combined to form an evaluation of an intermediate abstraction, such as when information on contribution margins and return on total assets is combined to form an evaluation of the profitability of a firm. If model complexity is increased, a hierarchy of intermediate abstractions can be introduced, in which new intermediate abstractions are formed on the basis of evaluations of other such abstractions. However, the simplest form only assuming one set of intermediate abstractions is often used. In traditional models, the intermediate abstractions are represented by concepts believed to be of diagnostic relevance.

A theoretical basis for identifying such diagnostic concepts can be found in prescriptive theory of financial analysis. However, their main basis is empirical, resulting from studies applying principal components analysis to financial statement information in order to find the "underlying dimensions" of this material (Pinches et al., 1973; Gombola & Ketz, 1983). Whether these "underlying dimensions" are diagnostic stimulus dimensions is, however, not clear.

A model introducing a set of represented abstractions intermediating original stimulus dimensions and diagnostic response is very similar to the simplest multilayered neural network models including one layer of hidden units representing a set of intermediate abstractions. Even though many different neural network models can be applied, and these can form different types of intermediate abstractions, the most widely known multilayered perceptron including one layer of hidden units is applied here as a model of the financial diagnosis task. Since financial diagnosis is a cognitive task with a behavioral outcome, we term the model a connectionist model of financial diagnosis.

3 Research design

To provide a data set of valid financial diagnoses, a controlled experiment was set up. Since information on small and medium sized firms' market values is often lacking, diagnosis depends even more upon financial statement information for such firms. A random sample of 75 firms was selected from an established small firms register maintained at the Norwegian School of Economics and Business Administration. Financial statement information from two consecutive years was collected and balance statements, income statements, funds flow statements and selected ratios were presented in a booklet to 108 subjects participating in a higher level financial analysis course for auditors. 89.9 % of the subjects had prior auditing experience and were familiar with the financial diagnosis task. The rest of the subjects had other accounting experience. Thus, the subjects were considered skilled diagnosticians.

To control for individual variation in diagnostic behavior, all subjects received a booklet of three financial statements for diagnosis. The procedure of distribution was randomized, so that on an average 4.3 skilled subjects diagnosed each firm. The subjects used a response form to characterize the profitability, financing, liquidity, and leverage of each firm on predefined 5-point Likert scales. A similar evaluation and a verbal characterization of the general financial situation of the firm were also given by the subjects.

From the data, a composite judge measure of the subjects' evaluation of the general financial situation was computed as the average value of their response on the general financial situation indicators. The use of composite judge measures has been recommended in financial diagnosis studies to reduce individual variation and increase diagnostic predictive value (Libby, 1981). In addition, the composite judge measure transforms the response of a classification task into an approximately interval scaled variable with good distribution properties without changing the classificatory character of the task itself.

Each subject also indicated the most important cues of the financial statements. Of the 108 subjects, 97.2 % indicated the use of one or more cues in any diagnostic area. Of these, 83.8 % indicated that cue values of two consecutive years, or the relationship between them, were used. Since the cue values of two consecutive years were highly correlated, the majority of the subjects indicated sensitivity to correlated stimulus dimensions. 55.4 % of all cues indicated were cues representing financial ratios, thus financial ratios seemed to represent the most important stimulus dimensions of the task. The main reason for the subjects using these ratios is probably that they are approximately firm size independent. By selecting 16 financial ratios with cue values from two consecutive years as preliminary input variables in the connectionist model, the most important stimulus dimensions were represented by variables with size independence and good distribution properties.

4 Simulation design

Clearly, 75 data sets of financial diagnoses are too few observations to properly set the weight values of a connectionist model with 32 input variables and one response variable. Since the number of valid diagnoses were restricted to 75, we reduced the number of input variables in the model, using sensitivity based selection of a smaller input variable set. By applying sensitivity analysis procedures similar to Moody and Utans (1995), a constrained set of 12 input variables giving the largest increase in training error when excluded, was selected. Not surprisingly, these input variables represented values from two consecutive years of the six most important financial cues as indicated by the diagnosticians.

A traditional multilayered perceptron model was set up applying the original principles of Rumelhart et al. (1986). The traditional asymmetric sigmoid output functions was used. Inputs and outputs were scaled to the [0,1] scale, but no other representational transformations were made. Consequently, the model had local variables representations at the input and output layers.

For model estimation, the original epoch-based learning of Rumelhart et al. (1986) was applied, setting η of the hidden layer to 0.5 and η of the output layer to 0.4. In addition, a small momentum term α of 0.1 was used. For each simulation, initial weights were randomly selected from a uniform distribution in the range [-0.2, 0.2] for the hidden layer and in the range [-0.7, 0.7] for the output layer.

As a basis for performance evaluation, n-fold cross validated mean square error (MSE) was used This performance measure have been recommended by several authors (e.g., White, 1990). To control model complexity, cross validated mean square errors were computed for models including 0, 2, 4, 6, 8, 10, 12 and 14 hidden units. Thus, the procedure was similar to a constructive algorithm, selecting the best model based upon n-fold cross validated performance measures.

Six benchmark models were developed in order to evaluate the performance of the connectionist model. First, two benchmark models were produced using a recommended procedure in the accounting and finance literature (e.g., Libby, 1975; Zavgren & Friedman, 1988). This procedure recommends using ordinary least squares regression analysis on a selected set of principal components of the original financial cues to avoid multicolinearity problems. Two such models were estimated using nine and five principal components respectively. Next, two benchmark models were produced using the original 32 variables selected by the subjects in an ordinary least squares regression and in a stepwise regression procedure selecting a restricted set of these 32 variables. The two final benchmark results were produced using the 12 input variables of the connectionist model in an ordinary least squares regression and a stepwise regression procedure selecting an even more restricted set of variables. The performance results of the benchmarks were produced using n-fold cross validation. Consequently, the mean square errors are averages of the performance of 75 models for each benchmark. The performance results of the six benchmarks models for the financial diagnosis data are shown in table 2.

Table 2. Performance results for the benchmark models.

Benchmark / Results	MSE	Corr. target	Corr. dist.
9-factor regression	0.232	0.059	0.252
5-factor regression	0.357	0.110	0.382
32-variables regression	0.435	0.179	0.010
32-var. stepw. regr.	0.275	0.147	0.095
12-variables regression	0.221	0.169	0.149
12-var. stepw. regr.	0.212	0.177	0.128

Table 2 shows the cross validated mean square errors and two measures illustrating the distribution of the models' error terms. Both correlations of the error terms with the target output values, and similar correlations of the error terms with distance from mean target value are shown. The first measure illustrates if model errors are larger for good or bad firms, whereas the second measure illustrates if the model is sensitive to extreme target values in general. These models should provide good benchmarks for evaluating the performance of the connectionist model.

5 Analysis and results

Performance results of the connectionist model are shown in table 3. The number of hidden units is indicated in the model name. Cross validated MSE is shown for every 5000 learning iterations.

As expected, MSE reached a flat minimum during learning and increased with learning beyond this minimum due to overtraining. Even though performance was best for the model with two hidden units, the larger difference in MSE was between the models with hidden units and the model without such units.

Table 3. Cross validated MSE for the connectionist model

Iterations:	5000	10000	15000	20000	25000	30000
Model:						
HID0	0.182	0.182	0.185	0.186	0.186	0.187
HID2	0.232	0.185	0.171	0.159	0.158	0.156
HID4	0.175	0.160	0.151	0.147	0.147	0.145
HID6	0.180	0.174	0.163	0.157	0.156	0.159
HID8	0.168	0.173	0.161	0.161	0.161	0.162
HID10	0.172	0.162	0.157	0.155	0.156	0.161
HID12	0.178	0.166	0.157	0.160	0.160	0.160
HID14	0.175	0.169	0.165	0.163	0.159	0.162

Simple t-tests of the differences between means can be used to evaluate of the propositions made earlier in this paper. First, a t-test of the difference in MSE between the best connectionist model stopped at the optimal number of training iterations (HID4) and the best benchmark model showed that the difference was significant and in favor of the connectionist model at α=0.05 (t=1.96, d.f.=74). This test indicated that the connectionist model was better at modeling the diagnostic outcome produced by our subjects. It was interesting to note that the t-value was relatively low despite the large difference in MSE. This indicated a large and unfortunate variance in the error terms of the best benchmark model.

The distributions of the error terms could be investigated by correlating the error terms with target values and distances from mean target values. For the best connectionist model, the correlation of the error terms with target values was 0.048, and the correlation of the error terms with distance from mean targets was -0.055. These measures indicated that the error terms had a uniform distribution over the range of target values. For the best benchmark model, the corresponding values were 0.177 and 0.128, indicating that errors were somewhat larger for the "healthier" and "extreme" firms. This unfortunate distribution of errors was eliminated in the connectionist model.

Further, a t-test of the difference in MSE between the best connectionist models with and without hidden units showed a significant difference in favor of the model with hidden units at α=0.05 (t=2.27, d.f.=74). This test supported the proposition that the improved performance could be explained by the ability of the more complex connectionist model to represent and utilize intermediate abstractions of relevance to the diagnosis.

It has been proposed that the intermediate abstractions represented by the hidden units have cognitive relevance. The most obvious presumption in the financial diagnosis area is that the hidden units are local representations of variables that can be interpreted as diagnostic concepts. The most obvious diagnostic concepts are profitability, financing, liquidity and leverage. Principal components analysis of the 12 input variables of the connectionist model showed that the factors with the highest eigenvalues could be interpreted as representing such concepts. Thus, it could be *suggested* that similar dimensions or "factors" were represented by the four hidden units of the best connectionist model.

To investigate this suggestion, analysis of the connectionist model representations was necessary. Experiments indicated that the final weights of the hidden units were very sensitive to initial weights. Consequently, 10 different models were developed using all cases of the data sets for learning, different initial weights, and by stopping the learning at the previously found optimal number of learning iterations. The MSE of these models averaged 0.112, and consequently, some overfit was present due to all cases being used in model development. Except from the somewhat lower MSE, the error terms had distributions very similar to the cross validated error terms, indicating that the 10 models were representative "versions" of the previously cross validated model. When analyzing the weights further, we found that the main reason for the differences in weight patterns were opposite signs of the weight patterns and different absolute weight values due to very different bias weights. After adjusting for opposite signs and differences in bias weights, a cluster analysis was performed using the weights from the input units to the hidden units of all hidden units in the ten models simultaneously.

This analysis revealed that the weight patterns were actually quite similar in the ten models. Some differences were still present due to the very flat error surface, but the cluster analysis was useful in detecting groups of hidden units with similar incoming weight patterns. All models had at least two very local hidden units. The absolute values of these units' weights were large, making them account for most of the models' response variation. Some models had more than two local hidden units, but in those cases, at least two of the local hidden units had almost similar weights. Thus, it could be concluded that the two functionally different local hidden units were most responsible for model response variation. In most of the models, the rest of the hidden units were more distributed, and only accounted for small variation in model response.

Since the local hidden units were so few, it could be suggested that the hidden units represented other dimensions of the financial cues than the diagnostic concepts profitability, liquidity, financing and leverage. If the hidden units had represented these concepts, four local hidden units with very different weight patterns should have been found. Hinton diagrams of two representative weight patterns from the two local hidden units of one of the models are shown in figure 1.

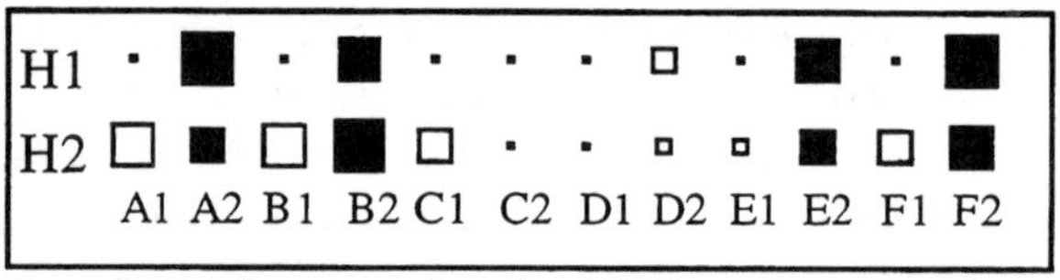

Figure 1. Weight pattern of two local hidden units.

In figure 1, the weights from six financial cues A - F to two local hidden units (H1 and H2) are shown. For each financial cue, two input units represent values of the first and second of two consecutive years. The financial cues are from left to right; operating margin (A), net income to total assets (B), net income to equity (C), average interest rate (D), acid test (E) and equity to total assets (F).

This weight pattern indicated very little specialization of each hidden unit on financial cues representing different diagnostic concepts. Instead, it seemed that the upper hidden unit (H1) used the second year values of a broad set of financial cues representing profitability, financing, liquidity and leverage. Thus, this hidden unit detected the level of the financial cues of the latest year. Thus, it was termed "level-oriented".

The lower hidden unit (H2) used both values of a broad set of financial cues, mainly representing profitability, liquidity and leverage. However, the weight pattern was interesting. It had negative weights from cues of the first year and positive weights from cues of the second year. Consequently, this unit was activated by the change in the level of a broad set of financial cues. The hidden unit actually computed the general trend in the financial cues from one year to the next. Consequently, this hidden unit was termed "change-oriented".

Further analysis of the outputs of these hidden units showed that the "change-oriented" hidden units had outputs that were approximately linear functions of the change in financial cues. The "level-oriented" hidden units had outputs that were highly non-linear functions of the level of the latest financial cues. This non-linearity gave under-proportional outputs for extremely high cue values.

To form the final diagnosis of the financial situation, the outputs of the two local hidden units were combined in an approximately linear function. Thus, it could be concluded that the diagnosis of the financial situation was performed by combining the response of two local hidden units representing the level of and the change in a broad set of financial cues.

6 Conclusion and discussion

To evaluate if the superior performance of neural networks for financial diagnosis could be explained by these models' ability to develop relevant internal representations, a behavioral approach was applied here. By setting up a behavioral experiment, a data set of valid financial diagnoses performed by skilled subjects under controlled conditions was provided. Based upon indications of the skilled subjects and sensitivity analysis, a set of important financial cues was selected as inputs to a multilayered perceptron model. Since the model was based upon behavioral data, we termed it a connectionist model of financial diagnosis. To evaluate the performance of the model, six different linear benchmarks were used.

Three findings were made. First, the performance of the connectionist model was significantly better than the benchmark models' performance when evaluated by the recommended n-fold cross validated mean square error. By comparing the error terms of the connectionist model and the best benchmark model, it was found that the error term distribution of the connectionist model was favorable. Consequently, we concluded that the superior performance of neural networks proposed for predictive models was also valid for models based upon behavioral financial diagnosis data.

Second, it was found that the connectionist model with hidden units significantly outperformed the model without hidden units developed with comparable parameter settings. This led us to conclude that the main reason for the superior performance of the connectionist model was the hidden units and not the nonlinearity of the output function, nor the method of parameter estimation (gradient descent). This finding was in correspondence with previously untested propositions made by several researchers applying neural networks to financial diagnosis.

Third, simple analysis of the internal representations of the connectionist models revealed no direct correspondence between the intermediate abstractions represented in the connectionist models and diagnostic concepts, such as profitability, financing, liquidity or leverage. The hidden units of the connectionist models seemed to represent the level and change in a broad set of financial cues. This was rather surprising, since principal components analysis of the same financial cues had revealed factors corresponding well to traditional diagnostic concepts. The underlying dimensions of level and change in the financial cues used by the connectionist models could be explained in two ways. First, the connectionist model may have implemented a functional heuristic not used by the skilled diagnosticians, but which still produced a behavior similar to that of the diagnosticians. Second, the diagnosticians may actually have used this functional heuristic, performing the diagnosis by an evaluation of the general level of a broad set of financial cues and an evaluation of the change in a similar broad set of cues. Some experiments were performed constraining the weight pattern of the connectionist model so that only representations of diagnostic concepts could be developed by the hidden units. In this case, performance deteriorated significantly. This indicated that the internal representations of the connectionist model had cognitive relevance, even though the representations were not as initially expected. A likely explanation of this finding was that the diagnosticians actually implemented a much simpler heuristic during diagnosis than prescriptive theory of financial diagnosis recommended.

There are several threats to the validity of these conclusions, such as lacking validity of the firms used as cases for diagnosis, or lack of skill among the diagnosticians. However, the firms were randomly selected, the diagnosticians had experience in financial diagnosis, and first of all, the diagnostic data were provided using a controlled experiment and randomization procedures not traditionally applied to tests of connectionist model performance. Several methods were used in evaluating model performance, all indicating superiority in favor of the connectionist model.

Our suggestion is that validation of neural network performance may not only be improved using multiple data sets and benchmarks, but as in any other empirical study, by using and reporting experimental procedures to demonstrate the validity of the data. In addition, evaluation of connectionist model performance can be improved by combining analyses of model performance. Even though cross validation improves the evaluation, analysis of the distributions of the models' error terms should be performed in a way similar to outlier analysis in linear models. Finally, analysis of the internal representations should be applied to compare the representations of the model to intermediate abstractions believed to be relevant in the application domain of the model. If the intermediate abstractions differ from these, their validity should be discussed and evaluated. Combining traditional performance measures, analysis of error term distributions and evaluation of internal representations constitutes a three-dimensional validation of a connectionist model.

References

Abdel-khalik, A.R., & El-Sheshai, K.M. (1980). Information choice and utilization in an experiment on default prediction. *Journal of Accounting Research*, autumn 1980 , 325-342.

Altman, E.I. (1968). Financial ratios, discriminant analysis and the prediction of corporate bankruptcy. *The Journal of Finance*, September 1968 , 589-609.

Altman, E.I., Avery, R.B., Eisenbeis, R.A. & Sinkey, J.F. (1981). *Application of classification techniques in business, banking and finance*. Greenwich, CT: The JAI Press.

Berry, R., & Trigueiros, D. (1993). Applying neural networks to the extraction of knowledge from accounting reports: A classification study. In Trippi, R.R. & Turban, E. (eds.), *Neural networks in finance and investing* (p. 103-123). Chicago, IL: Probus Publishing.

Biggs, S.F., Selfridge, M., & Krupka, G.R. (1993). A computational model of auditor knowledge and reasoning processes in the going-concern judgement. *Auditing: A Journal of Practice & Theory,* 12(supplement), 82-99.

Bouwman, M.J., Frishkoff, P.A., & Frishkoff, P. (1987). How do financial analysts make decisions? A process model of the investment screening decision. *Accounting, Organizations and Society*, 12, 1-29.

Chalos, P. (1985). Financial distress: A comparative study of individual, model and committee assessments. *Journal of Accounting Research*, 23, 527-543.

Frydman, H., Altman, E.I., & Kao, D. (1985). Introducing recursive partitioning for financial classification: The case of financial distress. *The Journal of Finance*, 40, 269-291.

Gombola, M.J., & Ketz, J.E. (1983). Financial ratio patterns in retail and manufacturing organizations. *Financial Management*, 12(2), 45-56.

Gorman, R.P., & Sejnowski, T.J. (1988). Analysis of hidden units in a layered network trained to classify sonar targets. *Neural Networks*, 1, 75-89.

Hanson, S.J., & Burr, D.J. (1990). What connectionist models learn: Learning and representation in connectionist networks. *Behavioral and Brain Sciences*, 13, 471-518.

Hopwood, W., McKeown, J.C., & Mutchler, J.F. (1994). A reexamination of auditor versus model accuracy within the context of the going-concern opinion decision. *Contemporary Accounting Research,* 10, 409-431.

Jones, F.L. (1987). Current techniques in bankruptcy prediction. *Journal of Accounting Literature,* 6, 131-164.

Kaplan, R.S. & Urwitz, G. (1979). Statistical models of bond ratings: A methodological inquiry, *Journal of Business*, 52, 231-261.

Kida, T. (1980). An investigation into auditors' continuity and related qualification judgements, *Journal of Accounting Research*, 18, 506-523.

Libby, R. (1975). Accounting ratios and the prediction of failure: Some behavioral evidence. *Journal of Accounting Research*, spring 1975, 150-161.

Libby R. (1981). *Accounting and human information processing: Theory and applications*. Englewood Cliffs, NJ: Prentice Hall.

Methlie, L.B. (1987). On knowledge based decision support systems for financial diagnosis. In Holsapple, C.W., & Whinston, A.B. (Eds.), *Decision support systems: Theory and application*. Berlin: Springer Verlag.

Moody, J.E., & Utans, J. (1995). Architecture selection strategies for neural networks: Application to corporate bond rating prediction. In Refenes, A.P. (Ed.), *Neural networks in the capital markets* (pp. 277-300). New York: Wiley.

Mutchler, J.F. (1985). A multivariate analysis of auditor's going-concern opinion decision. *Journal of Accounting Research*, 23, 668-682.

Newell, A., & Simon, H.A. (1972) *Human problem solving*. Englewood Cliffs, NJ: Prentice-Hall.

Ohlson, J.A. (1980). Financial ratios and the probabilistic prediction of bankruptcy. *Journal of Accounting Research*, 18, 109-131.

Pinches, G.E., Mingo, K.A., & Caruthers, J.K. (1973). The stability of financial patterns in industrial organizations. *Journal of Finance*, 28, 389-396.
Raghupathi, W., Schkade, L.L., & Raju, B.S. (1991). A neural network approach to bankruptcy prediction. Reprinted in Trippi, R.R., & Turban, E. (Eds.), *Neural networks in finance and investing* (pp. 141-158). Chicago, IL: Probus Publishing.
Rodgers, W. (1991). How do loan officers make their decisions about credit risks? A study of parallel distributed processing. *Journal of Economic Psychology*, 12, 243-265.
Rumelhart, D.E., Hinton, G.E., & Williams, R.J. (1986). Learning internal representations by error propagation. In Rumelhart, D.E., & McClelland, J.L. (Eds.), *Parallel distributed processing; Explorations in the microstructure of cognition.* Cambridge, MA: MIT Press.
Simnett, R., & Trotman, K.T. (1989). Auditor versus model: Information choice and information processing. *The Accounting Review*, 64, 514-528.
Singleton, J.C., & Surkan, A.J. (1995). Bond rating with neural networks. In Refenes, A.P. (Ed.), *Neural networks in the capital markets* (pp. 301-307). New York: Wiley.
Smith, E.E., & Medin, D. (1981). *Categories and concepts*. Cambridge, MA: Harvard University Press.
Srinvasan, V., & Kim, Y.H. (1987). Credit granting: A comparative analysis of classification procedures. *The Journal of Finance*, 42, 665-683.
Srivastava, R.P. (1992). Automating judgmental decisions using neural networks: A model for processing business loan applications. *Proceedings of the 20the Annual ACM Computer Science Conference* (pp. 351-357), New York: ACM
Surkan, A.J., & Singleton, J.C. (1990). Neural networks for bond rating improved by multiple hidden layers. In Trippi, R.R., & Turban, E. (Eds.), *Neural networks in finance and investing*. Chicago, IL.: Probus Publishing.
Tam, K.Y. (1991). Neural network models and the prediction of bank bankruptcy. *OMEGA International Journal of Management Science*, 19, 429-445.
Tam, K.Y., & Kiang, M.Y. (1992). Managerial applications of neural networks: The case of bank failure predictions. *Management Science*, 38, 926-947.
White, H. (1990). Connectionist nonparametric regression: Multilayer feedforward networks can learn arbitrary mappings. *Neural Networks*, 3, 535-549.
Wilson, R., & Sharda, R. (1994). Bankruptcy prediction using neural networks. *Decision Support Systems*, 11, 545-557.
Yoon, Y., Swales, G., & Margavio, T.M. (1993). A comparison of discriminant analysis versus artificial neural networks. *Journal of the Operations Research Society*, 44, 51-60.
Zavgren, C.V., & Friedman, G.E. (1988). Are bankruptcy prediction models worthwhile? An application in securities analysis. *Management International Review*, 28, 34-44.
Ziebart, D.A., & Reiter, S.A. (1992). Bond rating, bond yields and financial information. *Contemporary Accounting Research*, 9, 252-282.

CREDIT RISK SCORING: RESULTS OF DIFFERENT NETWORK STRUCTURES, PREPROCESSING AND SELF-ORGANISED CLUSTERING

DANILO BASSI
Departamento de Ingeniería Informática
Universidad de Santiago de Chile
Av. Ecuador 3659
Santiago, CHILE
dbassi@toqui.usach.cl

CARLOS HERNANDEZ
RedNova S.A.
Malaquías Concha 024
Santiago, CHILE

Abstract

We present the results of neural networks models for personal credit risk evaluation. Different kind of networks structures, preprocessing and unsupervised learning are analised, looking at improvements in the network performance. In first place, the preprocessing of variables is studied. Particularly, the recoding of categorical variables (non-numerical) which increases greatly the number of variables, since an input is associated with each category. For those variables we propose to reduce the number of inputs by using an unsupervised network, the Kohonen self-organizing map, which can automatically group similar categories. This results in a smaller classification network, improving learning. Looking for a convenient architecture, we searched among diferent multilayer perceptron based structures, obtaining the best results with modular or expert networks, which are non fully-connected feedforward networks. Finally we show classification results with different pre-processing of input variables.

1 Introduction

Risk estimation has been one of the first applications of neural networks into the financial world (Dutta *et al* 1988, Collins *et at* 1988). These neural based risk models have many inputs, (all the variables that may have influence), and usually a single output, the risk measure. For assessing personal credit risk, this function is based on individual antecedents of clients, like personal information and commercial records. To build this credit risk model, actual historical information of credit outcome must be used. Patterns of populations with better or worse risk are expected to be detected, and the financial institution will have the choice to improve its risk by giving more credit to perceived less risky population and less credit to more risky groups.

1.1 The credit risk function

The risk model is a regression function over the input variables. This model has been conventionally based on a linear functions which weights the influence of each parameters. The application of neural networks can improve the fitness of data due to the enhanced modelling capabilities provided by its non-linearity and adaptability. However, finding a suitable neural models is not that simple since networks are prone to overfitting, especially the bigger one with many input variables, like the one required to assess the credit risk. Moreover this large number of inputs is increased by usual preprocessing of non-numerical variables, which is tipically encoded into bit vector of class membership (one for each category). Thus intelligent preprocessing of input variable is advised and exploring different network structures is always recommended.

1.2 Pre-processing

In this paper we look at different preprocessing, trying to find good encoding for non-numerical (categorical) data. The recomended solution is to use one neural input for each category. This may result in very large networks because each categorical variable is multiplied by the number of actual categories. It generates more inputs weights, making more complicated to adjust them, especially if the real data base is limited in the number of exemplars. Looking more carefully at the categories, we observed oftentimesthat the very fragmented categories are not influencial by themselves but they could be grouped with other similar cases obtained more global classes which may be more relevant for final classification. That is clearly the case for geographical variable of the client (the district). We found that payment patterns are dependent on the district where the clients live. However there are too many districts and the particular information provided by one of them in particular is not that relevant. Nevertheless, it may indicate some information about more global categories which are more important for classification purpose. Therefore we set up to make groups of districts according to certain socioeconomical global variables. This clustering can be done unsupervisedly by the Kohonen self organizing maps network (Kohonen, T. 1992).

1.3 Network architectures

Extensive tests have been performed searching for a good network architecture. Several structures were tested, but finally we settled down for multilayer perceptron and modular networks. With the latter architecture we tried to make subgroups among several categorical variables, obtaining non-fully connected networks with less parameters to adjust. Pursuing our investigation on self-organizing networks we also explored other clustering using more variable, ultimately using all the available input variables In this way all clients are clustered in natural classes. And the enormous input space dimensionality is reduced greatly, resulting in an easier learning of the risk function.

2 Objectives

The main objective of this work is to design advanced neural networks based system for doing risk assessment of personal credit clients. The variables used for this risk modelling are personal, comercial and operational. The personal and comercial variable are related with personal characteristics that may have some influence on paying behaviour, like profession, age, income, total debts, marital status. The operational variable are those related with the desired credit: amount, number of instalments (term), payment, etc., which are in some way, cotrollable by the creditor. More precisely, the objective is to find the *best* conditional probability of non-payment giving some personal, comercial and operational variables. The fitness of the model is measured by the test classification rate.

After an initial study that allowed us to select a family structure of networks (multilayer perceptron and modular networks), we explored the influence of preprocessing of variables, mostly of categorical one. In particular we have a geographical variable that have many categories: residence districts. We set the objective of grouping or clustering this category, since a straightforward coding produces a large input network, resulting too many parameters to adjust. With clustering we may reduce the information contents, but we have a smaller network expected to have better prediction capabilities. Other analysis are done for procedures like findind a good sampling strategy, and the optimal cutting points.

3 Credit database and pre-processing

The information used in this study was obtained from sample of credit operations at a large national bank. These credit operations were started many years ago, therefore there was a known outcome (either good or bad). However since the proportion of default clients is very low (less than 3%) we directed our sample in order to select a given number of bad clients and good clients. In this way a database was built, containing information of 17 client input variables and having 552 cases, half of them being good standing credits and the other half bad or default credits. The neural network model is trained to learn one output variable (credit goodness), given the 17 input variables (Table 1).

Variable	Name	Kind	Range or number of values
1	Residence district	categorical	33
2	Occupation	categorical	5
3	Sex	logical	2
4	Age	numerical	20 - 63
5	Marital status	categorical	4
6	Retired	logical	2
7	Net income	numerical	29433 - 598334
8	Direct debt	numerical	0 - 25181918
9	Indirect debt	numerical	0 - 690269734
10	Employer	categorical	6
11	Seniority	numerical	0.17 - 37
12	Protests	numerical	0 - 13
13	Noncleared protests	numerical	0 - 8
14	Credit amount	numerical	60418 - 22308000
15	Term (months)	numerical	10 - 36
16	Payment	numerical	4310 - 156570
17	Payment/Income ratio	numerical	0.029 - 0.407
18	Credit classification	logical	2

Table 1:Variable definition, classification and value ranges or numbers.

The input variables are classified according to its type: there are *numerical* variables (like income), *categorical* or symbolic variables (like occupation) and *logical* variables (like sex). All the variables require some kind of preprocessing before entering to the network. Numerical variables are normalised to fit the entire input range (-1,1), usually with a linear transformation. In other cases a non-linear function, like the logarithm, is better suited, especially when data is not evenly distributed. Each categorical variable is converted into a set of logical variables where each one is asociated with a category. In this way, variables with many categories implies many inputs in the network. This is the case of the residence district variable which has 33 different values.

4 Self-organised preprocessing with Kohonen networks

Standard preprocessing may rise dramatically the number of network inputs, particularly if a categorical variable has many classes. In our study, after this *recoding* of variables, the number of inputs inflates from 17 original into 64 codified inputs. That number implies necessarily networks with many weights to be adjusted, resulting in poorer models. In this example, the recoding of *residence district* variable explain more than half (33) of final inputs! Although that variable may give valuable information for building the classification model, it cannot justify more than half of adjusted parameter (at the input layer). So it is advisable to compress that information, for example by lumping together certain district according to some similarities. This is the case of the location variable, which may be too spread.

To solve this problem of lumping or clustering variables we can use Kohonen self-organising networks (Kohonen, T. 1992). This procedure has the advantage of being unsurpervised, situation that helps since this grouping is done automatically. Which criteria can be used to make this self-organization? In principle similarity can be searched looking at the other variables of the samples. But we can obtain a more global criteria looking at complementary aggregate variables, which are not used in the individual inputs. In our case we decided to use socioeconomic infomation asociated with each district. This infomation is available from population census or polls, and the variable used are listed in Table 2.

For doing this self-organising procedure it also convenient to perform previously a slight preprocessing. In this case instead of using directly the number of inhabitants for each stratum, we computed the ratio over the total population. Thus for each district we used 5 population ratios and the number of persons per household ratio. These vectors are fed to a small Kohonen map which automatically clusters similars district vectors. This similarity is measured as an Euclidean distance among vectors. Finally, we have that similar district maps to a same unit and that, by the topology preserving property, neighbour units are also close together. We used two-dimensional maps of 2x2 and 3x2 units. After this network is trained its output corresponds exactly to a global category of district, reducing the number of inputs of the classification network from 33 to 6 or 4. In Fig. 1 is shown this self-organising preprocessing of *district* variable and its relationship with the whole classification system

Variable	Description	Ranges
Inhabitants	Total population	39954 - 328767
ABC1	Population in highest stratum	0 - 114435
C2	Population in second stratum	3222 - 98787
C3	Population in third stratum	3222 - 121785
D	Population in fourth stratum	2162 - 114489
E	Population in fifth stratum	0 - 42003
Persons/household	Average number of person in each home	2.91 - 4.68

Table 2: Global socioeconomic variables for geographic districts

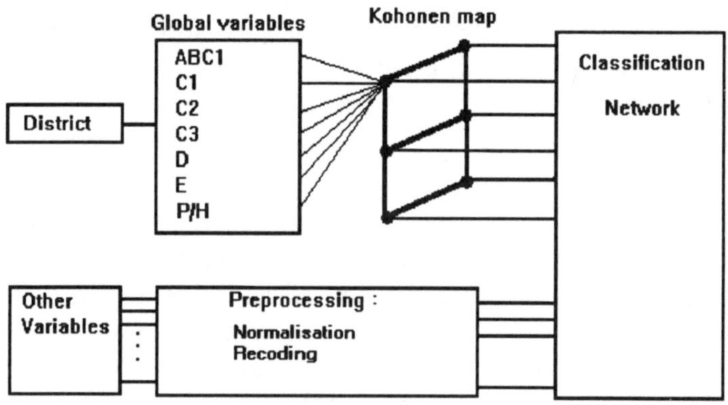

Fig. 1: Data preprocessing including a Kohonen map self-organising clustering

5 Classification networks, learning and evaluation

Different neural networks architectures for building the risk function were tested. Most of these networks are based on multilayer perceptron feedforward structure (Hecht-Nielsen, R. 1990), in which inputs are processed orderly layer by layer until getting the output. These networks use the well-known backpropagation learning procedure, which starts with the supervised error at the output (difference between the desired and the obtained value) and propagates it towards the input. After the network is trained, a test is run to assess the classification properties, using data not shown during the training phase.

5.1 Evaluation

The designed structures are evaluated with the previously built database containing personal and comercial antecedents and historical outcome personal credit operations. The input vectors are preprocessed according to its type, and a self-organised map is used for the *residence district* variable, as depicted above. This evaluation was based in a standard five-fold cross-validation process. For doing this,. five partitions of data set are used. Each partition is composed by a group of 80% of data (442 records) for network training and 20% (110 records) for testing. The evaluated result is a classification rate over the testing data. This number is computed by averaging the good data classified as good by the network with the bad data classified as bad by the network. For this classification a threshold was needed at the output; we assumed it at the middle of the range (0). The final results corresponds to the mean of 5 individual testings. Additionally, we computed the spread or standard deviation of each classification rate.

5.2 Network structures

The first network structure tested was a standard multilayer perceptron, with one hidden layer and with fully connections between layers. The design parameter is the number of hidden elements, which was selected to be 4. This number can be estimated, when building a phenomenological model, from the following empirical formula:

$$h = \frac{\#\ of\ training\ patterns}{4(m+n)} \tag{1}$$

Where *h* is the number of hidden units, *n* the number of input units and *m* the number of output units. In this case we have after the pre-processing (including self-organised clustering) 30 or 32 input variable (*n*) and 1 output variable (*m*). Therefore the number of hidden units is close to 3 or 4 ($h \approx 442/4(30+1)$).

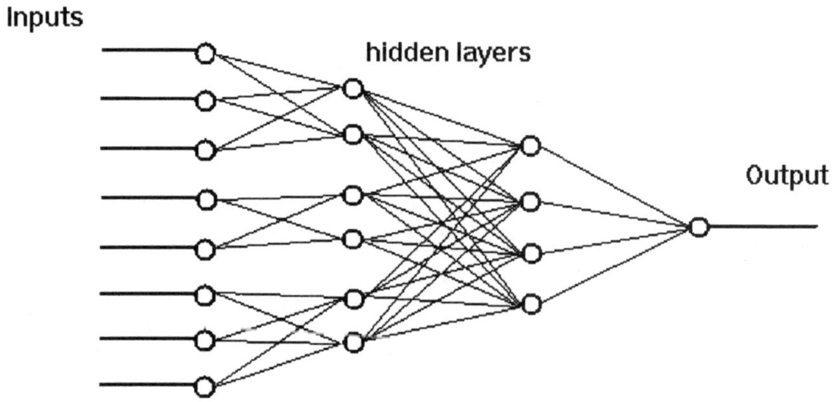

Fig. 2: Multilayer perceptron neural network with specialised sub-networks.

Other studied structure are modular networks, either with specialised sub-networks (Fig. 2) or with competing experts including a gating network (Jacobs & Jordan 1993). In these cases we have non-fully connected networks with a more elaborated structure. Like the modular with expert networks based on a special gating networks that decides which expert will provide the final output. In this way, each expert becomes specialised over certain input zones.

5.3 Results

The best results, which are reported here, corresponds to modular or expert architecture. In this case we tested structure with 2 experts networks, each one with 3 hidden units. We tested the effects on the results of different pre-processing of input variables:

- For self-organising clustering of district variable: either having a 2x2 map (4 groups) or 3x2 map (6 groups).

- For some variables (protests, noncleared protests and term) which could be treated as numerical or categorical we tested both kinds of pre-processing (normalisation and recoding). The number of inputs obviously increased as variables were considered as categorical instead of numerical. This number of inputs (excluding the district variable) corresponded to 26 and 48 respectively.

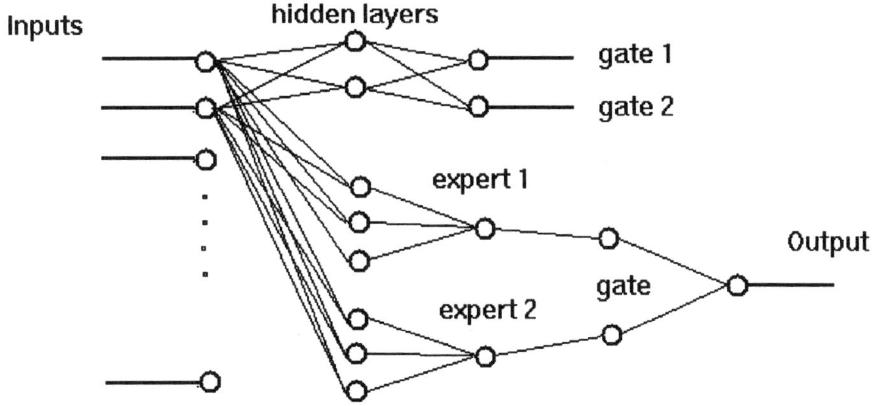

Fig. 3: Modular (expert) neural network structure, including gating network.

Geographical clustering:	**Test classification rate %** *4 groups*	*6 groups*
11 numerical, 6 categorical variables	70.0 ± 2.5	69.0 ± 3.7
8 numerical, 9 categorical variables	67.4 ± 3.6	70.0 ± 2.0

Table 3: Classification rate for different self-organization clustering.

The classification rates are computed using the standard five-fold cross-validation test above-mentionned. The range (plus-minus) is the standard deviation over 5 tests.

Those results were obtained using directed sampling of database, i.e. keeping the same proportion of good and bad credits en each generated subset (training and testing) of data while choising at random in each case. When entirely randomly generated testing and training sets were used, the resulting networks were less performant. Other improvement is to modify the classification, by optimising the cutting point, not assuming necessarily that it is at the center of the output range.

6 Conclusions and discussion

We have discussed different issues that can improve performance of a neural network based credit risk scoring system. We focused at the problem of finding and evaluating good preprocessing of non-numerical variable. The standard solution of transforming categorical variable into logical, having one variable for each category, may increment a lot the number of inputs. The solution of clustering some spatial categories into bigger groups, using global characteristics, produces a smaller network with better performance. This clustering is also done automatically, by means of a self organising features network. Other variations were also tested, like using numerical codification instead of categorical (in some suitable variables), obtaining smaller input networks with, sometimes, slight improvement in final results. We conclude that it is not always convenient to use of straight categorical codification, especially if there are many input variables and a small number of cases to train with. Reducing the inputs by clustering and grouping is convenient, producing more compact and reliable networks.

For the classification neural network we looked at several structures, all based on multilayer perceptron. Modular neural networks seem convienent when we need to process a large amount of input variables. This is explained by the fact of having not fully-connected networks which resulted in less trained parameters. Other architectures that are being explored at this time, are the self-organising maps, which besides its usefullnes for single variable preprocessing, could be used to perform a deeper preprocessing of the large number of variables required by this kind of application. In this way it could be possible to reduce the dimensionality of the input space, since all the input variable could be mapped into a smaller two-dimensional space, while conserving topological properties. Then the output of this self-organised model could be fed to a simpler classification network, making it easier to learn the relationship.

7 Acknowledgements

We would like to thank the support given by Conicyt (Fondef Project IN-03) and Rednova which helped us in pursuing this research.

8 References

Dutta, S. and Shekhar, S., Bond Rating: "A non-conservative application of neural networks", in *Proceedings of 1988 International Conference on Neural Networks*, Vol. 2, pp. 459-466.

Collins, E., Gosh, S. and Scofield, C., "An application of multiple neural network learning system to emulation of mortgage underwriting judgements", in *Proceedings of 1988 International Conference on Neural Networks*, Vol. 2, pp. 443-450.

Kohonen, T., "The Self-Organizing Map", *Neural Networks: Theoretical Foundations and Analysis*, Clifford Lau, Editor, IEEE Press, 1992.

Jacobs, R. and Jordan, M., "Learning piecewise control strategies in a modular neural network architecture", in *IEEE Transactions on System, Man and Cybernetics*, Vol. 23, Nr. 2, March 1993.

Hecht-Nielsen, R., *Neurocomputing*, Addison Wesley, 1990.

SIMULATING INTEREST RATE STRUCTURE EVOLUTION ON A LONG TERM HORIZON
A KOHONEN MAP APPLICATION

M. COTTRELL
SAMOS
Université Paris 1 - Sorbonne
E-mail: cottrell@univ-paris1.fr

E. DE BODT
E.F. HENRION
CEGF
Université Catholique de Louvain
E-mail: debodt@fin.ucl.ac.be

PH. GREGOIRE
CeReFIM
University of Namur
E-mail: philippe.gregoire@fundp.ac.be

In the 90s, a new approach to model risk was proposed and named Value at Risk (VaR). Pioneered by JP Morgan (RiskMetrics), VaR has initiated a lot of debate. One of the major shortcoming of RiskMetrics is its inability to generate scenarios on a long term horizon (the Monte-Carlo procedure proposed does not produce the classical mean-reverting properties of interest rate structure dynamics). In this paper, we propose an alternative approach, also based on a Monte-Carlo simulation procedure, but using a Kohonen map quantization to construct conditional probability distributions of interest rate structure shocks. The procedure is not only able to produce interest rate structure scenarios which are stable on a long term horizon (five years) but also these scenarios exhibit properties compatible with the historical interest rate structure evolution used to compute the conditional probability distributions.

1 Introduction

Financial institutions run different kinds of risks. The credit risk corresponds to the risk of failure of a counterpart. The market risk results from unanticipated movements of prices, interest rates or foreign exchange rates. The liquidity risk is associated with the impossibility of closing a position within a short delay. With derivatives, the liquidity risk also consists in the inability to face the margin call. The operational risk is the consequence of human or system errors. Finally, the legal risk occurs when the contract is not enforceable. In this paper, we limit ourselves to the market risk and more precisely, the interest rate risk. Management of interest rate risk is one of the key tasks of bank and insurance financial supervision. The $500 billions cost of the Savings and Loan (S&L) mess in the 80s shows what mismanagement of interest rate risk can do to an industry and its deposit-insurance.

The latest advancement of Wall Street in risk measurement is the so called Value at Risk (VaR). VaR is an estimate of the maximum loss to be expected over a given period a certain percentage of the time (Beder 1995). The calculation of VaR depends on assumptions and methodology. There is two common methodologies, historical simulations and Monte-Carlo simulations over a single short term horizon. In our paper, we present a methodology to estimate VaR over a long term horizon. We propose an alternative approach, also based on a Monte-Carlo simulation procedure, but using Kohonen map classification to construct conditional probability distributions of interest rate structure shocks. Using them, we are able to produce interest rate structure scenarios which are not only stable even over a five year horizon but also exhibit properties compatible (sharing common statistical features) with the historical interest rate structure evolution used to compute the conditional probability distributions.

The first section of the paper is devoted to a short presentation of Value at Risk (VaR) methodology. There we will specify the precise position of this work. The second section presents the Kohonen algorithm. Some useful references on this algorithm and its theoretical properties will be given. The data set is presented in the third section. The fourth section presents the proposed approach in three steps : the previous works, the relation between initial interest rate structure and interest rate shocks and the simulation procedure. In the last section of the paper, we will indicate the direction some future work might take.

2 Value-at-Risk methodology

The classical approach to model risk is to assume that the asset's returns are normally distributed or that the prices are lognormal. With this assumption, the classical tradeoff between risk and return is represented in a two dimensional space, mean (return) and variance (risk). With the assumption that the returns have normal multivariate distribution, the risk of a portfolio only depends on the matrix variance-covariance of the returns.

Value-at-Risk (VaR) is an estimate of the maximum potential loss to be expected over a given period a certain percentage of the time. Risk is model on the maximum potential loss which can be estimated by historical or Monte-Carlo simulations. Historical simulations give the maximum loss over a period of time. The limits of the historical approach are that the results depend on a past period while the Monte-Carlo simulations depend on the matrix variance-covariance. A recent study (Beder 1995) shows that the magnitude of discrepancy among these methods deviates by more than 14 times for the same portfolio. Moreover, the VaR results that are calculated by an historical simulation depend on the behavior of the return during the period. For example, during a period of decreasing interest rates, risk may be underestimated. Historical simulations face all the problems encountered by the non experimental science while Monte-Carlo simulations are well adapted for very short periods of time (from 1 day to 1 month). For example, the conceptual framework developped in RiskMetrics (JP Morgan) assumes that historical returns are generated from a multivariate normal distribution. From this assumption, future price paths can be simulated by the Cholesky decomposition. This procedure is adapted to short term horizon but fails when applied to the long term. The generated scenarios tend to be explosive because the resulting dynamics of the interest rate structure do not have mean reverting properties. The generation of those long term scenarios, while crucial for a bank in the management of assets and liabilities (ALM)[1], still remains a problem hard to solve. In this paper, we propose a methodology which tries to solve this particular problem.

In the first step, we will propose the use of the Kohonen algorithm

---

[1] For example, today, several assets have CAP or FLOOR. A CAP(FLOOR) is a clause assuring that the interest rate will not be higher (lower) than a certain level. These clauses affect the profit over a long period and this illustrate why one needs to model the interest rate structure evolution over a long term horizon.

to overcome the limitations due to the use of the variance-covariance matrix. Using it, we will show that it is possible to empirically estimate the relation between the interest rate structure and the distribution of movements it can undergo.

In the second step, the Monte-Carlo technique will be used to generate a large number of future interst rate paths on a long term horizon.

3 The Kohonen algorithm

The Kohonen algorithm (Kohonen, 1995; Cottrell, Fort, 1987; Cottrell, Fort, Pagès, 1994) is a well-known unsupervised learning algorithm which produces a map composed by a fixed number of units. A physical neighborhood relation between the units is defined and for each unit i, $Vr_{(i)}$ represents the neighborhood with radius r centered at i.

Each unit is characterized by a parameter vector W_i of the same dimension as the input space.

After learning, each unit represents a group of individuals with similar features (this group is named Voronoi region of the unit). The correspondence between the features and the units (more or less) respects the input space topology : similar features correspond to the same unit or to neighboring units. The final map is said to be self organized map which preserves the topology of the input space. The learning algorithm takes the following form :

- at time 0, $W_{i(0)}$ is randomly defined for each unit i;
- at time t, we present a vector $x_{(t)}$ randomly chosen among the rows of the data matrix and we determine the winning unit i*, which minimizes the Euclidean distance between $x_{(t)}$ and $W_{i(t)}$;
- we then modify the W_i in order to move the weights of the winning unit i* and its physical neighbors towards $x_{(t)}$, using the following relations :

$$W_{i(t+1)} = W_{i(t)} + \left[\varepsilon_{(t)} \times \left[x_{(t)} - W_{i(t)}\right]\right] \text{ for } i \in Vr_{(t)}(i^*) \quad (1)$$

$$W_{i(t+1)} = W_{i(t)} \quad (2)$$

where $\varepsilon_{(t)}$ is a small positive adaptation parameter, $r_{(t)}$ is the radius of $Vr_{(t)}$ and $\varepsilon_{(t)}$ and $r_{(t)}$ are progressively decreased during the learning.

The results have been obtained after 100 learning cycles (at each one, we present all the individuals composing the data). The input space dimension is 15. We have used a one-dimension map.

While the asymptotic properties of this algorithm remain partly unknown, some of its theoretical properties have been demonstrated during the last 10 years. One of them is of particular interest as regards this paper and concerns the density approximation property of this algorithm. In (Pages, 1993), the Kohonen algorithm terminating with a 0 neighbor at the end of learning is studied. According to the comment at the end of section 3, the convergence of this algorithm is thus equivalent to the convergence of a classical VQ technique as "competitive learning". The author shows that the units after VQ are a good discrete skeleton for reconstructing the initial density f(x), provided that each unit is weighted by the probability (estimated by the frequency) of its Voronoi region. In other terms, if $y_1, y_2, \ldots, y_n$ are the units after learning, and $C_1, C_2, \ldots, C_n$ the corresponding Voronoi regions, the following convergence (in law) is guaranteed:

$$\sum_{i=1}^{n} P(C_i)\delta_{y_i} \xrightarrow{\text{law}} P \tag{3}$$

when n goes on to infinity, and δ_{y_i} is a Dirac function on y_i. This is equivalent to saying that the empirical measurement defined by units $y_1, y_2, \ldots, y_n$, weighted by the probabilities of the associated Voronoi regions, converges (in law) on the initial probability P.

Provided that units are adequately weighted, this result shows that it is possible to reconstruct the initial law, and the result is exact when the number of units goes on to infinity. Pagès also showed that the speed of convergence is better than with data obtained by independent random drawings.

This remarkable theoretical property justifies the choice of the Kohonen algorithm to quantify the distributions of interest rate structures and interest rate shocks (see section 5) and largely explains the compatibility of the generated scenarios with the historical data set used.

4 The data set

To classify the observed shocks on the interest rate structure, we used data from the US bonds market. Our data are daily interest rate structures for maturity from 1 to 15 years. The interest rate for each maturity has been calculated by JP Morgan from the prices of US T-Bills and T-Bonds. The sample covers the period from 1/5/1987 to 5/10/1995, altogether 2088 entries. Using these data, we calculate the shocks which are the differences between the observed term structure at time t (given that we have only 15 rates corresponding to maturity ranging from 1 year to 15 years) and time t–10 working days (time delay recommended by the Basle Committee on Banking Supervision). Figure 1 shows the evolution the short-rate (1-year) et the long-rate (15-year) during the period 1987-1995. Using several other data sets, results presented in this paper have been confirmed.

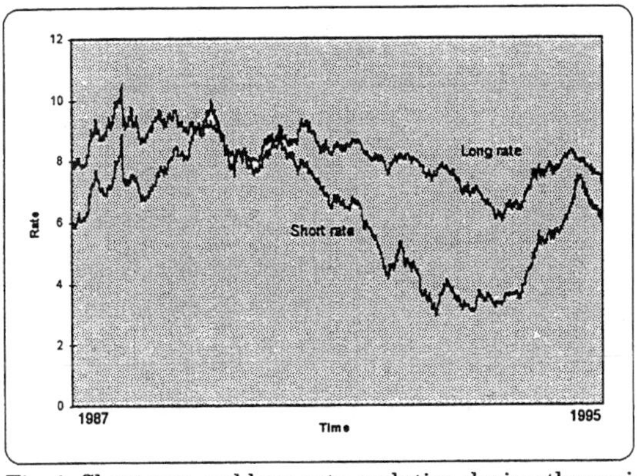

Fig. 1: Short-rate and long-rate evolution during the period 1987-1995 on the US market.

5 Using Monte-Carlo on a Kohonen Map

5.1 Previous works

The approach proposed in this paper is based on several previous works. The first work (Cottrell, de Bodt, Henrion, Grégoire, 1996a) was oriented towards the classification of the observed shocks on the interest rate structure. We used the Kohonen Algorithm and compared its performances to the classical hierarchical clustering approach (HCA). To compare the two algorithms, we used several statistics. First, for each dimension (maturity), we compare the ratio of the intra-class sum of squares to the total sum of squares and the classical Fisher statistic. Then, to compare the clustering power of each approach with all sets of maturities, we have used four multidimensional extensions of the Fisher test : Wilk's Lambda, Pillai's Trace, Hotelling-Lawley Trace and Roy's Greatest Root. These preliminary results clearly show the power of the Kohonen algorithm as compared to HCA.

On the basis of these results, in (Cottrell, de Bodt, Henrion, Grégoire, 1996b), we analyzed the information used by the Kohonen algorithm to form clusters of interest rate structure shocks. Using a canonical correlation analysis, we show that the level, spread and curvature are the three variables most correlated with the unsupervised classification produced.

It also seems important to mention that the structural stability of the data set have been tested and that, in all our analysis, we choose the number of units of the Kohonen map by studying the decrease of the intra-class sum of squares on the total sum of squares ratio as the number of units increase.

5.2 The relation between initial interest rate structure and interest rate shocks

A large number of term structure models are based on specific assumptions about the stochastic process determining the state variables, especially the instantaneous interest rate. Various empirical studies (Chan et al. 1992 ; Dalquist 1996) conclude that a class of models seems to outperform other models. This class of models takes into account the mean-reverting feature of the interest rates and the fact that the variance in interest rate changes appears to be dependent on the interest rate level. The method we have proposed in this article does not impose a priori an analytical form of the process governing the instantaneous interest rate. If there is a mean-reverting feature or a link between the level of the interest rates and the variance, our approach will take it into account. In fact, as we characterized the relation between the class of shocks and the initial structure, we take into account the magnitude of the shocks (variance) in respect to the initial structure (conditional variance) and the lower (higher) probability of an upper (downer) shock when the level of the initial structure is high (mean-reverting). Moreover, as we do not impose the processes governing the state variables, we hope to reproduce the statistical properties of the historical evolution of the interest rate structure.

To study the empirical relation between the initial interest rate structure and the interest rate shocks, we proceed in three steps. First, a clustering of the initial interest rate structure has been realized. A 9 unit one-dimensional Kohonen map has been used. Then, a clustering of the shocks on the interest rate structure has been done, in this case using a 30 unit one-dimensional Kohonen map. While it is behind the scope of this paper to present in full detail those results, it is interesting to mention the Fisher statistics obtained, for each maturity, on the clustering of shocks (Table 1). These statistics confirm the highly discriminate cluster formed by the Kohonen algorithm.

Dimension	Fisher	Dimension	Fisher
1	898	8	2840
2	1579	9	2803
3	2099	10	2840
4	2472	11	2544
5	2853	12	2221
6	3161	13	1894
7	3038	14	1574
		15	1279

Tab. 1 : Fisher statistics for each maturity obtained after clustering by a 30 unit one-dimensional Kohonen map.

Analysis of the relation between the initial interest rate structure and the shocks that apply to them has been conducted on this basis. To understand this procedure, we have to remember that each shock to the interest rate structure is related by its date to a specific initial interest rate structure. In other words, a specific deformation of the interest rate structure is obtained by the difference between the state of the interest rate structure at a specific date and the state of the interest rate structure 10 days later. It is therefore possible to identify the shock subset associated with each of the 9 interest rate structure classes and to calculate the conditional frequency distributions. We then test the statistical independence between the 9 empirical conditional distributions of shocks and the global population of shocks using a χ^2 test. Results are shown in Table 2. All 9 tests are statistically significant.

In other words, this is equivalent to saying that the conditional distributions of shocks are statically different from the distribution of the global population of shocks, with a very high level of confidence. The empirical relation between shocks and interest rate structure is confirmed.

Initial interest rate classes	*Independence test*
1	140
2	42.04
3	85.48
4	54.58
5	151.07
6	244.39
7	55.38
8	73.37
9	59.87

Tab. 2 : χ^2 tests between each of the nine conditional distributions of shocks and the global population of shocks.

5.3 Simulating interest rate structure evolution's on a long term horizon

Using these empirical conditional distributions of frequencies, we propose a Monte-Carlo procedure to simulate the interest rate structure evolution. The procedure is the following :

- first, we randomly draw an initial interest rate structure.
- the winning unit of the Kohonen map associated with the interest rate structure is then determined.
- using the conditional distribution of frequencies of the interest rate shocks, we randomly draw a shock.
- we then apply the shock to the interest rate structure.
- the procedure is repeated 125 times to construct an interest rate structure evolution on a five year horizon (125 times the 10 days covered by the interest rate shock).
- for each simulation, we then repeat the procedure 1000 times to build the distribution of probability of interest rate structures, starting from the same initial interest structure.

Figure 3 and 4 respectively show the distribution of the short-rate and the long-rate for three simulations. The first two have been realized using the same interest rate initial shape (for which unit 6 is the winning one). The third one has been done using an initial interest rate structure attached to unit 1 (the only inverted interest rate structure mean profile). Based on these figures we see that the procedure is stable and that, on a five year basis, the initial interest rate structure mainly influences the short rate level. We also see that, for all simulations, the level of the short-rate and the long-rate are compatible with the historical one. Figure 5 presents five interest rate structures obtained in simulation 1, drawn from among the 1000 produced. We see that they are well-shaped. This property has been verified in all the results. Figure 6 presents, still in the case of simulation 1, one trajectory of the short and the long rate over 5 years. They clearly represent possible paths. While not presented here, we should also mention that in all simulations and at all steps all forward interest rate are positive.

6 Future works

In this paper, we have described a method for generating different scenarios of the evolution of the interest rate structure. The scenarios reproduce the characteristics of the historical data and seem to be stable over a long term horizon. To measure the interest rate risk of financial institutions by the VaR numbers, we need to calculate the prices, at some future date, of the securities whose payoff are dependent on the interest rate process. The standard techniques for valuation of these securities are, implicitly or explicitly, application of a risk-neutral valuation principle. The compensation for risk is made explicitly by adjusting the discount factors or implicitly when we impose the martingale property on the simulated sample paths of the underlying security price. Our future work will focuse on the valuation of the contingent claims.

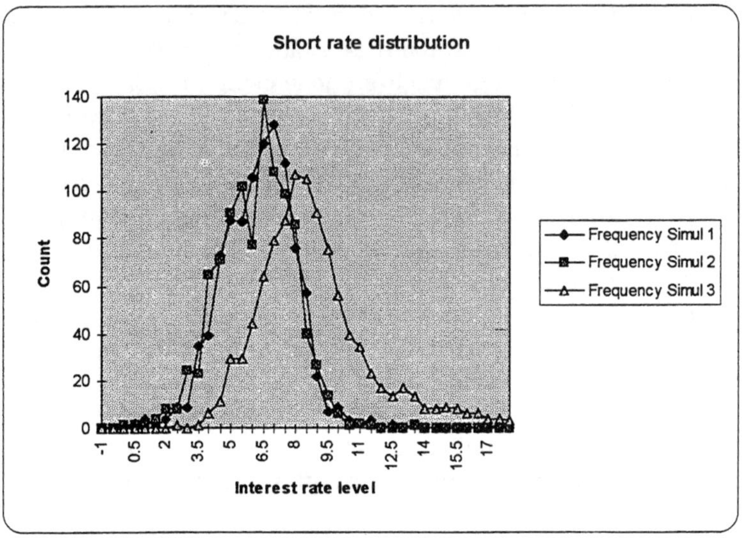

Fig. 3 : The short rate distributions produced by simulation 1 and 2 (starting from the same initial interest rate structure) highlight the stability of simulation procedure.

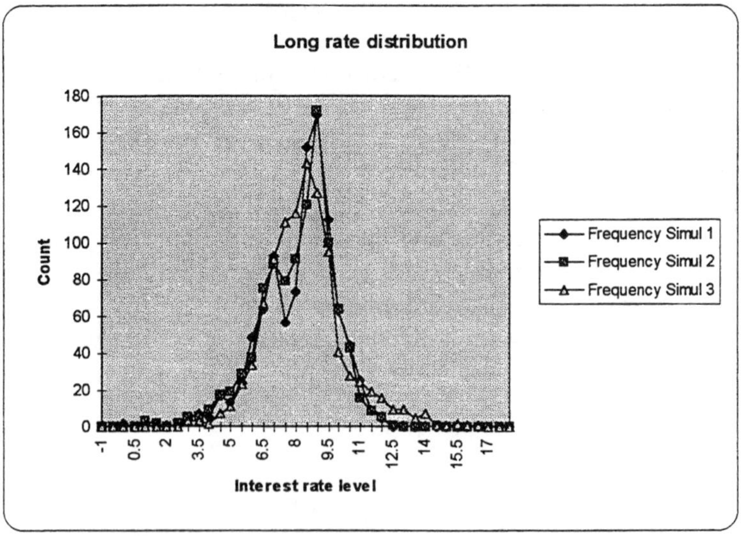

Fig. 4 : The long-rate distributions produced by simulation 1 and 2 (starting from the same initial interest rate structure) highlight the stability of simulation procedure.

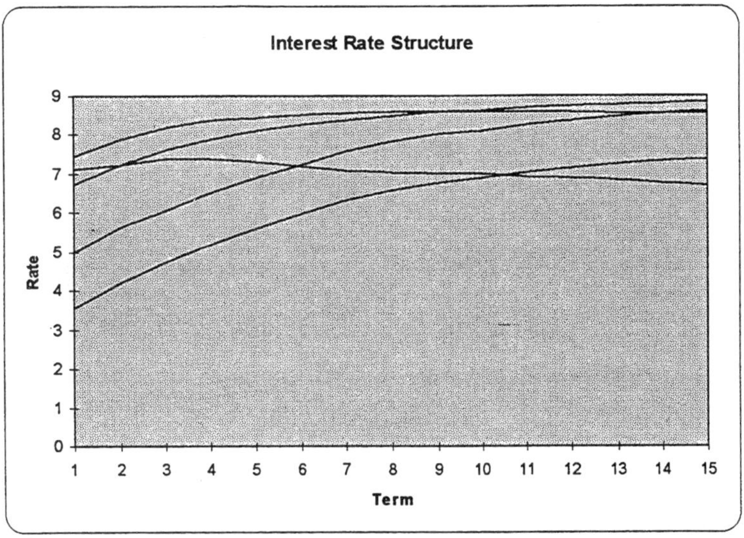

Fig. 5 : Five interest rate structures obtained in simulation 1, randomly drawn among the 1000 produced.

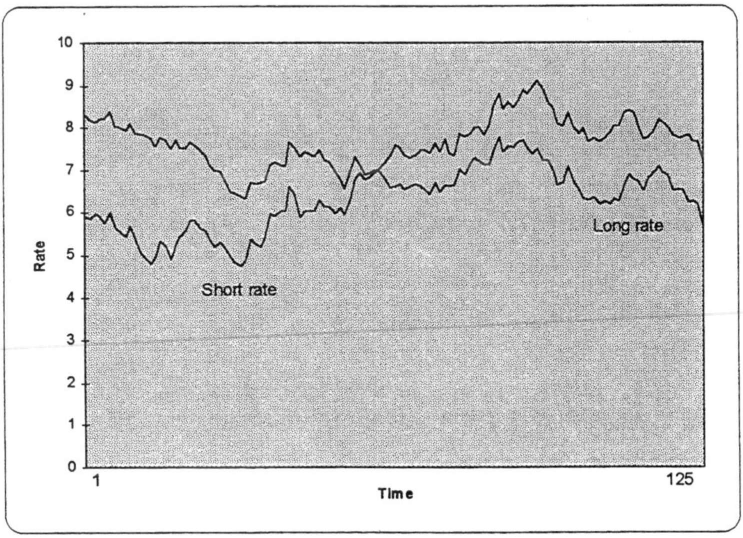

Fig. 6 : One trajectory of the short and long rate over 5 years, chosen among the 1000 produced by simulation 1.

7 References

Beder T.S. (1995), *VAR : Seductive but Dangerous*, Financial Analysts Journal, p. 12-24

Chan K.G., Karolyi G.A., Longstaff F.A., Sanders A.B. (1992), *An Empirical Comparison of Alternative Models of the Short-Term Interest Rate*, Journal of Finance 48, p. 1209-1227.

Cheyette O. (1996), *Implied Prepayments - Addressing anomalies in modeling MBS value and risk*, The Journal of Portfolio Management, p. 107-115.

Cottrell M. de Bodt E., Grégoire Ph., Henrion E.F. (1996), *Analyzing Shocks on the Interest Rate Structure with Kohonen Map*, Conference on Computational Intelligence for Financial Engineering - New York, IEEE, 1996, p. 162-167.

Cottrell M. de Bodt E., Grégoire Ph., Henrion E.F. (1996), *The Relation between Interest Rate Shocks and the Initial Interest Rate Structure : An Empirical Study using a Kohonen Map*, Congress of the Association Française de Finance Internationale, Genève.

Cottrell M., Fort J.C., (1987), *Etude d'un algorithme d'auto-organisation*, Annales de l'Institut Poincaré, Vol. 23, 1, p. 1-20.

Cottrell M., Fort J.C., Pagès G. (1994), *Two or three things that we know about the Kohonen algorithm*, in Proc of ESANN, M. Verleysen ED., D Facto, Bruxelles.

Dahlquist M. (1996), *On alternative interest rate processes*, Journal of Banking & Finance, vol. 20, p. 1033-1119.

Kohonen T. (1995), *Self-Organizing Maps*, Springer Series in Information Sciences Vol 30, Springer, Berlin.

Ho T.S.Y., Chen M.Z.H. & Eng F.H.T. (1996), *VAR Analytics : Portfolio Structure, Key Rate Convexities, and VAR Betas - A new approach to determining the VAR of a portfolio*, The Journal of Portfolio Management, p. 89-98.

Pagès G. (1993), *Voronoï tesselation, Space quantization algorithms and numerical integration*, Proc. ESANN'93, M.Verleysen Ed., Editions D Facto, Bruxelles, p. 221-228.

NEURAL NETWORKS FOR RISK ANALYSIS IN STOCK PRICE FORECASTS

MARJORIE KLENIN
Physics Department
North Carolina State University
Raleigh, North Carolina 27695-8202
E_mail: m_klenin@ncsu.edu

The present work integrates backpropagation networks into a hierarchical system and develops a simple probabilistic approach to timed price forecasts. A standard neural net is critiqued by a second, simpler network, whose output is used as the predictor. It is argued that network output should not be treated as a single-valued answer, but rather as a variable that determines an empirical likelihood function. The technique has been tried on a portfolio of 34 stocks, trained over a several-year period and tested on approximately a year's worth of daily data. Two conclusions are drawn: [1] Actual returns correlate better with the discrete "critic" predictions than with the "evaluator" net's price estimates, and [2] the set of probability distributions p(r|s) contains significantly more information than a random walk distribution based on overall stock volatility.

1 Introduction

Backpropagation networks have been used extensively to gauge behavior of stock prices. They are particularly suited to this application because they are able to extract statistically significant trends from noisy data in a model-independent manner. There are, however, also particular difficulties which arise. The mixing of statistical noise with systematic dynamical information is a problem in itself. Furthermore, the absence of a model makes it difficult to isolate non-redundant parameter sets for input, or to estimate timescales over which network training should occur. A number of modifications to standard backpropagation have been introduced to deal with these problems, and all seem to be important in improving performance (Azoff 1994, Beltratti *et al.* 1996). The purpose of this paper is to isolate two of those modifications, using them in their simplest form, and to examine their effect on the analysis of real stock data.

Specifically, consider the role of hierarchical structure and the use of the network as a *probabilistic* component in a prediction scheme. Both of these elements can be implemented in highly sophisticated ways, but to date this has been possible only in relatively small-scale problems, even with large computing resources. The approach here is to simplify the implementation drastically, in the hope that, even in a minimal form, these features will retain some of their important advantages, while requiring only modest computing power when scaled up to real datasets.

Hierarchical architectures

Most often hierarchical structures are used in conjunction with a feedback mechanism. They may, for example, be used in reinforcement learning (Sutton 1988), in gating systems that combine estimators (Jacobs, *et al.* 1991, Weigand *et al.* 1995) , or as a means of tuning control (Myers 1992). Although often part of delay-learning schemes, the notion of hierarchy is separate from that of delay or memory. In the form used here, hierarchy permits a second ("higher") module to make commentary on the output of a standard backpropropagation network. In talking *about* predictions made by the "lower" network, the higher network is in effect dealing in metalanguage, and the sophistication of the resulting prediction may be changed qualitatively. The higher network is used here in a *summative* way: it issues a prediction based on the lower network's output. It is in no way *formative*: it does not influence that output.

It should also be emphasized that the present structure does not attempt to partition the input space into distinct domains. The problem of regime switching cannot be studied with this system.

Probabilistic interpretation of neural network output

Neural networks are not usually used as stochastic predictors. The nets may be trained to match intrinsic noise in the dataset (Weigend *et al.* 1995, Klenin 1996), or post-training Bayesian model comparison may be used (Mackay 1992, 1995). The network parameters that result from such analyses are probabilistic in the sense that they are best estimates (by some criterion) for fitting the data, and their reliability (by the same criterion) is approximately known. The aim, however is to produce a single network output. It is assumed that that output represents the expectation of a distribution, and that the only other interesting stochastic parameter is the variance of the true data from the mean.

Things may be considerably more complicated in dealing with real stock data. Although the goal may be to extract any deterministic components of the time series, such components are always masked by stochastic fluctuations in the real data. This creates two problems for any neural network model: First, the trained network may include noise as well as the desired "clean" predictor. Second, even if the estimate is clean, random behavior about that estimate will occur in the real system. One solution is to derive conditional probability distributions for return that depend both on the series input data and on the neural network output. To do this properly is a serious computational undertaking. Such calculations on paradigm data sets, however, indicate that detailed information about the distributions may be crucial in making investment decisions. In particular, market instability may be characterized by the onset of extreme divergence between mean network output and actual data, and by catastrophic decrease in the reliability of the network predictor (LeBaron and Weigend 1996). It has also been shown empirically that multimodal distributions are by no means uncommon (Weigend and Srivastava 1995).

In the present work, a "quick and dirty" scheme is used to characterize the performance of the single neural net used for each stock price forecast. The conditional probability of return is computed, given the network's output value; this is done as an independent analysis, once the network's prediction is in. It turns out that certain average measures derived from the distributions correlate about as well with test data as does the direct network output. However considerably more material is available for the decision-making process, especially when the errors are not normally distributed.

Specific project task

The forecasting objective was to predict price changes for a number of stocks thirty trading days into the future. The raw input data included the time series for price and volume of each stock, as well as side information consisting of standard indicators. These included such factors as U.S. Treasury rates, foreign exchange rates, and Standard and Poor's industry composites. For each stock considered, four to six indices were chosen from a bank of about fifty. The data pertaining to the stock itself were daily price changes, volume, and, in some cases, standard technical indicators, such as relative strength index.

The network system was used primarily to distinguish classes of probable outcome. Expected returns were sorted into categories, and distributions of true returns were obtained for each category. Network errors were logged for about a year's worth of daily data. Their distributions were generally non-Gaussian, and in some cases multimodal. Several measures were defined to characterize mean expected return, and to evaluate performance over the entire collection of stocks studied.

Finally, the information content of the derived probability densities was compared with that of the random-walk Gaussian corresponding to the trend and volatility of each of the stocks studied. The measure used was the Kullback-Leibler entropy. This was computed for each of thirty-four stocks over the same year-long period. The values obtained indicate significant differences, and suggest that these reflect primarily differences in the means if the two distributions.

2 Learning procedure

The architecture of the entire learning system is shown in Fig. 1. For present purposes, the most important components are the two neural networks. The first of these (which will be denoted as the "evaluator" network) incorporated a number of standard enhancements. The second net (to be denoted as the "critic") has a much simpler structure, and receives several input parameters derived from the time series generated by the first net. Details of the network structures are given in Table 1, at the end of this section.

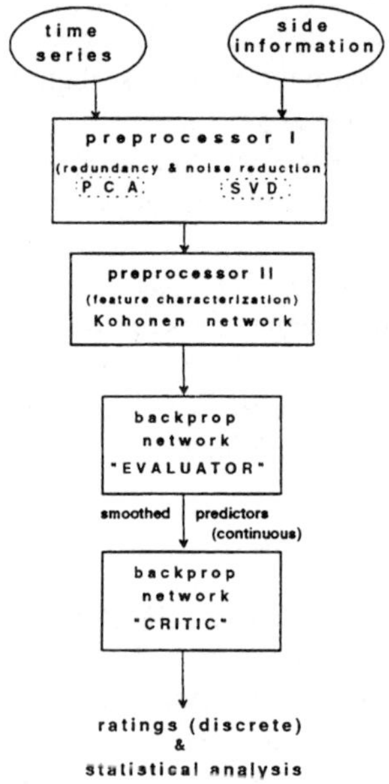

Fig. 1. Modular structure of the hierarchical learning system.

Evaluator

The following features were incorporated into the evaluator network.

- recursion: The main module is permitted a time-lagged response to its own previous output. This allows it to model system dynamics, including the capacity for cyclic behavior.[1]
- incremental learning: The network adapts continuously as new data are processed. This permits it to capture system drift over longer timescales.
- unsupervised feature extraction: A preprocessing module prepares data for the main network module. The raw time series were first subjected to principal component analysis and singular value decomposition (Press *et al.*, 1988; Azoff, 1994). The resulting data were then transformed to a coordinate system prescribed by a Kohonen network.[2]

---

1 The form used here is that suggested by Medio, 1992, It was chosen because it can be parameterized simply. Although the parameters were chosen arbitrarily and held fixed during training. It is in principle possible to optimize them (Principe and Kuo, 1994). This possibility will be investigated in the future.

2 A modified Kohonen network was used to map the trajectories of the input parameters. The usefulness of Kohonen nets as preprocessing modules is well known; for an example of standard usage see the paper by Lawrence, Tsoi, and Giles in these proceedings. The implentation in the present work is nonstandard, in that the Kohonen network was used to supply coordinates for phase space trajectories rather than to provide a discrete classification scheme. It was found that backpropagation network size could be substantially reduced when the Kohonen module was used. Improvement may in part be attributable to the fact that the module creates extra input nodes, although simply using the random fan-out procedure suggested in Gallant and Smith, 1987 did not seem to work as well. A systematic study

Target values were set to $\log(<price(t+\Delta)>/<price(t)>)$ .The brackets indicate an exponential average over a several day period. t is the date on which the prediction is made and Δ was taken to be 30 days. The evaluator was thus required to produce an explicit time series of predicted returns. The typical mean square error (MSE) was of the order of several percent on both training and cross-validation data. The evaluator generally recognized both trends and shifts in trends, but could not time the shifts consistently.

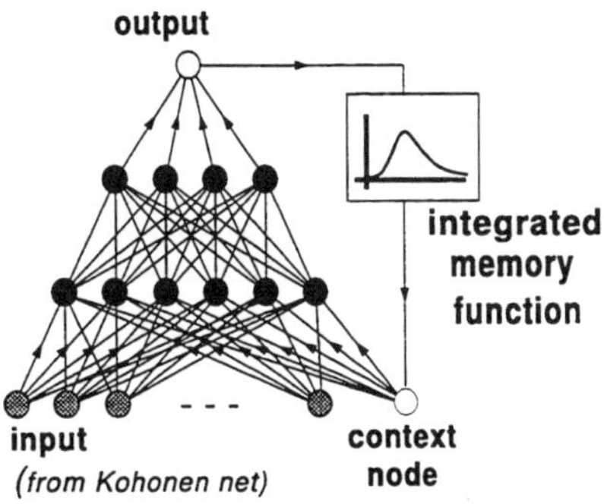

Fig. 2.Structure of the evaluator

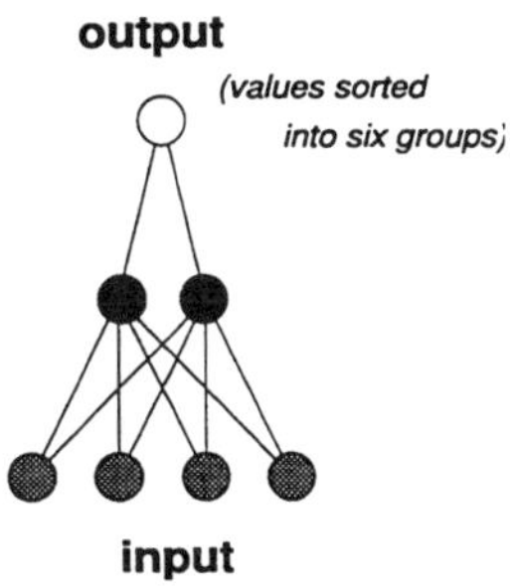

Fig. 3. Critic network

Critic

The critic's main role was to compensate for the timing problem. It was a second, simpler net that received the first net's output. The job of the critic was to obtain a graded rating (on a scale of -1 to 1) based only on quantities derived directly from the output of the evaluator. Because this net produced a discrete output, it was possible to characterize its performance as a conditional probability distribution, describing the relationship between returns actually realized and the critic's estimate of return.

The input values summarized the evaluator output over the prediction period Δ, as shown in Fig.4. The evaluator's output during the entire period Δ was monitored. Maximum and minimum values were fed to the critic, together with two average values, one taken during each half of the prediction period. Comparison of the averages permitted the critic to compute time rates of change for evaluator predictions.

---

of this aspect of the model will be described elsewhere. For a description of the self-organizing mapping, see Kohonen, 1989 or Hertz, *et al.*, 1991, Chapter 9.

The target values were rated returns, drawn from a period beginning in June, 1994. In this dataset the actual returns were grouped into categories with the lowest rating corresponding to losses greater than 12.5% over the six-week period; the highest corresponding to gains greater than 12.5%. The critic's continuous output was then discretized -- i.e., rounded to the nearest rating value.

The table summarizes training details.

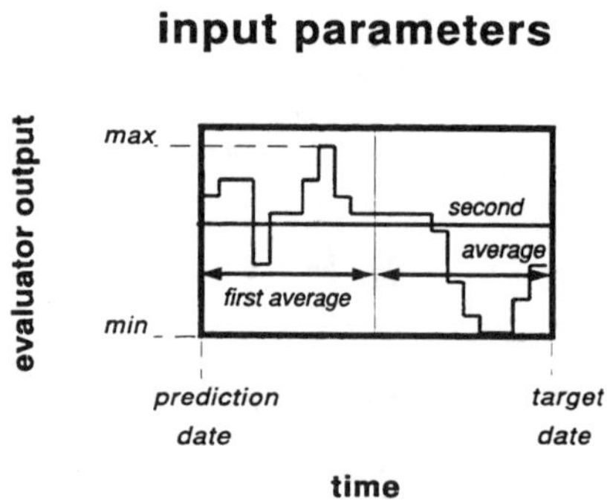

Fig. 4. Deriving critic input parameters from the evaluator output. The horizontal axis represents the time between between the date of prediction and the target date Δ days in the future. The evaluator's prediction of fractional return for each date is shown on the vertical scale.

	EVALUATOR	CRITIC
STRUCTURE	nonlinear activation: tanh function two hidden layers; typical size was four to eight nodes	nonlinear activation: tanh function one hidden layer with four nodes
LEARNING ALGORITHM	gradient descent cost function: mean square error incremental: new data added continuously	gradient descent cost function: mean square error regularization penalizes trivial (constant) response. non incremental -- occasional retraining as new data become available.
TRAINING/TEST DATA	temporally disjoint input time series: stock data and standard indicators training: Jan 1990 - Jun 1994 test: Jun 1994 - Mar 1995	disjoint, but with temporal overlap input: output from evaluator training: Jun 1994 - Feb 1995
STATISTICAL ANALYSIS	————————	computed from out-of-sample data Oct 1994 - present

Table 1. Summary of evaluator and critic network parameters.

3 Raw results and statistical analysis

Predictions obtained from both evaluator and critic nets are displayed for a typical (if particularly volatile) stock in Fig. 5. The evaluator results are just the direct network output. The critic predictors are derived from empirical probability distributions, as described below.

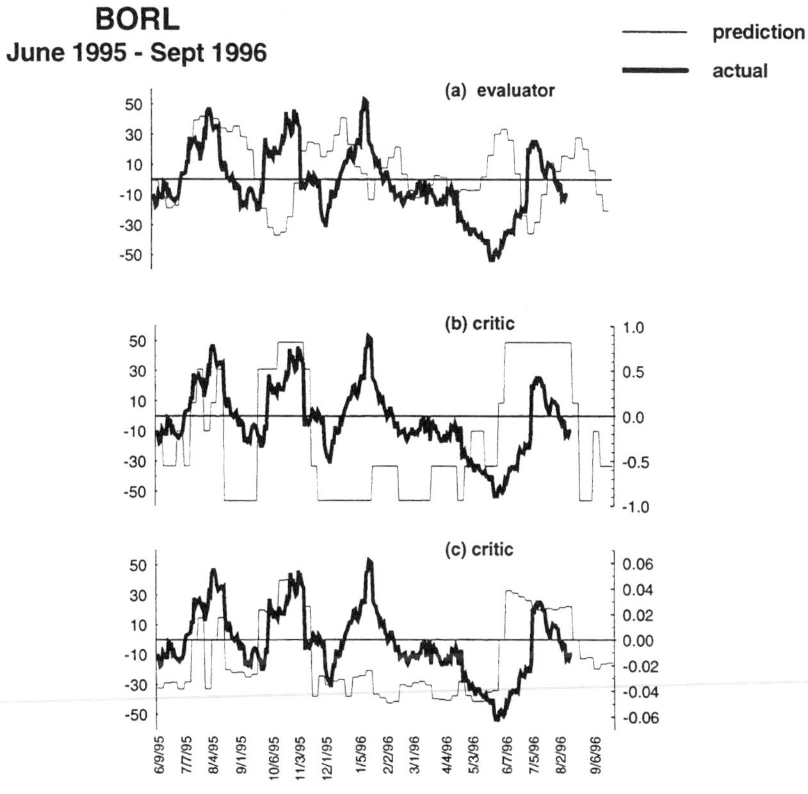

Fig. 5. Forecasts of evaluator and critic networks. The horizontal scale represents the time t at which predictions were made. The heavy line compares the actual log return at the corresponding target date t+Δ. The evaluator output represents log returns. These values are plotted using the left axis. Critic predictions use the right-hand axis. Critic (b) is a mean prediction derived from an empirical Dirichlet distribution. Critic (c) is a mean utility function derived from Parzen's kernel density estimate. (See text.) Note that critic predictors appear to correct the phase shifts evident in the evaluator forecasts.

Conditional distributions and summary parameters

In the spirit of empirical Bayesian analysis, data-adaptive probability densities were derived from the discrete critic output (Maritz and Lwin 1989). Both discrete and continuous distributions were obtained for each critic category. Fig. 6 shows the continuous functions corresponding to the forecasts of Fig. 5 The critic was usually extremely optimistic or pessimistic, and data for intermediate predictions is statistically less significant. The empirical density function is non-Gaussian. Its form indicates significant regime switching -- either the network makes a reasonable estimate or it does not understand the input data at all.

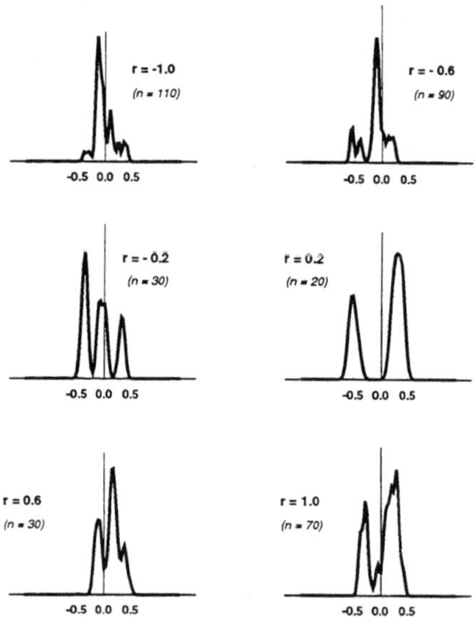

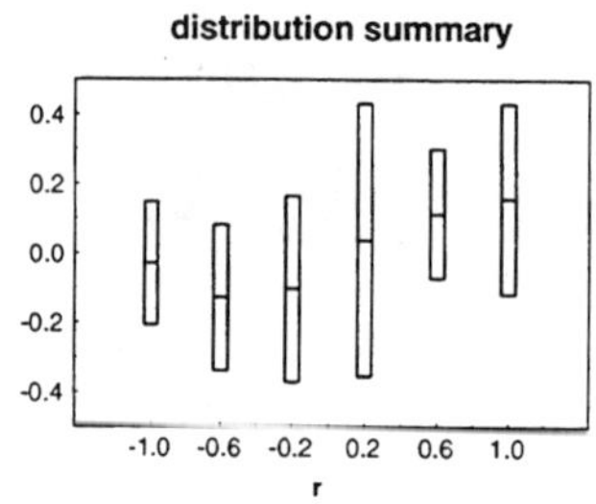

Fig. 6. Distribution of return for each of the critic ratings r, for the data of Fig. 5. n is the number of samples. The densities at left are summarized above. Median lines of the bars represent distribution means, bar length represents standard deviation. Means correspond roughly (but not precisely) to rating.

Dirichlet estimator (discrete):

Actual return data corresponding to a rating r were sorted into six categories r'_k in the same way as the network output. The estimator yields a set of probabilities $\{\pi_k\}$ for the various categories k, together with measures of their reliability (Heckerman 1995):

$$\mathcal{P}\left(\{\pi_k(r)\},\{N\}\right) \quad \propto \quad \prod_k (\pi_k)^{N_k+N_k^{(0)}-1}$$

N_k is the number of observations of category k. $\{N^{(0)}_k\}$ are integers used to fix the prior. In practice, the expectation of π_k over the distribution $\mathcal{P}$ is used as the conditional probability $\pi(r'_k|r)$. As more observations are made, $\mathscr{P}$ becomes sharper, and $<\pi_k>$ approaches the value one would obtain simply by averaging over the observations. The rating r, averaged over $<\pi_k>$ is the series "critic (b)" of Fig.5

Kernel density estimator (continuous)

The adaptive distribution is constructed from kernels centered at the observed values v_j of the data. The probability of finding return x, given (discrete) critic rating r is taken as (Parzen 1962):

$$p_n(x|r) = \frac{1}{n\sqrt{2\pi}\,\sigma(n)} \sum_j K\left(\frac{x-v_j}{\sigma(n)}\right)$$

n is the total number of observations corresponding to rating r; K has been taken to be a normal distribution with mean v_j and standard deviation $\sigma(n) \sim 1/\sqrt{n}$. As n increases, both mean and variance approach values obtained directly from the data.

Mean utility function

A useful measure for predicted performance is derived from the continuous distributions. Defining the utility as $u(x|r) = x \cdot p(x|r)$, consider the average of its maximum and minimum values over the distribution p: $u_{avg} = (u_{\max} + u_{\min})/2$. This quantity depends on both expectation and uncertainty. To restrict the parameter to values between +1 and -1 $\tanh(u_{avg})$ was used. For a Gaussian this quantity depends only on the ratio of mean to standard deviation -- it is essentially just the Sharpe ratio. Its interpretation is in general more complex, but it factors in both expectation and volatility of return. This is the quantity plotted in Fig. 5 as the series labeled "critic (c)," and it is shown below to correlate well with actual price behavior.

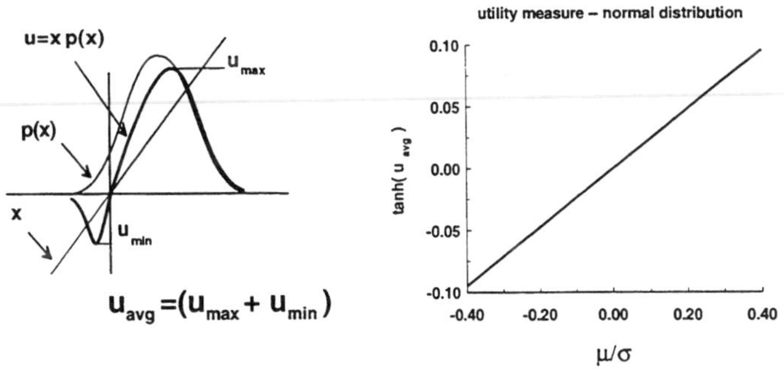

Fig. 7. Utility parameter, as used to determine correlation functions. Its behavior in the special case of the normal distribution N(μ,σ) having mean μ and standard deviation σ, is displayed for the range of μ/σ appropriate to stockmarket time series.

4 Discussion -- quantitative summary results[3]

Correlation functions as a measure of predictive capacity

The various evaluator and critic predictors were compared with actual returns. In each case the quantity

$$C(\{x(t_j)\},\{y(t_j)\}) = \frac{\sum_j [(x(t_j)-\bar{x})\cdot(y(t_j)-\bar{y})]}{\sqrt{\sum_j (x(t_j)-\bar{x})^2 \cdot \sum_j (y(t_j)-\bar{y})^2}}$$

was computed for individual stocks over the time sequence $\{t_i\}$. A value of +1 indicates perfect correlation; -1, perfect anti-correlation; 0, no correlation.

$y(t_i)$ was in all cases the true fractional return averaged over the week preceding the target date; the value was either used directly or rounded into discrete categories. The x values are listed in Table 2. Summary data are displayed in Fig. 8. The figure also shows the fraction of events in which the evaluator and critic had the correct *direction* of change. In all cases critic predictions represent a dramatic improvement over the original evaluator output.

chart label	$x(t_j)$	$y(t_j)$ --avg. target return
evaluator	discrete network prediction	actual value
critic:1	discrete network prediction	discretized
critic:2	continuous network prediction	discretized
critic:3	mean utility: $(u_{max}+u_{min})/2$	actual value
critic:4	average Dirichlet rating	actual value

Table 2. Correlation functions summarized in Fig. 8

Kullback-Leibler entropy: information content and random walk theory

If $N(x,\mu,\sigma)$ is the normal distribution for return x, with time-dependent mean $\mu(t)\sim t$ and standard deviation $\sigma(t)\sim\sqrt{t}$ determined by the appropriate random walk parameters (Ison 1994, Gibson 1991, Kittel 1969), then the relative entropy (Kullback 1959) provides a quantitative measure of the *difference* in information content between this distribution and the empirical distributions $p(x|r)$ for x,

[3] The box plots have been drawn to the following prescription: Box length encloses 50% of data. Box width is proportional to the number of samples. Median line is determined by the *enclosed* data. Lines above/below may have a maximum falue of 1.5 imes the box length. They actually extend to the data points farthest from the box but within this range. Outliers (x symbols) lie outside this range.

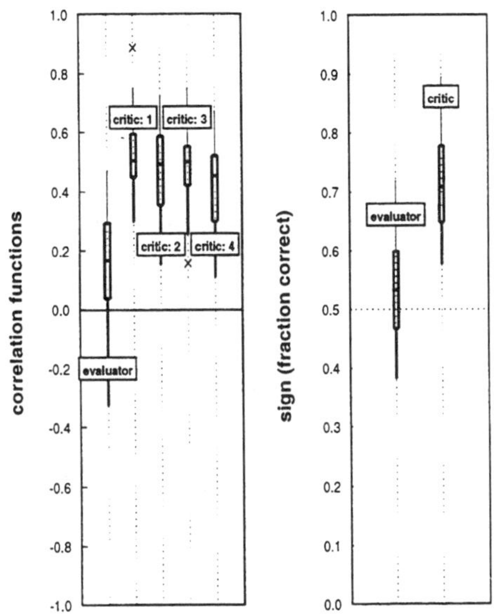

Fig. 8. Comparison of evaluator and critic performance. Correlation functions were computed for a collection of 34 stocks over the period from June 1995 through Sept. 1996.

given critic rating r:

$$S\{p(x|r), N(x,\mu,\sigma)\} = \int dx \left[p(x|r) \cdot \ln\left(\frac{p(x|r)}{N(x,\mu,\sigma)} \right) \right]$$

S depends on difference in both mean and variance -- and in general, on differences in higher moments as well. (See Fig. 9.)

Fig. 10 shows that the network predictions differ from those of a random walk analysis; the difference is greatest when the network predicts a significant gain or loss.

Fig. 9. Comparison of two normal distributions $N(x,\mu,\sigma)$ and $N(x,0,1)$. The contour labels designate values of S for various σ, μ

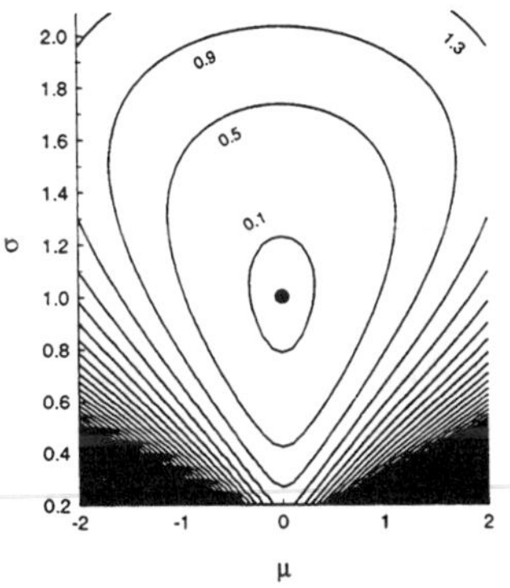

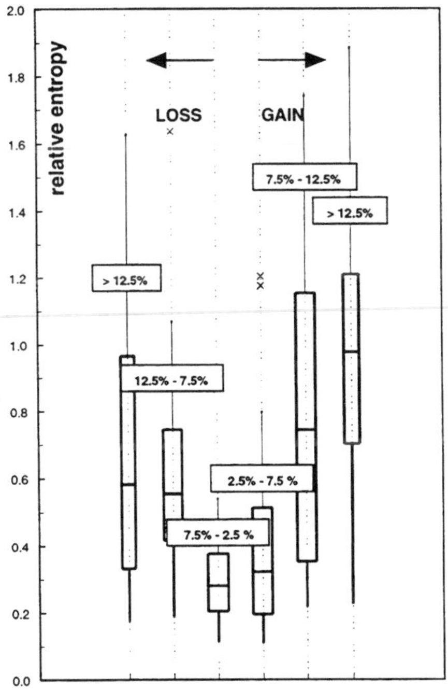

Fig. 10. Summary plot of Kullback-Leibler entropy calculated for the same stock data as the correlations of Fig . 8. The comparison is between the conditional distributions determined by the critic network and a random walk Gaussians whose mean and variance are determined by individual stock trends and volatilities. The labels indicate critic predictions.

5 Conclusions

This work has compared the performance of a standard multilayer neural network predictor with that of a hierarchical critic model, which is simple in structure. Judging by the visual appearance of the time series generated, the use of the critic as predictor improves the timing of forecasts.

Four different rating measures were derived from the output of the critic net. Two of these were taken directly from the network output, and two were calculated from the empirical distribution of returns. Correlation with actual return was computed for each of the four predictors, and the correlation between evaluator network output and actual return was computed as well. Over a sample set of 34 stocks, all four of the critic functions performed better than the evaluator output

The critic output also correctly predicted the direction of change significantly more often. The critic's worst performance was 58%, compared with the evaluator's 38%.

Relative entropy was used to determine the <u>difference</u> in information content between each of the empirical distributions and the normal distribution corresponding to mean six-week return and overall volatility. (This measure says nothing about which description is more accurate, only whether the two are distinguishable in a meaningful way.) The results do indicate important differences. In part this may be attributable to the non-Gaussian form of the empirical distributions, but the summary chart suggests that the main difference results from shifts in the mean and most probable return.

6 Acknowledgments

I am indebted to my colleagues at NCSU for many useful conversations, in particular to Mark White and three of his students, Jeff Joines, Chris Houck and Tim Wiwel. Thanks to Roger Ison of Mantic Corporation for helpful correspondence. I am also grateful to the Triangle Area Neural Network Society for providing a forum in which very preliminary versions of this work could be discussed.

7 References

Azoff, M. (1994) *Neural Network Time Series Forecasting of Financial Markets* (John Wiley & Sons, New York)

Beltratti, A., Margarita, S., and Pietro Terna (1996) *Neural Networks for Economic and Financial Modeling* (International Thomson Computer Press, London).

Gallant, S. and Smith, C. (1987) *in Proceedings of the IEEE International Conference on Neural Networks*

Gibson, Rajna (1991) *Option Valuation (McGraw-Hill, NewYork)*

Heckerman, D. (1995) *A Tutorial on Learning Bayesian Networks.* Microsoft Technical Report MSR-TR-95-06.

Hertz, J., Krogh,A., and Palmer, R.G. (1991) *Introduction to the Theory of Neural Computation* (Addison Wesley, Redwood City).

Ison, Roger (1994) *A Model of Runs and Cycles in Price Data,* available from http://www.manticsoft.com

Jacobs, R.A., Jordan, M.I., Nowlan, S.J., and Hinton, G.E. (1991) Neural Computation *3*, 79-87

Kittel, C. (1969) *Thermal Physics* (John Wiley & Sons, New York).

Klenin, Marjorie (1996) in *Computational Learning Theory and Natural Learning Systems 4,* Greiner, R., and Petsche, T., ed. (MIT, Cambridge)

Kohonen, T. *(1989) Self-Organization and Associative Memory, 3rd edition* (Springer-Verlag, Berlin).

Kullback, S. (1959) *Information Theory and Statistics* (John Wiley & Sons, New York).

LeBaron, Blake and Weigend, Andreas S. (1996) *Forcasting Financial Data: A Method for Evaluating Predictors.* available from http://www.econ.wisc.edu/~blake/research.htmld

MacKay, David J.C.(1992) *Advances in Neural Information Processing Systems 4, 839-846* (Morgan Kaufman, San Mateo).

MacKay, David J.C.(1995) Network **6**, 469-506.

Maritz, J.S., and Lwin, T. (1989) *Empirical Bayes Methods, 2nd edition* (Chapman & Hall, London).

Medio, A., (1992) *Chaotic Dynamics: Theory and Application to Economics, pp. 195-201*(Cambridge, Cambridge).

Myers, Catherine E. (1992) *Delay Learning in Artificial Neural Networks* (Chapman & Hall, London)

Parzen, E. (1962) *Ann. Math Statist. 33, 1065-1076.*

Press, W.H., Flannery, B.P., Teukolsky, S.A., and Vettering, W.T (1988) *Numerical Recipes in C, pp. 60-72.* (Cambridge, Cambridge).

Principe, J.C., Hsu, H.-H., Kuo, J.-M. (1994) *Advances in Neural Information Processing Systems **6**, 1011-1018.* (Morgan Kaufman, San Mateo)

Sutton, R.S. (1988) Machine Learning 3, 9-44.

Weigend, Andreas S. and Srivastava, Ashok N. (1995) International Journal of Neural Systems **6**.

Weigend, A.S., Mangeas, M., and Srivastava, A.N. (1995) International Journal of Neural Systems **6**, 373-399, and references contained therein.

OPTIMIZING NEURAL NETWORK CLASSIFIERS FOR BOND RATING

ALEXEI N. SKURIKHIN

Mathematics Department, Institute of Physics & Power Engineering, 249020 Obninsk, RUSSIA

Email: alexeisk@hotmail.com Fax: 095 883 3112

ALVIN J. SURKAN

Computer Science and Engineering Department, University of Nebraska Lincoln, NE 68588-0115, USA

Email: surkan@cse.unl.edu Fax: 402-472-7767

Three variants of probabilistic neural networks were developed using a data base of corporate financial parameters paired with their corresponding bond ratings. The classification efficiency in the estimation of these ratings was studied for three kinds of Bayesian neural networks, namely: a probabilistic neural network (PNN), a Gram-Charlier neural network (GCNN) and Edgeworth's modification of Gram-Charlier method (EWNN). The accuracy obtained by these three methods in assigning ratings to bond issues for collections of set-aside test-set patterns of 11 variables were 54.0%, 55.6%, and 53.3%, respectively. On the basis of inferred sensitivities of each of the variables obtained in constructing a PNN with an 11 variable data set, the number of variables was reduced to 8 and finally to 6. With this final reduced number of selected variables, the EWNN method outperformed the other two kinds of probabilistic neural networks.

1 Introduction to the Bond Rating Problem

Publishers of financial data retain experts who rate corporate bond issues. The public-domain availability of these data and a growing need for rapid, reproducible predictions of bond ratings make construction of computer-implemented models attractive for implementing automatic methods. These are designed to extract classification information from financial data bases. Models based on the trained neural network paradigm can capture components of the expertise applied by experts in the rating process. These models also shed some light on mechanisms for objectively using financial ratios to obtain reliable and improved bond ratings (see Surkan and Singleton 1990, 1992, 1995). To preprocess these data, specialists define, normalize and nonlinearly scale financial quantities to derive more predictive ratios. These are used to provide credible estimates of various bond ratings which can help investors assess risks.

Inherently, there is a year-to-year correlation between the ratings assigned to bond issues. This correlation may persist significantly for a number of years. The neural network models for predicting bond ratings were experimentally studied with four years of data records from about 700 corporations.

Table 1. Statistics of the Financial Data Base Used in Ratings

CATEGORY NUMBER	CLASS CODE	RATING SYMBOL	TOTAL NUMBER OF PATTERNS	NUMBER OF TRAINING PATTERNS	NUMBER OF TEST PATTERNS
1	2	AAA	62	32	30
2	4	AA+	25	15	10
3	5	AA	115	65	50
4	6	AA-	121	61	60
5	7	A+	187	107	80
6	8	A	302	152	150
7	9	A-	197	107	90
8	10	BBB+	197	107	90
9	11	BBB	281	141	140
10	12	BBB-	200	100	100
11	13	BB+	132	72	60
12	14	BB	237	127	110
13	15	BB-	275	145	130
14	16	B+	324	164	160
15	17	B	92	52	40
16	18	B-	42	22	20
17	19	(*)	31	21	10
Total number of patterns			2820	1490	1330
(*) - This category combined the rating classes CCC+, CCC, and CCC-					

Data for the period 1990 to 1994 were provided by Standard and Poor's and were used to construct PNNs. For these experiments there were a total of 2820 data patterns of 11 financial ratios and/or scores. These patterns were supplied with their ratings which populated the categories as described by the statistics in Table 1.

For this study, an integer scale of ratings ranging from 2 to 19 labeled the data patterns. Standard and Poor's experts converted the ratios to scores by applying non-linear scaling to map the majority of these prediction variables onto a 0-20 interval. Before using these data, each of its variables were individually converted to standardized Z-scores by subtracting their means and dividing by their standard deviations. The data set summarized by the previous statistics was used for all experiments. The data set was divided so that first $n_1 = 1490$ samples were used for training and the remaining $n_2 = 1330$ samples were used for testing.

2 Bayesian Neural Networks and their Application

The PNN (Spacht 1990), GCNN (Kim et al 1992), and EWNN (Masters 1995) methods belong to a family of classifiers based on Bayesian likelihood tests. Their differences depend on what functions are used for approximating the probability density function (PDF). A Parzen (1962) window approximates the PDF for a PNN. The GCNN and EWNN use the Gram-Charlier series expansion for the PDF.

In comparison with the PNN, the last two methods require negligible storage. All three of the methods are very fast because they are constructed in a single pass. Mathematically, the problem of bond rating is one of classifying an input vector into one of several classes with Bayesian optimality. Baye's optimal decision rule states that an input vector **x** is to be classified as a member of class i according to the following inequality.

$$h_i c_i f_i(\mathbf{x}) > h_j c_j f_j(\mathbf{x}) \tag{1}$$

where: h_i is the prior probability of an unknown sample being drawn from class i, c_i is the cost associated with misclassifying a sample from class i, f_i is the PDF for class i. The above equation requires an approximation of the probability density function. In the standard PNN of Specht (1990) method, the Gaussian function is the weighting function used for PDF estimation:

$$f(x)=\frac{1}{(2\pi)^{p/2}\sigma^p m}\sum_{i=1}^{m}e^{-1}\left[-\frac{\|x-x_i\|^2}{2\sigma^2}\right] \tag{2}$$

where: m is the total number of training patterns;
p is the dimension of the input vector;
σ is a smoothing parameter (standard deviation of a Gaussian distribution.)

In the GCNN method, the PDF is approximated by the Gram-Charlier series expansion (Kendall, 1969 and Kim et al, 1992) as follows:

$$f(x)\approx\alpha(x)\left[c_0+c_1H_1(x)+c_2H_2(x)+c_3H_3(x)\ +\ldots\right] \tag{3}$$

where:

$$\alpha(x)=\frac{1}{2\pi}e^{-x^2/2} \tag{4}$$

$$H_k(x)=xH_{k-1}-(k-1)H_{k-2} \tag{5}$$

and $H_k(c)$ are the Hermite polynomials,

$$H_0(x)=1,\ \ H_1(x)=x^2-1,\ \ H_2(x)=x^3-3x \tag{6}$$

Edgeworth's method (Cramer, 1946 and Kendall et al, 1969) uses the same series as does the Gram-Charlier but there is a reordering of the terms within the expansion shown in Eq. (7). When these two series are summed to infinity, they become equivalent. Different truncations of the series yield the two different approximations. Edgeworth's modification provides an opportunity for improving the accuracy of the results over those above that possible from the GCNN.

$$f(x)\approx\alpha(\mathrm{x})\begin{bmatrix}1+c_3H_3(x)+c_4H_4(x)+c_6H_6(x)+\\ +c_5H_5(x)+c_7H_7(x)\ \ldots\end{bmatrix} \tag{7}$$

3 Architecture of a Probabilistic Neural Network or PNN

The PNN can be viewed as having its structure organized as a layered neural network. Following the input layer, the PNN has two hidden layers and a single output layer. The input pattern layer has one neuron for each pattern. Each input neuron computes a distance between the input pattern and the training pattern represented by that neuron. These distances provide values for the weights for the neuron's activation function. The summation layer has one neuron for each class. A layer following the summation neurons collects the activations of pattern layer neurons from the members of the class corresponding with each summation neuron. The final activation of the ith summation neuron provides directly an estimate of the PDF at the ith population. The output neuron is a threshold unit that decides which of its inputs receives the largest contribution.

4 Parametric Description of the PNN Architecture

Finding a good value of the variance σ is critical to the performance of the PNN. In these experiments σ was defined in three ways. The first way gives a single value of σ parameter to all the variables for all the classes with an assumption of equal prior probabilities. The second approach uses a separate σ for each variable which suppresses effects of variance in those of less importance. Also, in these experiments two methods are used for specifying and comparing the effects of prior probabilities.

These methods differ as to how prior probabilities are obtained. The prior probabilities are either set equal for all classes or they are set to be proportional to the number of training patterns in each class. In combination with these two methods one can employ either different σs for each variable or, under the assumption of equal prior probabilities, one may use a different σ for each class. To estimate the σ's, a gradient-based method is used. The range of σ used in the optimizing search was 0.0001 to 15.

5 Preprocessing the Raw Variable Data Values

For these experiments, the data patterns were partitioned into 17 classes (see Table 1) with some combination of the three most sparsely populated rating classes. Before using the data patterns,, individual components were standardized to a Z-score. This normalization equalizes the contribution of each variable by removing the effects of offset and different measurement scales. As a rule, normal (non-outlier) patterns were slightly concentrated in the training set by choosing those patterns which are more closely clustered, relative to each other, and are not outliers. However, several outliers may also be intentionally included in each class for training. Because some of the outliers were avoided for inclusion in the training set, the test data set has a bias that gives it a higher density of outliers compared with the training set.

6 Finding Parameters for the PNN, GCNN and EWNN Models

Finding good values for the σs and coefficients of series is required for maximizing the performance of the PNN, GCNN and EWNN classifiers. The approach used for the PNN has a separate σ for each variable. This suppresses the effects of variance in unimportant variables. The GCNN and EWNN methods used three and four moments, respectively, in approximating the PDF. For the GCNN, only the first two elements inside the brackets of Eq (7) are used. The first four terms are used for the EWNN method. Using all four terms provides σs having greater relative stability under noisy conditions. To calculate σs and coefficients, gradient-based methods are used. In all of the experiments the prior probabilities for the classes were equal.

7 Simulation Results

Simulation results follow in Tables 2-7. Experiments began with the PNN being applied to a data sample with all of the available 11 variables. Confusion matrixes from the training and test sets are in Tables 2 and 3. Based on the results from the training set, the σ values shown in Table 4 were obtained. Analysis of these values enabled the selection of two subsets of more significant variables. These two subsets were used for all of the comparison experiments. The first subset consists of eight variables, specifically, those numbered by 4 through 11. This second subset consists of six variables which are numbered 10 and 4 through 8. Comprehensive experimentation was done with the three neural network algorithms for these subsets of the data variables. Tables 3-6 indicate the accuracy of classification results grouped by class.

Table 2. **Confusion Matrix Obtained by the PNN Using 11 Variables in the Training Set**

CLASS INDEX	1	2	3	4	5	6	7	8	9	10	11	12	13	14	15	16	17	PERCENT CORRECT
1	30	2	-	-	-	-	-	-	-	-	-	-	-	-	-	-	-	100.
2	-	15	-	-	-	-	-	-	-	-	-	-	-	-	-	-	-	100.
3	6	1	58	-	-	-	-	-	-	-	-	-	-	-	-	-	-	90.76
4	-	1	-	60	-	-	-	-	-	-	-	-	-	-	-	-	-	98.36
5	3	1	7	4	91	-	1	-	-	-	-	-	-	-	-	-	-	88.78
6	-	3	4	8	3	129	3	1	1	-	-	-	-	-	-	-	-	88.81
7	1	-	1	1	-	-	98	5	-	1	-	-	-	-	-	-	-	96.26
8	2	1	-	1	-	-	3	100	-	-	-	-	-	-	-	-	-	96.26
9	-	-	-	-	-	-	-	1	135	3	2	-	-	-	-	-	-	98.58
10	-	-	-	-	-	-	-	-	-	100	-	-	-	-	-	-	-	100.
11	-	-	-	-	-	-	-	-	-	-	72	-	-	-	-	-	-	100.
12	-	-	-	-	-	-	-	-	-	-	2	123	-	-	-	1	1	98.42
13	-	-	-	-	-	-	-	-	-	-	3	-	136	1	1	1	3	94.48
14	-	-	-	1	1	-	-	-	-	-	-	4	2	147	-	3	6	90.85
15	-	-	-	-	-	-	-	-	-	-	-	-	-	-	50	2	-	100.
16	-	-	-	-	-	-	-	-	-	-	-	-	-	-	-	22	-	100.
17	-	-	-	-	-	-	-	-	-	-	-	-	-	-	-	-	21	100.
AVERAGE NUMBER OF PREDICTED RATINGS EQUAL TO THAT ASSIGNED OR TO ONE OF ITS ADJACENT NEIGHBORS																		96.6

Table 3 **Confusion Matrix Obtained by PNN for the Test Set with 11 Variables**

CLASS INDEX	1	2	3	4	5	6	7	8	9	10	11	12	13	14	15	16	17	PERCENT CORRECT
1	18	10	2	-	-	-	-	-	-	-	-	-	-	-	-	-	-	93.33
2	6	3	-	-	-	-	-	-	-	-	-	-	1	-	-	-	-	90.
3	3	10	15	14	5	-	2	-	-	-	1	-	-	-	-	-	-	78.
4	3	7	7	17	13	4	1	4	3	-	-	1	-	-	-	-	-	61.66
5	-	2	12	6	22	10	11	8	4	5	-	-	-	-	-	-	-	47.5
6	2	7	24	13	35	19	20	9	6	9	3	2	-	1	-	-	-	49.33
7	-	1	5	9	6	15	1	13	20	4	7	1	5	3	-	-	-	32.22
8	-	-	1	5	7	13	5	12	10	19	6	5	3	-	-	3	1	30.
9	-	-	2	10	24	12	18	12	17	18	5	14	3	1	-	4	-	33.57
10	-	-	-	1	2	4	15	4	16	18	13	14	6	-	5	2	-	47.
11	-	-	2	1	1	3	5	3	4	9	8	15	4	3	1	-	1	53.33
12	-	-	-	4	4	2	2	6	12	11	8	26	12	6	8	5	4	41.81
13	-	-	-	4	2	2	3	5	5	13	8	25	17	15	15	5	11	43.84
14	-	-	-	1	-	1	1	-	6	4	5	15	48	31	19	8	21	61.25
15	-	-	-	1	-	-	-	-	-	1	3	3	10	8	3	5	6	40.
16	-	-	-	-	-	-	-	-	-	-	1	3	2	3	6	1	4	55.
17	-	-	-	-	-	-	-	-	-	-	1	-	-	1	2	3	3	60.
AVERAGE NUMBER OF PREDICTED RATINGS EQUAL TO THAT ASSIGNED OR TO ONE OF ITS ADJACENT NEIGHBORS																		55.00

A smaller σ is expected to indicate a less significant variable. Since each variable appears in the PDF in proportion to the value of $\exp(-1/\sigma^2)$, it is possible to use these values for identifying the most significant variables.

Table 4 **Values of σ Obtained for 11 Variables when Using all the Training Patterns**

CLASS INDEX	NAME OF FINANCIAL RATIO OR SCORE	σ	$1/\sigma^2$	$exp(-1/\sigma^2)$
1	Market Capitalization	0.35	7.96	0.00035
2	SALES	0.26	14.85	0.00000
3	ASSETS	0.18	29.52	0.00000
4	OPERATING MARGIN	0.95	1.11	0.32840
5	PRETAX INTEREST	1.11	0.81	0.44562
6	EBITDA_COV	0.77	1.67	0.18797
7	ROPC	2.13	0.22	0.80151
8	FFO_TDEBT	0.88	1.30	0.27358
9	TD_TCAP	0.58	2.97	0.05123
10	FREE OPERATING CASH FLOW	2.27	0.20	0.81747
11	Market_TD/TC	0.61	2.65	0.07065

Table 5 **Accuracy of PNN, GCNN, & EWNN Algorithms Using all 11 Variables**

CLASS INDEX	TRAINING DATA SET			TEST DATA SET		
	PNN	GCNN	EWNN	PNN	GCNN	EWNN
1	100.	50.	46.9	93.3	66.7	63.3
2	100.	60.	40.	90.	60.	50.
3	90.8	49.2	43.1	78.	70.	64.
4	98.4	63.9	57.4	61.7	51.7	43.3
5	88.8	61.7	57.9	47.5	31.3	28.8
6	88.8	52.6	50.7	49.3	44.7	46.
7	96.3	52.3	62.6	32.2	44.4	41.1
8	96.3	48.6	52.3	30.	45.6	41.1
9	98.6	42.6	56.0	33.6	54.3	57.9
10	100.	54.	54.	47.	47.	47.
11	100.	43.1	44.4	53.3	40.	48.3
12	98.4	33.9	56.7	41.8	37.3	42.7
13	94.5	37.2	62.8	43.8	61.5	62.3
14	90.9	50.6	75.	61.3	71.5	77.5
15	100.	69.2	76.9	40.	55.	57.5
16	100.	77.3	63.6	55.	80.	85.
17	100.	38.1	38.1	60.	50.	50.
AVERAGE	96.6	52.0	55.2	53.99	53.6	53.3

Table 6 Accuracy of PNN, GCNN, and EWNN Algorithms Using Selected 8 Variables

CLASS INDEX	TRAINING DATA SET			TEST DATA SET		
	PNN	GCNN	EWNN	PNN	GCNN	EWNN
1	93.8	40.6	3.1	90.	50.	0.
2	100.	66.7	6.7	70.	40.	10.
3	86.2	38.5	30.8	64.	46.	56.
4	73.8	52.5	59.0	25.	28.3	46.7
5	54.2	48.6	62.6	28.8	33.8	35.
6	46.1	37.5	44.7	26.7	27.3	39.3
7	62.6	47.7	51.4	27.8	30.	28.9
8	60.7	34.6	33.5	31.1	32.2	36.7
9	61.0	39.	40.4	44.3	47.9	39.3
10	64.	36.	39.	38.	27.	33.
11	77.8	27.8	37.5	43.3	11.7	18.3
12	59.8	33.1	39.4	16.4	21.8	30.
13	47.6	42.8	47.6	30.	47.0	43.8
14	47.0	48.2	50.	25.	50.	58.8
15	82.7	65.4	63.5	25.	45.	52.5
16	100.	68.2	54.5	50.	65.	55.
17	100.	33.3	38.1	30.	60.	20.
AVERAGE	71.6	44.7	41.3	39.1	39.	35.5

Table 7 Accuracy Obtained by PNN, GCNN and the EWNN Algorithms Using 6 Variables.

CLASS INDEX	TRAINING DATA SET			TEST DATA SET		
	PNN	GCNN	EWNN	PNN	GCNN	EWNN
1	71.9	37.5	0.	90.	60.	0.
2	100.	73.3	0.	70.	40.	10.
3	75.4	40.	32.3	62.	58.	56.
4	44.3	47.5	73.8	21.7	31.7	46.7
5	28.0.	47.7	47.7	28.8	31.3	35.
6	31.6	42.8	45.4	26.	38.7	39.3
7	38.3.	50.5	39.3	18.9	28.9	28.9
8	35.5.	35.5	28.0	23.3	35.6	36.7
9	46.1	34.0	27.0	35.7	38.6	39.8
10	45.	30.	27.	39.	32.	33.
11	44.4.	26.4	38.9	36.7	21.7	18.3
12	29.9.	31.5	44.9	13.6	26.4	30.
13	12.4	38.6	48.3	13.8	40.8	43.8
14	7.3	56.1	49.4	13.1	59.4	58.8
15	57.7	71.2	53.8.	0.	57.5	52.5
16	100.	68.2	59.1	65.	60.	55.
17	85.7.	14.3	14.3	80.	30.	20.
AVERAGE	50.2.	43.8	37.0	39.3	40.60	35.5

Each of the three methods gave nearly the same average accuracy. At the same time, the accuracy for classes which are more populated give better results with the GCNN or EWNN algorithms.

Analysis of other confusion matrices (not included in this paper) using different numbers of variables indicated the possibility of detecting the subsets for certain classes. It is observed that for class 1 nearly all the test cases were predicted as exactly the expert-assigned rating class or one of the two neighboring classes with the selected 6 and 8 variables. The full complement of 11 variables gave the greatest number of correct classifications for class 1 [see Table 3].

8 Conclusions

Considering the high complexity of the bond rating problem and the very significant context sensitivity of financial data, the modest accuracy of prediction on the set-aside test data is realistic enough to be encouraging.

Since the objective of this work is not only to achieve accuracy but to improve reliability in real-world situations, it will be advantageous to pool the results of a number of different methods to estimate the ratings. Since the PNN is intrinsically a classifier based on Bayes theory, it is a promising model for providing a better explanation and a deeper insight into the network's operation as a classifier.

This research has demonstrated that the σ values from a PNN are useful for selecting more significant variables. A comparison of the results indicates that different sensitivities of selected variables can serve as a basis for performing variable deletion that depends on a more quantitative analysis.

9 Acknowledgments

Although all of these data used for these experiments is in the public domain and could be compiled and derived directly from the open literature, the task of preparing it would be prohibitively time-consuming. We are grateful for the cooperation of Standard and Poor's in making their data available in a machine readable form.

10 References

Cramer, H., 1946, *Mathematical Methods of Statistics*, Princeton University Press, Princeton, New Jersey 1946.
Kendall, M., and Stuart, A., 1969. *The Advanced Theory of Statistics,* Volume 1, Hafner, New York, 1969.
Kim, M.W., and Arozullah, M., 1992 *Generalized Probabilistic Neural Network-Based Classifiers*, Proceedings of the International Joint Conference on Neural Networks, Baltimore, MD, 1992.
Masters, T., 1995, *Advanced Algorithms for Neural Networks: A C++ Sourcebook*, John Wiley & Sons, Inc., ISBN 0-471-10588-0, 1995.
Parzen, E., 1962, *On Estimation of a Probability Density Function and Mode*, Annals of Mathematical Statistics, 33:1065-1076, 1962.
Singleton, J.C. and Surkan, A.J., 1990, *Modeling the Judgment of Bond Rating Agencies*, at the Midwest Finance Association Annual Meeting, March 28-31, 1990, Chicago, IL.
Singleton, J.C. and Surkan, A.J., 1995 *Neural Networks in Bond Rating*, invited chapter in the 1995, 376 page book titled: Neural Networks in the Capital Markets, edited by A-Paul Refense, London Business School, London England. Chapter 20, pages 301-307, John Wiley & Son's.
Specht, D.F., 1990, *Probabilistic Neural Networks*, Neural Networks Volume 3, pp. 109-118, 1990.
Surkan, A.J. and Singleton, J.C., 1990, *Neural Network Performance in Emulations of Professional Bond Rating Judgments,* Proceedings of the INNC International Neural Networks Conference, Volume 1, page 394, July 3-9, 1990, Paris, France.
Surkan, A.J. and Singleton, J.C., 1992, *Neural Networks as Bond Rating Tools*, HICSS92 25th Hawaii International Conference on Systems Science, Volume 4, pp 499-503, January 7-10, 1992, Koloa, Hawaii.
Surkan, A.J. and Singleton, J.C., 1990, *Neural Networks for Bond Rating Improved by Multiple Hidden Layers*, Proceedings of the IJCNN International Joint Conference on Neural Networks, Volume II, pp 157-162, June 25, 1990, San Diego, CA.
Surkan, A.J., and Skurikhin, A.N., 1996 *Experiments in Bond Rating with Probabilistic Neural Networks*, (ICONIPS'96), page 777, The Proceedings of the International Conference on Neural Information Processing, September 20, Hong Kong 1996).

Part 3
Statistical Learning for Financial Problems

A COMPARISON OF NON-PARAMETRIC REGRESSION TECHNIQUES FOR THE PRICING OF OPTIONS USING AN OPTIMAL IMPLIED VOLATILITY

P. LAJBCYGIER
A. FLITMAN
Department Of Business Systems,
Monash University
Clayton Vic 3168 Australia
E-mail:PLAJBCYG@fcit-m1.fcit.monash.edu.au

A technique is chosen from each of the three general classes of non-parametric regression techniques and tested to see which can best enhance option pricing accuracy. It is well known that conventional option pricing models have inherent, persistent and systematic deviations/biases. The non-parametric regression techniques are used to model these biases. Of the techniques compared artificial neural networks are the most accurate.

1 Introduction

In this work, an optimally weighted implied volatility (IV) (in the sense of being (virtually) unbiased and the most efficient estimator of expected future return standard deviations) is used as an input into a conventional option pricing model. There are systematic and persistent deviations from actual transaction prices when using this implied volatility and these deviations are modelled using various comparable non-parametric, non-linear regression techniques.

2 Financial Preliminaries

In this section the financial background to the paper is discussed. For the sake of brevity the reader is referred to previous work (Lajbcygier et al 1996a) for details on the Sydney Futures Exchange (SFE), the All Ordinaries Share Price Index (AO SPI) options on futures, calls, puts, American, European and other general finance terms and definitions.

2.1 *The Modified-Black Model*

Black 1976, extended the work of Black and Scholes 1973 to options on futures, and provided a solution for European boundary conditions. The Black differential equation is given below:

$$\frac{1}{2}\sigma^2 F^2 \frac{\partial^2 f}{\partial F^2} - rf + \frac{\partial f}{\partial t} = 0 \tag{1}$$

where F is the current futures price, t is the time, and σ is the volatility of the underlying. f can represent European or American style call or put options on futures.

The SFE uses a system of deposits and margins for both long and short option positions which requires a modification in the Black equation. This modification reflects the fact that no interest can be earned on a premium that has not been paid fully up front. Essentially the interest rate, r is set to zero in the Black solution. This is the SFE recommended model. Lajbcygier *et. al.* 1996a has shown that the modified Black model outperforms all other competing conventional models when using historical volatility.

The solution of the Black differential equation Eq.(1), when appropriate boundary conditions are imposed and the interest rate set equal to zero, is the modified Black equation, given below:

$$c' = FN(d'_1) - XN(d'_2) \tag{2}$$

where

$$d'_1 = \frac{\ln(F/X) + (\sigma^2/2)(T-t)}{\sigma\sqrt{T-t}} \tag{3}$$

$$d'_2 = d'_1 - \sigma\sqrt{T-t} \tag{4}$$

c' is the premium , X is the strike price, T-t is the time to maturity (in years) and the other variables are defined above.

Even though the AO SPI options on futures are American style, Lieu 1990, claims that the early-exercise premium is negligible due to the peculiar margin requirements of the SFE. This is why the European Black formula can be used for the American style options on futures.

2.2 Moneyness Bias & Time to Maturity Bias

The conventional option pricing models (such as the modified Black model in section 2.1) are considered to be amongst the most successful models in the social sciences. However, the models are systematically and persistently biased and despite their success, these models are becoming less reliable over time in the markets where one would expect them to be most accurate (Rubinstein 1985). Persistent option pricing biases have been noted in the empirical option pricing literature by Eales *et. al.* 1990 and Shastri *et al.* 1986. It is well known that these empirical anomalies or biases are a function of the options 'moneyness' - ratio of underlying price to strike price - F/X, and 'time to maturity'- T-t (Jordan *et al.* 1987).

There are a number of plausible reasons for the bias of the conventional models. Hull et al. 1987 have proven that that this bias is consistent with a stochastic and time-varying volatility. Ncube *et al.* 1995 have derived a bias-adjusted Black-Scholes option pricing formula by relaxing the assumption of a constant volatility and replacing it by the notion of stochastic volatility. In general, the approaches are unsatisfactory because they require strong assumptions. An alternative approach is discussed below.

3 Artificial Neural Networks and Nonparametric Regression

Regression is the problem of estimating a function of several variables $\varepsilon = \hat{f}(\vec{x}) + error$. The aim of this work is to determine which non-parametric regression technique can enhance option pricing accuracy best by modelling the biases inherent in the conventional option pricing approaches discussed in section 2.2.

The fundamental advantage of nonparametric regression is that it makes very few assumptions about the unknown function to be estimated. A taxonomy of non-parametric regression techniques is presented in Cherkassky 1992. There are three general classes :- *global parametric methods* assume that the estimating function can be represented as a combination of some basis functions, *local parametric methods* approximate the function by fitting simple parametric functions to different sub-regions of the domain and *adaptive computation methods* adjust their strategy to take into account the behavior of the function to be approximated.

This work compares at least one model from each of the above classes. There are two global parametric techniques used in this work - the linear regression and the non-linear ANN. The local parametric technique is represented by kernel regression. Finally, the adaptive technique used is Projection pursuit regression.

Each of these techniques models the difference between the conventional option pricing model and the real transactions data as a function of the input data (see section 4.4) :-

$$\varepsilon = (c'/X)_{Model} - (c/X)_{Real} \tag{5}$$

where ε is modelled as :-

$$\varepsilon = \hat{f}_j(\vec{x}) \tag{6}$$

$$\text{where, } x_i = \begin{cases} F/X & i=1 \\ T-t & i=2 \\ \sigma & i=3 \end{cases}$$

F, X, T-t,c' and σ are defined in section 2.1 and c is the actual transaction price.

The regressions are represented mathematically as follows:-

$\hat{f}_j(\vec{x}) =$

Multi-variate linear regression, j=1,

$$\varepsilon = \hat{f}(\vec{x}) = \delta_0 + \sum_{i=1} \delta_i x_i \tag{7}$$

Multi-variate non-parametric kernel regression, j=2,

$$\varepsilon = \hat{f}(\vec{x}) = \frac{\sum_{i=1} f_i K(\chi - x_i)}{\sum_{i=1} K(\chi - x_i)} \tag{8}$$

Projection pursuit regression, j=3,

$$\varepsilon = \hat{f}(\vec{x}) = \sum_{i=1} \delta_i h_i (\vec{\beta}_i \vec{x}) + \delta_0 \tag{9}$$

ANN, j=4,

$$\varepsilon = \hat{f}(\vec{x}) = h(\sum_{i=1} \delta_i h(\beta_{0i} + \vec{\beta}_{1i}' \vec{x}) + \delta_0) \tag{10}$$

For the linear regression, j=1, the δ_i are coefficients, for the kernel regression j=2, the K() represent kernel functions (such as the gaussian kernel)[1]. For the projection pursuit regression j=3, h_i ( ) are estimated from the data, k is the number of projections, δ_i and $\vec{\beta}$ are coefficients[2]. For the ANN, j=4, h(.) is a typically a smooth monotonically increasing function (such as the sigmoid), k is the number of hidden units, δ_i and $\vec{\beta}$ are coefficients[3].

---

[1] NeuroShell2 was used for the Kernel regression and the ANN. Tanh input scaling was used for Kernel regression. The smoothing factor was set automatically by determining optimal performance on a test set.

[2] The S-plus language was used to estimate the projection pursuit regression model.

[3] The ANN's architecture was a 3,15,1 tanh input scaling with logistic activation functions in the hidden and output layers and using standard back-propagation with learning rate=0.05 and momentum=0.5. Training was halted when performance did not improve on a test set.

4 Method

4.1 *Weighted Implied Volatility*

In conventional option pricing models the volatility σ is the only variable which is not known with complete certainty. There are two ways of estimating volatility - historical volatility or implied volatility. Historical volatility is calculated using an arbitrary rolling window of the log returns of the underlying[4]. The implied volatility is defined as the volatility which equates the conventional model price with the observed option price. Lajbcygier et al. 1996a and Hutchinson et al. 1995 have shown that an ANN can out-perform conventional option pricing models when historical volatility is used. The present work uses implied volatilites instead. This is significant because, empirically, implied volatility (IV) has been found to be a more accurate and efficient a predictor of option prices (and ex-ante volatility) than historical volatility. (Park et al. 1985, Jordan et al. 1987, Chiras et al. 1978, Turvey 1990)

There can only be a unique underlying volatility. However, the implied volatility from any given option is not unique, but is biased and is a function of its moneyness and maturity. WIV's are needed to mitigate this bias and to obtain an optimal estimate of the markets expected ex-ante volatility.

Theoretically, Corrado et al. 1996 has shown that implied volatilities from 'at the money options' (or implied volatility weighting schemes using 'at the money options') are the most efficient and also (virtually) unbiased estimators of the ex-ante underlying volatility when return volatility is stochastic (ie. non-constant).

Lajbcygier *et al.* 1996a compared various IV weighting schemes and found, for the data sample under consideration, consistent with Corrado's et al. 1996 theoretical work and Turvey's 1990 empirical study that the most accurate WIV is an 'at the money'/vega based WIV - the DERIV IV.

---

[4] Lajbcygier 1997 has shown that a window of near sixty days is optimal for the AO SPI options on futures.

The DERIV uses a weighting scheme based on vega[5],

$$\text{VEGA} = \Lambda_{imp} = F\sqrt{T-t}\,N'(d_1') \tag{11}$$

where N'() is the standard normal distribution and d_1' is from Eq. (3).

$$\text{DERIV} = \left(\sum_{i=1}^{K} \sigma_{imp}^{2}\,\Lambda_{imp}^{2}\right)^{1/2} \Big/ \left(\sum_{i=1}^{K} \Lambda_{imp}^{2}\right)^{1/2} \tag{12}$$

In preceding studies (Martini et al. 1995, Park et al. 1985) WIV's are calculated using each of the IV's obtained from the previous day. This WIV is then used to calculate prices for the next day. However, in this work the WIV is calculated intraday using the previous transacted options on the same day. It was felt that this approach would provide more accurate results because the exchange traded options are not traded overnight and therefore significant overnight news events may influence the next days markets ex-ante volatility estimate.

To insure only prior information was used for any day, only the implied volatility's derived from each option transaction prior to the one under consideration could be used. For example, if on a given day, there were ten call options transacted and we wished to forecast the volatility for the tenth, we could only use the first nine transaction IV's - σ_{imp}, to calculate a WIV volatility for the tenth.

4.2 The Use of Ratios For Variable Input

Similarly to Hutchinson *et al.* 1994, Merton's theorem (8.9) (Merton 1973) allows us to use F/X and C/X in place of F, X and C. Although using this result has been criticized because it assumes that the volatility and underlying price are independent (Ait-Sahalia and Lo, 1995) we still use it because it offers the competing non-parametric regression techniques information about strike bias in an explicit

---

5 Vega is the partial derivative of the option price with respect to volatility. Vega is at a maximum for at the money options so at the money options are most sensitive to changes in volatility and therefore are the most efficient.

manner. Also, using a ratio means that the output can be independent of underlying level.

4.3 *Data & Data Synchronicity*

The data is SFE intraday PIT data, it is time stamped to the second ,and transacted from January 1993 to December 1995. There are over 5,200 transactions after filtering out all those transactions where no WIV could be calculated[6].

In previous studies (Hutchinson *et. al.* 1994), the underlying futures price often used is the closing price of the day. In this study we priced intraday option transactions. Hence, it was decided to extract the nearest recent SPI futures price that was recorded before the time that the option was transacted. This resulted in underlying values that in most cases were recorded only seconds before the option was transacted. If, however, the underlying future transacted more than 60 seconds prior to the option, the option transaction was discarded.

4.4 *The Hybrid Approach*

The *hybrid* approach is motivated by the fact that the conventional option pricing model - the modified Black (see section 2.1), provides a good fit to the data to begin with - if the entire pricing surface[7] provided by the conventional option pricing model provides a reasonable fit to the real data why not just fit the residual errors between the model and the real data?

The basis of the hybrid approach to the problem of option pricing is in using a conventional option pricing model (ie. the modified-Black equation, Eq.'s 2-4) as a base, and allowing the nonparametric regression techniques (see section 3) to augment its performance.

The values of F, X, $T\text{-}t$, C are obtained directly from the SFE whilst volatility is estimated as described above in section 4.1. Essentially, the nonparametric regression technique (eg. ANN) is presented with targets - the difference between the modified-Black equation and the C/X value taken from the real data.(see Eqn. 5) The nonparametric regression is

---

[6] The first transaction on each day was used for WIV but not included on its own.

[7] The pricing surface is the price of the option over the strike price C/X as a function of T-t and F/X.

thus estimated to produce an appropriate deviation from the conventional OPM (ie. modified-Black) according to the input parameters (see section 4.1). Therefore, when the system is used for pricing, the difference between the conventional OPM and the nonparametric regression output should produce a bias adjusted *C/X value.*

4.5 Error Measures

In order to reasonably compare the neural network approach with conventional approaches, more than one measure of closeness-of-fit was used. In Table 1 below, we used the following:

$$R^2 = \frac{(n\sum xy - (\sum x)(\sum y))^2}{(n\sum x^2 - (\sum x)^2)(n\sum y^2 - (\sum y)^2)} \tag{13}$$

$$NRMSE = \sqrt{\frac{\Sigma(y-x)^2}{\Sigma(y-\bar{y})^2}} \tag{14}$$

$$MAE = \frac{1}{n}\Sigma|y-x| \tag{15}$$

Where x is the actual, or target value and y is the model, or estimated value. The R^2 value is best when nearest to 1, the *NRMSE* is best when nearest to 0, and the *MAE* is also best near 0.

4.6 Outliers

A simple filter rule was used to strip outliers - if an IV > 30% or if IV< 5% then the transaction was deemed to be an outlier and not used in the calculation of any of the WIV's. In this way, 50 outliers were discarded. Sixty percent of the outliers had time to maturities of less than 3 days - presumably there is a 'very short time to maturity' effect. There were another one hundred and sixty 'very short time to maturity' options which were not outliers and these were included in WIV calculations.

5 Results and Discussion

The data was divided into six monthly periods, this was done to reduce data snooping bias and mitigate the non-stationarity effect of the data (as in Hutchinson *et al.* 1994). For each period, an $\varepsilon = \hat{f}_j(\vec{x})$ for j=1,...,4 model is estimated. For each sample the model was estimated and then this estimated model was tested on the next period.

For example, ANN931 is the out-of sample pricing performance for an artificial neural network estimated on the first half of 1993, and tested on the next half. M.BLK is the conventional modified Black model, KERN is the non-parametric kernel regression, PPR is the projection pursuit regression and LIN is the linear regression. The number of data points is also given for each sample.

The most important point to note is that the ANN model performs consistently best except for the model estimated on the second half of 1994. The KERN model is the next best regression model. The LIN model is the next best, surprisingly more accurate than the PPR model. The non-parametric ANN and KERN regressions are more accurate than the LIN model and all three are more accurate than the conventional M.BLK model. The PPR regression on the other hand performs inconsistently - better than the conventional model only twice.

A number of studies have compared one or the other of these techniques to ANN's (Ripley 1996 , Atlas *et al.* 1990). The results of these studies using simulated functions have shown that ANN's provide no large and consistent benefit over other conventional statistical nonparametric regression techniques. Cherkassky 1992 suggests that since no single method is best for all applications and the only analytical proofs of performance are usually proofs of convergence in an asymptotic sense the ultimate test for a nonparametric regression technique is a measure of its performance on many different data sets. The work is significant because it shows that for the problem of estimating the residuals between the conventional model and the market transactions the ANN approach is optimal.

Table.1 Out-of-sample sample performance.

	931 ANN	931 KERN	931 PPR	931 LIN	931 M.BLK
RSQ	0.9951727	0.9952012	0.9942523	0.9949971	0.9947835
NRMSE	0.0698509	0.0702922	0.0772302	0.0713105	0.0814473
MAE	0.0008286	0.0008395	0.0009316	0.000856	0.0009488
	932 ANN	**932 KERN**	**932 PPR**	**932 LIN**	**932 M.BLK**
RSQ	0.9956733	0.9955597	0.9951718	0.9954902	0.9954536
NRMSE	0.0683826	0.0672248	0.0829654	0.0704286	0.0754421
MAE	0.0009312	0.0009545	0.0012036	0.0010087	0.0010046
	941 ANN	**941 KERN**	**941 PPR**	**941 LIN**	**941 M.BLK**
RSQ	0.9937131	0.9923633	0.9932386	0.993678	0.9929989
NRMSE	0.0795772	0.089005	0.0862601	0.0818747	0.0887273
MAE	0.0007394	0.0008416	0.0008179	0.0007702	0.0008099
	942 ANN	**942 KERN**	**942 PPR**	**942 LIN**	**942 M.BLK**
RSQ	0.9960207	0.9956835	0.9950373	0.995724	0.9958351
NRMSE	0.0688387	0.0679805	0.0810613	0.0691352	0.0722735
MAE	0.0007597	0.0007239	0.0008945	0.0007657	0.0007062
	951 ANN	**951 KERN**	**951 PPR**	**951 LIN**	**951 M.BLK**
RSQ	0.9966417	0.996486	0.9953673	0.9963922	0.9962533
NRMSE	0.0580769	0.0595331	0.0688122	0.0607768	0.0660859
MAE	0.0005438	0.0005572	0.0006653	0.0005781	0.0006126

6 Conclusion and Further Work

In this study, we have chosen a technique from each class of non-parametric regression techniques and have compared it with various conventional non-linear, non-parametric regression techniques from other classes. We have found ANN's to perform marginally better on the whole. This work can be extended in various ways; statistical tests on the difference between the models can be included. Other comparable techniques such as regression trees, MARS and k-nn regressions can be considered. Also, attempts should be made to model the entire option pricing surface rather than only the residuals between conventional models and the market to insure that the approach is inferior to the hybrid approach. Finally, it would be interesting to see if the regression surfaces estimated by each of the techniques are similar to each other and constant over time too.

7 Acknowledgments

Thanks to Brian Ripley for suggesting the most appropriate conventional statistical non-parametric regression techniques for comparison.

8 References

Y.Ait-Sahalia and A.Lo, 1995, *Nonparametric estimation of state-price densities implicit in financial assets*, MIT - Sloan School, Working paper No.LFE-1024-95.

Atlas, L, 1990, *A Performance comparison of trained multilayer perceptrons and trained classification trees* , 1990 Transactions on neural nets.

F.Black, 1976, *The Pricing Of Commodity Contracts*, Journal Of Financial Economics, 3, p.167-179,

F.Black, *1975, Fact and Fantasy in the use of options* , Financial Analysts Journal 3, p.36-41.

F.Black and M.Scholes, 1973, *The pricing of options and corporate liabilities* , Journal Of Political Economy 81, 637-654, May-June.

C.Boek,P.Lajbcygier, P., M.Palaniswami,A.Flitman, 1995, *A Hybrid Neural Network Approach to the Pricing Of Options*, Proceedings of ICNN'95, Neural Networks for signal processing II, Helsingoer, Denmark, 31 Aug 1992, IEEE Press, NY, USA.

V. Cherkassky, 1992, *Neural Networks and Nonparametric regression*, Neural networks for signal processing II, Helsingoer, Denmark, Aug 1992, IEEE press, NY, USA.

D.Chiras, S.Manaster, 1978, *The informational content of option prices and a test of market efficiency* ,Journal Of Financial Economics,6:213-234.

C.Corrado, T.Miller, 1996, *Efficient Option-Implied Volatility Estimators*, The Journal Of Futures Markets, Vol. 16, No.3, pp.247-272

J.Eales and R.Hauser, 1990, *Analyzing biases in valuation models of options on futures, Journal of futures markets*, Vol.10,No.3.

Hull and White, 1987, *The pricing of options on assets with stochastic volatilities*, Journal Of Finance, Vol. XLII, No.2.

J.Hutchinson, A.Lo and T.Poggio, 1994, *A Non-parametric* approach to pricing and hedging derivative securities via learning networks , Journal of Finance, Vol. XLIX, no.3, July 1994.

J.Jordan,W.Seale,N.McCabe,D.Kenyon, 1987, *Transactions Data Tests of the Black model for Soybean Future Options* ,Journal of Futures Markets, 5:539-577.

P.Lajbcygier, 1997, ***Pricing and trading options with artificial neural networks and bootstrap***, unpublished Ph.D dissertation, Department Of Business Systems, Monash University, Australia

P. Lajbcygier, C Boek, M Palaniswami and A. Flitman, 1995, *Neural Network Pricing of All Ordinaries Options on Futures* , Proceedings NNCM 95, London, England, October 1995, World Scientific, pp.64-77.

P.Lajbcygier,C.Boek,A.Flitman and M.Palaniswami, 1996a, *Comparing conventional and artificial neural network models for the pricing of options on futures* , Neurovest Journal, September 1996, pp.16-24.

P.Lajbcygier, A.Flitman and M.Palaniswami, 1997, *A Hybrid non-parametric approach to the intraday pricing of options on futures using implied volatility*, Proceedings on CCE,(ed.) S.Keen et al., Cambridge University Press, 1997.

D.Lieu, 1990, *Option Pricing with futures style margining*, Journal of Futures Markets, 10, pp.327-38

C.A. Martini and S.D. Taylor, 1994, *A Test of the (Modified) Black Model for Options on the SPI Futures Contract,* University of Melbourne, Dept. Finance, Research Paper Series No. 94-05.

Merton, 1973, *Theory Of Rational Option Pricing*, Bell Journal Of Economics.

N.Ncube and S.Satchell, 1995, *A bias-adjusted Black-Scholes Option Pricing Model,* Applied Financial Economics, p.51-60.

H.Park,R.Sears, 1985, *Estimating stock index futures volatility through the price of their options* , Journal Of Futures Markets, 5:223-237.

B.Ripley, 1996, *Pattern recognition and neural networks* , Cambridge University Press.

M.Rubinstein, 1985, *Nonparametric tests of alternative option pricing models*, Journal of Finance, XL, no.2.

K.Shastri and K.Tandon, 1986, *An empirical test of a valuation model for American options on futures contracts* , Journal Of financial and quantitative analysis, 21,4,p.377-392.

C.Turvey, 1990, Alternative Estimates of Weighted Implied Volatilities from Soybean and Live Cattle Options, The Journal Of Futures Markets, Vol.10, No.4, pp.353-366

FORECASTING VOLATILITY MISPRICING

P. J. BOLLAND AND A. N. BURGESS
London Business School
Department of Decision Science
Sussex Place, Regents Park
London NW1 4SA
Phone -(+44) 71-262-5050
FAX - (+44) 71-724-7875
E-Mail - pbolland@lbs.lon.ac.uk
E-Mail - nburgess@lbs.lon.ac.uk

A simple strategy is employed to exploit volatility mispricing based on discrepancies between implied and actual market volatility. The strategy uses forward and Log contracts to either buy or sell volatility depending on whether volatility is over or under priced. As expected, buying volatility gives small profits on average but with occasional large losses in adverse market conditions. In this paper multivariate non-linear methods are used to forecast the returns of a Log contract portfolio. The explanatory power of implied volatility and the volatility term structure from several indices (FTSE, CAC, DAX) are investigated. Neural network methodologies are benchmarked against linear regression. The use of both multivariate data and non-linear techniques are shown to significantly improve the accuracy of predictions.

1 Introduction

The overall aim of the analysis is to produce a model that will directly relate to an options trading strategy. The analysis shown in this paper extends and complements previous work in the area. We compare linear models and non-linear semi-parametric techniques for forecasting the price series of two option portfolios. The first option portfolio measures the mispricing of volatility on a stock index, identifying when volatility is over or under-priced. The second option portfolio measures the relative mispricing of the major European stock indices, showing which index has a greater mispricing. The models incorporate information from several sources such as international implied volatilities (FTSE, CAC, DAX), the dynamics of the returns series, and the term structure of volatility.

Several methodologies have been widely employed to forecast future option prices. Examples include, ARCH / GARCH models, stochastic volatility models, implied volatility regressions. The comparative advantage of the different methodologies is still an open question. Schmalensee and Trippi, 1978, show results which suggest that implied volatilities yield better forecasts of market volatility than simple estimates based on standard deviation of past returns. There have been many subsequent studies, the results of which are both contradictory and ambiguous (for critique, see Canina and Figlewski, 1993). Henon and Kat, 1994 compare the GARCH, EGARCH and stochastic volatility models, and show that the performance of the different models strongly depends on the specific asset class under consideration.

One of the main problems with volatility forecasting is that volatility is an unobserved variable, so there is no natural performance metric to compare different volatility forecast methodologies. An obvious performance metric is the profitability of an option trading strategy. Several authors have used option trading performance as a frame work within which to assess different volatility forecasting algorithms (Harvey and Whaley, 1992, Engle, Kane and Noh 1993). Noh, Engle and Kane, 1994, compares the prediction of an implied volatility regression against a GARCH model for predicting the price of an option straddle. By comparing their predicted volatility with the observed implied volatility they determine whether to buy or sell options straddles. Only when mispricing is identified can profitable trades be executed.

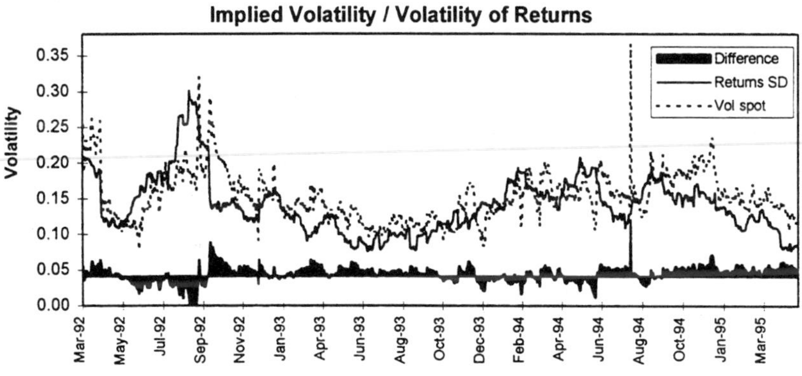

Figure 1 : Mispricing of Volatility on the FTSE

In this paper we do not forecast market volatility directly rather we forecast the volatility mispricing (market vol. - implied). We obtain exposure to volatility mispricing via Log contract portfolios (Neuberger, 1994) described in section 2. The Log contract portfolio offers a very efficient mechanism for taking an outright position on volatility. The decision to buy or sell volatility depends on whether implied volatility is over or under- priced. By predicting the mispricing rather than the actual volatility we focus on estimating only the relevant dynamics (i.e. the market inefficiencies). Using a Log contract trading rule as a performance metric to evaluate volatility forecasts has several advantages. Firstly, there is no need to delta hedge the trading strategy as would be needed for a single option strategy. Secondly, the Log contract would be relatively insensitive to dividend payoffs. Furthermore, the Log contract can be viewed as the average of many straddles, so the performance results are not sensitive to the specific choice of straddle. Also, because the Log contract payoff is quadratic, the total profits are sensitive to the accuracy of the predictions.

2 The Log contract Portfolio

The Log contract portfolio described by A. Neuberger consists of two positions, long 1 Log contract and short 1% forward contract. The Log contract is especially designed so that its payoff is related to the difference between market volatility and implied volatility. The contract is not exchange traded. However, it may be purchased O.T.C. The price of a Log contract, for which the pay off at time t is Log(S_t), is defined as,

$$\text{Price}_{\text{log-c}} = \ln(S_0) + R_g t - 1/2\,\sigma_{isd}^2 t \quad , \tag{1}$$

where S_0 in (1) is the current spot price, t is the length of the Log contract, R_g is the adjusted interest rate (= interest rate - dividend yield), and σ_{isd}^2 is the implied market volatility. Defining r_s, as the percentage return of the underlying spot, then $S_t = S_0(1+r_s)$. The return of the Log contract at time t in the future is defined,

$$\begin{aligned} \text{Return}_{\text{log-c}} &= \ln(S_0(1+r_s)) - (\ln(S_0) + R_g t - 1/2\,\sigma_{isd}^2 t) \\ &= \ln(1+r_s) - R_g t + 1/2\,\sigma_{isd}^2 t \\ &= (r_s - 1/2\,r_s^2 + O(r_s^n)) - R_g t + 1/2\,\sigma_{isd}^2 t \end{aligned} \tag{2}$$

To construct the Log contract portfolio we need to hedge the Log contract with 1% of a forward contract. The price of a forward contract is, $\text{Price}_{\text{Foward}} = S_0 e^{R_g t}$. The forward contracts return at time t, is defined as,

$$\begin{aligned} \text{Return}_{\text{Forward}} &= S_0 = (1 + r_s) - S_0 e^{R_g t} \\ &= S_0(1 + r_s) - S_0(1 + R_g t + O((R_g t)^n)) \\ &= S_0(r_s - R_g t) \end{aligned} \tag{3}$$

Buying a single Log contract and selling 1% of a forward contract enables us to construct a payoff which is immunized against the level of the underlying spot. The portfolio only has exposure to the difference in the actual volatility ($\sigma_m^2 = r_s^2/t$) and the implied volatility (σ_{isd}^2).

$$\begin{aligned} \text{Difference } &= (r_s - 1/2\, r_s^2 - R_g t + 1/2\,\sigma_{isd}^2 t) - \frac{1}{S_0}\left(S_0(r_s - R_g t)\right) \\ &= 1/2(\sigma_{isd}^2 - \sigma_m^2)t \end{aligned} \tag{4}$$

If the volatility is expected to be higher than the implied volatility, then we sell one unit of a Log contract and buy 1% of a forward contract. If the volatility is expected to be lower than the implied volatility, then we buy one unit of a Log contract and sell 1% of a forward contract. The payoff from the Log contract is a quadratic saddle, where the profit at the strike price (S_0) is proportional to the level of implied market volatility.

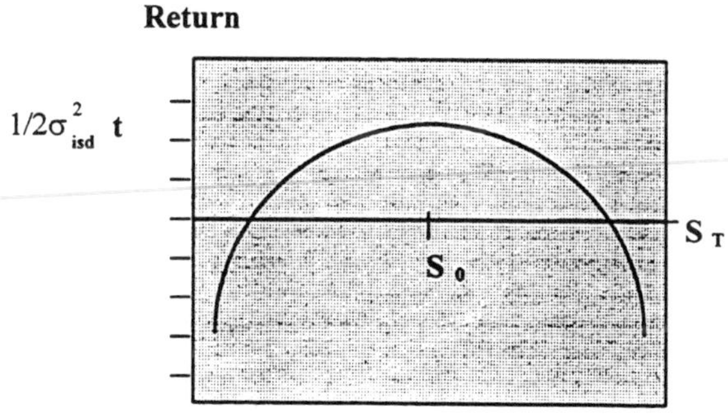

Figure 2 Log contract Pay Off

Similar exposure to volatility mispricing can be obtained by buying or selling delta hedged options. However delta hedging is expensive to implement and it also incurs exposure to other sources of risk. Figure 3 shows the weekly returns of the volatility portfolio on the major European stock indices.

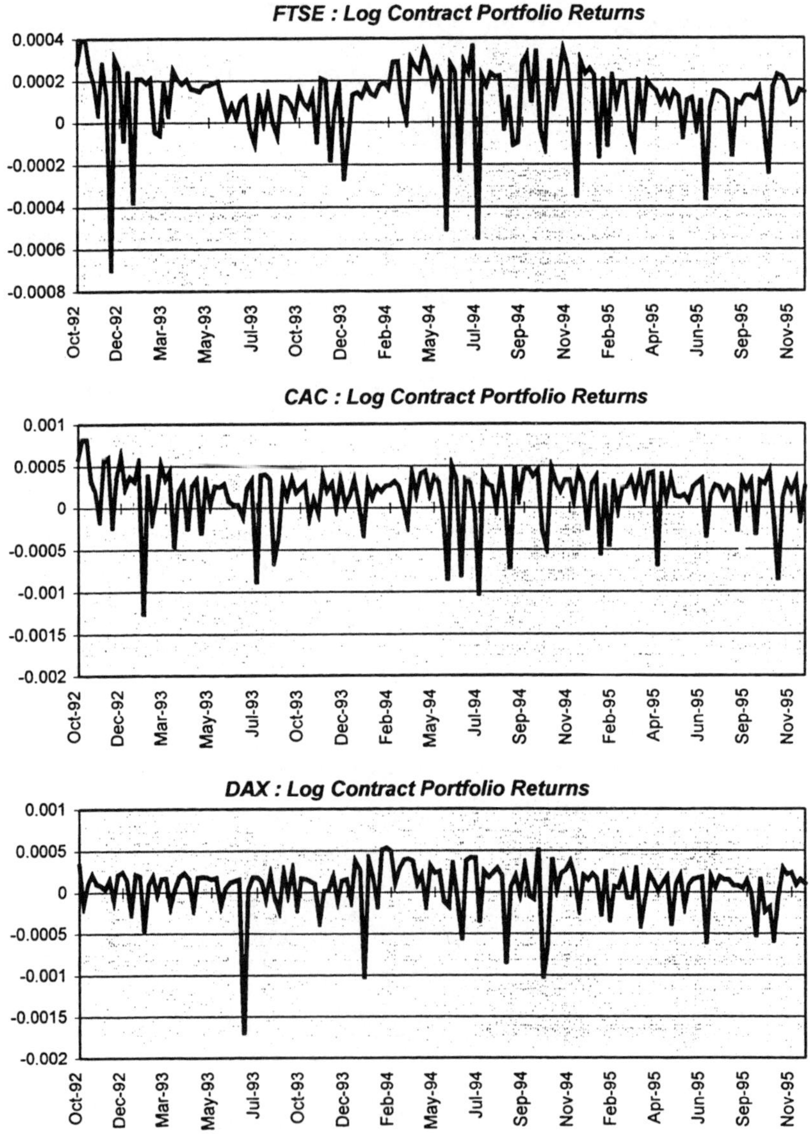

Figure 3 Log contract / Forward contract Returns

It is clear by inspection that for all markets implied volatility is usually slightly higher than actual. So on average the markets make a slight profit from over pricing (insurance risk premium). However, the portfolios incur occasional large losses during adverse market conditions. The prediction of this series would allow us to buy and sell volatility profitably. Note that the upside pay off does not have a constant level (as in a saddle), rather the pay off of this portfolio is directly related to the level of implied volatility.

3 Data

The data required to produce the Log contract / forward contract portfolio included, the implied volatilities, spot prices, and the adjusted growth rate. Data was available for the major European Markets (FTSE, DAX, CAC) from Jan. 92 - Jan. 96. In addition to the monthly implied volatilities the volatility term structures were also available.

Foreign & Colonial	Indices	Options	Term Structure (Months)			
	CAC	C&P	1	3	6	12
	DAX	C&P	1	3	6	12
	FTSE 100	C&P	1	3	6	12

Table 1: Implied Volatilities

Observation noise can be clearly identified when financial data from different data suppliers are compared. Implied volatilities were examined from two sources, Foreign and Colonial and Liffe exchange. The overall trends in the data set are the same. However, over a shorter time horizon the differences can be significant. In addition the contamination level of the two series are also different. By conducting a comparison of the two series several spurious outliers were identified and removed.

4 Models

Two sets of models were estimated, volatility mispricing models for each stock index (r_{FTSE}, r_{CAC}, r_{DAX}), and relative volatility mispricing models for each pair of indices (r_{FTSE} - r_{CAC}, r_{FTSE} - r_{DAX}, r_{DAX} - r_{CAC}.). Three sets of explanatory variables were investigated for each return series.

(i) Auto-regression models on the return series:

$$\hat{r}_t = f(r_{DAX_t},\ldots,r_{DAX_{t-n}},r_{FTSE_t},\ldots,r_{FTSE_{t-n}},r_{CAC_t},\ldots,r_{CAC_{t-n}}) \quad (5)$$

It is well documented that volatility has some auto-regressive structure. The first set of models investigates whether this predictive property is also found in the returns of the option strategy. The model's predictions utilize the lagged returns from each of the European index portfolios.

(ii) International volatility term structure regression:

$$\begin{aligned}\hat{r}_t = f(&\Delta V^{1M}_{DAX_t},\Delta V^{3M}_{DAX_t},\Delta V^{6M}_{DAX_t},\Delta V^{12M}_{DAX_t},\ldots\\ &\Delta V^{1M}_{CAC_t},\Delta V^{3M}_{CAC_t},\Delta V^{6M}_{CAC_t},\Delta V^{12M}_{CAC_t},\\ &V^{3M}_{DAX_t}/V^{1M}_{DAX_t},V^{6M}_{DAX_t}/V^{1M}_{DAX_t},V^{12M}_{DAX_t}/V^{1M}_{DAX_t},\ldots\\ &V^{3M}_{CAC_t}/V^{1M}_{CAC_t},V^{6M}_{CAC_t}/V^{1M}_{CAC_t},V^{12M}_{CAC_t}/V^{1M}_{CAC_t})\end{aligned} \quad (6)$$

The term structure of implied volatility represents the markets opinion / expectation of the future values of market volatility. The second set of models investigate the predictive power of the change in volatility term structure and the relative level of volatility term structure for each of the European indices.

(iii) Combined auto-regression and term structure model.

$$\begin{aligned}\hat{r}_t = f(&r_{DAX_t},\ldots,r_{DAX_{t-n}},r_{FTSE_t},\ldots,r_{FTSE_{t-n}},r_{CAC_t},\ldots,r_{CAC_{t-n}},\\ &\Delta V^{1M}_{DAX_t},\Delta V^{3M}_{DAX_t},\Delta V^{6M}_{DAX_t},\Delta V^{12M}_{DAX_t},\ldots\\ &\Delta V^{1M}_{CAC_t},\Delta V^{3M}_{CAC_t},\Delta V^{6M}_{CAC_t},\Delta V^{12M}_{CAC_t},\\ &V^{3M}_{DAX_t}/V^{1M}_{DAX_t},V^{6M}_{DAX_t}/V^{1M}_{DAX_t},V^{12M}_{DAX_t}/V^{1M}_{DAX_t},\ldots\\ &V^{3M}_{CAC_t}/V^{1M}_{CAC_t},V^{6M}_{CAC_t}/V^{1M}_{CAC_t},V^{12M}_{CAC_t}/V^{1M}_{CAC_t})\end{aligned} \quad (7)$$

The final set of models combines the auto-regression and the exogenous variables of the volatility term structure to capture overall explanatory power of the two sets of variables.

Where $\hat{r}_t$ is the return the portfolio at time t (either the return from of the mispricing portfolio or of a relative mispricing portfolio), $\Delta\nabla^1_{DAXt}$ denotes the change at time t in the 1 month implied volatilities of the DAX index. The relationship , f, is modeled by both linear regression and neural network algorithms. The linear regression imposes a strict parametric form on the functional relationship. Neural networks relax the parametric restriction and determine the functional relationship from the data.

5 Results

The results shown in this section are only for the relative volatility mispricing models. The complete set of results for both mispricing models and relative mispricing models can be found in Bolland and Burgess 1996. The data set was split into an estimation set (Oct. 92 - Oct. 94) and an out of sample test set (Oct. 94 - Dec. 95). A subset of the estimation set was used to validate the parameter estimation. A prediction horizon of one week was examined. The models were compared using three performance metrics (correlation, percent of correct in direction (POCID), and the cumulative return of a simple trading strategy). The performance of the auto-regression models, term structure models (TSM) and the combined models are shown Table 2, Table 3 and Table 4.

FTSE CAC	Estimation Set			Out of Sample		
	Correl	POCID	Profit	Correl	POCID	Profit
Linear AR Model	0.432	0.695	37.2%	0.122	0.516	20.5%
Non-linear AR Model	0.459	0.711	42.7%	0.143	0.526	20.2%
Linear TSM	0.426	0.688	47.7%	0.059	0.500	4.5%
Non-linear TSM	0.448	0.723	51.4%	0.132	0.554	4.2%
Linear AR TSM	0.422	0.679	37.7%	0.178	0.536	31.0%
Non-linear AR TSM	0.528	0.670	45.9%	0.112	0.536	29.3%

Table 2 : *FTSE CAC* Modeling Results

FTSE DAX	Estimation Set			Out of Sample		
	Correl	POCID	Profit	Correl	POCID	Profit
Linear AR Model	0.354	0.552	45.8%	0.321	0.543	50.5%
Non-linear AR Model	0.409	0.561	46.7%	0.345	0.536	56.2%
Linear TSM	0.388	0.571	48.3%	0.393	0.538	70.5%
Non-linear TSM	0.468	0.634	70.9%	0.425	0.558	71.4%
Linear AR TSM	0.418	0.616	57.5%	0.367	0.577	74.5%
Non-linear AR TSM	0.477	0.634	61.7%	0.465	0.558	79.2%

Table 3 : *FTSE DAX* Modeling Results

DAX CAC	Estimation Set			Out of Sample		
	Correl	POCID	Profit	Correl	POCID	Profit
Linear AR	0.320	0.552	30.2%	-0.012	0.471	10.5%
Non-linear AR	0.401	0.611	36.7%	0.025	0.506	15.2%
Linear TSM	0.416	0.625	41.6%	0.039	0.518	21.5%
Non-linear TSM	0.440	0.652	55.7%	0.053	0.518	19.7%
Linear AR TSM	0.429	0.634	52.6%	0.089	0.536	37.6%
Non-linear AR TSM	0.490	0.679	67.4%	0.079	0.571	52.1%

Table 4 : *DAX CAC* Modeling Results

On the whole all models show reasonable performance, with the combined non-linear model generally being superior. The results appear consistent across the different markets. The simple trading strategy indicate positive results. It should be noted that the profit and loss analysis does not include any transaction costs.

Figure 4 and Figure 5 show the in sample and out of sample equity curves for a non-linear auto regression term structure model of the relative *FTSE DAX* volatility mispricing. Based on the models predictions the trading strategy chooses to buy volatility in the market which is forecast to be most over priced.

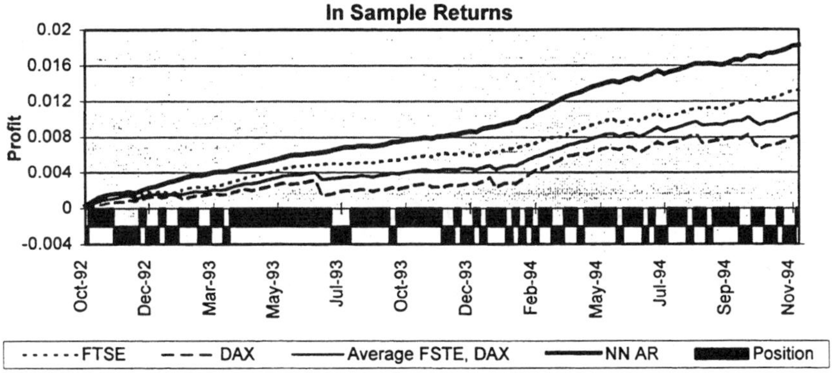

Figure 4 : In Sample P & L for *FSTE DAX* Portfolio Model

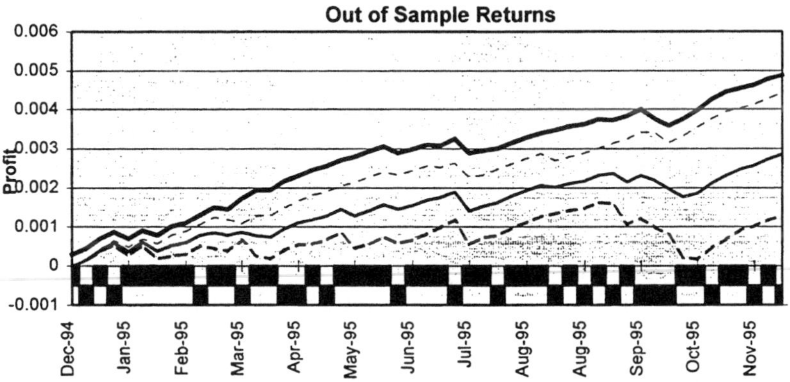

Figure 5 : Out of Sample P & L for *FSTE DAX* Portfolio Model

The model produces consistent profits both in and of sample with no major draw downs. The performance of the strategy is compared to a simple buy and hold strategy (dotted lines) and a naïve portfolio holding 50% of each market (thin solid lines). The model's predictions allow the portfolio to switch between the two indices, out performing the simple strategies both in and out of sample.

6 Conclusions

The overall goal of the analysis was to produce a statistical model of volatility that would form the basis of a profitable trading strategy. The profitability of the strategy being the crucial performance criterion for the volatility predictor. The methodology we propose focuses on predicting the volatility mispricing as opposed to forecasting the actual market volatility. The Log contract portfolio provides an ideal mechanism for gaining exposure to volatility mispricing.

Our results demonstrate that the returns of the Log contract portfolio have predictable time series dynamics. In addition, the markets expectations of the future volatility (the volatility term structure) also has explanatory power. When the both sets of explanatory variables are combined in one model, consistent stable profits can be made on all the major European indices.

7 References

Bolland, P. J. and Burgess, A. N., 1996, *Multivariate Forecasts of Volatility Mispricing*, Working Paper, London Business School.

Canina, L., and Figlewski, S., 1993, *The Information Content of Implied Volatility,* Review of Financial Studies, **6**, 3, 659-681.

Harvey, C., R., and Whaley, R., E., 1992, *Marker Volatility Prediction and the Efficiency of the S&P 100 Index Options Market*. Journal of Financial Economics, **31**, 43-73.

Henon R., C., and Kat, H., M., 1994, *Volatility Prediction: A Comparison of the Stochastic Volatility, GARCH(1,1), And EGARCH(1,1) Models.* Journal of Derivatives, Winter, 50-65.

Neuberger A., 1994, *The Log Contract: A New Instrument to Hedge Volatility*. Journal of Portfolio Management, Winter, 74-80.

Noh, J., Engle, R., F., and Kane, A., 1994, *Forecasting Volatility and Option Prices of S&P 500 Index*. Journal of Derivatives, Fall, 17-30.

Schmalensee, R., and Trippi, R., R., 1978, *Common Stock Volatility Expectations Implied By Option Prices*. Journal of Finance, **33**, 129-147.

INTRADAY MODELLING OF THE TERM STRUCTURE OF INTEREST RATES

J. T. CONNOR & P. J. BOLLAND
London Business School
Sussex Place, Regents Park
London NW1 4SA
Phone (+44) 71-262-5050
Fax (+44) 71-724-7875
E-Mail - jconnor@lbs.lon.ac.uk
E-Mail - pbolland@lbs.lon.ac.uk

P. LAJBCYGIER
Department Of Business Systems
Monash University, Clayton
Victoria, Australia 3168
Phone (+61) 3-9905-5801
Fax (+61) 3-9905-55159
E-Mail - PLAJBCYG@fcit-m1.fcit.monash.edu.au

The term structure of interest rates is composed of the most fundamental quantities which define the price of fixed income products. This work seeks to track movements of the term structure on a tick by tick basis. Each observed bond future will induce movements into the term structure, in order to obtain the most up to date estimate. Arbitrage relationships for fixed income models are incorporated into state space models, which leads to a state vector that is equivalent to the term structure of interest rates. Observed prices can be both linear an nonlinear functions of the term structure. We show how less frequently observed elements of the term structure can be inferred from the most heavily traded parts of the term structure. Results show how predictions of the present for less traded elements of the term structure can be modelled efficiently.

1 Introduction

Arbitrage relationships which price fixed income securities in terms of an underlying term structure of interest rates are well understood, see for example Fabozzi (1993). If a set of bonds spanning the entire term structure is observed simultaneously, the term structure is uniquely determined for that instant of time.

At the intraday time scale, rarely is more than a single bond or bond future observed at the same time. If a price is observed which is different from that derived from the estimated term structure, the term structure has moved. Since only one price is observed, at best only one element of the term structure is known. It is possible, even probable, that the rest of the term structure has also moved. The rest of the term structure must be estimated statistically. Despite the wide use of the term structure and the issues which arise at the intraday time scale, very little research has been done on intraday term structure modelling.

The methodology we propose is flexible enough to incorporate arbitrage relationships, dynamics of the term structure, correlation between different points on the term structure, erratic arrival of information, and price bond futures through the extended Kalman filter. Our model is demonstrated on the intraday term structure of Australian 90-day bank bills. Bank bill future transaction data (1993-1994) is used to model the Australian future rates out to 3 years. Modelling inter-relationships between different points on the term structure allows for us to update estimates of the whole curve upon the arrival of each new transaction price.

2 State Space Models for Term Structure

The term structure is put into a state-space model similar in form to that used in Bolland and Connor (1995) for foreign exchange modelling. The underlying states of the model describe the term structure. For the data used here, all future expiry dates and coupon payments fall on the same day at quarterly or semi-annual periods which allows the term structure to be described as a function of these dates alone. The state is given by the vector

$$\mathbf{s}_t = \{e^{-r_1\tau_1}, e^{-r_2\tau_2}, \cdots, e^{-r_n\tau_n}\} \tag{1}$$

where r_i denotes the forward rate between time t_{i+1} and t_i and τ_i is equal to the interval $t_{i+1} - t_i$. The state given by (1) has equivalent information to a term structure of interest rates. This particular state description was chosen for the ease of which it describes the bond bill future described in section 2. Alternative choices of states such as spot rates, forward rates, and zero coupon bonds have equivalent information and are discussed at fuller length in a longer version of this abstract.

The observations of the state space model are the prices of bond or bill futures, $p_{i,t}$, at time t

$$p_{i,t} = h_i(\mathbf{s}_t) + v_t \tag{2}$$

where $h_i()$ is the function which links the price of security i to the underlying term structure described by $\mathbf{s}_t$. For simple bill futures where the price is given by $e^{-r_i\tau_i}$ equation (2) reduces to a linear model,

$$h(s_t) = [\mathbf{0}_{1\times(i-1)}, 1, \mathbf{0}_{1\times(N-i-1)}]\mathbf{s}_t \tag{3}$$

where the position of the 1 depends on the expiry of the particular future. More complex bond futures with multiple coupons have a price of the form $\sum_{i=k}^{k+N} C_i \prod_{j=k}^{i} e^{-r_j \tau_j}$ which is a nonlinear function of the states denoted by $h(\mathbf{s}_t)$.

Additive noise is denoted by v_t in (2) and represents distortions between the observed price and the true price. There are several sources of observation noise encountered when modelling high frequency financial data. When modelling transaction data, the observations are of both bid and offer prices. The bid-ask spread influences the dynamics of the time series. Roll (1984), showed that bid-ask bounce induced strong negative auto-correlation into financial data, an effect empirically observed in many studies (Fama 1965). When no new information arrives the true value remains constant, however, any observed variation is caused by the difference in bid and ask price. Bouncing between bid and ask prices gives rise to a strong negative auto-correlation shown in figure 1.

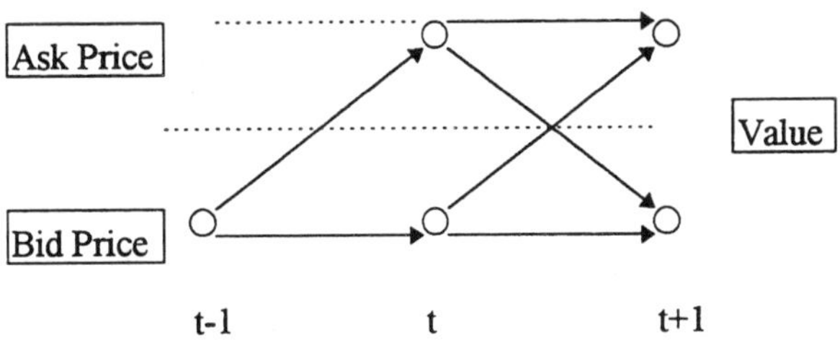

Figure 1: Bid-Ask Bounce

A second source of observation noise is price quantisation. Futures prices on bills and bond are only quoted to certain degree of accuracy (Australian 90-banks bills yield is quoted in multiples of 0.01%, three year bonds 0.005%, ten year bonds 0.01%). Limiting the accuracy of price quotation induces structure into the time series of prices (Harris 1990). Similar to the effect of the Bid-Ask bounce, the price quantisation induces auto-correlation and increases return variance. Gottlieb and Kalay found that the influence of this quantisation was greatest at small time intervals and low yield. In order to model transaction data these artifacts have to be incorporated. In the Kalman filter framework these effects can be modelled as observation noise and incorporated into the observation noise covariance matrices. The level of observation noise in transaction data is significantly less then found in quote data (Bolland and Connor (1996)).

The dynamics of the term structure can be described as a linear system

$$\mathbf{s}_t = \Phi \mathbf{s}_{t-1} + \mathbf{e}_t \tag{4}$$

where $\mathbf{e}_t$ describes the random innovations in the states and Φ gives a predicted state $\hat{\mathbf{s}}_t$ based on $\mathbf{s}_{t-1}$. For the simples case, the dynamics can be described as a random walk model where Φ would be the identity matrix. Vasciek (1977) incorporates mean reversion into term structure models which can also be incorporated into equation (4) with the appropriate choice of Φ. The covariance of $\mathbf{e}_t$ is an important part of the system because most of the rates tend to move together. Proper modelling of the covariance structure leads to accurate predictions of infrequently observed futures even when a random walk model is assumed as shown in section 3. It is possible to generalise equation (4) to be nonlinear as done in Bolland and Connor (1995).

The term structure is estimated from the observed bill future prices by a linear Kalman filter operating on the system described by (2), (3) and (4). The Kalman filter is used because it is the optimal predictor for the linear system described by (2), (3) and (4) excited by Gaussian noise. For the case of bond futures, an **extended Kalman filter** is used on the nonlinear system described by (2) and (4). Details on the EKF are given in the longer version of this paper.

3. Australian Future Data

In this study, intraday Australian 90-day bank bill, three year and ten year bond futures, for January 1995 and December 1994, are used to estimate an intraday model of the Australian future rates.

A bank bill is a discount security issued by a bank representing a promise to pay the full face value of the bill at maturity. The 90 day bank bill futures market was launched in 1979. It was the first fixed interest future launched outside the United States and is similar to the CME's Eurodollar contract and LIFFE's 3 month Sterling contract. It is Australia's most liquid fixed interest derivative instrument with a daily average volume of 43,037 contracts representing a turnover of five times the underlying cash market of $3 billion AUD. It has become one of the world's most liquid short term interest rate products. The bank bills futures expire each quarter : in March, June, September and December; up to 3 years ahead.

Commonwealth Treasury bonds are fixed interest securities issued by the Federal government of Australia. They are issued with a fixed term to maturity and pay a fixed coupon each half year until the bond matures. The ten year and three year bond futures were launched in 1984 and 1988 respectively. The average daily volume for the ten year and three year bond futures is 25,340 and 39,990 contracts respectively. These Australian futures contracts are similar to the CBOT's US Treasury Bonds and LIFFE's Gilt contracts. Each year, bank bill futures expire quarterly - in March, June, September and December; up to half a year ahead.

The SFE is an open out-cry double auction market. The intraday futures data represents every transaction which occurred on the floor of the Sydney futures Exchange (SFE) in the Bank bill, the three year and the ten year pits. Each transaction is communicated from the pit via pit supervisors and is time stamped to the second. The fixed instrument futures transactions are quoted in yield (not price) and include the volume per transaction.

4. Results

Trades in Australian bill futures are dominated by the first two bill futures which are typically traded more than all other bill futures combined. Often, the first two bill futures are undergoing considerable movement while none of the other bill futures are being observed. A good model of the term structure will result in accurate predictions of bill futures even after long periods in which they are not observed.

An example of improved prediction performance for longer term bill futures is shown in Fig. 2. The first and second expiring futures are frequently traded and their prices are fairly well determined. The underlying future prices are estimated for each future and are displayed as lines in Fig. 2. The futures with longer term expiry dates have relatively few data points. The correlation's between the traded futures and the unobserved futures enable the Kalman filter to predict most of the resulting price shifts on the less frequently observed futures.

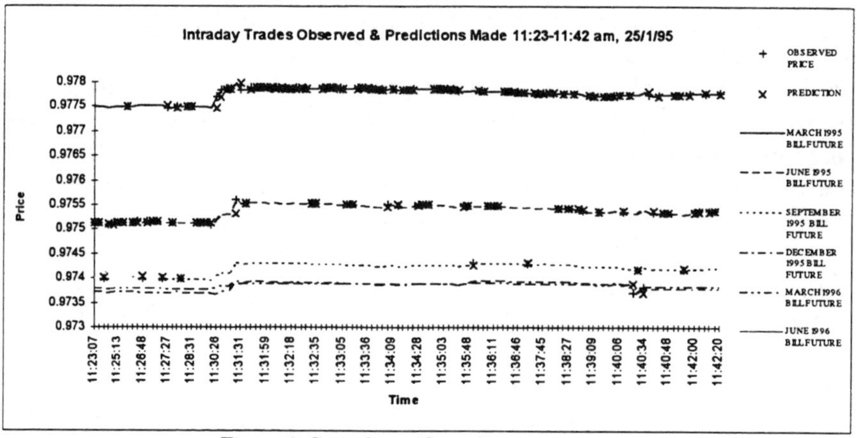

Figure 2: Snapshot of Intraday term structure

The Kalman filter estimates of the future rates are compared with a naive predictor. The naive predictions are simply based on the last observed price of each of the individual bill futures. Table 1 and 2 show the in- and out of sample mean squared error performance of the two models. Tables 1 and 2 have different expiry dates because the in-sample data occurs after the Dec. 1994 future expiry date. The prediction performance of the Kalman filter is often twice as good as a naive predictor for bill futures with the longer expiry dates on both in- and out of sample data. Note that a considerable amount of data is used to compute the following tables, ranging from 7291 data points for the March 1995 expiry date to 290 data points for June 1996 expiry date on the in-sample data, the amount of data for out of sample testing ranges from 3363 to 450.

	March 1995	June 1995	Sept. 1995	Dec. 1995	March 1996	June 1996
Kalman STD	1.43	1.35	1.88	2.33	3.59	3.20
Naive STD	1.39	1.82	3.26	3.55	6.22	6.65

Table 1: Standard Deviation of prediction error for a 1 A$ Australian 3 month bill future given in terms of .00001A$ for various expiry dates on insample data for the month of January 1995.

	Dec. 1994	March 1995	June 1995	Sept. 1995	Dec. 1995	March 1996
Kalman STD	1.511	2.046	3.884	2.280	3.154	2.918
Naive STD	1.962	2.590	4.757	5.423	5.835	6.705

Table 2: Standard Deviation of prediction error for a 1 A$ Australian 3 month bill future given in terms of .00001A$ for various expiry dates on out of sample data for the month of November 1995.

	March 1995	June 1995	Sept. 1995	Dec. 1995	March 1996	June 1996
Kalman STD	1.1098	1.576	1.674	2.420	1.517	2.569
Naive STD	1.1107	1.527	1.554	2.393	1.375	2.286

Table 3: Standard Deviation of prediction error for a March 1995 1 A$ Australian 3 month bill future given in terms of .00001A$ as a function of the most recently observed future expiry dates for insample data during the month of January 1995.

	Dec. 1994	March 1995	June 1995	Sept. 1995	Dec. 1995	March 1996
Kalman STD	0.746	1.946	1.719	1.745	1.357	2.427
Naive STD	0.747	2.384	3.423	1.638	1.238	2.228

Table 4: Standard Deviation of prediction error for a March 1995 1 A$ Australian 3 month bill future given in terms of .00001A$ as a function of the most recently observed future expiry dates for out of sample data *for the month of November 1994.*

The Kalman filter out performs the naive predictor on all futures except the future closest to expiry (the most heavily traded contract). The quality of the prediction depends upon which future was previously observed. The prediction error for the future closest to expiry can be broken down into several components. Each of the components correspond to the previously traded future and are shown in table 3 and 4 for both in and out of sample. The Kalman filter prediction does better when the preceding price observation also has a March 1995 expiry date on in-sample data. If the preceding price observation has a longer expiry date, the naive prediction does better on in-sample data. This trend is observed on out of sample data where the Kalman filter predictor does better than the naive predictor when the first future is preceded by futures closer to the present. This leads us to believe that correlation's of longer term future should not influence the shortest future date. The first future expiry drives the market.

5 References

Bolland, P. J. and Connor, J. T. " A Robust Nonlinear Multivariate Kalman Filter for Arbitrage Identification in High Frequency Data", *Proceedings of Neural Networks in the Capital Markets,* 1996, World Scientific.

Burgess, A. N. "Statistical Yield Curve Arbitrage in Eurodollar Futures using Neural Networks", *Proceedings of Neural Networks in the Capital Markets*, 1996, World Scientific.

Fabozzi, F. "Bond Markets Analysis and Strategies", Second Edition, Prentice Hall International Editions, 1993.

Fama, E. F., "The Behaviour of Stock Market Prices", *Journal of Business*, Vol. 38, pp 34-105, Jan 1965.

Gottlieb, G., and Kalay, A., "Implications of the Discreteness of Observed Stock Prices", Journal of Finance, Vol. XL, 1, pp 135-153, March 1985.

Harris, L., "Estimation of Stock Price Variance and Serial Covariance's from Discrete Observations", Journal of Financial and Quantitative Analysis, Vol. 25, 3, pp 291-306, 1990.

Roll, R. "A Simple Implicit Measure of the Effective Bid-Ask Spread in an Efficient Market", *Journal of Finance*, Vol. 39, pp 1127-1140, Sept. 1984.

Vasicek, O.A, "An Equilibrium Characterization of the Term Structure," *Journal of Finance*, 44, 1989, pp. 205-9.

APPLICATION OF STOCHASTIC DIFFERENTIAL GEOMETRY TO THE TERM STRUCTURE OF INTEREST RATES IN DEVELOPED MARKETS

YURI TARANENKO AND CHRIS BARNES

Los Alamos National Lab, XCM, MS-F645, Los Alamos, NM 87545, USA; email: yuri@lanl.gov

This paper deals with further developments of the new theory that applies stochastic differential geometry (SDG) to dynamics of interest rates. We examine mathematical constraints on the evolution of interest rate volatilities that arise from stochastic differential calculus under assumptions of an arbitrage free evolution of zero coupon bonds and developed markets (i. e., none of the party/factor can drive the whole market). The resulting new theory incorporates the Heath-Jarrow-Morton (HJM) model of interest rates and provides new equations for volatilities which makes the system of equations for interest rates and volatilities complete and self consistent. It results in much smaller amount of volatility data that should be guessed for the SDG model as compared to the HJM model. Limited analysis of the market volatility data suggests that the assumption of the developed market is violated around maturity of two years. Such maturities where the assumptions of the SDG model are violated are suggested to serve as boundaries at which volatilities should be specified independently from the model. Our numerical example with two boundaries (two years and five years) qualitatively resembles the market behavior. Under some conditions solutions of the SDG model become singular that may indicate market crashes. More detail comparison with the data is needed before the theory can be established or refuted.

1 Introduction

1.1 Dynamics of Forward Interest Rates in Heath-Jarrow-Morton Model

In the HJM model [*Heath, Jarrow, Morton*, 1992] forward interest rates $F(t,T)$ evolve according to

$$dF(t,T) = \sum_k \nu_k(t,T)\sigma_k(t,T)dt + \sum_k \sigma_k(t,T)dW^k \tag{1}$$

under the equivalent martingale probability measure. Where t is time at which one can contract for a loan at continuously compounded interest rate $F(t,T)$ starting at time T and maturing an instant later, dW^k are independent Brownian motions, $\sigma_k(t,T)$ are corresponding volatilities of forward rates,

$$\nu_k(t,T) = \int_t^T \sigma_k(t,u)du \tag{2}$$

are corresponding volatilities of pure discount bonds that are given by

$$P(t,T) = \exp\{-\int_t^T F(t,s)ds\} \tag{3}$$

Heath, Jarrow, Morton [1992] have shown that under a simple non-singularity condition on the volatility functions $\sigma_k(t,T)$

$$\int_0^T \sigma_k^2(t,T)dt < +\infty \quad a.e. \quad Q \tag{4}$$

the equivalent martingale measure (for the pure discount bonds) is unique that guarantees unique prices of contingent claims if one can solve equations (1) for forward rates $F(t,T)$. That brings us to the following question.

1.2 What is Needed to Solve HJM Equations?

First, we have to provide the initial term structure of interest rates $F(0,T)$ and the initial term structure of volatility $\sigma_k(0,T)$ for all $0 \leq T \leq T_{max}$ where T_{max} is maximum maturity we are interested in. Such information can be obtained from market observations. Then we have to make some *guess* about the future dynamics of volatility. We want to underline that only after making an additional assumption about dynamics of interest rate volatilities $\sigma_k(t,T)$ for $t > 0$ we can solve equations for forward rates and then derive prices of contingent claims.

For example, if we assume that there is only one Wiener process driving the yield curve and that its volatility is independent of time and maturity, that is

$$\sigma(t,T) = \sigma_o = const \tag{5}$$

then we can solve equations (1) for a particular case of first arbitrage free model introduced by *Ho and Lee* [1986]. Let us give another example suggested by *Heath, Jarrow, Morton* [1992]

$$\sigma_k(t,T) = \sigma_k^{ln}(T-t) \times \min(F(t,T), \lambda) \tag{6}$$

where $\sigma_k^{ln}(T-t)$ is a function of time left to maturity that is for forward rate of given maturity this function is constant and λ is a positive constant. For small interest rates $\sigma_k^{ln}(T-t)$ is close to lognormal volatility of interest rates. When we examined market data for normalized perturbations of forward interest rates, that is

$$\frac{F(t+\Delta t,T) - F(t,T)}{F(t,T)\sqrt{(\Delta t)}} \tag{7}$$

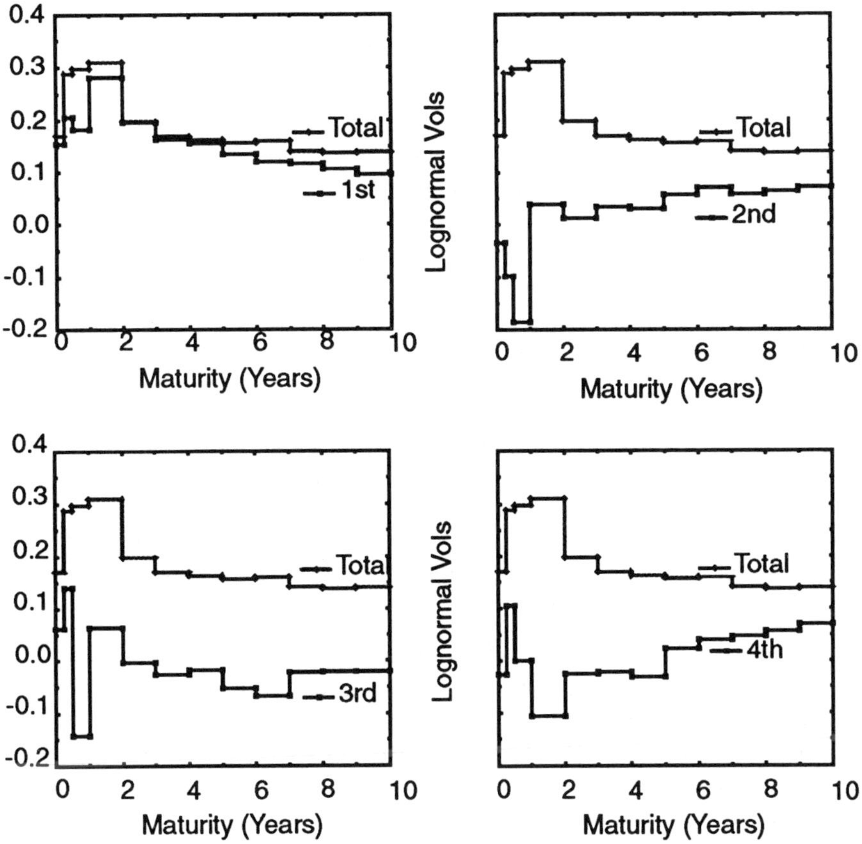

Figure 1: Principal components of lognormal volatilities.

we found that functions $\sigma_k^{ln}(T_{const})$ changes slowly with time showing normalized variations of up to 25 %-per-year. An example of principal components of lognormal volatilities of forward rates is shown in Figure (1).

1.3 How to Do Better on Volatilities?

The volatility assumption (6) discussed in the previous section is a good one to start with, but how can we do better than that? One of the ways to go is to use neural nets or other methods that predict future volatility variations without identifying driving forces for that or as an alternative for curious minds one can try to find fundamental principles that provide dynamic equations for volatility functions. In the rest of the paper we explore one of the latter possibilities.

2 Relating Stochastic Differential Geometry to Interest Rates

In this section we give qualitative introduction to stochastic differential geometry (SDG), show how we conform general SDG equations to the HJM model, and then discuss what is needed to solve them and what advantages they provide in comparison to HJM equations.

2.1 Qualitative Understanding of Stochastic Differential Geometry,

The goal of this section is to describe a Brownian motion on a curved manifold.

We consider an example of a two-dimensional manifold [*Makhankov et. al.*, 1995]. Let us consider a point X_1 on the surface and a patch of a tangential plane in this point, we denote it T_{X_1}. Then we proceed to a neighboring point X_2 and construct T_{X_2}. In such a way, we can cover the entire surface with such patches obtaining a polyhedron. Crucial points of this construction are: *i)* the surface is a manifold, *ii)* the covering is a Euclidean space. A Wiener process (a martingale)

$$dW^q dW^p = \delta^{qp} dt \tag{8}$$

is defined in a Euclidean space. This means that a Wiener process appears on the covering while a particle is moving on the surface. Now we should adjust both phenomena. Consider for that a surface with fluctuating forces (Wiener processes) and a particle in the point X_1 on the surface. This point also belongs to the covering T_{X_1}. Hence the particle undergoes a random shock

$$d\vec{X}_1 = \hat{\sigma}_1 d\vec{W}_1 \tag{9}$$

jumping to a point X_2 on the surface. In this new point it again undergoes a shock

$$d\vec{X}_2 = \hat{\sigma}_2 d\vec{W}_2 \tag{10}$$

and so forth. The matrix $\hat{\sigma}$ defines mobility of a particle. Here we should emphasize that all differentials considered in this section are of the Stratonovich's type, which allows us to use the standard differential calculus [*Gardiner*, 1994].

Now our task is to connect σ_1 and σ_2. Note for that that matrix $\hat{\sigma}$ being in fact a rotating operator, can be constructed of two vectors $\vec{j}_1$ and $\vec{j}_2$

$$\hat{\sigma} = \begin{pmatrix} j_1^x & j_2^x \\ j_1^y & j_2^y \end{pmatrix}$$

which gives a frame of reference for the patch considered. While moving from one patch to another, this frame changes its orientation. Let us recall that the total change of a vector, $\vec{B}$, due to moving from one point to another consists of two parts [*Dubrovin et. al.*, 1992]

$$\delta\vec{B} = d\vec{B} + \Gamma\vec{B}d\vec{X} \tag{11}$$

Where Γ is the connexion. The first term in (11) is the conventional differential

$$d\vec{B} = \frac{\partial\vec{B}}{\partial X^i}dX^i \tag{12}$$

and the second one allows for a change of the frame of reference. Since matrix $\hat{\sigma}$ is constructed of two vectors $\vec{j}_1$ and $\vec{j}_2$ it is transformed following the same rule,

$$\delta\hat{\sigma} = d\hat{\sigma} + \Gamma\hat{\sigma}d\vec{X} \tag{13}$$

Now we make an assumption of fair game or we also call it an assumption of developed markets, which means that none of a single party/factor can influence the whole market. In mathematical terms it means that the total change of $\hat{\sigma}$ should be zero

$$\delta\hat{\sigma} = 0 \tag{14}$$

that results in

$$d\hat{\sigma} = -\Gamma\hat{\sigma}d\vec{X} \tag{15}$$

what along with the equation for the elementary shock

$$d\vec{X} = \hat{\sigma}d\vec{W} \tag{16}$$

gives us the equations of *Stochastic Differential Geometry* on a curved manifold.

2.2 Fitting SDG Equations to HJM Model, [Makhankov et. al., 1995]

To have SDG equations that describe evolution of the interest rates and their volatilities we have to find the connexion Γ that satisfies the arbitrage free model (1) of interest rates. For the purpose of comparing SDG equations with HJM equations for forward interest rates we have to write them in the same form of stochastic differentials. We chose to write SDG equations in the Ito representation that will make them compatible with HJM equations that are given in the Ito form (1). Assuming that the phase space is a Riemannian manifold, the inverse of the Riemannian metric is given by

$$g^{ij} = \sum_q \sigma_q^i \sigma_q^j, \; g_{ij} g^{jk} = \delta_i^k \tag{17}$$

So the Ito form of equations (16) written in a component form is

$$d_I X^i = -\frac{1}{2} \sum_{kj} \Gamma^i_{kj} g^{kj} dt + \sum_q \hat{\sigma}_q^i dW^q \tag{18}$$

Where $d_I X^i$ indicates Ito differentials. Whereas if we go from continuous maturity in HJM equations (1) to finite maturity then they become

$$dF^i = \sum_k \nu_k^i \sigma_k^i dt + \sum_k \sigma_k^i dW^k \tag{19}$$

with index $i = 1, N_m$ where N_m is the number of maturities. If we match volatilities and drifts in both equations then

$$\Gamma^i_{kj} = -\frac{2}{N_m} g_{kj} \sum_q \nu_q^i \sigma_q^i \tag{20}$$

Substituting this expression for Γ^i_{kj} into equation (15) we get equations for volatilities

$$d_S \sigma_j^i = 2\nu_j^i \sum_k \sigma_k^i dW^k \tag{21}$$

where sub-index S underlines that equations are written for Stratonovich differentials. Equations for forward rates are

$$d_S F^i = \sum_k \sigma_k^i dW^k \tag{22}$$

Same equations written in Ito differentials are:

$$d_I F^i = \sum_k \nu_k^i \sigma_k^i dt + \sum_k \sigma_k^i dW^k \tag{23}$$

$$d_I\sigma_j^i = 2\sum_k \sigma_k^i(\nu_j^i\nu_k^i + \sum_{l\leq i}\sigma_k^l\Delta T_l\nu_j^l)dt + 2\nu_j^i\sum_k \sigma_k^i dW^k \tag{24}$$

where $\nu_j^i(t)$ are

$$\nu_j^i(t) = \sum_{k=1}^{i}\sigma_j^k\Delta T_k + \nu_j^0(t) \tag{25}$$

and ΔT_k is the time interval between maturities for $k > 1$ and $T_1 - t$ for $k = 1$.

Equations (21), (22) is Stratonovich form of SDG equations conformed to the HJM model of interest rates, Ito form of SDG equations for the interest rates and volatilities is given by (21), (22).

2.3 What is Needed to Solve SDG Equations?

Before we give answer to the above question let us quickly examine our set of equations. We note that a set of equations for forward interest rates (23) is exactly the same as in the HJM model (1) which makes the SDG model arbitrage free. In addition to the rate equations the SDG model provides a set of equations (24) for volatilities. This extra set of equations restricts possibilities of volatility changes and consequently guarantees that we have to provide smaller amount of extra information to solve for forward rates and volatilities. In terms of *initial conditions* for interest rates and volatilities the SDG model has the same requirements as the HJM model, i.e. $F^i(0)$ and $\sigma_j^i(0)$ are needed. If we assume that the whole yield curve satisfies the developed market condition (i.e., the fair game assumption (14)) and conforms to the SDG model then we do not need anything else to predict volatility and interest rate dynamics for time range up to T_{max} (i.e., the maximum maturity range for which initial conditions were specified). Here we see an advantage of the SDG model as compared to the HJM model as the latter requires additional assumptions (see section (1.2) for more details) about the volatility dynamics before it can solve for interest rates.

On the other hand, the assumption of developed markets may be not satisfied around some particular maturities. If the whole yield curve conforms to the SDG model then on average the dependence of volatilities versus maturity would be given by a smooth curve. However, our analysis of market data indicates a persistent perturbation in volatility functions around the two year term. Such a perturbation is clearly seen in all important principal components shown in Figure (1). We *guess* that such anomaly may be due to high demand for two year borrowing on the part of some strong party (e.g., US government) that drives the whole market. So, what it means for the SDG model? We have to identify maturities around which the SDG model may not hold true and treat volatility and/or interest rate values at those maturities as *boundary conditions* when solving SDG equations (23), (24). Again, if we compare this case to the HJM model we see the advantage of the SDG model. The SDG model needs inputs of volatilites $\sigma_k(t, T-t = T_{fixed})$ for very few maturities (e.g., T_{fixed} equal to two years, seven years, and ten years) and then it solves for all other interim maturities whereas the HJM model requires input of future dynamics of all volatilities, e.g., T_{fixed} has to cover zero to ten years with a step equal to one quarter.

3 Solutions of SDG Model

General equations for forward interest rate volatilities (24) are nonlinear and indicate interconnection of volatility functions of different principal components and maturities $\sigma_k^i(t)$. So in general there is little hope for solving such equations analytically and most of the information is expected to be obtained through numerical solutions.

3.1 Analytical Solution for Volatilities in Case of Single Factor Model

Even if it is difficult to find analytical solutions of SDG equations (24) in the general case it turns out that we can find solutions for a case when the interest rates are driven by a single Wiener process [*Makhankov et. al.*, 1995]. In this particular case the volatility equations can be represented as

$$d_S\sigma^i = 2(\nu^{i-1} + \sigma^i \Delta T_i)\sigma^i dW \tag{26}$$

that gives a chain type solution for σ^i

$$\sigma^i(t) = \frac{\sigma^i(0)\exp[2\int_0^t dw_\tau \nu^{i-1}(\tau)]}{1 - 2\sigma^i(0)\int_0^t dw_\tau \Delta T_i \exp[2\int_0^\tau dw_x \nu^{i-1}(x)]} \tag{27}$$

It is seen from the denominator of this expression that the solution may become singular. At the same time, under different initial and boundary conditions the solution may be regular. More investigation is necessary before we can make definite conclusions about the nature of solutions of SDG equations (23), (24).

3.2 Numerical Solution For Constant Boundary Conditions

As it was noted in section (1.2) lognormal volatilities of forward interest rates demonstrate quasi steady behavior. In our following example we concentrate on finding a steady state solution of the SDG equations that might resemble such

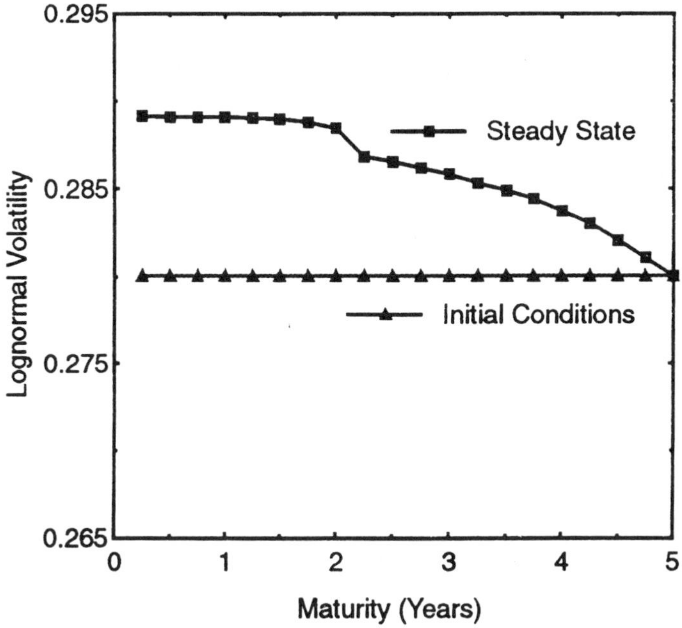

Figure 2: Initial volatility structure and the steady state solution.

market behavior. For this purpose we solve SDG equations (24) numerically with the following assumptions: we use a single factor model, the initial term structure of volatility is flat (see Figure (2)), we introduce two "boundaries" (at two years and five years) at which volatilities are kept constant. In Figure (2) we show the initial term structure of lognormal volatility that is flat at 0.28 (i.e., 28 %-per-year) and the steady state that is established after a transition period. The steady state curve is expected value of volatilities obtained from Monte Carlo modeling of equations (24). Comparison of the steady state curve with a typical term structure of volatilites from the market shows qualitative agreement of two curves.

4 Conclusions

We examine mathematical constraints on the evolution of interest rate volatilities that arise from stochastic differential calculus under assumptions of an arbitrage free evolution of zero coupon bonds and developed markets/fair game (i. e., none of the party/factor can drive the whole market). The resulting new theory incorporates the HJM model of interest rates and provides new equations for volatilities which makes the system of equations for interest rates and volatilities complete and self consistent. It results in much smaller amount of volatility data that should be guessed for the SDG model as compared to the HJM model. Limited analysis of the volatility data suggests that the assumption of the developed market is violated around maturity of two years. Such maturities where the assumptions of the model are violated are suggested to serve as boundaries at which volatilities should be specified independently from the SDG model. Our numerical example with two boundaries (two years and five years) qualitatively resembles the market behavior. Under some conditions solutions of the SDG model become singular that may indicate market crashes. The present analysis does not allow us to make strong statements about validity of the theory. More detail comparison with the data is needed before the theory can be established or refuted. Especially valuable should be comparisons for dynamic situations in the market with high volatility and market crashes.

References

[1] Dubrovin, B. A., A. T. Fomenko, S. P. Novikov, *Modern Geometry – Methods and Applications*, Springer-Verlag, 1992.

[2] Gardiner, C. W., *Handbook of Stochastic Methods in Physics*, Springer, Heidelberg, 1994.

[3] Heath, D., R. Jarrow, A. Morton, Bond Pricing and the Term Structure of Interest Rates: A New Methodology for Contingent Claims Valuation. *Econometrica*, vol. 60, pp. 77-105, 1992.

[4] Ho, T. S., and S. Lee, Term Structure Movements and Pricing Interest Rate Contingent Claims, *Journal of Finance*, vol. 41, pp. 1011-1028, 1986.

[5] Makhankov, V. G., Y. N. Taranenko, C. C. Gomez, and R. D. Jones, Stochastic Differential Geometry and the Term Structure of Interest Rates. *Report No. LA-UR-95-2998*, Los Alamos National Laboratory, 1995.

NEURAL MODEL IDENTIFICATION, VARIABLE SELECTION AND MODEL ADEQUACY

A-P. N. REFENES, A. D. ZAPRANIS AND J. UTANS
Department of Decision Science
London Business School
Regents Park, London, NW1 4SA, UK

In recent years an impressive array of publications have appeared claiming considerable successes of neural networks in modeling financial data but skeptical practitioners and statisticians are still raising the question of whether neural networks really are "a major breakthrough or just a passing fad". A major reason for this is the lack of procedures for performing tests for mispecified models, and tests of statistical significance for the various parameters that have been estimated, which makes it difficult to assess the model's significance and the possibility that any short term successes that are reported might be due to "data mining". In this paper we describe a methodology for neural model identification which facilitates hypothesis testing at two levels: model adequacy and variable significance. The methodology includes a model selection procedure to produce consistent estimators, a variable selection procedure based on variable significance testing and a model adequacy procedure based on residuals analysis.

1 Introduction

Neural networks are essentially devices for non-parametric statistical inference. From the statistical viewpoint, they have a simple interpretation: given a sample $D_n = \{(\mathbf{x}_i, y_i)\}_{i=1}^{n}$, generated by an unknown function $\varphi(\mathbf{x})$ with the addition of a stochastic component ε, i.e.,

$$y = \varphi(\mathbf{x}_i) + \varepsilon_i \tag{1}$$

the task of "neural learning" is to construct an estimator $g(\mathbf{x};\mathbf{w};\ D_n)$ $\equiv\hat{\varphi}(\mathbf{x})$ of $\varphi(\mathbf{x})$, where $\mathbf{w} = \{w_1, w_2, w_3, \ldots, w_p\}^T$ is a set of free parameters (known as "connection weights") and D_n is a finite set of observations. Since, no *a priori* assumptions are made regarding the functional form of $\varphi(\mathbf{x})$, the neural model $g(\mathbf{x};\mathbf{w})$ is a *non-parametric* estimator of the conditional density $E[y|\mathbf{x}]$, as opposed to a *parametric* estimator where the functional form is assumed a priori. Neural networks are a relatively recent development in the field of the non-parametric estimation. Well studied and frequently used members of the family include nearest neighbours regression and kernel smoothers (Haerdle, 1989), projection pursuit (Friedman & Stuetzle, 1981), alternating conditional expectations or "*ACE*" (Breiman & Friedman, 1985), average derivative estimation "*ADE*" (Haerdle & Stoner, 1989), classification and regression trees or "*CART*", (Breiman *et al*, 1984), etc. Because of their universal approximation properties, neural networks provide an elegant formalism for unifying all these paradigms.

These methods select a model from a number of competing alternatives on the basis of a discrepancy criterion (e.g., least squared error) which is minimised or, a gain function, (e.g., log likelihood) which is maximised. However, the selected model is not necessarily a faithful representation of the underlying function $\varphi(\mathbf{x})$. This may be due to a number of reasons, for example:

- omission of relevant variables,
- inclusion of irrelevant variables,
- measurement errors in the explanatory and dependent variables,
- incorrect specification of the functional form, or error term
- inadequacies of the estimation (learning) algorithm, e.g., convergence to a unique solution,
- inefficiencies of the model selection method, e.g., underfitting.

Any of the above reasons can lead to *specification bias*. However, unlike most of the other methods neural networks are not, as yet, supported by the rich collection of specification and diagnostic tests (commonly deployed in statistical and econometric modeling) which form the basis for a coherent model identification procedure to provide a degree of comfort that the estimated model corresponds to reality and has a plausible theoretical interpretation. In this paper we describe a methodology for neural model identification which facilitates hypothesis testing at two levels: model adequacy and variable significance. The methodology includes a model selection procedure to produce consistent estimators, a variable selection procedure based on variable significance testing and a model adequacy procedure based on residuals analysis.

2 Model Identification, Variable Selection & Model Adequacy

The objective of a <u>model identification</u> procedure is to construct a "well-specified" estimator of the unknown function $\varphi(\mathbf{x})$. A well-specified

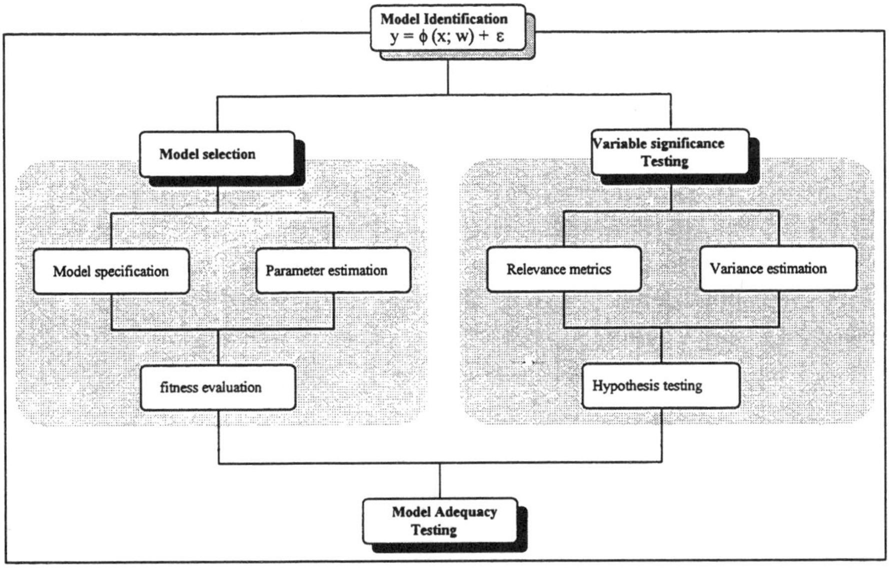

Figure 1: Model Identification.

estimator will be: **i)** a faithful representation of the regression $E[y|\mathbf{x}]$ (i.e. provides a comfortable fit with the data), **ii)** all the parameters and variables used by the estimator will be significant, and **iii)** the expectation of $E[\varepsilon|\mathbf{x}]=0$. In theory it may be possible to devise a model identification procedure which attempts to satisfy all these goals simultaneously. In practice however it is much easier to separate these goals into three distinct tasks: model selection, variable significance testing, and model adequacy testing. These stages are shown in Figure 1.

2.1 Model Selection

The task of model selection is to chose a functional form from a number of possibly competing alternatives, and to estimate the parameters in a way that satisfies a fitness criterion. Assuming that the input variables $\mathbf{x}$ remain fixed, there is a clear distinction between the problems of *estimation* (i.e. estimating the parameters of the model) and model *specification* (i.e. identifying the appropriate functional form). In the setting of parametric estimation, this distinction is clear and model selection is relatively straightforward: the *model specification* procedure consists of simply **assuming** a functional form; the *parameter estimation* procedure is required to compute (or **converge** to) a (**unique**) set of values for the parameter vector **w** which maximise an explicit fitness criterion, and *fitness* is measured by a simple criterion (e.g. least squares error, likelihood, $R^2, \overline{R}^2$, AIC, etc.). In the setting of non-parametric (neural) estimation, the search over the specification and the parameter space is performed simultaneously. Moreover, the dependencies on initial conditions, control parameters and regularisation terms have prompted statisticians to claim that neural networks do not posses the asymptotic property of *consistency*: i.e. that they are asymptotically unbiased in that $\lim_{n \to \infty} E[g(\mathbf{x}; \mathbf{w}; D_n)] = \varphi(\mathbf{x})$ and that its variance approaches zero as the sample size tends to infinity i.e. $\lim_{n \to \infty}(\mathrm{var}(g(\mathbf{x}; \mathbf{w}; D_n))) = 0$.

This is only partially true: neural networks can be made to be consistent estimators if they satisfy the properties of **convergence** and **uniqueness** together with a further requirement that the model contains no **redundant** parameters in **w**. These are essential requirements for the estimator to posses the asymptotic property of *consistency* and can be easily tested by checking that **i**) the error Hessian has no negative eigenvalues (convergence), **ii**) the empirical distribution of the weights produced by the resamling technique is multivariate normal (uniqueness), and **iii**) the model contains no redundant parameters in **w** (by using a irrelevant connection elimination scheme e.g. OBD, OBS, ICE). However, with the notable exception of Moody and Utans (1995) who were the first to introduce a numeric procedure facilitating such tests, this is rarely practiced. Our model selection procedure (section 3) is a development of their work but clearly any algorithm that satisfies the conditions above can be used.

2.2 Variable Significance Testing

The second leg of the model identification process deals with the estimation of the statistical significance of the explanatory variables. Irrelevant variables are removed in a way analogous to stepwise variable selection in linear regression. It involves three stages:

- define a variable's "relevance" to the model,
- estimate the sampling variation of the relevance measure,
- test the hypothesis that the variable is "irrelevant".

With linear models of the form:

$$y = b_0 + \sum_{i=1}^{m} b_i x_i + \varepsilon \tag{2}$$

this is a straightforward process; the relevance of variable x_i is measured by the magnitude of the partial derivative of y w.r.t. x_i, that is the coefficient b_i of x_i, i.e., large changes in x_i induce large changes in y; the sampling variation of the variable's relevance measure is the variation of b_i; and testing the hypothesis that the variable is relevant simply consists of testing $H_0 : b_i = 0$ against the alternative $H_0 : b_i \neq 0$. With non-linear models, however, this is not straightforward. In fact there are complications on all three counts.

The first difficulty arises with the definition of a variable's "relevance". Unlike the linear case, the partial derivative of the network's outcome $\hat{y}$ with respect to the variable x_i is not a constant but varies through the range of x_i. As yet there does not exist a universally accepted relevance criterion. In fact, with the notable exception of White's χ^2-test on the model's individual weights (White 1991) there is hardly any work in the field of hypothesis testing. Zapranis (1996), demonstrated that testing whether the weights are significantly different than zero can be a misleading way of testing the overall significance of an explanatory variable. A number of criteria each measuring different aspects of "relevance" are proposed. Amongst others, the *average magnitude* of the partial derivative $\hat{y}$ w.r.t. x_i the *average elasticity* of $\hat{y}$ w.r.t. x_i,, *maximum sensitivity* etc. are discussed in section 4.

The second difficulty arises with estimating sampling variation. Clearly, for a formal statistical test of a variable's significance, an estimate of the "relevance" measure's standard error is also needed. In the setting of parametric estimation, the sampling variability is a by-product of the model specification process and the assumptions made therein. Since, by specification, the true model has a fixed functional form it is often also **assumed** that the variance of the partial derivatives follows a particular distribution, thus, providing the basis for using asymptotic arguments to estimate standard error. In the setting of non-parametric estimation, asymptotic arguments are only rarely used. It is much more common to carry out stochastic simulations, such as bootstrapping, to provide empirical probability distributions for the relevance measures. Unfortunately, with the exception of Baxt and White (1995), this is rarely practiced (hardly surprising, given the extreme computational requirements). Zapranis *et al*, (1996) evaluated a number of common ways for estimating sampling variability (of relevance measures) including, (*a*) bootstrapping with a fixed set of random initial values for the parameter vector **w**, (*b*) bootstrapping in a local minimum, and (*c*) bootstrapping close to a local minimum. The results were compared with the asymptotic variance. It is shown that, due to the sensitivity of the model to initial conditions, control parameters etc. the common bootstraps have a tendency to over-estimate the variance. A parametric bootstrap was proposed which produces acceptable estimates and it is computationally attractive (see section 4).

The third task involves testing the hypothesis of irrelevance. Once the empirical distribution of the relevance measure is obtained, hypotheses can be tested by forming confidence intervals either, of the crude form $\hat{\theta} \pm z_a \hat{\sigma}$, with $\hat{\theta}$ being the estimated relevance measure and z_a being the 100(1-a) percentile point of the standard normal distribution or, non-parametric confidence intervals, e.g.,

$$\theta \in [\hat{\theta}(a), \hat{\theta}(1-a)] \qquad (3)$$

which uses the 100a and 100(1-a) percentiles of the empirical distribution of $\hat{\theta}$. Then, based for example, on the non-parametric (1-2a) central confidence interval, one can test the null hypothesis $H_0 : \theta = \theta_0$, with θ_0 usually being zero (alternative hypotheses might also be relevant, e.g., elasticity being less or equal to a threshold suggested by empirical or theoretical arguments).

2.3 Model Adequacy Testing

The last leg of the model identification methodology is about ensuring that the estimated model is a faithful representation of the regression $E[y|\mathbf{x}]$. It is concerned with testing that the residuals of the model conform with our assumptions about the nature of the stochastic component ε of the data generating process. Typically, one will assume that the stochastic and therefore unpredictable component is i.i.d. with zero mean and standard deviation σ. All that this assumption implies, is that the variables which are not explicitly included in the model, and therefore subsumed in ε, do not systematically affect $E[y|\mathbf{x}]$. Satisfying the model adequacy tests is not a *sufficient* condition for the model to qualify as the optimum solution, but it is a *necessary* condition for the model to qualify as a reasonable fit to the data. If the existence of a systematic component is detected in the error model, that indicates specification bias because for example, the functional form being of inadequate complexity or, some relevant variables were omitted, etc. or, simply because the estimation procedure failed to converge.

The stage of model adequacy checking should be an integral part of model identification. Any of the conventional tests for randomness can be applied here e.g. Box-Pierce, Ljung-Box, Durbin-Watson, F-test etc. It should be noted however, that the common critical values cannot be used since these are both data and model dependent. Ideally, one would need to re-compute critical values, again by stochastic simulation once the model has been estimated, which may be computationally intensive. Nevertheless we would encourage researchers to supply these statistics even if one cannot make strong inferences regarding their significance.

3 Model Selection

Over the years of neural network development an impressive array of model selection procedures have been proposed. They differ in the way in which they evaluate fitness: although most penalyse for complexity in the model specification they do so using different criteria. They differ in the way in which they estimate the model's parameters: the majority make a clear distinction between model specification and parameter estimation but many tackle the problem of searching over the specification space and the parameter space simultaneously. Finally and, from the perspective of testing hypotheses about variable significance and model adequacy, perhaps most importantly, they differ in the way in which dependencies upon initial conditions, control parameters and regularisation terms effect the consistency properties of the estimator. The basic requirement of *any* method is convergence of the training algorithm to a *locally unique* minimum. Clearly, a number of algorithms (can be made to) fulfill this requirement. In this paper we propose a relatively simple method termed *hierarchical minimisation of prediction risk* (*HMPR*). It is a structured procedure based on algebraic estimation of prediction risk, including a stage of model adequacy tests.

Our methodology for model selection traces its origins to Moody and Utans (1995). It is based on an incrementally constructed hierarchy of network classes $S_1 \subset S_2 \subset ... \subset S_k ...$ (see figure 2). Since, no more than one hidden layer is necessary for universal function approximation, each class comprises all possible one-hidden-layer networks with the same architecture A_λ. The number of hidden units λ uniquely indexes each class. Given the architecture A_λ the network is trained to convergence, that is we select the member of the class S_λ with parameter vector estimated from equation (4), i.e.,

$$\hat{\mathbf{w}}_n = \arg\min\{L_n(\mathbf{w}) : \mathbf{w} \in \mathbf{W} \quad \text{where} \quad \mathbf{W} \subseteq \Re^p,\ p = h(A_\lambda) \tag{4}$$

where the empirical loss is given form equation (5), i.e.,

$$L_n(\mathbf{w}) = \frac{1}{2n}\sum_{i=1}^{n}[y_i - g(\mathbf{x}_i;\mathbf{w})]^2 \tag{5}$$

The actual estimation (training) algorithm used, is of no consequence. The procedure is repeated several times for increasing values of λ. (initially $\lambda = 1$). The upper limit in the value of λ is determined by sample size (n). For m variables, the number of parameters $p = (m+2)\lambda + 1$, should be less than n (in practice, that limit is much lower; for a good fit it is widely accepted that the ratio n/p should be at least in the order of 5). For each neural network obtained from the above procedure, its associated prediction risk is estimated algebraically (e.g. Moody & Utans 1995):

$$\hat{E}[L(\hat{\mathbf{w}}_n)] \approx L_n(\hat{\mathbf{w}}_n) + \frac{tr\hat{\mathbf{A}}_n^{-1}\hat{\mathbf{B}}_n}{n} \tag{6}$$

Equation (6) requires that $\hat{\mathbf{w}}_n$ is indeed the solution to the minimisation problem (4) and not an intermediate vector of the training process. We can check this by examining the eigenvalues of the Hessian $\hat{\mathbf{A}}_n$. A further requirement, is that $\hat{\mathbf{w}}_n$ is "locally unique" (it does not have to be a global minimum, but it must contain only the necessary parameters). If this is not the case some eigenvalues of $\hat{\mathbf{A}}_n$ will have very small magnitudes.

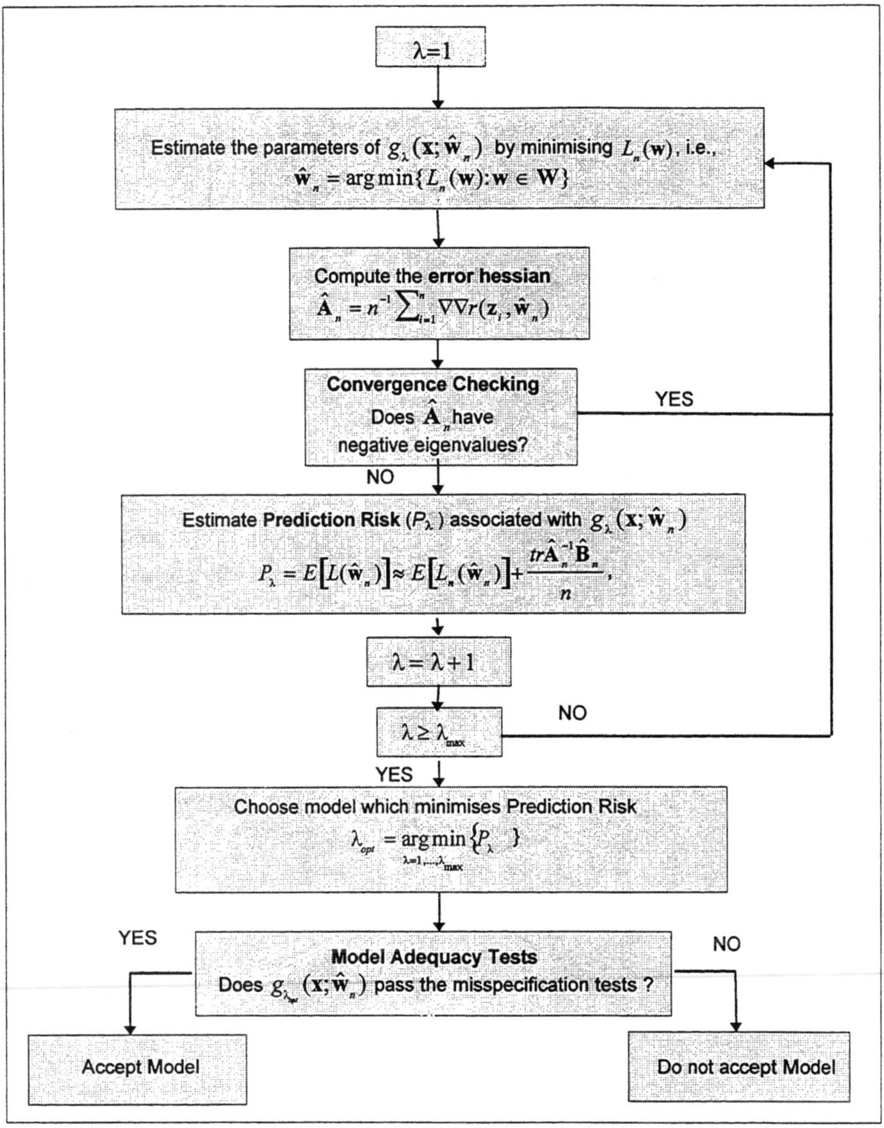

Figure 2 : Incremental *ANN* model selection procedure using prediction risk.

By setting their inverse to zero when calculating $\hat{\mathbf{A}}_n^{-1}$, we effectively exclude the irrelevant connections. These computational issues are discussed separately in Zapranis (1996). After the model with the least associated prediction risk has been identified, its adequacy is tested

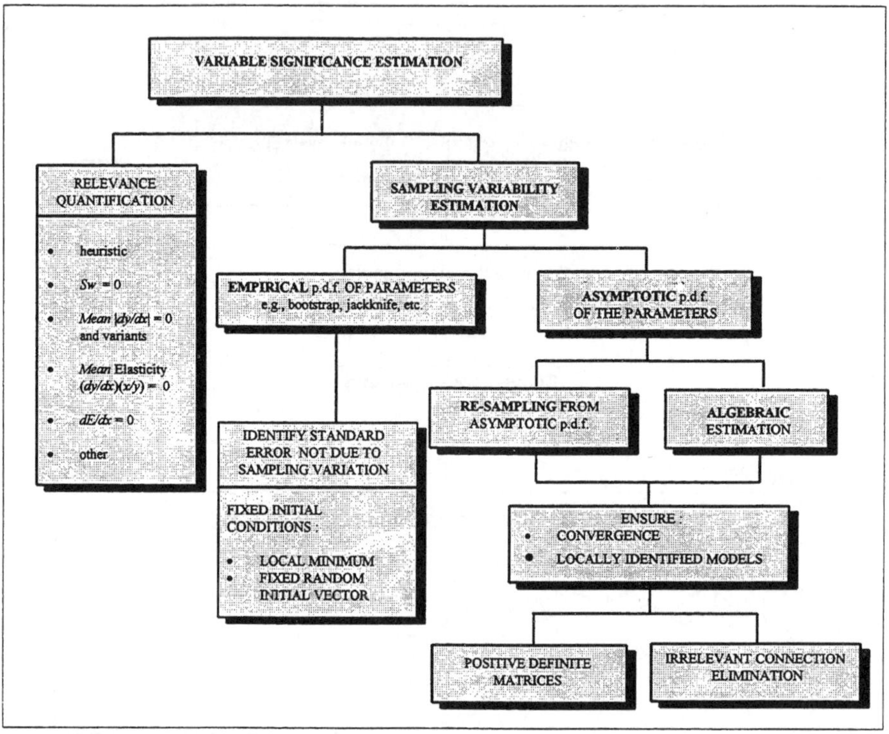

Figure 3: Variable Significance Estimation.

(relevant tests are given in section 5). Passing the misspecification tests is a "***necessary but not sufficient***" condition. However, failure to pass these tests indicates that either, more hidden units are needed or, some relevant variables were omitted. In section 4, we discuss how the significance of each explanatory variable can be estimated.

4 Variable Selection

The procedure for variable selection deals with the statistical significance of the explanatory variables. It involves quantifying the "relevance" measure, estimating the sampling variability of this measure and testing the hypothesis of insignificance. This is shown diagramatically in Figure 3.

Of the three legs by far the most important is that of estimating sampling variability. The two main choices are either using the distribution of the empirical p.d.f of the parameters or the asymptotic p.d.f. Both have disadvantages. Empirical estimation is computationally intensive, whilst asymptotic estimates have the tendency to underestimate the true variance (see for example Zapranis, *et al* 1996). For the results in this paper (see section 4.2) we use a novel resampling method which draws random weight vectors from the asymptotic distribution of the weights (see Zapranis *et al* 1996).

4.1 Relevance Metrics

Not surprisingly, the most commonly used measure of relevance is the average derivative since, the average change in $\hat{y}$ for a very small perturbation $\delta x \to 0$ in the independent variables x_j, is simply:

$$AvgD(x_j) = \frac{1}{n}\sum_{i=1}^{n}\frac{\partial \hat{y}_i}{\partial x_{ij}} \equiv mean\left(\frac{\partial \hat{y}}{\partial x_j}\right) \tag{7}$$

However, because of cancellations between negative and positive values, the average derivative might not be representative of the effect of x_j on $\hat{y}$. For example, the average derivative of a periodic symmetric function (e.g., a sinus wave) over one period will be zero. In an attempt to rectify this problem we propose using their absolute values or the squares of derivatives, to compute the average; suitable measures are:

$$AvgDM(x_j) = \frac{1}{n}\sum_{i=1}^{n}\left|\frac{\partial \hat{y}_i}{\partial x_{ij}}\right| \tag{8}$$

$$\theta = n^{-\frac{1}{2}}\sqrt{\sum_{j=1}^{n}\left(\partial \hat{y}_i / \partial x_i\right)^2} \times \frac{\sigma_x}{\sigma_\varepsilon} \tag{9}$$

where σ_x is the standard deviation of the independent variable and σ_ε is the standard deviation of the residual error. Under certain mild assumptions this is analogous to the t-statistic. In fact, unbeknown to us at the time, a version of (9) was presented independently by White and his co-author at NnCM-96 and should appear in these proceedings.

Sometimes although $\hat{y}$ is sensitive to x_j only in a small percentage of input vectors, x_j this can be quite important in the context of a particular application. This is quite common in certain financial applications, e.g., constructing risk-neutral portfolios, where downside risk is quantified by the magnitude of the negative derivatives $\partial\hat{y}_j/\partial x_{ij}$ ($\hat{y}$ being the portfolio return). Such special requirements give rise to the following measures:

$$MaxD(x_j) = \max_{i=1,\dots,n}\left\{\frac{\partial\hat{y}_i}{\partial x_{ij}}\right\} \quad \text{and} \quad MaxDM(x_j) = \max_{i=1,\dots,n}\left\{\left|\frac{\partial\hat{y}_i}{\partial x_{ij}}\right|\right\} \tag{10}$$

$$MinD(x_j) = \min_{i=1,\dots,n}\left\{\frac{\partial\hat{y}_i}{\partial x_{ij}}\right\} \quad \text{and} \quad MinDM(x_j) = \min_{i=1,\dots,n}\left\{\left|\frac{\partial\hat{y}_i}{\partial x_{ij}}\right|\right\} \tag{11}$$

Obviously, these measures are sensitive to influential observations and inflection points, where derivatives can take extremely values. Extra care must be taken to identify such problems before applying these measures.

We propose another quantification of $\hat{y}$'s sensitivity to x_j, which is especially relevant to financial applications: the average percentage change in $\hat{y}$ for a one-percent-change in x_j, or more commonly known as the average elasticity of $\hat{y}$ to x_j, which is computed as:

$$AvgL(x_j) = \frac{1}{n}\sum_{j=1}^{n}\left(\frac{\partial\hat{y}_i}{\partial x_{ij}}\right)\left(\frac{x_{ij}}{\hat{y}_i}\right) \quad \text{where} \quad \hat{y}_i \neq 0 \tag{12}$$

The average elasticity apart from having a natural interpretation, takes into account the differences in magnitude between $\hat{y}$ and x. For example, assume that for the exemplars $z_1 = \{x_1, y_1\}$ and $z_2 = \{x_2, y_2\}$ the derivatives of $\hat{y}$ w.r.t. x are equal. Then in general, the same change in x (in value or percentage terms) will not induce the same change in $\hat{y}$, because of the differences in magnitude between x_1 and x_2 and y_1 and y_2, although $dy_1/dx_1 = dy_2/dx_2$. However, cancellations between negative and positive values can sometimes create a misleading picture. This problem can be addressed whenever necessary by computing its <u>magnitude</u>:

$$AvgLM(x_j) = \frac{1}{n}\sum_{j=1}^{n}\left(\left|\frac{\partial \hat{y}_i}{\partial x_{ij}}\right|\right)\left(\left|\frac{x_{ij}}{\hat{y}_i}\right|\right) \qquad \text{where} \quad \hat{y}_i \neq 0 \tag{13}$$

A further proposal we put forward here, is computing, x_j's average contribution to the magnitude of the gradient vector $\nabla_x \hat{y}$, as a way of "standardising" $\partial \hat{y}_i / \partial x_{ij}$, since, the local gradient is calculated from all the derivatives (Zapranis, 1996). Locally, the relative contribution of $\partial \hat{y}_j / \partial x_{ij}$ to the gradient magnitude is simply the ratio:

$$r_{ij} = \frac{(\partial \hat{y}_i / \partial x_{ij})^2}{\|\nabla \hat{y}_i\|^2} = \frac{(\partial \hat{y}_i / \partial x_{ij})^2}{\sum_{i=1}^{m}(\partial \hat{y}_i / \partial x_{ij})^2} \tag{14}$$

and x_j's <u>average contribution to the gradient magnitude:</u>

$$AvgSTD(x_j) = \frac{1}{n}\sum_{i=1}^{n} r_{ij} \tag{15}$$

Yet another proposal for quantifying sensitivity, is the <u>standard deviation</u> of the derivatives across the sample, which measures the dispersion of the derivatives around their mean, i.e.,

$$SDD(x_j) = \left[\frac{1}{n}\sum_{i=1}^{n}\left(\frac{\partial \hat{y}_i}{\partial x_{ij}} - AvgD(x_j)\right)^2\right]^{1/2} \tag{16}$$

Dividing $SDD(x_j)$ by the mean, provides us with the <u>coefficient of variation</u>, that is the standard deviation per unit of sensitivity.

$$CVD(x_j) = \frac{SDD(x_j)}{AvgD(x_j)} \tag{17}$$

As a standardised quantity (17) is suitable for comparing different inputs.

Finally, the notion of *model-fitness sensitivity* can be used. This was introduced by Moody and Utans (1995); as a method for "sensitivity-based-pruning". It is a simple criterion measuring the effect of x_i on the estimation error. Its obvious advantage is that it does not vary across different cross-sections of $\phi(\mathbf{x})$ but it is a unique figure associated with each particular variable. A variable is removed from the model if its effect is negligible. In this paper we consider the measure $\theta = \partial L(w) / \partial x_i$ where

$$L(w) = n^{-1} \sum_{j=1}^{n} \left(\varphi(\mathbf{x})_j - g(\mathbf{x};\mathbf{w})_j \right)^2 . \tag{18}$$

Evidently there are potentially many possible quantifications of $\hat{y}$'s sensitivity to the independent variable x_j. For example, one might use the median instead of the average value. Understandably, however, any proposed measure reflects different aspects of the relationship between x_j and $\hat{y}$, thus being inevitably subjective to a degree. This has been demonstrated in Zapranis (1996).

Provided that the probability distribution of the above sensitivity measures is known or it can be estimated, confidence intervals can also be constructed and hypotheses can be tested. For example, in the context of sensitivity analysis, one might want to test the null hypothesis that $H_0\!: AvgDM(x_j) = 0$, or that $H_0\!: AvgL(x_j) > 15\%$, if that is suggested by empirical or theoretical arguments.

4.2 Estimating sampling variability

Estimating sampling variability is an integral part of the model specification process. However, for complex functionals of the parameter vector $\hat{\mathbf{w}}_n$, such as the relevance measures defined earlier (let us denote such composite measures as $\hat{\theta} = h(\hat{\mathbf{w}}_n)$) providing estimates for the standard error $\sigma(\hat{\theta})$ can be quite tedious. We can distinguish between two general approaches: (*i*) obtain the empirical p.d.f. of $\hat{\mathbf{w}}_n$, by means of a computationally intensive resampling scheme (bootstrap, jackknife, etc.), and then use that to estimate $\sigma(\hat{\theta})$, and (*ii*) provide an analytical estimate of $\sigma(\hat{\theta})$ based on asymptotic arguments.

The first approach requires fitting a large number of networks to data samples generated from the original, through some sort of resampling process. Given that there is not a closed form solution to the minimisation (maximisation) problem of neural learning, the associated computational overheads can be quite considerable. Moreover, the accuracy of the estimated $\sigma(\hat{\theta})$ can also be affected by computational problems, such as sensitivity of the learning algorithm to initial conditions, multiple local minima, flat local minima, etc. For example, Tibshirani (1996), reported that by simply changing the initial conditions for a fixed sample, the induced variability of the forecasts average accounted for 12% to 37% of the total variability. For these reasons in Zapranis, Utans & Refenes (1996), we evaluated various "local bootstrap" schemes adjusted to take into account the idiosyncrasies of neural learning. The idea, originally due to Moody and Utans (1995), is simply to start each bootstrap run from a fixed point in the weight-error surface obtained by minimising the expression in (4).

The second approach requires the derivation of an analytic form for $\sigma(\hat{\theta})$ which is of course tied to the specific functional $h(\circ)$. If this were possible, this is the preferred approach (as it requires no computation), but for complicated functions of $\hat{\mathbf{w}}_n$, such as the measure in (18) this is not straightforward. To overcome this drawback, we proposed stochastic sampling from the asymptotic distribution of $\hat{\mathbf{w}}_n$, and then estimating $\sigma(\hat{\theta})$ in a manner similar to the classic resampling schemes mentioned above. This is a cross between the analytical derivation of $\sigma(\hat{\theta})$ and its estimation is based on purely resampling schemes. The scheme is independent of the functional $h(\circ)$ and much less computationally demanding, compared to bootstrap for example, since, the estimate $\hat{\mathbf{w}}_n$ has to be obtained only once. Its added advantage is that it provides an equally (and in some cases more) accurate estimates of the variance of the parameters. This is illustrated by an example in Table 1 which shows a comparison of the estimates for the average value of the relevance measure in (8) for the well known (Wahba's) function :

$$y = 4.26(e^{-x} - 4e^{-2x} + 3e^{-3x}) + \varepsilon \qquad (19)$$

where x is uniformly distributed in [0, 2.5] and ε is i.i.d. and normally distributed as N~(0, 0.05), sample size n = 100.

TABLE 1: Sampling Variability of | *dy/dx* | - Wahba's Function (B=50 trials)

		AvgDM^G	| *dy/dx* |/*stdev*
1. Pairs Bootstrap			
1.1 Local[a]	average	0.93725	
	stdev	0.01547	60.60
1.2 Local/Perturbed IC[b]	average	0.93137	
	stdev	0.01681	55.40
1.3 Common/Random IC[c]	average	0.4880	
	stdev	0.0480	10.16
1.4 Common/Fixed IC[d]	average	0.5115	
	stdev	0.0732	6.98
2. Residuals Bootstrap			
2.1 Local	average	0.9391	
	stdev	0.0152	61.78
2.2 Local/Perturbed	average	0.9378	
	stdev	0.0201	46.65
2.3 Common/Random IC	average	0.4641	
	stdev	0.0212	21.89
2.4 Common/Fixed IC	average	0.4895	
	stdev	0.0274	17.86
3. Parametric Sampling[e]			
	average	0.9353	
	stdev	0.0070	133.61

a. Initial conditions (IC), i.e., starting weights, (fixed) as in row 4.
b. Initial conditions (fixed) as in row 5.
c. ICs randomly drawn from [-0.5,0.5]. Different in each bootstrap trial.
d. IC's randomly drawn from [-0.5,0.5] and fixed forall 50 bootstrap trials.
e. Random sampling from the asymptotic distribution of the parameters.

Besides Zapranis' scheme referred to as *parametric bootstrap* in Table 1, there are two other types: *pairs* and *residuals* bootstrap. With each of these principle types of bootstrap 4 different variations are shown. Clearly, the *local* types of bootstrap give far better estimates of both the variance and the mean of the relevance measure in (8), whilst the parametric bootstrap gives a more accurate estimate of its standard deviation (this is more pronounced when we formulate a composite measure of significance, see the last column).

5 Experimental Results

In this section we use some experimental results to illustrate the process of variable selection in the context of neural model identification. The experimental set-up uses the model selection procedure described in section 3 and the relevance-measures/variance-estimates described in section 4. We use an artificial dataset generated by:

$$y = 1 - x_1 + e^{-200(x-0.5)^2} + x_2 + \varepsilon \tag{20}$$

A cross-section of (20) along the x_1-axis is shown in figure 4; x_2 is white noise.

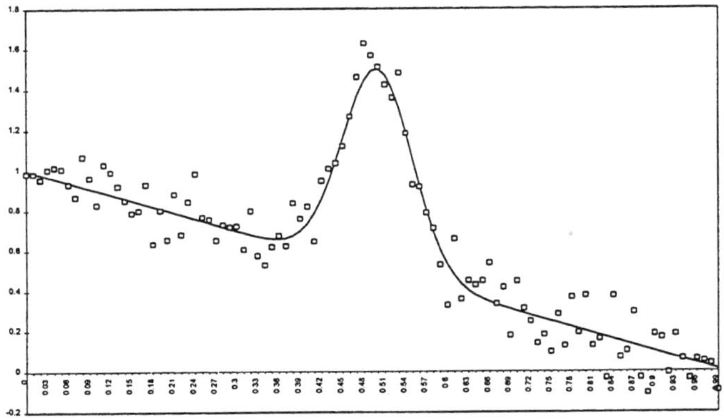

Figure 4: Cross-section of y (20) along x_1-axis.

Table 3 shows sensitivity (upper rows) of y to the two variables (x_1 and x_2) measured by seven[1] different "relevance" measures (columns) as well as the standard deviations of these measures (lower rows). For each "relevance" measure, say ϑ, the shaded rows show $t = \vartheta/\sigma(\vartheta)$ (the larger this value the higher the probability that the variable is significant).

Table 3: Variable significance statistics

SENSITIVITY OF Y TO X1 AND X2							
VAR	**MAXD**	**MIND**	**MAXDM**	**MINDM**	**AVGD**	**AVGDM**	**AVGEL**
X 1	15.305534	-15.287400	15.50540	0.04887	-1.38317	2.96351	-2.48979
	0.844462	0.410908	0.62747	0.04055	0.02533	0.06435	0.15460
	18.124600	-37.204100	24.71070	1.20493	-54.59312	46.05292	-16.10466
X 2	0.244480	0.008711	0.24485	0.01175	0.05192	0.05406	-0.00028
	0.091812	0.014546	0.09088	0.00861	0.02213	0.01910	0.00022
	2.662853	0.597917	2.69418	1.364437	2.34179	2.82911	-1.25301

---

[1] These are only a small subset of relevance measures described in section 3.

Table 4: Variable significance testing - (Moody and Utans' metric).

mean									
VAR	**DSSE**	**St.Dev.**	**t-value**	**p-value**	**1pc**	**10pc**	**50pc**	**90pc**	**99pc**
X 1	11.24243	1.16899	9.6172	0	8.46935	9.60197	11.23798	12.71668	13.5661
X 2	0.0005	0.0012	0.41681	0.6777	-0.00287	-0.00123	0.00036	0.00182	0.0026

The most important observation here is that according to all measures, by far the most relevant variable is correctly identified as x_1 (see shaded rows). The minimum derivative magnitude (MINDM) is an exception but both x_1 and x_2 have such a low t value that are insignificant.

Table 4 shows how the statistics can be used for hypothesis testing. For the purposes of completeness and comparison we use Moody and Utans' (1995) *model fitness sensitivity* measure. Clearly, x_1 is identified as the most significant of the two with a probability of wrongly entering the model being equal to zero at the 95% level of confidence, whilst the probability of wrongly accepting x_2 is 0.68.

Space restrictions prohibit any discussion on model adequacy but details can be found in Zapranis (1996). An application of the methodology to a real life problem in tactical asset allocation can be found elsewhere in these proceedings.

6 Conclusions

Neural Networks are a relatively recent development which can be seen as a consistent if extreme example of non-parametric estimation. However, much of the application development with neural networks has been done in an ad-hoc basis without due consideration for model identification. In this paper we described a methodology to facilitate model identification.

7 References

Baxt W. G. and White H. (1995), "Bootstrapping confidence intervals for clinical input variable effects in a network trained to identify the presence of acute myocardial infraction", *Neural Computation*, 7, 624-638.

Breiman L. & Friedman J., (1985), "Estimating optimal transformations for multiple regression and correlation", *Journal of the American Statistical Association*, 80, 580-619.

Breiman L., Friedman J. Olshen, R. & Stone, C. J. (1984). "Classification and regression trees", Belmont, Wadsworth, CA.

Haerdle & Stoner, (1989), "Investigating smooth multiple regression by the method of average derivatives", *Journal of the American Statistical Association*, 84, 986-95.

Haerdle, W. (1989) "Applied Nonparametric Regression", Econometric Society Monographs, Cambridge University Press.

Moody J. and Utans J. (1995), "Architecture Selection Strategies for Neural Networks: Application to Bond Rating Prediction", in Refenes A-P. N. (ed), "Neural Networks in the Capital Markets", Willey & Sons, (1995).

Tibshirani R. (1996), "A comparison of some error estimates for neural network models", *Neural Computation*, 8, 152-163.

White H., (1991), "Learning in artificial neural networks: a statistical perspective", *Neural Computation* 1, 425-464.

Zapranis A. D, (1996), Utans J. and Refenes A-P. N. "Local Bootstrap for Neural Models", Technical Report, Department of Decision Science, London Business School, Nov. (1996).

Zapranis, A. D. (1996), "Neural Model Identification: a structured approach", Ph.D. Transfer Document (Nov. 1996), also in Zapranis (1997), Ph.D. Dissertation, London Business School, (1997), in preparation.

SPECIFICATION TESTS FOR NEURAL NETWORKS: A CASE STUDY IN TACTICAL ASSET ALLOCATION

A. D. ZAPRANIS, J. UTANS, A-P. N. REFENES
Department of Decision Science
London Business School
Regents Park, London, NW1 4SA, UK

A case study in tactical asset allocation is used to introduce a methodology for neural model identification including model specification and variable selection. Neural models are contrasted to multiple linear regression on the basis of model identification. The results indicate the presence of non-linear relationships between the economic variables and asset class returns.

1 Introduction

With multiple-factor CAPM and APT, practitioners explain asset returns as a weighted combination of the different factors i.e.:

$$R_i = a_i + b_{i1}f_1 + b_{i2}f_2 + \ldots + b_{in}f_n + \varepsilon_i \tag{1}$$

where $R_{i\,i}$ is the return of asset i, f_j the determinant factors, b_{ij} the exposure of asset i to factor j, ε_i the non-predictable part of the return, i.e. the error of the model

However, there is no reason to assume that the relationship between asset returns and their determinants is linear and independent. In other words, it is highly possible that these remaining price fluctuations ε are due to some extent to *non-linear and interrelated* processes at work in the market place. Therefore it might be possible with non-linear models such as neural networks to model more of the market's price structure on the basis of partially *deterministic* but *non-linear* dynamics. However, unlike linear methods neural networks are not, as yet, supported by the rich collection of specification and diagnostic tests, which are common place in statistical and econometric modeling. Thus, their widespread exploitation neural networks is inhibited by the perceived difficulty of ensuring that a estimated model is well specified and the various variables/parameters included in the model are of statistical significance.

This paper, deploys the methodology described in Refenes, Zapranis and Utans (1996) to construct well specified, multi-factor models of relative returns between different asset classes. The results are compared with an multiple linear regression model and confirm the presence of non-linear relationships between the economic variables and the asset class returns.

2. A Regression Model for Tactical Asset Allocation

Tactical Asset Allocation refers to the task of allocating funds between different asset classes. The main asset classes considered here are equities, bonds and cash. This is done on the basis of forecasted (or expected) differences in returns between equities and cash versus (estimated) differences in returns between bonds and cash. Expected returns for $t+1$ are computed on the basis of the values of several economic (and other) variables at time t. We use monthly data on economic variables to estimate relative returns between equities and cash one month ahead.

These economic variables are to be selected from a universe of 17 variables and we use stepwise regression to reduce them to a manageable level. The variables selected through the stepwise regression are then used to forecast out-of-sample relative returns. For the forecasts we compare the performance of linear regression against a neural model constructed through a similar processes using the identification procedure in Refenes, Zapranis and Utans. (1996). Our purpose is to see if a non-linear estimator can provide some incremental value to the model. Furthermore, to the extent that one of the criticisms of neural modeling methods is their lack of statistical explainability, we provide a methodology enabling us to work from a platform of statistical understanding and looking for incremental value over a conventionally understood set of input variables.

The total sample covers the period August 1978 to August 1996 (the last three years are kept for out of sample testing). The resolution is one month. The total number of independent variables is 17. Some of them must be used lagged due to availability constraints. All the relevant information is summarized in Table 1.

Table 1: Leading Indicators

Variable	Description	Lag	Originally	Transformation
X_1	Expected Return	0	1M % Change	logarithm
X_2	Financial	0	level	first differences
X_4	Financial	0	level	first differences
X_5	Financial	0	level	first differences
X_6	Market Valuation	0	level	first differences
X_7	Business Cycle	0	level	first differences
X_8	Investor Risk	0	level	detrended (a)
X_9	Investor Sentiment	-1 M	1M % Change	logarithm
X_{10}	Market Risk	-1 M	1M % Change	na
X_{11}	International	-1 M	1M % Change	na
X_{12}	International	-2 M	1M % Change	na
X_{13}	Economic Conditions	-2 M	1M % Change	logarithm
X_{14}	Inflation	-2 M	1M % Change	logarithm
X_{17}	Inflation	-3 M	1M % Change	na
Y	Stocks-TBbills Return	+1 M	1M % Change	na

(a) $z_{6,t} = x_{8,t} - b_1 - b_2 t$

(b) Aug. 78 - Aug. 96

2.1 *Model Identification*

We use multiple linear regression to estimate the linear relationship between the independent variables (x_j^i) and the dependent variable (y). The least-squares technique is used to estimate the coefficients (b_i) in an equation of the form given in (1). The regression coefficient b_i represents the expected change in y associated with a one-unit change in the *ith* independent variable.

Backwards stepwise variable selection will be used to determine which of the of the 17 independent variables to include in the final regression equation which estimates expected returns. This procedure starts by including all the variables and then deleting variables one at a time. The criterion for deleting variables is to select the ones which reduce the sum of squared errors the most. One problem which can occur especially with financial data is multicollinearity. Among other implications (e.g., stability of estimates) it can result in making it difficult to obtain accurate estimates of the individual effects on variables. The regression statistics for the whole universe of 17 input variables are summarized in Table 2. The t-values and significance levels are used to eliminate the low sensitivity variables.

Table 2: Multiple Regression Analysis - Full Model

	Estimate	strd error	t-value	p-value
Constant	0.65715	0.02710	24.2485	0.0000
Z_1	0.01977	0.00683	2.8939	0.0044
Z_2	0.00265	0.00849	0.3128	0.7548
Z_3	0.00158	0.00991	0.1603	0.8729
Z_4	0.00133	0.01074	0.1242	0.9013
Z_5	-0.00785	0.01184	-0.6634	0.5081
Z_6	0.00900	0.00560	1.6062	0.1105
Z_7	-0.00969	0.00677	-1.4308	0.1547
Z_8	-0.01234	0.01112	-1.1093	0.2692
Z_9	0.01651	0.01098	1.5032	0.1351
Z_{10}	-0.00139	0.00695	-0.2005	0.8413
Z_{11}	-0.00543	0.00633	-0.8585	0.3921
Z_{12}	-0.01015	0.00716	-1.4178	0.1585
Z_{13}	0.00321	0.00452	0.7093	0.4793

Analysis of Variance

source	sse	Df	mean square	F-ratio	p-value
Model	0.18758	13	0.0144298	1.27	0.2400
Residual	1.58298	139	0.0113884		
Total (Corr.)	1.77057	152			
R^2	10.59470	%			
R^2 (adj.)	2.23307	%			
SE	0.10671				
MAE	0.07621				
D.W.	2.13589				

The ANOVA table is used to decide whether or not there is evidence of a linear relationship between the dependent variable Y and at least one of the independent variables. The F-statistic in that table is 1.27 with a corresponding p-value of 0.24. That means that there is 24% chance of wrongly rejecting the null hypothesis that *all* coefficients of the regression equation are simultaneously equal to zero.

The single most important variable (judging by its t-value) is variable Z_1. This is hardly surprising since Z_1 is the logarithm of the expected return (X_1). Other potentially important variables appear to be Z_6 (investor sentiment), Z_9 (international conditions), Z_7 (market risk) and Z_{12} (inflation). Quite appropriately the coefficients of expected return and investor sentiment are positive while the coefficients of market risk and inflation are negative.

Before proceeding further (or indeed giving up), it is desirable to test the assumption of regression to see if it is possible to make any improvements. This is a procedure which should be followed for all estimation methods. The main areas of investigations include: **i)** testing for serial correlation in the residuals (the presence of which may indicate that there is a systematic error component which could be modeled separately through an error correction term); **ii)** testing for possible non-linear transformations of the input variables (the presence of which may lead to an additive regression approach as shown in equation (1); **iii)** investigating the effect of influential observations in the data (the presence of which can be dealt with in various ways e.g. robust regression methods or simple removal); and **iv)** investigating the effects of possible non stationarities in the data.

2.2. Testing the Assumptions of Linear Regression

The reported *Durbin-Watson* statistic (DW) is 2.14. The DW is used to detected autocorrelation of first order in the residuals of a linear regression model. From the statistical tables for k = 13 and n = 153 we read d_L = 1.568 and d_U = 1.907. However, for these values of d_L and d_U the test is inconclusive since, 2.13589 falls in the indecisiveness region between 4 - d_U = 2.093 and 4 - d_L = 2.432. Residual plots were also constructed in search of a consistent pattern. The standardised residuals were plotted against time but no obvious time dependency was detected. The residuals were also plotted against all independent variables. The pattern of the residuals appears to be random (see Zapranis 1996).

We can check the normality the residuals visually by means of examining the normal probability plot. There we compare the studentised (or standardised) residuals (the actual residuals divided by their estimated standard deviation) with the normal distribution. If they are normally distributed they should follow very closely the diagonal. This was not found to be the case for this regression.

In addition to examining the normal probability plot, statistical tests can be used to asses the normality of the residuals. The simplest is a rule of the thumb based on *skewness* value. The critical value is from a z distribution based on the significance level we require. For example at the 0.05 error level we can reject the assumption about the normality of the distribution if z is less than -1.96 or, greater than 1.96. The statistic z is computed as $z = skweness / (6/n)^{1/2}$. For this regression we computed *skewness* = -0.9461 and z = -4.7775 confirming that the residuals are not normally distributed.

2.3 Influential Observations

Influential observations in an estimated regression equation are those that make a relatively large contribution to the values of the estimates and potentially include leverage *outliers* and *leverage points* but may include other observations as well. Once identified, they are usually removed and their effect on the model evaluated.

Outliers are observations that have large residual values and can only be identified with respect to a specific regression model. Studentised residuals can be used to identify outliers. Since studendised residuals are divided by the estimated standard deviation they are really t-values and they should be greater than -2 or less than 2. Any observation with a studentised residual outside this range indicates an outlier. In table 6 there are seven observations listed as outliers.

The most common influence measure for the observation $\mathbf{Z}_t$ on the fitted line in regression is know as the *leverage* of that observation. The leverage value h_t is the tth diagonal element of the "hat" matrix $\mathbf{H} = \mathbf{Z}(\mathbf{Z}'\mathbf{Z})^{-1}\mathbf{Z}'$ and its values lie between 0 and 1 and have an average value of p/n, where p is the number of parameters and n the sample size. For this regression the average leverage value is 0.091503 (14/153) and observations can be regarded as influential when their leverage exceeds 0.274509 (3×0.091503). As we can see from table 3 observations 23 and 108 have leverage values above the threshold.

Another statistic for estimating the influence of an individual observation on the fitted regression line is DFFITS. Both leverage and prediction error affect DFFITS. An observation $\mathbf{Z}_t$ has significant influence if it has an absolute value of DFFITS that is greater than 2 times the square root of the number of parameters divided by the number of observations, that is $|DFITS_t| = 2(p/n)^{1/2} = 2(14/153)^{1/2} = 0.60499$.

For this regression the critical DFFITS value is 0.60499. Table 4 shows that there are nine observations with DFFITS above the critical value.

Table 3: Unusual Points

Row	Y	Predicted Y	Residual	Studentised Residual
15	0.445897	0.695514	-0.249617	-2.57
33	0.290129	0.644698	-0.354569	-3.64
65	0.421117	0.647821	-0.226704	-2.22
106	0.1	0.563523	-0.463523	-5.33
108	0.822576	0.621486	0.201090	2.57
121	0.9	0.680597	0.219403	2.17
141	0.461173	0.676147	-0.214974	-2.15

Table 4: Influential Points

Row	Leverage	Mahalanobis Distance	DFFITS
3	0.117928	19.1944	0.638923
15	0.140267	23.6425	-1.039360
23	0.296233	62.5663	0.298196
33	0.091917	14.2911	-1.157040
35	0.181264	32.4372	0.616519
106	0.204739	37.8814	-2.703960
108	0.439631	117.4720	2.274020
121	0.076281	11.4763	0.622851
141	0.097031	15.2328	-0.703894
Average leverage of single data point	0.091503		

Finally, *Mahalanobis distance* is statistic that can also be used for identifying unusual values for the independent variables of the regression. This statistic measures the distance of observations from average values of the independent variables.

The influential observations identified in Tables 3 and 4 are removed from the sample. After repeated applications this stepwise procedure retains only 2 independent variables (Z_1, and Z_6), which account for the 3.13% of the variability in the dependent variable. We shall however, err on the side of safety and allow variables which are significant at the 80% level of confidence to enter the model. Table 5 summarizes the most important performance metrics for the reduced model.

Clearly, the percentage of explained variability is very low, although the estimates of the coefficients of the regression equation are statistically significant (the significance levels are ranging from 0 for the constant, to 0.1751 for Z_6). This, however is not unusual in financial analysis.

Table 5: Multiple Regression Analysis (Reduced model)
(Backwards Elimination, F-to-enter : 1.0, F-to-remove : 1.0)

	estimate	standard error	t-statistic		p-value
CONSTANT	0.65666	0.0128484	51.10820		0.0000
Z_1	0.01822	0.0063511	2.86956		0.0047
Z_6	0.00938	0.0054016	1.73775		0.0844
Z_7	-0.00904	0.0063762	-1.41864		0.1581
Z_8	-0.01322	0.0104541	-1.26484		0.2079
Z_9	0.01578	0.0104726	1.50746		0.1339
Z_{12}	-0.01098	0.0066114	-1.66192		0.0987
		Analysis of Variance			
source	**ssse**	**Df**	**mean square**	**F-ratio**	**p-value**
Model	0.16149	6	0.0269165	2.44	0.0280
Residual	1.60907	146	0.011021		
Total	1.77057	152			
R^2	9.12129	percent			
R^2 (adj.)	5.38654	percent			
SE	0.10498				
MAE	0.07765				
D.W.	2.14939				

Having identified a well specified linear model for Tactical Asset Allocation, in the next section we shall deploy the model identification procedure described in Refenes, Zapranis and Utans (1995). The objective is to investigate whether incremental value can be obtained by a nonlinear model.

4. A Neural Model for Tactical Asset Allocation

4.1. Model Identification

The experimental set up uses the model selection procedure described in Refenes, Zapranis and Utans (1996). The model fitness criterion is based the estimated prediction risk. The procedure for estimating sampling variability is as described in the same paper. The statistics for the full neural model are shown in Table 6. As a measure of "relevance" for each variable we use Moody and Utans' (1995) *model-fitness sensitivity* (MFS).

The p-values denote the probability of wrongly rejecting the null hypothesis that a variable's MFS is zero. Note the shaded areas.

Table 6: Statistics for the Full Neural Network Model (4 hidden units).

Variable	MFS (*a*)	St.Dev.	p-value (*b*)	1pc (*c*)	10pc	50pc	90pc	99pc
Z_1	1.13753	0.33581	0	0.50471	0.74937	1.05518	1.57944	2.06001
Z_2	1.51922	0.32325	0	0.62202	1.08297	1.50705	1.82050	2.28146
Z_3	1.00832	0.42693	0	0.26081	0.41478	0.87669	1.56099	2.10844
Z_4	0.40030	0.18484	0	0.01338	0.14774	0.37717	0.65598	0.84584
Z_5	0.52542	0.19240	0.00266	-0.00776	0.25925	0.47540	0.74750	0.90771
Z_6	0.22512	0.18103	0.19936	-0.52207	0.00354	0.23714	0.44155	0.55835
Z_7	0.20884	0.17419	0.21918	-0.28843	-0.08119	0.18649	0.40582	0.59234
Z_8	0.56338	0.24430	0.06912	-0.14754	0.25484	0.49977	0.83654	1.19081
Z_9	0.99248	0.31734	0	0.18641	0.57168	0.93613	1.36305	1.87328
Z_{10}	0.29201	0.29164	0.11261	-0.23429	-0.08381	0.16342	0.74386	1.04483
Z_{11}	1.89023	0.40729	0	1.01938	1.40433	1.92926	2.34920	2.87413
Z_{12}	0.21467	0.17877	0.11508	-0.10752	-0.03752	0.17548	0.40795	0.75160
Z_{13}	0.48919	0.24261	0.00378	-0.02456	0.16083	0.43891	0.79115	1.04143

Standard error of the estimate (SE)	0.05112
Empirical loss (Ln)	0.00130
Prediction risk (E[L])	0.00266
Generalised Cross Validation (GCV)	0.00722
Final Prediction Error (FPE)	0.00608
R-squared	77.44641
DW statistic	2.10804
Box-Pierce Q statistic	48.18286
Ljung-Box LB statistic	56.98613

(*a*) Model Fitness Sensitivity: the effect on the loss function of replacing a variable by its mean.
(*b*) The probability of wrongly rejecting the null hypothesis that a variable's MFS is zero.
(*c*) Characteristic points of the cumulative probability distribution of MFS.

The variable selection procedure is performed in a backwards fashion (cf. linear regression) by removing the variable with the highest p-value but we impose a further restriction namely, that the overall loss function (i.e. prediction risk) does not increase by more than 5%. As shown in Table 6 the variable with the highest p-value is z_7. Table 7 shows the effect of removing z_7 and re-estimating the model (z_6 is now to be removed).

Table 7: statistics for the Neural Network Model when Variable Z_7 is removed

Variable	MFS (*a*)	St.Dev.	p-value (*b*)	1pc (*c*)	10pc	50pc	90pc	99pc
Z_1	2.61448	0.83422	0	0.71698	1.07395	2.71005	3.53872	4.04867
Z_2	1.01671	0.35861	0	0.28683	0.39664	0.99091	1.41465	1.66269
Z_3	1.28231	0.26150	0	0.47705	0.88930	1.25003	1.55922	1.86841
Z_4	0.91244	0.32642	0.06425	0.08299	0.40024	0.93293	1.24534	1.53251
Z_5	0.32089	0.15729	0.01766	-0.05669	0.10102	0.28650	0.50877	0.68476
Z_6	1.20132	0.35364	0.21862	0.10054	0.66810	1.20728	1.53836	1.80322
Z_8	1.01169	0.25856	0	0.39825	0.64562	1.00371	1.27228	1.56912
Z_9	0.77171	0.28069	0.17542	0.01782	0.32533	0.79758	1.02822	1.18198
Z_{10}	0.96924	0.60526	0.01063	-0.18065	0.08853	0.84456	1.74958	2.43895
Z_{11}	0.75353	0.20219	0.07839	0.17353	0.44982	0.76755	0.93925	1.16818
Z_{12}	1.37626	0.71955	0.19307	-0.24490	0.04156	1.32769	2.07130	2.66059
Z_{13}	1.39051	0.76731	0.02087	-0.06797	0.26374	1.33208	2.34873	3.29646

Table 8: Stepwise variable selection with backwards elimination

	(a)	*(b)*		*(c)*		*(d)*	*(e)*
Step	**To Remove**	**To Enter**	**Variables in Model**	**Hidden Units**	**Empirical Loss**	**Prediction Risk**	**Ljung-Box Statistic**
	-	-	13	4 (61)	0.00130	0.00266	56.986
1	Z_7	-	12	4 (57)	0.00177	0.00232	45.118
2	Z_6	-	11	4 (53)	0.00187	0.00250	38.159
3	Z_2	-	10	4 (49)	0.00185	0.00304	38.620
4	Z_{12}	Z_2	10	4 (49)	0.00227	*0.00323*	35.243
5	Z_4	Z_{12}	10	4 (49)	0.00199	*0.00346*	31.734
6	Z_5	Z_4	10	4 (49)	0.00202	*0.00289*	57.240
7	Z_{10}	-	9	5 (56)	0.00167	0.00278	62.062
8	Z_{11}	-	9	5 (56)	0.00161	*0.00319*	36.497
9	Z_2	Z_{11}	8	6 (61)	0.00147	0.00256	31.572

Variables in final model	Variables removed as insignificant	Variables removed as multicolinear
1. $Z_1 = \log(X_1)$	1. $Z_7 = \log(X_9)$	1. X_6
2. $Z_3 = \Delta X_4$	2. $Z_6 = X_8 - b_1 - b_2 t$	
3. $Z_4 = \Delta X_5$	3. $Z_5 = \Delta X_7$	
4. $Z_8 = X_{10}$	4. $Z_{10} = X_{12}$	
5. $Z_9 = X_{11}$	5. $Z_2 = \Delta X_2$	
6. $Z_{11} = \log(X_{13})$		
7. $Z_{12} = \log(X_{14})$		
8. $Z_{13} = X_{17}$		

a) The variable with the largest p-value is removed. The procedure terminates when all variables have very small p-values, e.g., below 0.05 at the 95% significance level.

b) A removed variable is re-entered in the model if the prediction risk increased above threshold.

c) Once a variable is removed the model is re-estimated.

d) An increase of up to 5% in prediction risk is acceptable. The threshold above which a variable is re-entered to the model is 0.00279 (0.00266×1.05). Unacceptable models are marked **.

e) The Ljung-Box statistic measures autocorrelation in the residuals of the regression.

Table 8 shows the results of repeated applications of the procedure to obtain the final model. The exact steps are as described in the footnotes of Table 8 (a)..(e).

The Ljung-Box statistic measures autocorrelation in the residuals of the regression. Asymptotically valid for non-linear regressions. For 50 lags at the a = 0.05 significance level the critical value is 67.50. Values exceeding this figure imply serial correlation in the residuals.

The statistics for the final model itself are shown in Table 9. All variables are significant (see p-values); and the Ljung-Box statistic is well below its critical value indicating no serial correlation in the residuals. (note that the R-Square value is not adjusted for degrees of freedom).

Table 9: Statistics for the final neural model

Variable	MFS (*a*)	St.Dev.	p-value (*b*)	1pc (*c*)	10pc	50pc	90pc	99pc
Z_1	1.48975	0.38747	0	0.33873	0.92638	1.43242	1.93030	2.42001
Z_3	0.60595	0.14955	0	0.26246	0.40387	0.59098	0.78461	0.86620
Z_4	0.72388	0.15822	0	0.31725	0.48237	0.71321	0.89015	1.07107
Z_8	0.46481	0.23219	0	0.04963	0.16766	0.42122	0.77095	0.98079
Z_9	1.22202	0.22047	0	0.66300	0.91229	1.19994	1.46840	1.69852
Z_{11}	1.76898	0.38792	0	0.79599	1.17910	1.73634	2.25876	2.57221
Z_{12}	1.06345	0.35137	0	0.26532	0.54588	0.95114	1.53720	1.94869
Z_{13}	1.17979	0.31176	0	0.30290	0.77646	1.14074	1.51716	1.94215

Standard error of the estimate (SE)	0.05425
Mean absolute error (MAE)	0.04226
Empirical loss (Ln)	0.00147
Prediction risk (E[L])	0.00256
Generalised Cross Validation (GCV)	0.00814
Final Prediction Error (FPE)	0.00684
R-squared	74.89826
DW statistic	1.85353
Box-Pierce Q statistic	26.26729
Ljung-Box LB statistic	31.57233

a) Model Fitness Sensitivity : the effect on the loss function of replacing a variable by its mean.
b) The probability of wrongly rejecting the null hypothesis that a variable's MFS is zero.
c) Characteristic points of the cumulative probability distribution of MFS.

The model shown above has four hidden units. As a final check the final neural model was re-estimated with 2, 3, 4, 5, and 6 hidden units without significant change in the statistics shown in Table 9.

Having identified a well specified neural model, our next task is to evaluate the performance of the models using out of sample data.

5. Performance Evaluation

To address the problem of possible non-stationarities all models, including the regression were re-estimated (without significant change in the statistics) using a rolling window for three periods: firstly the model were estimated with data from Dec. 78 to Sept. 91. They were tested out-of sample one year i.e. Sept. 91 to Sept. 92. The models were then re-estimated using data from Dec. 78 to Sept. 92 and tested for the period Sept. 92 to Sept. 93. This was repeated for the next year.

Table 10: Optimal Weights for UK Portfolio (*a*)

	Levels of Risk Tolerance				
	A	**B**	**C**	**D**	**E**
Asset Class Weights	**Minimum Risk**	**Low Risk**	**Average Risk**	**High Risk**	**Maximum Return**
Cash	95.6	73.4	48.9	24.5	0
Gilts	2.4	0	0	0	0
Equities	2.0	26.6	51.1	75.5	100
Total Portfolio	**100**	**100**	**100**	**100**	**100**
Portfolio Return	5.5	7.1	8.6	10.3	11.9
Portfolio Risk	1.2	1.9	3.3	4.7	6.2

(*a*) From the BZW Equity & Guilt Study, Barclays de Zoete Wedd Research, January 1993.

To compare the results of this analysis, we use a set of benchmark portfolios in Tactical Asset Allocation taken form the BZW Equity & Guilt Study, Barclays de Zoete Wedd Research, January 1993. Table 10 shows the optimal weights for five different portfolios with varying levels of risk tolerance (as well as their average returns).

Table 11, shows the returns of there variations of the benchmark and a the neural model in the hold-out sample (Period : Oct. 1991 - Sept. 1994).

Table 11: Model Performance Evaluation in the Holdout Sample

Portfolio	Annual Return	Standard Deviation	Return per Unit Risk (*a*)	Sharpe Ratio (*b*)	Max. Drawdown (*c*)
Benchmark					
Equities/Cash (100/0)	10.70	16.15	0.66	0.19	15.2
Equities/Cash (70/30)	10.05	10.91	0.92	0.22	10.1
Equities/Cash (0/100)	7.58	2.35	3.22	0	0
Neural Network					
NN#1 (*d*)	16.49	12.30	1.34	0.72	6.76
NN#2 (*e*)	15.80	12.66	1.25	0.65	6.78
NN#3 (0.1/0.2) (*f*)	13.59	10.15	1.34	0.59	5.35
NN#4 (0.1/0.3) (*g*)	12.74	8.82	1.44	0.58	4.64
NN#5 (0.1/0.4) (*h*)	11.88	7.53	1.58	0.57	3.92

a) The annualised return divided by the standard deviation of returns.
b) Annualised excess return of the portfolio, i.e., annualised return of the portfolio minus the annualised return of the risk free asset (cash), for a unit of risk (standard deviation).
c) Maximum drop of the cumulative return curve for subsequent months of negative growth.
d) Naive allocation, with no transactions costs; this strategy takes a position according to the sign of the forecasted differential return - fully flexible 100% allocation in either equities or cash.
e) Naive allocation as in (*d*) but with transactions costs of 10 basis points (0.1%).
f) Restricted allocation : equities not less than 10 percent, and cash not less than 20 percent of the asset mix; transactions costs of 10 basis points (0.1%).
g) Restricted allocation : equities not less than 10 percent, and cash not less than 30 percent of the asset mix; transactions costs of 10 basis points (0.1%).
h) Restricted allocation : equities not less than 10 percent, and cash not less than 40 percent of the asset mix; transactions costs of 10 basis points (0.1%).

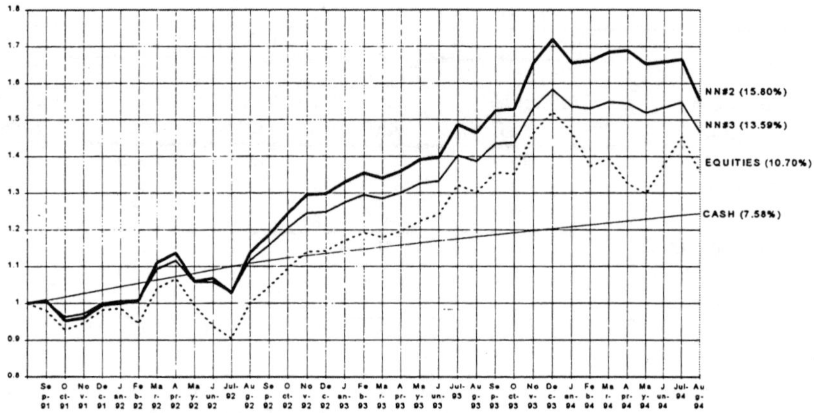

Figure 1 : Cumulative return of neural network models versus market return: (i) NN#1 takes a position every time a buy/sell signal is generated, (ii) NN#2 requires that the coefficient of variation (CV=standard deviation of the forecast) is less than 2, and (iii) NN#2 as NN#2 but with equities not less than 20 percent and cash not less than 2 percent of the asset mix.

The allocation strategies for the predictions of the neural model are shown in the footnotes to Table 11.

Figure 1 shows the cumulative returns of the neural model versus market returns for the same period. Two allocation strategies are shown: (i) NN#1 takes a position every time a buy/sell signal is generated, (ii) NN#2 requires that the coefficient of variation (CV = standard deviation of the forecast / forecast) is less than 2, and (iii) NN#2 as NN#2 but with equities not less than 20 percent and cash not less than 2 percent of the asset mix.

6 Conclusions

We have used a case study in tactical asset allocation to introduce a methodology for neural model identification including model specification and variable selection.

We have produced models well-specified models for tactical asset allocation; both linear and non-linear. The two models differ in the variables which are allowed to enter the equation. The results indicate the presence of non-linear relationships between the economic variables and asset class returns.

7 Acknowledgments

We would like to thank Masood Javaid at Hermes Investment Management for providing the data for this application and also for his constructive comments during the development of the models.

8 References

Moody J. and Utans J. (1995), "Architecture Selection Strategies for Neural Networks: Application to Bond Rating Prediction", in Refenes A-P. N. (ed), "Neural Networks in the Capital Markets", Willey & Sons, (1995).

Refenes A-P. N. Zapranis A. D. and Utans J (1996). "Neural Model Identification, Variable Selection and Model Adequacy", in Proc. NnCM-96, Weigend A. et al, World Scientific.

Zapranis A. D, Utans J. and Refenes A-P. N. (1996),"Local Bootstrap for Neural Models", Technical Report, Department of Decision Science, London Business School, Nov. (1996).

Zapranis, A. D. (1996), "Neural Model Identification: a structured approach", Ph.D. Transfer Document (Nov. 1996), also in Zapranis (1997), Ph.D. Dissertation, London Business School, (1997), in preparation.

ASSET ALLOCATION ACROSS EUROPEAN EQUITY INDICES USING A PORTFOLIO OF DYNAMIC COINTEGRATION MODELS

A. N. BURGESS
Department of Decision Science
London Business School
Sussex Place, Regents Park, London, NW1 4SA, UK
E-mail: N.Burgess@lbs.lon.ac.uk

In modelling financial time-series, the model selection process is complicated by the presence of noise and possible structural non-stationarity. Additionally the near-efficiency of financial markets combined with the flexibility of advanced modelling techniques creates a significant risk of "data-snooping". These factors combine to make trading a single model a very risky proposition, particularly in a situation which allows for high leverage, such as futures trading. We believe that the risks inherent in relying on a given model can be reduced by combining a whole set of models and, to this end, describe a population-based methodology which involves building a portfolio of complementary models. We describe an application of the technique to the problem of modelling a set of European equity indices using a portfolio of cointegration-based models.

1 Introduction

In recent years much interest has been shown in the possibility of using novel modelling techniques, such as neural networks and genetic algorithms, as the basis of trading systems which will "beat the market". Intuitively the reasoning behind this general approach is that the markets are only truly "efficient", or unpredictable, with respect to information and modelling techniques which are commonly available to the market participants, and that new modelling techniques in effect create new information with respect to which the markets are not necessarily efficient. We might call this the "Relatively Efficient Markets" hypothesis.

In practice, however, financial markets are noisy, non-stationary and very close to being efficient. These factors combine to make it very difficult to determine whether a particular model actually has significant predictive ability or not. This problem is further exacerbated by the fact that advanced modelling techniques are typically very flexible and increase the risk of "data snooping" (Lo and MacKinlay, 1990) or finding models which appear to be statistically significant if we only consider the explicit degrees of freedom of the models but not when we take into account the additional degrees of freedom contained either in the experimental procedure itself or in prior knowledge.

We believe that the risks inherent in relying on a given model can be reduced by combining a whole set of models, in effect trading a **portfolio of models**. In the remaining sections of the paper we describe a methodology which involves building a portfolio of complementary models. Section 2 introduces the econometric concept of "cointegration" which provides the motivation for the individual models. Section 3 describes the "evolutionary" algorithm by means of which a population of complementary models are generated. Section 4 presents an application to modelling relative returns on a set of European equity indices. The paper concludes with a brief discussion and summary in section 5.

2 Cointegration

Cointegration (Engle and Granger, 1987) is an econometric concept which can be thought of as "dynamic correlation" (Alexander and Johnson, 1994). Hypothesizing that a set of financial markets is co-integrated is equivalent to suggesting that whilst the short-term movements of the markets may be very different, they will be "tied together" in the longer term. From the perspective of modelling financial asset prices, cointegration is important because it provides a method of dealing with non-stationary data which can capture relationships between the *levels* of the time-series which are destroyed by the more common approach of *differencing* the time-series (Burgess, 1996).

2.1 Testing for Cointegration

The cointegration hypothesis is essentially that from a set of time-series which are individually non-stationary (difference stationary) it is possible to form a linear combination which is stationary. We can test if a given time-series y_1 is cointegrated with the time-series $y_2,..,y_n$ by perfroming a standard regression, of the form:

$$y_{1,t} = \beta_2 \cdot y_{2,t} + \beta_3 \cdot y_{3,t} + \ldots\ldots + \beta_n \cdot y_{n,t} + r_t \qquad (1)$$

The test for cointegration is then equivalent to testing the residuals r_t of the regression for stationarity according to a Dickey-Fuller "unit root" (Dicky and Fuller, 1979) or similar test. Stationarity of the residuals is equivalent to saying that divergences between y_1 and the "cointegrating vector" ($\beta_2 \cdot y_{2,t} + \beta_3 \cdot y_{3,t} + \ldots\ldots + \beta_n \cdot y_{n,t}$) are only temporary and will tend to be mean-reverting.

2.2 Implicit Cointegration Models

In the context of financial markets, the mean-reversion which is a property of sets of assets which are cointegrated can be considered as an opportunity for trading "statistical arbitrage" (Burgess and Refenes 1996).

If we define the cointegrating portfolio for y_1 according to:

$$CP(y_1)_t = \beta_2 \cdot y_{2,t} + \beta_3 \cdot y_{3,t} + \ldots\ldots + \beta_n \cdot y_{n,t} \tag{2}$$

Then we see from Eq. (1) that:

$$E[\, y_1 - CP(\, y_1 \,)] = 0 \tag{3}$$

From this perspective the cointegrating regression can be viewed as defining a "fair price" relationship in which the long run prices of y_1 and $CP(y_1)$ have a tendency to revert towards each other. The cointegration residual r_t can be considered a "mis-pricing" in that it measures the current divergence from the "fair price" relationship. We can define a portfolio p which consists of a position in y_1 together with an offsetting short position in its cointegrating portfolio $CP(y_1)$:

$$p = y_1 - CP(y_1) \tag{4}$$

Where the value of p at time t is equal to that of the cointegration residual r_t and hence we expect the value of p to be mean-reverting around zero. From this perspective a non-zero value of r_t represents an opportunity for statistical arbitrage: if r_t is negative we take a long position in portfolio p, if r_t is positive we take a short position in portfolio p. In each case the trade will be profitable if the fair price relationship is restored. We refer to this approach an *implicit* cointegration model because the trading positions are not based on an explicit model of asset returns. Note that because p contains both long and short positions we prefer to calculate "returns" relative to the total exposure rather than to the "value", i.e.:

$$\Delta p_t = (\, \Delta y_{1,t} - \Delta CP(y_1)_t \,) \,/\, (\, y_{1,t} + CP(\, y_1 \,)_t \,) \tag{5}$$

As an example we consider the French Cac and German Dax indices. If we regress the Cac on the Dax for daily closing prices from August 1988 to August 1990 we find:

$$CAC_t = 0.888 * Dax_t + 388 + r_t \tag{6}$$

We can plot the price of the Cac against the "fair price" of 0.888 times the price of the Dax plus 388 points, as shown in Figure 1 below:

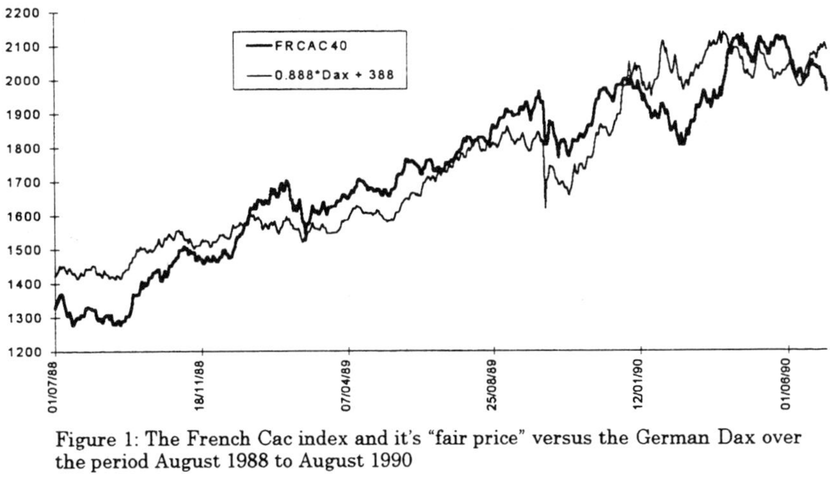

Figure 1: The French Cac index and it's "fair price" versus the German Dax over the period August 1988 to August 1990

The cointegrating regression in itself will induce a certain degree of mean-reversion on the residuals during the in-sample period. Thus in order to evaluate the effectiveness of the "statistical arbitrage" we simulate trading on subsequent data. The results are shown in table 1, below; there are six entries representing yearly periods from August to August. The final entry summarises the performance over the whole period.

Period	90-91	91-92	92-93	93-94	94-95	95-96	90-96
Return	11.3%	22.4%	17.7%	7.1%	-4.2%	-7.2%	47.2%
S.R.	0.72	1.78	1.18	0.53	0.25	-0.56	1.30

Table 1: paper-trading performance of implicit cointegration model for Dax-Cac (S.R. is annualised Sharpe Ratio, trading costs NOT included)

In this simple analysis the model does continue to perform well, returning good profits for each of the first four years. Note that factors such as slippage, transactions costs, leverage etc. are not included in the results above. Notice also that the model performance deteriorates over time, an issue to which we will return in section 2.4 below.

2.3 Error-correcting Models

A more sophisticated approach is to use the cointegration residual as an explanatory variable in a model of asset price returns. In fact, an important corollary of the existance of cointegration in a given set of variables **y** is provided by the "Granger Representation Theorem". This tells us that if a set of variables **y** are cointegrated then there is an error-correction model (ECM) of the form:

$$\Delta y_{1,t} = \alpha_{1,1}.\Delta y_{1,t-1} + \dots + \alpha_{2,1}.\Delta y_{2,t-1} + \dots + \gamma.r_{t-1} + e_t \tag{7}$$

We can modify this approach so as to immunise the model to level shifts in the asset prices by replacing the $\Delta y_{1,t}$ of Eq. (7) with returns Δp_t on a portfolio p as defined in Eq. (5) and Eq. (4) respectively. This leads to a model of the form:

$$\Delta p_t = \alpha + \beta.r_t + \mathbf{x}_t'\mathbf{b} + e_t \tag{8}$$

Where r_t is the cointegration residual and the vector **x** represents the various autoregressive terms together with any desired exogenous variables.

In previous work we have suggested that it can be advantageous to dispense with the assumptions of linearity and independence which are inherent in the model of Eq. (8). A feedforward neural network can be used to estimate a model of the form:

$$\Delta p_t = f(r_t, \mathbf{x}_t) + e_t \tag{9}$$

Applying this approach to modelling relative asset returns between the FTSE 100 index and a cointegrating portfolio of international equity indices, we reported (Burgess and Refenes, 1996) that the neural network model had consistently higher generalisation performance than the equivalent linear model. It was suggested that the improved performance of the neural network "conditional cointegration" model is due to the flexible functional form, which allows the strength of the cointegrating effect to be modelled as a function of market conditions, as represented by the exogenous variables **x**.

2.4 Dynamic Cointegration Models

The models discussed above all assume that the underlying cointegrating relationship is itself stable through time. There is, however, every reason to believe that the market's opinion as to what constitutes a "fair price" of one asset relative to another will change over time, with changes in the underlying economics, politics and even sentiment.

The implication of this is that even cointegration models which have worked well in the past are liable to "break down". In table 1 we noted a marked decline in the performance of the "implicit" cointegration model of the Dax-Cac. In fact the reason for this is clear when we view the two time-series in figure 2:

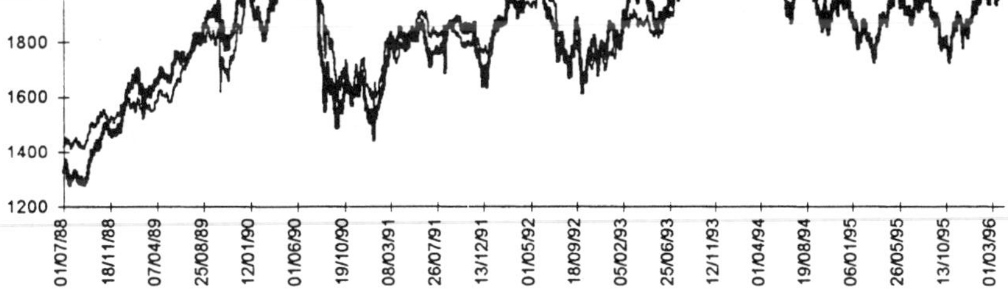

Figure 2: Price series for the Cac and (scaled) Dax indices, showing a cointegration relationship which subsequently breaks down

We see that from early 1994 the two series begin to diverge and, contrary to the cointegration hypothesis, do not move back into line with each other. Whatever relationship was present truly has "broken down".

This phenomenon has been noted for other financial time series. In modelling the FTSE against a basket of international equity indices Burgess and Refenes (1996) adjust for a changing relationship by periodically re-calculating the coefficients of the cointegrating regression using a "rolling window" approach. Bruce, Connor and Martin (1996) use a more sophisticated approach which is robust to both level and trend shifts and find that it significantly improves the stability of a cointegrating relationship between the FTSE and the U.S. S&P index.

Both of these approaches create discontinuities in the beta parameters which may effect the accuracy of any subsequent modelling procedure. Instead, we prefer to allow the cointegration coefficients to evolve slowly according to a "random walk parameter" model.

The random walk time-varying parameter model which is analogous to the cointegration regression given in Eq. (1) is:

$$y_{1,t} = \beta_{2,t} \cdot y_{2,t} + \beta_{3,t} \cdot y_{3,t} + \ldots\ldots + r_t \tag{10}$$

Where $r_t \sim \mathrm{NID}(0, \sigma^2)$ and the parameters β_i are generated by the process:

$$\beta_{i,t} = \beta_{i,t-1} + \eta_{i,t} \qquad \eta_{i,t} \sim \mathrm{NID}(0, \sigma^2 q_i) \tag{11}$$

This is a state-space model in which the states are the cointegration coefficients β_i and which can easily be implemented within the framework of a standard Kalman filter. The scale parameters q_i determine the rate at which the coefficients may evolve through time; in the special case of all the q_i's = 0 the model collapses to a (fixed coefficient) regression model. Further discussion of the random walk parameter model and related models can be found in (Harvey, 1993).

As an illustration, we apply the algorithm to the Dax-Cac problem considered previously; the single parameter which must be specified is the scale parameter q which controls the rate at which the parameters are allowed to vary. Table 2 shows the performance for a model with different levels of sensitivity q.

Period	90-91	91-92	92-93	93-94	94-95	95-96	90-96
q=0	11.3%	22.4%	17.7%	7.1%	-4.2%	-7.2%	47.2%
q=25	12.9%	11.3%	20.9%	11.1%	0.3%	3.2%	59.8%
q=1600	15.4%	7.9%	19.4%	5.4%	13.6%	9.9%	71.5%
q=102400	23.3%	-5.5%	-16.9%	9.7%	14.6%	13.7%	38.9%

Table 2: performance of time-varying cointegration model for Dax-Cac with different levels of sensitivity q (Note: $q = 0$ is equivalent to fixed model)

We see that even with a low level of sensitivity (q=25) the model adjusts sufficiently to be marginally profitable even when the cointegration breaks down in early 1994; with a moderate level of sensitivity (q=1600) the system performance is consistent across all periods with the least profitable period being the one in which the major adjustment is made. When the sensitivity is too high (q=102400) the system becomes unstable and performs less well than even the fixed parameter model.

3 Reducing Risk by using a Portfolio of Models

When modelling financial time-series the issue of model selection is complicated by the fact that the high level of noise makes it difficult to evaluate accurately the performance of the models, particularly when the probability distribution of returns may be heavy tailed and/or heteroskedastic. A second major complication is that the relationships within and between markets are changing over time - hence future performance, which is a composite of current performance and performance degradation due to non-stationarity, is almost impossible to assess with any real degree of confidence.

These factors combine to make trading a single model a very risky proposition, particularly in a situation which allows for high leverage, such as futures trading. In our view this situation can only realistically be dealt with in one way: by **model combination**.

3.1 Pareto-optimality

Our objective is to reduce the risks which are inherent in trading a single model, by generating a whole portfolio of different models, each independently profitable but with different susceptibilities to over-fitting, non-stationarity, etc. In fact, we would like to emulate natural evolution, in which a whole plethora of environmental niches are filled by species which each have their own strengths, weaknesses and susceptibilities to changing conditions. This property of natural evolution is echoed by the statistical concept of "Pareto Optimality".

Pareto Optimality is a notion which applies to "multi-objective" optimisation problems. A "pareto optimal" or "non-dominated" solution is one which does not lose, on all criteria, to any single individual. In the context of financial markets, the "Efficient Market Frontier" is actually the set of Pareto-optimal solutions to the multiple objectives of maximising expected return whilst minimising risk in the form of standard deviation of return.

Population-based algorithms such as Genetic Algorithms and other "evolutionary" algorithms present the opportunity of solving multi-objective optimisation tasks without the need to prespecify a fixed trade-off between the different objectives. This realisation has resulted in algorithms such as the "non-dominated sorting genetic algorithm" (Srinivas and Deb, 1995) which explicitly aim to find sets of pareto-optimal solutions. In order to apply such an algorithm to the problem of building a set of trading models, however, we need to define the multiple-objectives with respect to which the pareto-optimality would be evaluated. The obvious candidates of "risk" and "return" can be jointly optimised directly by means of a trade-off such as Sharpe Ratio or some other measure of "risk-adjusted-return".

Ideally perhaps, the multiple objectives would be *profitability under different market conditions*. Although this approach merits consideration we believe that the problem of defining sets of "market conditions" is significant in it's own right and have instead chosen to avoid this issue by adopting a slightly different approach.

3.2 Generating a portfolio of complementary models

We have developed an approach which avoids the need to define explicit sets of market conditions. Instead we allow the models themselves to do this implicitly, through the use of *correlation* between the profits and losses of different models. We calulate a measure of "success" which modifies the raw fitness to take into account the effects of competition:

$$\mathrm{SUCCESS}_i = \mathrm{FITNESS}_i - \sum_{j \neq i} C(\,\mathrm{FITNESS}_i, \mathrm{FITNESS}_j, \mathrm{CORREL}(i,j)\,) \tag{12}$$

To date we have used competition functions C of the form:

$$C(\,\mathrm{FITNESS}_i, \mathrm{FITNESS}_j, \mathrm{CORREL}(i,j) = \begin{cases} \mathrm{FITNESS}_i > \mathrm{FITNESS}_j : 0 \\ \mathrm{FITNESS}_i < \mathrm{FITNESS}_j : \mathrm{CORREL}(i,j)^d . \mathrm{FITNESS}_j \end{cases} \tag{13}$$

We set the parameter d to the value 7, which implies that an individual should lose 50% of its fitness if it 90% correlated with a marginally fitter "competitor". Clearly other competition functions along broadly similar lines could also be investigated.

In penalising correlations between model profitability we can see analogies both to portfolio theory and also to statistical results which indicate that the advantages of combining models in order to provide more robust estimation are related to the extent to which the various models are uncorrelated (Krogh and Vedelsby, 1995).

4 Application to modelling a set of European Equity Indices

In this section we present the results of applying the methodology described above to the problem of modelling returns on a set of European equity indices, namely FTSE 100 in the UK, the Dax in Germany, the Cac in France, the EOE in Holland and the SMI in Switzerland.

Our approach involves modelling relative returns on portfolios consisting of long and short positions on the underlying indices and hence is most suitable to implementation through the futures markets. In principle the results are applicable either to a "statistical arbitrage" trader interested in taking highly leveraged futures positions or to a more conservative fund manager. In the latter case the positions indicated by the models would be considered as "overlays" on an underlying asset allocation, with the size of the overlays being dependent on the risk tolerance of the fund manager.

4.1 The data

The dataset consists of daily closing prices from August 1990 through to July 1996. A total of 1583 daily observations were available, which we divided into four periods: the most recent 300 observations as a true out-of-sample period; the next 300 as an evaluation period for calculating the fitness of individual models; another 400 observations are used as the "training period" which is used to optimise the parameters (weights) of the models; the remaining data, prior to October 1992, is the pre-ERM-crisis period and was only used for purposes of initialisation.

4.2 The models

The details of each model are encoded in a "genome" which consists of a sequence of real numbers, scaled to lie in the range 0-1. The specific details of this encoding are presented as a "gene map" in table 3.

Number	Short Description	Comment
5	Target market ?	The market which has the highest value will be used as the target variable
5	Cointegrating market ?	Those markets (other than that selected as the dependent) with values > 0.5 are used in the cointegrating portfolio
1	Sensitivity	Used to scale Kalman Filter sensitivity
3	Claims for different model types	The model type (implicit, linear, neural) used is the one with the highest value
1	Random number seed	Used to generate random weights*
1	Number of hidden units	scales from 1-5 hidden units *
1	Training time	scales to 0-2000 epochs *
1	Trading Horizon	Scales holding-period from 1..MAX

Table 3 : The parameters which define each model in the population
(Note: genes marked * are "recessive" except for the neural models)

The first part of the coding specifies the target, cointegrating variables and "sensitivity" which together define a dynamic cointegration model. Note that we only use one parameter for sensitivity which is then scaled according to the variances of the different cointegrating variables.

The second part of the coding specifies the type of model which is used to estimate the relative returns of the two sides of the cointegration. The *Implicit* models take positions based simply on the sign of the cointegration residual. The *Linear* and *Conditional* models are error-correcting models of a form similar to Eq. (8) and Eq. (9) respectively. These models include additional variables which indicate (i) lagged relative returns on the model portfolio and (ii) a moving-average of the profitability of the "implicit" strategy applied to the appropriate portfolio, this latter taken as an indication of the degree of cointegration exhibited recently by the portfolio.

We use a stochastic population-based algorithm to generate sets of 20 models for each of the three model classes: Implicit, Linear and Conditional. Using information up to $Close_t$ the models produce forecasts for the relative returns between the period $Close_{t+1}$ and $Close_{t+2}$ i.e. daily returns but one-day-ahead in order to avoid trading artefacts. The positions indicated by the population of models are then consolidated to give a net position in each of the five markets.

4.3 Results

The performance of the models during the out-of-sample period, June 1995 to July 1996, is summarised in table 4 below. The "Overall" column represents the system which is produced by combining all three populations.

	Implicit	Linear	Conditional	Overall
Sharpe Ratio	1.16	1.48	2.28	2.33
'z' stat (SR > 0)	1.11	1.41	2.16*	2.21*
Profitable Periods	50.0%	52.3%	53.3%	54.7%
Total Return	7.2%	7.4%	10.2%	8.3%

Table 4: Results during out-of-sample period, averaged across each population of models (20 in each population, 60 overall) *=significant at 95% level of confidence

The Sharpe Ratio is an annualised measure of the average return divided by risk as represented by standard deviations of returns; all models generate positive returns with the neural-network based Conditional model representing a slightly over 50% improvement on the Implicit and Linear models. The "best" model, in terms of risk-return performance, is actually the "Overall" model which gains from the additional diversification obtained by combining all three populations.

5 Conclusions

We have described a methodology which is intended to reduce the risk of trading financial models. Our general approach is to use a population-based algorithm in which the "fitness" of individual models is adjusted to penalise correlations with the profits and losses of more profitable models. The objective of the algorithm is to evolve a well-diversified population which can then be traded as a "portfolio of models".

We have motivated the use of the econometric notion of cointegration as a suitable basis for the models, whether in the form of *implicit* "statistical arbitrage" strategies or as explicit models of the relative returns of the two sides of a cointegrated portfolio. Within this framework the use of neural networks allows the linear error-correction model to be generalised in a way which allows us to model cointegration effects which are conditional upon other factors. Further, we describe a "dynamic" cointegration in which the cointegrating vector is generated by a random-walk parameter model. This allows the cointegration to adapt, and to track the changing view of the markets over time as to what constitutes a "fair price" relationship. This contrasts to the fixed-parameter approach which can be prone to catastrophic break-down when applied to financial time-series.

We describe an application in which we use the technique to model a set of European equity indices using a portfolio of cointegration-based models. Comparing the different families of models, we find that they all generate positive profits during an out-of-sample period. The conditional, neural-network, models out-perform both the implicit and the linear models by just over 50%. The best performance, in terms of risk-return trade-off, is obtained by combining all three populations into a single model.

In future work we intend to investigate the relative merits of different measures of "fitness" and "competition" and the way in which they influence population diversity; to extend the individual models in order to include true exogenous variables in addition to the current time-series and technical variables; and to evaluate the profitability of the system under realistic trading conditions.

6 References

Alexander, C. and Johnson, A., 1994, "Dynamic links", *RISK,* Vol. 7(2).

Bruce, A., Connor, J. T. and Martin, R. D., 1996, "Prediction with Robustness Towards Outliers, Trends, and Level Shifts", in *Neural Networks in Financial Engineering,* (Singapore: World Scientific)

Burgess, A. N., 1996, "Modelling Conditional Cointegration in Financial Time-Series", *Proceedings of Intelligent Systems for Finance and Commerce,* 25-26 April 1996, London, (Unicom).

Burgess, A. N. and Refenes, A. N., 1996, "Modelling Non-linear Cointegration in International Equity Index Futures", in *Neural Networks in Financial Engineering,* (Singapore: World Scientific)

Dickey, D. A. and Fuller, W. A., 1979, "Distribution of the estimators for autoregressive time series with a unit root", *Journal of the American Statistical Association,* **74**

Engle, R. F. and Granger, C. W. J., 1987, "Cointegration and error-correction: representation, estimation and testing", *Econometrica,* 55

Harvey, A. C., 1993, "Time Series Models", (Harvester-Wheatsheaf)

Krogh, A. and Vedelsby, J., 1995, "Neural network ensembles, cross-validation and active learning", *NIPS 7,* MIT Press

Lo, A. W. and MacKinlay, A. C., 1990, "Data-Snooping Biases in Tests of Financial Asset Pricing Models", *Review of Financial Studies,*Vol.3, No.3

Srinivas, N. and Deb, K., 1995, "Multiobjective Optimization using Nondominated Sorting in Genetic Algorithms", *Evolutionary Computation,* Vol. 2, No. 3

REPRESENTING DYNAMICAL SYSTEMS IN FEED-FORWARD NETWORKS: A SIX LAYER ARCHITECTURE

HANS GEORG ZIMMERMANN
Siemens AG, Corporate Research
Otto-Hahn-Ring 6, D-81730 München, Germany
georg.zimmermann@mchp.siemens.de

ANDREAS S. WEIGEND
Department of Information Systems
Leonard N. Stern School of Business, New York University
44 West Fourth Street, MEC 9-74, New York, NY 10012
aweigend@stern.nyu.edu
www.stern.nyu.edu/~aweigend

Predictive models for financial data are often based on a large number of plausible inputs that are potentially nonlinearly combined to yield the conditional expectation of a target, such as a daily return of an asset. This paper introduces a new architecture for this task: On the output side, we predict dynamical variables such as first derivatives and curvatures on different time spans. These are subsequently combined in an ***interaction output layer*** to form several estimates of the variable of interest. Those estimates are then averaged to yield the final prediction. Independently from this idea, on the input side, we propose a new ***internal preprocessing layer*** connected with a diagonal matrix of positive weights to a layer of squashing functions. These weights adapt for each input individually and learn to squash outliers in the input. We apply these two ideas to the real world example of the daily predictions of the German stock index DAX (Deutscher Aktien Index), and compare the results to a network with a single output. The new six layer architecture is more stable in training due to two facts: (1) More information is flowing back from the outputs to the input in the backward pass; (2) The constraint of predicting first and second derivatives focuses the learning on the relevant variables for the dynamics. The architectures are compared from both the training perspective (squared errors, robust errors), and from the trading perspective (annualized returns, percent correct, Sharpe ratio).

1 Introduction

Historically, time series prediction has often been reduced to mere regression or pattern recognition.[a] This popular approach ignores any explicit relation between adjacent patterns in time. In fact, the presentation order of the pat-

[a] A pattern typically consists of a target and several inputs, such as lagged values of the time series variable.

terns is often randomized during training in order to avoid local minima and to improve the training speed.

On the other extreme, fully recurrent networks allow for a perfect representation of temporal dependencies. Unfortunately, despite a lot of effort in the last decade, fully recurrent networks have proven difficult to train, in particular for long-term dependencies.

Recently, two new classes of approaches have been applied to financial markets that are located between these two extremes. The first class employs the idea of a hidden state that cannot be inferred from a finite window in time. This state can be continuous (see Timmer & Weigend (1997) for the application of state space models to volatility prediction), or it can describe the switching between several discrete models (see Shi & Weigend (1997) for the application of Hidden Markov experts for predictions of returns). These examples of the first class rely on heavy statistical machinery to estimate the hidden states.

The second class, described in this paper, focuses on the variables used for the targets of the network. It incorporates dynamics as architectural constraints, such as the first and second derivatives of the dynamical system. It turns out that this architecture has improved learning behavior since it uses several outputs that are variations of the quantity of interest. Apart from providing perspectives of the problem on different time scales, this approach enables an information flow in the backward pass of an amount similar to that in the forward pass. In contrast to the first class of approaches mentioned in the previous paragraph, this second class maintains the training simplicity of a feed-forward network and does not introduce the notion of hidden states.

We begin by discussing the first point, the use of variables that formulate the problem in terms of adequate dynamic quantities. A common approach to time series prediction uses (potentially nonlinear) ARMA models. Their main goal is to obtain a point prediction of a future value by taking the point to be predicted and performing regression onto past values of the same observable, as well as on external variables.

When such simple point predictions are carried out with a very rich nonlinear model class, such as a neural network or connectionist model, they often lead to the serious problem of overfitting. For noisy data in particular, the small amount of information contained in a single point does not suffice in determining the structure of the model and the values of all the parameters. Because of high flexibility and usually insufficient constraints, the model tends to memorize the training points well, but the out-of-sample performance does not improve beyond chance.

In this paper we exploit the additional structure that originates from the nature of a dynamical system. This is in contrast to the assumption of arbitrary mappings between random inputs and random outputs, typically made in machine learning. Specifically, we use the following two features:

- Inspired by physics and economics, we use variables, both for the inputs and the targets, that characterize *dynamic behavior* (such as curvatures, corresponding of accelerating that are proportional to driving external forces).
- It is well known that the information provided by the input needs to capture the state of the system. We take the idea of state seriously also for the output side, by providing a *sufficient number of outputs* to describe the subsequent state of the systems, as opposed to almost all other prediction models that only use information from a single target (e.g., the value to be predicted).

Thus far, one might think that it would suffice to just predict several such dynamical system quantities. This more symmetrical approach between inputs and outputs would indeed have the added advantage to accelerate iterative learning procedures such as error backpropagation, since more information is "flowing back" from the target side. However, networks trained on many such outputs tend to learn the individual mappings quite well, ignoring the fact that they are related in time. In many cases, just sharing hidden units does not stipulate sufficient interactions between these outputs, particularly when the complexity of the problem requires many hidden units.

We thus add a third feature to the specification of the network architecture for time series prediction: an additional layer that we call the *interaction layer*. The interaction layer encodes the relationship between its neighbors. Examples include derivatives and curvatures on different scales between predicted points. This feature is missing in standard multivariate regression where the different outputs typically do not have a relation to one another.

The general ideas are made concrete in Section 2 through two specific architectures: (1) point predictions followed by an interaction layer, and (2) an indicator layer of dynamical system variables followed by an interaction layer combining the dynamical system variables. Section 3 introduces another useful ingredient for modeling that is inserted between the inputs and the hidden units. This internal preprocessing layer connects each input with one preprocessing hidden unit with a hyperbolical tangens (tanh) transfer function. Adapting the corresponding weights allows for a problem-driven suppression of outliers. These architectural elements are combined in Section 4 and applied to daily forecasts of the German equity index DAX (Deutscher Aktien Index). The learning performance is shown to be more stable compared to a standard network with a single output unit, and the performance is comparable to a state-of-the-art neuro-fuzzy model (Zimmermann *et al.*, 1996). Section 5 discusses why the observed stability cannot be reached by simply reducing the learning rate.

2 Taking relations to neighbors into account: the interaction layer

This section presents two new architectures that take relations between neighboring values in time into account. The first architecture adds an interaction layer on top of a layer with individual point predictions. The second architecture (which will be used for the DAX example) first computes dynamical quantities on several time scales such as first derivatives and curvatures, and subsequently combines them to predictions of the desired value.

2.1 Architecture 1: Point-predictions followed by the interaction layer

In most applications of neural nets in financial engineering, the number of inputs is huge (of the order of a hundred), but only a single output is used. This can be viewed as a large "inverted" funnel; the hard problem is that the only information provided in learning is that of the single output. This is one of the reasons for the "data-hungryness" of single-output neural networks, i.e., a large set of training data is often required in order to distinguish nonlinearities from noise.[b]

One approach to increase the information flow from the output side to the input side is to increase the number of output units. In the simplest case, two outputs can be used, one to predict the return, and the other one to predict the sign of the return, see Weigend *et al.* (1991), as well as the experiments described by Caruana (1994).

While the idea of increasing the information flow through multiple outputs can generally be used, the specific task of time series allows us to exploit yet another source of information. We would like to provide enough information to characterize the state of the autonomous part of the dynamics on the output side, similarly to Takens' theorem for the notion of state on the input side, see e.g., Gershenfeld (1989). In this time series context, this embedding of the output can be done analogously to the input side of a tapped "delay" line, indicated in Fig. 1 as *point prediction layer.*

The forecast we are interested in is y_t, the t-step ahead forecast of variable y. Additionally, we here also predict y_{t-1} and y_{t+1}. However, the experiments with this architecture were disappointing; contrary to our original hopes, sharing hidden units does not promote significant interactions between the outputs. This prompted us to add an explicit second output layer, the *interaction layer.* It computes the next-neighbor derivatives $(y_t - y_{t-1})$ and $(y_{t+1} - y_t)$, as well as the curvature $(y_{t+1} - 2y_t + y_{t-1})$.

[b]Too small data sets also imply a bias towards linear models. This is not to be confused with the bias towards linear models that is a consequence of some overfitting techniques such as early stopping or weight decay.

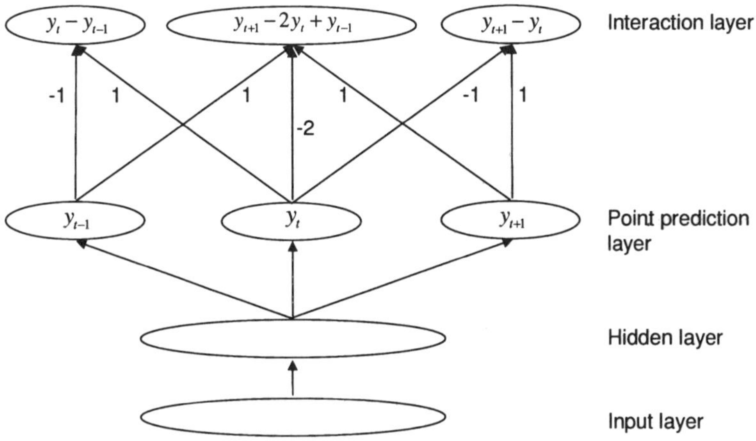

Figure 1: The first architecture, where point predictions are followed by the interaction layer.

Since the differences between neighbors are encoded as fixed weights, they do not have to be estimated and thus do not enlarge the number of free parameters that have to be determined from the data. The overall cost function is the sum of all six contributions. Here we weigh all individual contributions evenly. An alternative is to give equal contribution to the error and down-weigh each error output by the average error of that output unit.

If the point forecasts were perfect, the interaction layer would have no effect at all. To explain the effect of non-zero errors, consider Fig. 2. Both predictions of the three points have the same pointwise errors at each of the three neighboring points. However, both the slopes and the curvature are correct in Model 1 (they do not give additional errors), but do add to the errors for Model 2.[c]

Despite all of these desirable features, this architecture has a disadvantage when viewed from the input side: In order to be able to make predictions on several time horizons on the output side, we have to use the preprocessing transformations (such as moving averages) on all corresponding time scales. This unfortunately increases the number of inputs dramatically, yielding once again a strong asymmetry between the information flow in the forward and in the backward pass, defying our original intention. Furthermore, the additional parameters increase the problem of overfitting.

[c]In the case of a quadratic error function, the interaction layer can be substituted by a single output layer of point predictions that are combined with a positive definite non-diagonal quadratic form to create an equivalent target function.

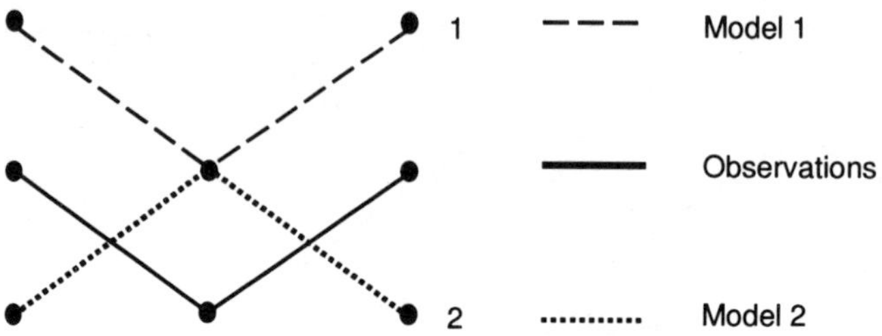

Figure 2: Geometric interpretation of the effect of the interaction layer on the cost function (schematic). Given are three curves connecting points at three adjacent steps in time. The solid line connects the target points. Model 1 (dashed line) is an example of a model that takes relationships between neighbors into account, as proposed in this paper. Model 2 (dotted line) only focuses on the quality of the point predictions. Note that we constructed this fictitious example such that both models have the same point-by-point errors, but when derivatives and curvatures are taken into account, Model 1 is favored.

2.2 Architecture 2: An indicator layer recombined by the interaction layer

The second architecture keeps the advantages of the model given above but avoids its disadvantages. Let us assume that the target of ultimate interest has the form:

$$\text{TARGET} = \frac{y_t - y_0}{y_0} = \frac{y_t}{y_0} - 1 \quad . \tag{1}$$

y denotes a price, y_0 is the value at the present time, and y_t is the price for t days into the future. This target thus corresponds to the relative return for t-day trading. We now define an indicator layer that adds a series of additional pairs of targets to this true goal:

$$\text{TARGET} = \frac{y_{t+n} + y_t + y_{t-n}}{3y_0} - 1 \tag{2}$$

$$\text{TARGET} = \frac{-y_{t+n} + 2y_t - y_{t-n}}{3y_0} \quad . \tag{3}$$

where n defines the *span* of the embedding. Eq. (2) describes a smoothed return centered at time t, and Eq. (3) is proportional to the curvature, normalized similarly to the average by the current price y_0. The curvature, as second derivative, can be seen to reflect an acceleration, revealing and underlying force, as well as drawing attention to the turning points. Note that these pairs are chosen such that they add up to the ultimate target, Eq. (1). All of the targets are centered around the same midpoint t. This indicator layer is followed by the interaction layer. It recombines the N pairs of smoothed returns and curvatures, yielding N estimates of the ultimate target.

The number N of such pairs used is one of the modeling choices. In the task of one-day forecasts discussed in this paper we use three pairs, covering in their union the forces of one week. In another problem of six-month forecasts, we find six spans useful; they can be seen as attempting to cover the forces of one year.

In the final step, all of the individual forecasts in the interaction layer will be averaged in a final output layer. Combining forecasts is beneficial to the degree to which the individual forecasts are uncorrelated, see Bates & Granger (1969) and Granger (1989), as well as the corresponding ideas in the mean variance framework of modern portfolio theory, e.g., Elton & Gruber (1995).

Experimenting with this architecture, we find that forecasts of the individual averages and the individual curvatures resemble each other more than we had hoped for. If the degree of correlation between the forecasts should be reduced, a remedy consists of including additional targets, such as combinations of dynamic variables, indicating to the learning algorithm that it should also consider the differences between the individual forecasts, not just their commonalities. In other work we use the pairwise differences of the point averages of the spans, as well as the pointwise differences of the curvatures of the spans. This corresponds to $2(N-1)$ additional targets for the interaction layer.

3 Internal preprocessing layer

In order to have potentially very different inputs on a comparable scale, we follow the common practice and standardize the input data to zero mean and unit variance. A problem with this approach is that outliers in the input can have a large impact. This is particularly serious for data in finance and economics that contain large shocks.[d] To deal with the shocks, we inserted an additional preprocessing layer between the inputs and the first hidden layer. The complete network architecture is shown in Fig. 3.

This additional preprocessing layer has the same number of hidden units as the input layer and uses standard tanh squashing functions. But the weight matrix between the input layer and the preprocessing layer is only a square diagonal matrix. The weights have initial values of 0.1, ensuring that the

[d]The same reasoning about shocks and outliers in the data lead us to use a robust error function on the output side. Rather than using squared errors between target and outputs, we minimize in all the examples in this paper $\frac{1}{2}\log(\cosh(2(\text{target - output})))$. This function approximates the parabola of the squared errors for small differences (Gaussian noise model), and is proportional to the absolute value of the difference for larger values of the difference (Laplacian noise model).

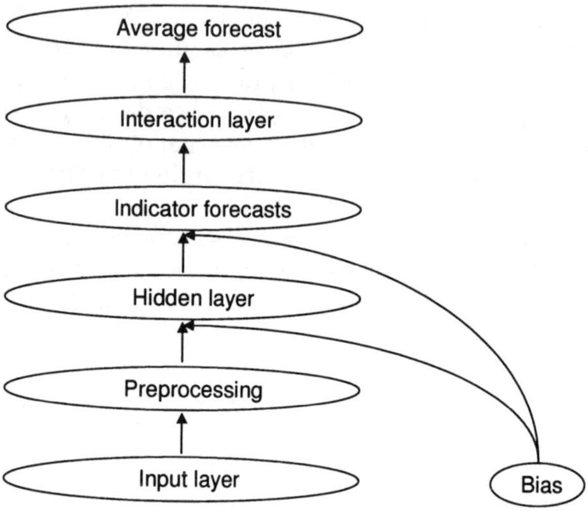

Figure 3: The second architecture, the six layer network. The novel features are the preprocessing layer that learns to scale the importance of the individual inputs, and the indicator forecasts of differences and curvatures followed by the interaction layer of individual predictions of the target that are averaged to the final forecast.

tanh is initially in its linear range, letting the external inputs pass through essentially unchanged.

The diagonal weights to the preprocessing layer are constrained to be positive. Furthermore, no bias term is included for the preprocessing layer to avoid numerical ambiguities. The weights are adaptive and updated in the same way as all the other weights in the network. In practice, we observe both growing and shrinking values for the weights. The growing values cause a larger proportion of the inputs to be compressed by the squashing function of the tanh. Shrinking diagonal elements indicate that the corresponding input might be a candidate to be pruned away. So as to not mix too many features in this analysis, we do not use pruning in the simple example presented in this paper.

4 Real-world application: One-day ahead predictions of DAX

We now apply the ideas about the interaction layer and the preprocessing layer introduced in the previous sections to a real world example. We chose the benchmark problem of predicting the German stock index (DAX, Deutscher Aktien Index). Section 4.1 describes the task and the data, and Section 4.2

presents the results, and compares the new six-layer architecture to a neural network with a single output.

4.1 Data

The task is a DAX one-day ahead return forecast based on twelve input time series that include various stock indices, bond indices, and inflation indicators.[e] We present information from these time series in a variety of ways to the network. The "momentum" in the market is represented by the first difference of the prices. If we only chose such first differences as inputs and nothing else, the forecast model will very likely be trending. In order to avoid the bias towards a trending model. Additional inputs include the underlying "forces" expressed as second derivatives, as well as a simple description of the "distances" to the estimated equilibria.

In the experiments reported here, we use the time period from the beginning of January 1986 up to the end of February 1993 as training set, and the period from March 1993 up to mid-August 1996 as the test set. We trained for 300 epochs without any early stopping nor pruning. (This justifies the omission of a validation set.) For performance comparison, a simple buy-and-hold strategy on this period gives an annualized return of 12 percent.

4.2 Results and Comparisons

We compare the six-layer network with a standard three-layer network using the same 44 inputs in both cases. Both networks have 40 hidden units. The resulting behavior during the first 300 epochs of learning is shown in Fig. 4 for

[e] In full detail, the variables used are:

1. DAX Price Index (30 firms);
2. DAX Price-Earnings Ratio;
3. DAX Composite (several hundred firms);
4. Dow Jones Industrial Average;
5. Nikkei 225;
6. 3-month German interest rate (reflecting decisions by the Bundesbank);
7. Yield of German circulating bonds (average over all maturities);
8. U.S. 30-year bond;
9. Morgan Stanley Price Index Germany (inflation indicator);
10. Morgan Stanley Price Index Europe (inflation indicator);
11. Gold price (inflation indicator);
12. DEM/USD exchange rate (Frankfurt closing);

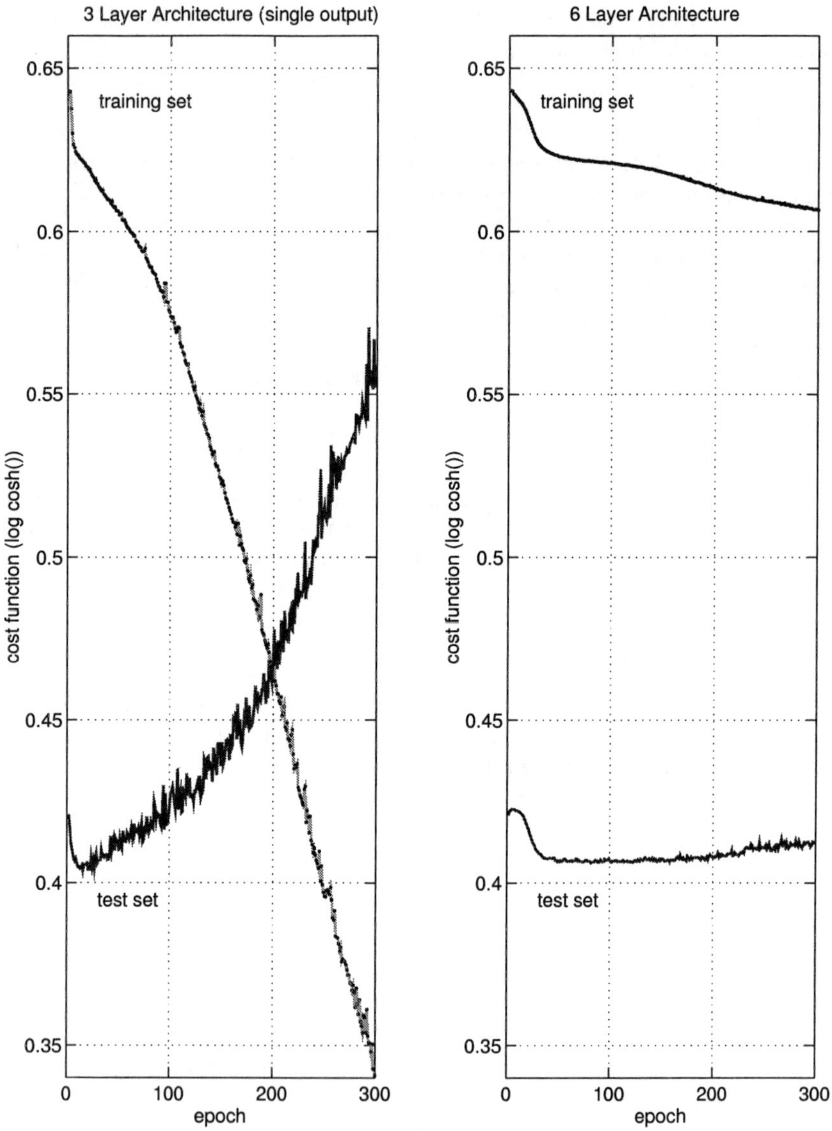

Figure 4: Learning curves for the DAX example. The left panel describes a standard network with a single output unit; the right panel gives the training and testing for the six-layer architecture. Each panel has the performance for both the training and test set. Note the clear overfitting on the network without interaction layer.

the log(cosh(.)) target function used to train the networks, and in Fig. 5, for the normalized mean squared error.

Fig. 4 compares a standard network with a single output unit (left panel) with the six-layer architecture (right panel). The level is not normalized but reflects the different volatilities of the training and test sets. The relative shape of each curve matters, not their absolute values.

Fig. 5 shows the normalized mean squared error, E_{NMS}, as a function of the training time. Note the stabilizing effect of the six layer architecture, in comparison to a single output on the left. Furthermore, the out-of-sample behavior measured by squared errors is better for a network trained on the robust log(cosh(.)) than for a network trained directly on squared error minimization.

The next three figures, Figs. 6–8, evaluate the network from a trading perspective. The forecast needs to be translated into a strategy in order to compute financial objectives. We use a simple strategy based on the sign of the forecasting model: We buy when the predicted return is positive, and we sell short when the predicted return is negative, both to the full position size.

Using this specification, Fig. 6 shows annualized return as a function of training iterations, Fig. 7 shows the percentage of correct predictions, and Fig. 8 shows the Sharpe ratio of the six layer architecture followed by the simple strategy. Here, we compute the Sharpe ratio simply by dividing the returns by the standard deviation of the returns, and annualizing it. In contrast to usual practice, no risk-free interest rate has been subtracted from the returns. For more details on the Sharpe ratio, as well as its explicit optimization with variable position sizes, see Choey & Weigend (1997). Furthermore, no transaction costs have been applied. The key point here is the comparison between the new and the standard architecture.

Using the forecast model as part of a decision model, especially in a trading application, it is important to interpret the major input influences at a given day. The input-output sensitivities can vary over time in a nonlinear model, depending on the current operating point. Fig. 9 shows as an example the sensitivities for the 20 days leading up to December 17, 1992. The rightmost column represents the values for the day of the evaluation. Variations over time indicate changes in the importance of the input indicators.

Summarizing the results, the six layer architecture stabilizes the learning process. Given the simple sign-based strategy of translating the forecast into a trading signal, this behavior carries over to the decision process.

5 Discussion and implications

This paper introduced a new architecture for time series prediction. The most important result is that this six layer architecture stabilizes learning in the

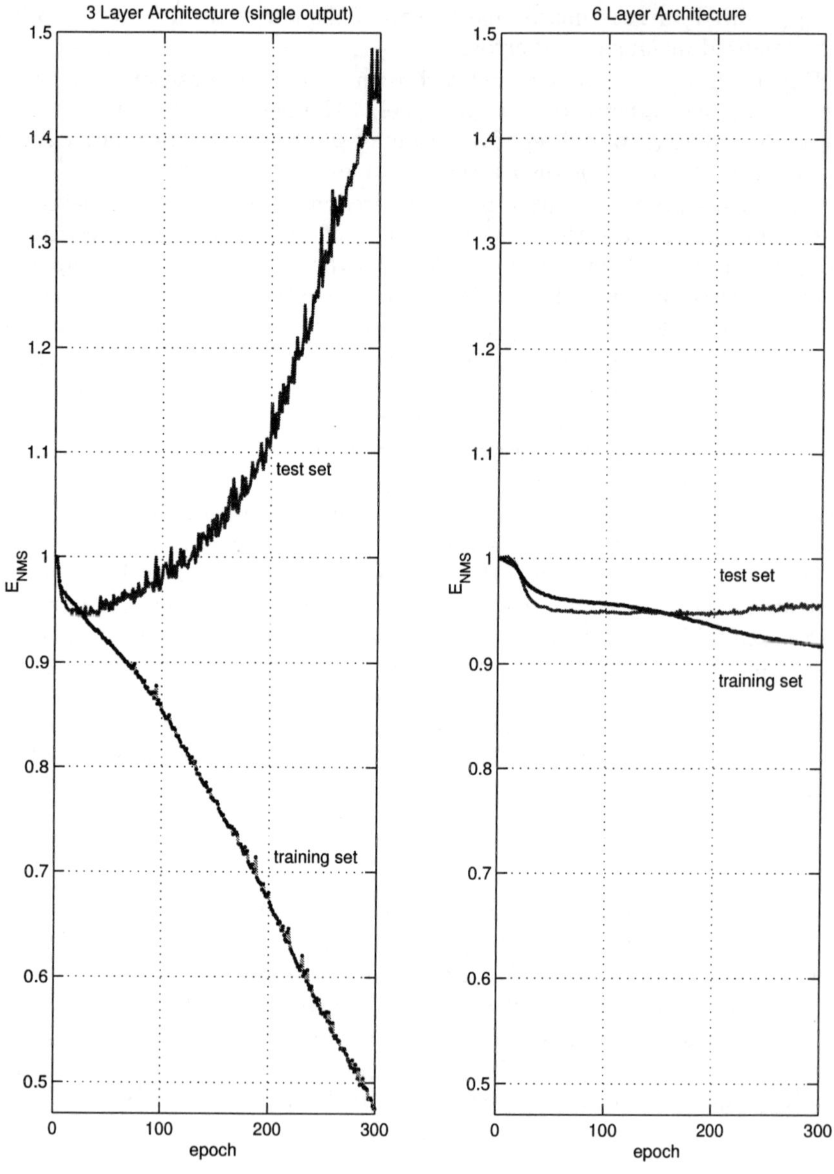

Figure 5: Normalized mean squared error as a function of the training time. The picture shows the stabilizing effect of the six layer architecture on the right, in comparison to a single output on the left.

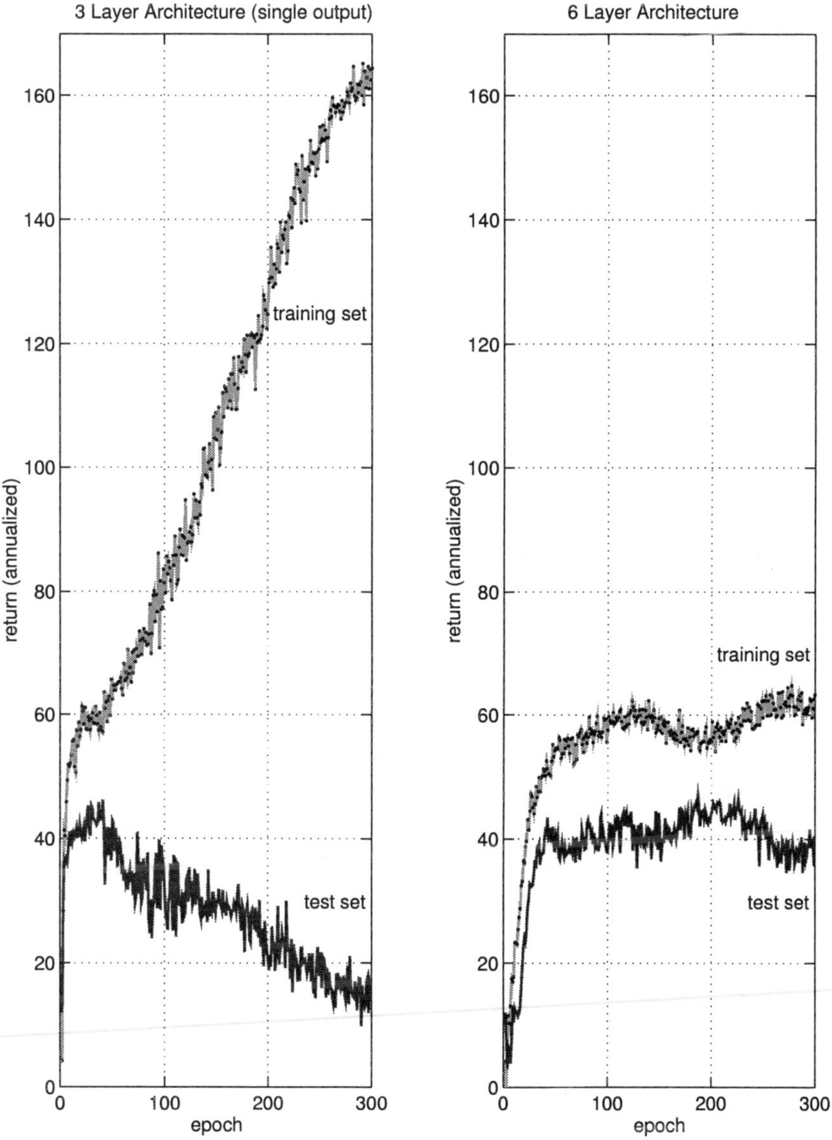

Figure 6: Annualized return as a function of the training time. Whereas the network with a single output (left) overfits dramatically, there is no strong deterioration of the out-of-sample performance for the six layer architecture on the right. (No transaction costs are taken into account.)

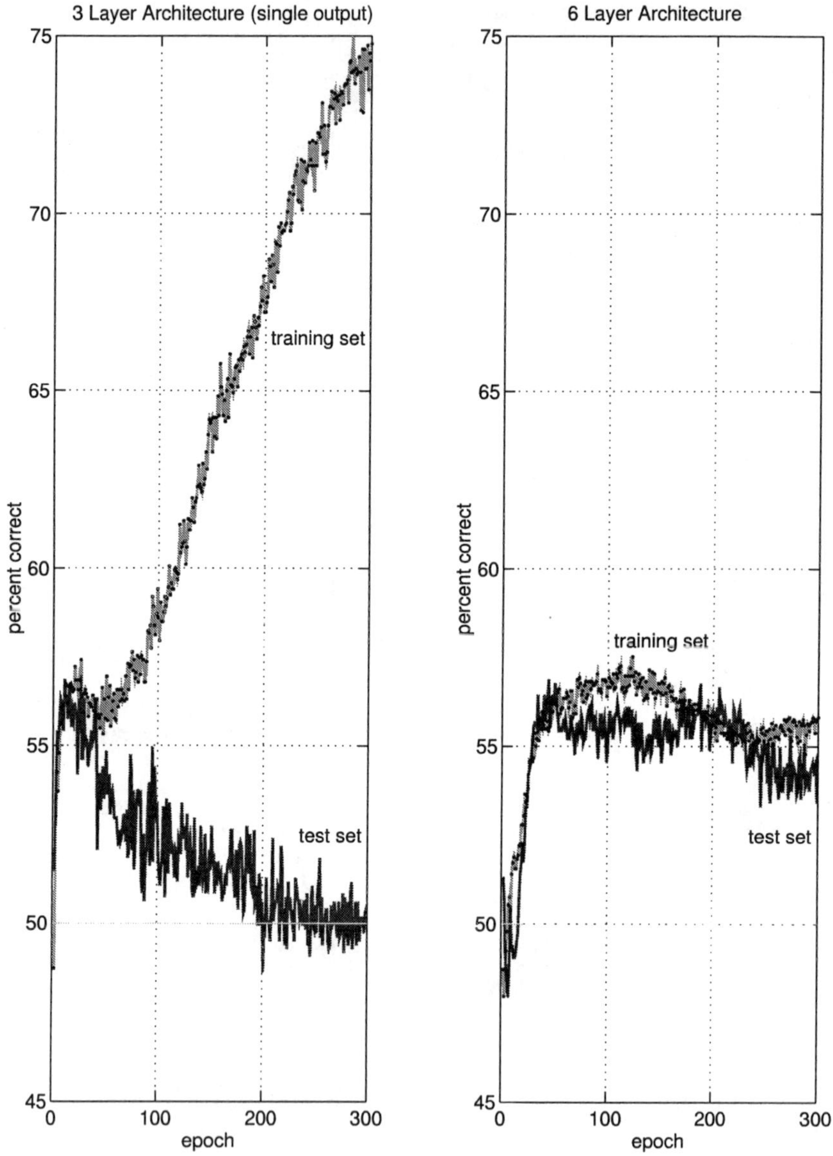

Figure 7: Probability of correct sign ("hit rate") as a function of the training time. Note the close proximity of training and test set values for the six layer architecture on the right.

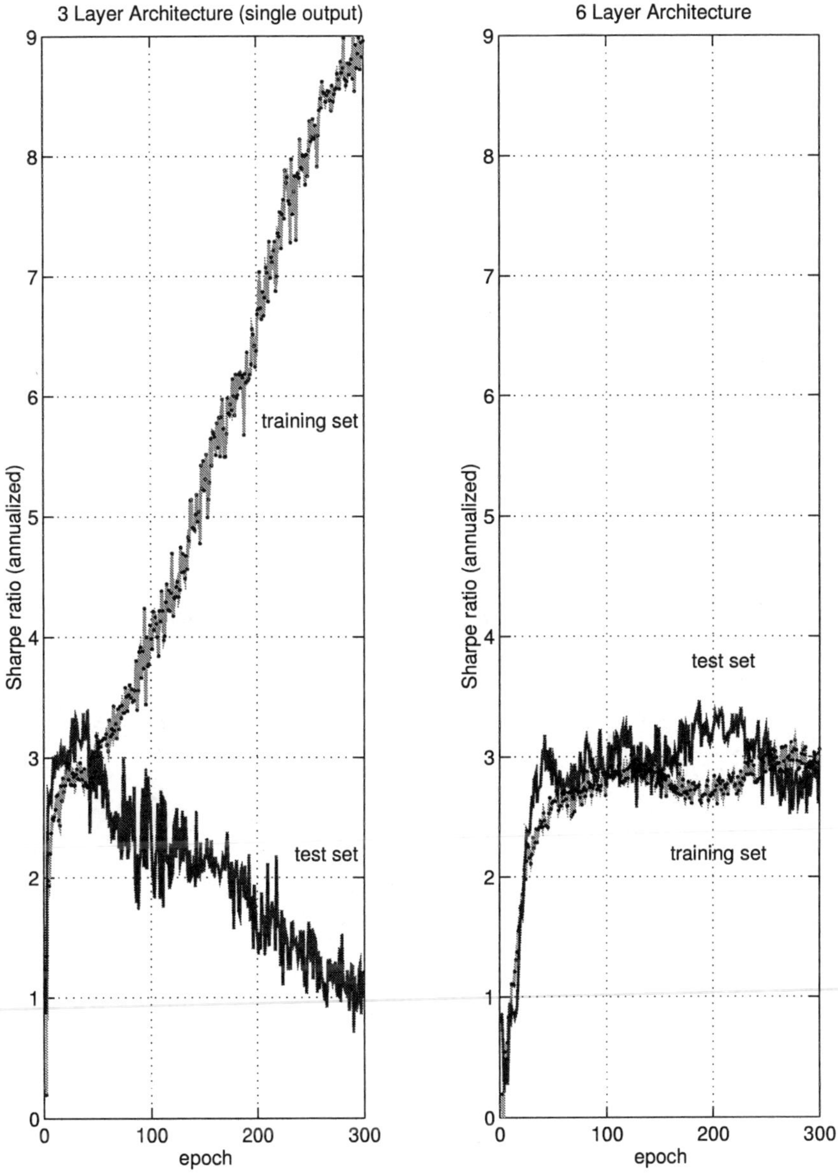

Figure 8: Sharpe ratio as a function of the training time. This network was not optimized on the risk-adjusted performance measure but only evaluated on the annualized return divided by the standard deviation of the returns. (No risk-free interest rate is taken into account.)

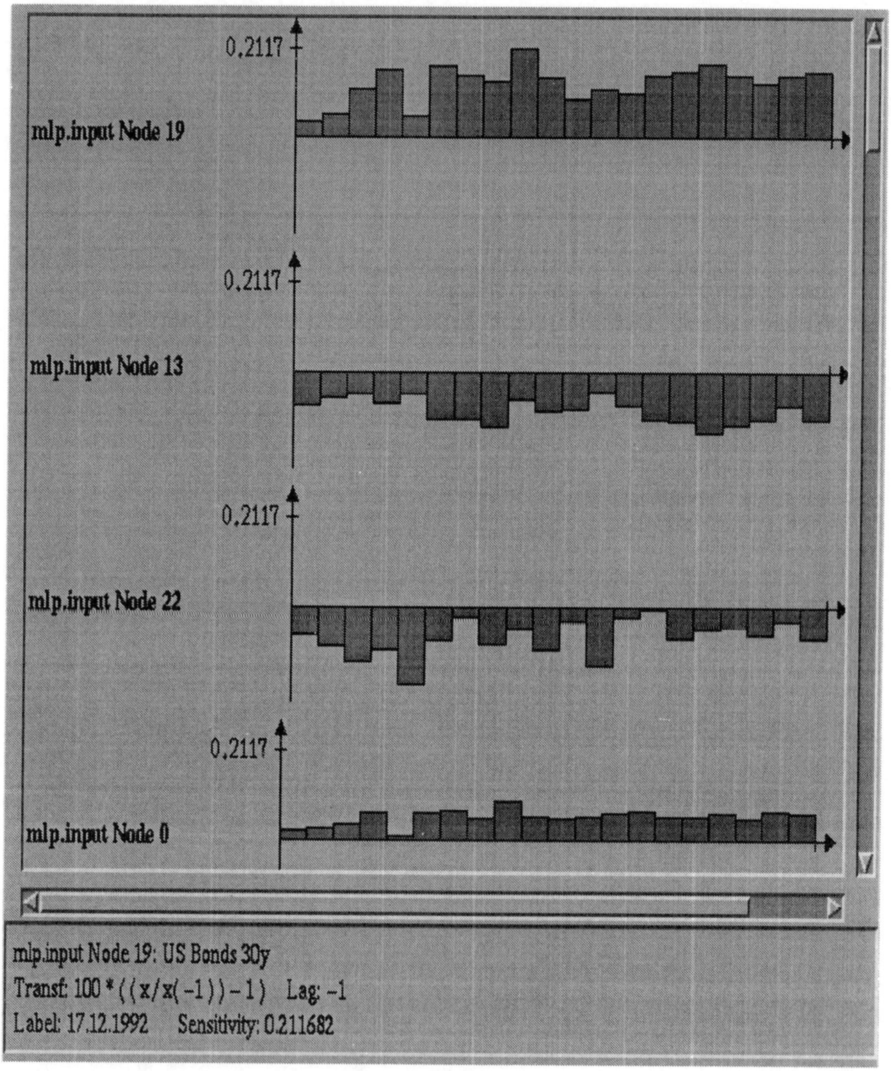

Figure 9: Sensitivity analysis from SENN (Software Environment for Neural Networks). The partial derivative of the final output with respect to each input is shown for the 20 days leading up to the date shown (December 17, 1992). The ranking of the input importance is, starting with the most important one: (1) U.S. 30-year bond (2) Dow Jones Industrial Average, (3) Gold price, and (4) DAX price.

sense that the network does not overfit on a learning time scale where a standard network has already overfitted strongly. This is mainly caused by the richer error evaluations in the interaction layer. We showed that this can be understood as a consequence of the penalty function effect of the interaction layer. Instead of this approach, we included features of the dynamics in the network architecture. This type of penalty is not a bias towards linear models or any structural feature unrelated to the task—the central point is to formulate the time series problem in terms of dynamics variable on several time scales.

From the viewpoint of early stopping, one may argue that a simple reduction of the learning rate would also stabilize the learning behavior. Beside the facts (1) that overfitting often starts already right in the first epoch, and (2) that there is a well-known bias towards a linear solutions,[f] a smaller learning rate would change the global stochastic search to a local optimization which may end in the nearest local minimum. On the other hand, if the local learning does not stop in the nearest local minimum, it has a bias towards maximum likelihood solutions instead of Bayesian solutions. In general, it is important to exploit noise as a central part of the training procedure. Furthermore, we introduced another idea for the input side, independent of the interaction layer on the output side. The new preprocessing layer on the input side consists of adaptive weights on the diagonal and zeros everywhere else (i.e., each input is connected to one tanh preprocessing hidden unit). The purpose is to allow for an adaptive outlier suppression for each input individually.

For the interaction layer, the penalty effect vanishes for noise-free data as well as for extreme overfitting on noisy data when the network completely memorizes the data. This paper does not focus on this situation; many approaches including additive noise on the inputs (Weigend *et al.*, 1991) and weight pruning methods (Zimmermann, 1994) have been proposed to curb overfitting. We did not want to clutter the discussion and obscure the results of the new architecture by also including methods against overfitting here. We would like to note, however, that the additional topology optimization by pruning methods rests on an evaluation of the error signals flowing through the network. We thus expect these techniques to also profit from the extended error signal created by the new six layer architecture proposed in this paper.

Acknowledgments

We thank Mark Choey for his kind help in the final production of this paper during his time with the Information Systems Department of NYU's Leonard N. Stern School of Business. The simulations were performed with the Software Environment for Neural Networks (SENN) by Siemens Nixdorf.

[f] LeBaron & Weigend (1997) give an empirical evaluation on financial data.

References

Bates, J. M. and C. W. J. Granger. 1969. The combination of forecasts. *Operations Research Quarterly* **20**, 451–468.

Caruana, R. A. 1994. Multitask connectionist learning. In *Proceedings of the 1993 Connectionist Models Summer School*, M. C. Mozer, P. Smolensky, D. S. Touretzky, J. L. Elman and A. S. Weigend (eds), pp. 372–379, Hillsdale, NJ. Lawrence Erlbaum Associates.

Choey, M. and A. S. Weigend. 1997. Nonlinear trading models through Sharpe Ratio maximization. In *Decision Technologies for Financial Engineering: Proceedings of the Fourth International Conference on Neural Networks in the Capital Markets (NNCM-96)*, A. S. Weigend, Y. S. Abu-Mostafa and A.-P. N. Refenes (eds), S'pore. World Scientific.

Elton, E. J. and M. J. Gruber. 1995. *Modern Portfolio Theory and Investment Analysis.* John Wiley and Sons, New York, fifth edition.

Gershenfeld, N. A. 1989. An experimentalist's introduction to the observation of dynamical systems. In *Directions in Chaos*, H. B. Lin (ed), vol. 2, pp. 310–384. World Scientific, Singapore.

Granger, C. W. J. 1989. Combining forecasts–Twenty years later. *Journal of Forecasting* **8**, 167–173.

LeBaron, B. and A. S. Weigend. 1997. A bootstrap evaluation of the effect of data splitting on financial time series. *IEEE Transactions on Neural Networks* **8**, forthcoming.

Shi, S. and A. S. Weigend. 1997. Taking time seriously: Hidden Markov experts applied to financial engineering. In *Proceedings of the IEEE/IAFE 1997 Computational Intelligence for Financial Engineering (CIFEr)*, pp. 244–252, Piscataway, NJ. IEEE Service Center.

Timmer, J. and A. S. Weigend. 1997. Modeling volatility using state space models. Technical Report IS-97-11, Leonard N. Stern School of Business, New York University. Accepted for *Computational Finance 97.*

Weigend, A. S., D. E. Rumelhart and B. A. Huberman. 1991. Generalization by weight-elimination with application to forecasting. In *Advances in Neural Information Processing Systems 3 (NIPS*90)*, R. P. Lippmann, J. Moody and D. S. Touretzky (eds), pp. 875–882, Redwood City, CA. Morgan Kaufmann.

Zimmermann, H. G. 1994. Neuronale Netze als Entscheidungskalkül. In *Neuronale Netze in der Ökonomie (In German)*, H. Rehkugler and H. G. Zimmermann (eds), pp. 1–87, München. Vahlen Verlag.

Zimmermann, H. G., R. Neuneier, H. Dichtl and S. Siekmann. 1996. Modeling the German stock index DAX with neuro-fuzzy. In *EUFIT'96, Fourth European Congress on Intelligent Techniques and Soft Computing*, H.-J. Zimmermann (ed), vol. 3, pp. 2187–2190.

MODELING OF NONSTATIONARY FINANCIAL TIME SERIES BY NONPARAMETRIC DATA SELECTION

G. DECO, R. NEUNEIER AND B. SCHÜRMANN
Siemens AG, R&D
Otto-Hahn-Ring 6
81739 Munich
Germany

We apply a new method for data selection to the task of predicting the daily relative differences of the DAX given 12 inputs which describe a so called technical model using only historical DAX prices and the total volume of the transactions at the stock market. The method consists of a nonparametric cumulant based statistical approach for detecting linear and nonlinear statistical dependences in non-stationary time series. The statistical dependence is detected by measuring the predictability which tests the null hypothesis of statistical independence, expressed in Fourier-space, by the surrogate method. Therefore, the predictability is defined as a higher-order cumulant based significance, discriminating between the original data and a set of scrambled surrogate data which correspond to the null hypothesis of a non-causal relationship between past and present. In this formulation nonlinear and non-Gaussian temporal dependences can be detected in time series.

1 Introduction

The dynamics of international stock market portfolios are receiving increasing attention. In this article, we focus on the German stock index DAX because the 30 companies forming the index are responsible for about 70% of the turnover at the stock market in Frankfurt. Since the DAX is a weighted mixture of stocks it behaves like a real portfolio. Therefore, the goal is the construction of efficient parametric models of a nonstationary time series based on data. Consequently, when neural networks are used for example, it is very important to train the model with a set of data which contains the underlying structure to be discovered. Information about the predictability can be used to select regions where a temporal structure is visible in order to select data for training a neural network for prediction. The regions where only a noisy behavior is observed are therefore ignored, avoiding in this fashion the learning of irrelevant noise which normally spoils the generalization characteristics of the neural network. The reliable detection of statistical dependence in the data is a task which has to be solved first before the final goal of extracting the dynamics of the system can be achieved. In the context of time series, the statistical dependence between the past points and the present point considered therefore yields a measure of the predictability of the corresponding system. An information-theoretic based redundancy reduction learning in data has also been formulated in the context of neural networks (see Deco and Schürmann (1995), Deco and Brauer (1995), and Deco and Obradovic (1996) for a rigorous mathematical formulation). Deco and Schürmann (1995) have applied this theory of redundancy minimization to the unsupervised parametric extraction of statistical dependences in time series. Deco and Brauer (1995) formulated a cumulant based method for the parametric extraction of statistical dependence in time series which does not involve the calculation of entropy but the estimation of higher order moments.

Some time ago, a very powerful method, called "the surrogate method", for the analysis of time series was introduced by Theiler et al. (1992) and used in combination with entropy based measures of temporal redundancy by Palus et al. (1993) and Palus (1995). A drawback of the redundancy measure of statistical dependence is that it is entropy based, and therefore usually box-counting algorithms should be used for the estimation of probability distributions involved in its calculation. In the case where the dimensionality involved is high, e.g. when the redundancy between several points in the past and the present should be measured, very unreliable results can be obtained, due to the difficulty of density estimations by histograms in high dimensions, especially when the number of data is small (see Grassberger, 1988 and Herzel et al., 1994).

The aim of the present paper is to formulate a nonparametric cumulant based statistical approach for detecting linear and nonlinear statistical dependences in time series. The statistical dependence is detected by measuring the discriminating significance which tests the null hypothesis of statistical independence, expressed in Fourier-space, by the surrogate method. The surrogate data used herein correspond to the null hypothesis of a non-causal relationship between past and present, i.e. of a random process with statistical properties equivalent to the original time series. The formulation of statistical independence in Fourier-space automatically and consistently leads to a cumulant based measure. In this formulation non-linear and non-Gaussian temporal dependences can be detected in time series. The cumulant based predictability offers a method for the estimation of temporal redundancy (i.e. statistical dependencies between past and present) which is possible even in the case of a small number of data because for calculating cumulants the probability density need not be explicitly known (unbiased estimators based on summation over the patterns are used). This fact permits us to avoid the assumption of stationarity and to use the sliding window based method for measuring the non-stationarity that can only be reliably employed when the estimation of predictability can be performed with a small number of data points. Let us remark that an entropy based measure of temporal redundancy cannot be applied in combination with the sliding window method if more than one point in the past should be considered due to the difficulty in the estimation of the involved high dimensional density with the small number of data contained in the sliding window.

2 Theory

Let us consider a time series $x(t)$ and let us define an embedding vector $\vec{x}(t) = (x(t), x(t-\Delta), \ldots, x(t-(m-1)\Delta)) = (x_1, \ldots, x_m)$ of dimensionality m and time-lag Δ. The vector $\vec{x}$ is a random variable distributed according to the probability distribution $P(\vec{x})$. A measure of the predictability of the present from the past is determined by how strongly the probability of the present (say the point $x(t)$) is conditioned by the past (i.e. by $(x(t-\Delta), \ldots, x(t-(m-1)\Delta))$). In other words, the predictability is a measure of how different from zero is the substraction $P(x_1) - P(x_1|x_2, \ldots, x_m)$. Equivalently, multiplying this quantity by $P(x_2, \ldots, x_m)$, the predictability is a measure of the statistical independence between the present and the past, i.e. of how different from zero is the substraction $P(x_1)P(x_2, \ldots, x_m) - P(x_1, x_2, \ldots, x_m)$ for all x. If this quantity is zero, then the present is independent of the past and therefore unpredictable from the past, i.e. there is no statistical structure underlying the time series data meaning that the data are just uncorrelated noise and therefore defined by a Bernoulli process.

Due to this fact we will measure in this work the predictability by testing the null hypothesis $H \equiv \{P(x_1, x_2, \ldots, x_m) = P(x_1)P(x_2, \ldots, x_m)\}$ of statistical independence. In order to be able to estimate the null hypothesis H from the data we would like to express H in terms of empirically measurable entities like higher order cumulants, which take into account the effect of non-Gaussianity and nonlinearity underlying the data. Therefore, let us consider the cumulant expansion of the Fourier transforms of the joint and marginal probability distributions:

$$\phi(K_1, K_2, \ldots, K_m) = \int dx_1 \ldots dx_m \; e^{i\left(\sum_{j=1}^{m} x_j K_j\right)} P(x_1, \ldots, x_m) = e^{\sum_{n=1}^{\infty} \frac{i^n}{n!} \sum_{i_1, \ldots, i_n = 1}^{m} \aleph_{i_1 \ldots i_n} K_{i_1} \ldots K_{i_n}} , \tag{1}$$

$$\varphi(K_1) = \int dx_1 \; e^{i(K_1 \cdot x_1)} P(x_1) = e^{\sum_{n=1}^{\infty} \frac{i^n}{n!} \aleph_1^{(n)} K_1^n} , \tag{2}$$

$$\lambda(K_2, \ldots, K_m) = \int dx_2 \ldots dx_m \; e^{i\left(\sum_{j=2}^{m} x_j K_j\right)} P(x_2, \ldots, x_m)$$
$$= e^{\sum_{n=1}^{\infty} \frac{i^n}{n!} \sum_{i_1, \ldots, i_n = 2}^{m} \aleph_{i_1 \ldots i_n} K_{i_1} \ldots K_{i_n}} \tag{3}$$

where $i = \sqrt{-1}$ and $\aleph_{i_1 \ldots i_n}$ are higher order cumulant tensors (Gardiner, 1990). In Fourier space the independence condition is given by $\ln(\phi(K_1, K_2, \ldots, K_m)) = \ln(\varphi(K_1)) + \ln(\lambda(K_2, \ldots, K_m))$. Hence, in the case of independence the following equality should be satisfied:

$$\sum_{n=1}^{\infty} \frac{i^n}{n!} \sum_{i_1, \ldots, i_n = 1}^{m} \aleph_{i_1 \ldots i_n} K_{i_1} \ldots K_{i_n} = \sum_{n=1}^{\infty} \frac{i^n}{n!} \aleph_1^{(n)} K_1^n + \sum_{n=1}^{\infty} \frac{i^n}{n!} \sum_{i_1, \ldots, i_n = 2}^{m} \aleph_{i_1 \ldots i_n} K_{i_1} \ldots K_{i_n} \tag{4}$$

and therefore

$$\sum_{n=1}^{\infty} \frac{i^n}{n!} \sum_{i_2, \ldots, i_n = 1}^{m} \left(1 - \delta_{i_2 \ldots i_n}\right) \aleph_{1 i_2 \ldots i_n} K_1 K_{i_2} \ldots K_{i_n} = 0 \,. \tag{5}$$

$\delta_{i_2 \ldots i_n}$ is Kroenecker's delta. Due to the fact that equation (5) should be satisfied for all $\vec{K}$, all coefficients in each summation of equation (5) must be zero. Therefore, a measure that can be used for testing statistical independence in time series can be defined by the cost function

$$D = \sum_{n=1}^{\infty} \sum_{i_2, \ldots, i_n = 1}^{m} \left(1 - \delta_{i_2 \ldots i_n}\right) \{\aleph_{1 i_2 \ldots i_n}\}^2 \,. \tag{6}$$

The quantity D is such that $D \geq 0$. In the framework of statistical testing, an hypothesis about the data can be rejected or accepted based on a measure which discriminates the statistics underlying a distribution consistent with the hypothesis from the original distribution of the data. The hypothesis to be tested is called *null hypothesis*. The measure which quantifies the above mentioned distinction between the statistics of the distributions is called *discriminating statistics*. In general it is very difficult to derive analytically the distribution of a given statistics under a given null hypothesis. The surrogate method proposes to estimate such distributions empirically by generating different versions of the data, called *surrogates*, such that they share some given properties of the original data and are at the same time consistent with the null hypothesis. The rejection of a null hypothesis is therefore based on the computation of the discriminating statistics for the original time series D_O and the discriminating statistics D_{S_i} for the i-th surrogated time series generated under the null hypothesis. The null hypothesis is rejected if the *significance* S given by

$$S = \frac{|D_O - \mu_S|}{\sigma_S} \tag{7}$$

is larger than $\hat{S}$ corresponding to a p -value $p = erfc(\hat{S}/(\sqrt{2}))$ (p being usually 0.05 which corresponds to $\hat{S}$=1.645). This means that the probability of observing a significance $\hat{S}$ or larger is p if the null hypothesis is true under the assumption of Gaussianity in the surrogates distribution (which is a realistic assumption if the number of surrogates is equal or larger than 100). In equation (7)

$$\mu_S = \frac{1}{N}\sum_{i=1}^{N} D_{S_i} \text{ and } \sigma_S = \sqrt{\frac{1}{N}\sum_{i=1}^{N}\left(D_{S_i} - \mu_S\right)^2} \tag{8}$$

are the estimated mean value and standard deviation of the discriminanting statistic under the surrogates distribution. In our case the concrete null hypothesis that we would like to test is the one corresponding to the assumption of a non-causal relationship between past and present, i.e. of statistical independency in time. In other words we are trying to answer the most modest question whether there is any dynamics at all underlying the data. The surrogates data used are generated from the original time series by mixing the temporal order, so that if originally any temporal dependence was present it is destroyed by this mixing process. The generated surrogates are scrambled surrogates and have the same statistical characteristics as the original data.

The histogram of the original data is preserved but with the particularity that these data do not possess any statistical temporal correlation. The discriminating statistics used here measures the statistical correlations by means of the cumulant expansion, i.e. by calculating the non-diagonal elements of the cumulants according to equation (6). In this paper we include cumulant terms up to fourth order.

If the assumption of stationarity of the observed time series cannot be accepted, then the test of the existence of a dynamics should be performed by the method of overlapping windows or sliding windows. In this method the statistical test of temporal independency at time t is performed in a window of the data of length N_W , i.e by using the data from time $t - N_W\Delta$ to t . Subsequently we slice the window into N_S time steps and perform again the statistical test by using the data from $t + N_S - N_W\Delta$ to $t + N_S$ and so on. In this case it is useful to plot the significance S as a function of the time t where the sliding window finished. It is clear that for stationary time series the value of S will be approximately the same for all times. In other cases this method can be used for the detection of regions in which a stationary behavior is observed, or regions in which a dynamics is actually underlying the process.

3 German Stock Index

In this section we demonstrate the selection of data in time series so that they can be used for learning the underlying dynamics. We use the method of sliding windows in combination with our cumulant-surrogates based testing of statistical correlations. The task is to predict the daily relative differences of the DAX given 12 inputs. These input variables describe a so called technical model using only historical DAX prices and the total volume of the transactions at the stock market. Table 2 describes the preprocessed input variables used in modeling the DAX data.

In order to select the regions where a temporal structure, i.e. predictability, exists, we apply the surrogate-cumulant based method. Figure 1 shows the significance for the daily DAX time series as a function of time for a sliding window with $N_W = 256$ and $N_S = 4$. The dimension of the embedding vector is $m = 11$ and the time lag is $\Delta = 1$. The number of surrogates used in this experiment is $N = 100$.

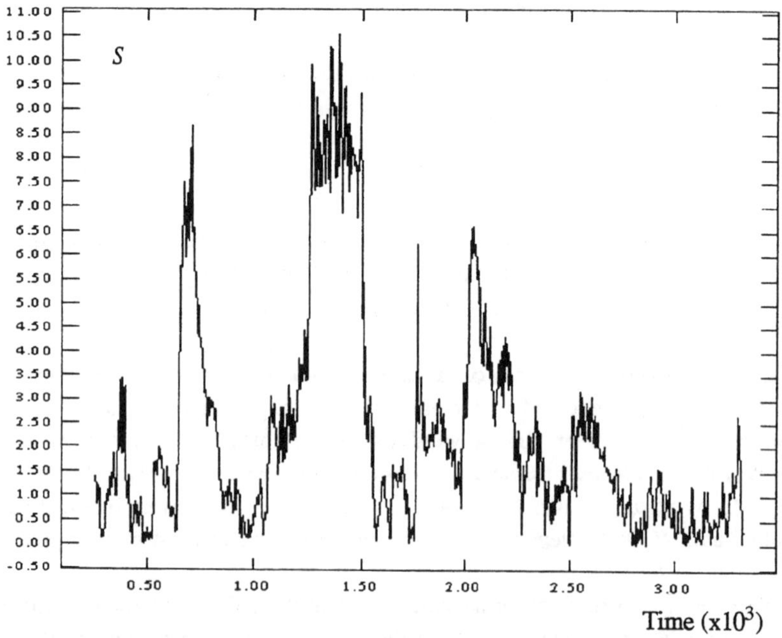

Fig. 1: Significance as a function of time. Daily German stock index (DAX).

Predicting noisy financial time series with neural networks is always a very difficult task, because the models typically exhibit a strong tendency of overfitting (Refenes, 1994). Therefore, to test the surrogate-cumulant based method, we decided to use the extended neuro-fuzzy approach of Neuneier and Zimmermann (1996), which transforms rules given by experts into parameters to initialize a RBF-like network. Like in the works of Takagi and Sugeno (1985), Wang and Mendel (1991), Tresp et. al. (1993), and others, a rule base is identified with a neural network of the form of equation (11). Each rule corresponds to a basis function b_i (i.e. a neuron) in the hidden layer. The output y for a given input vector x is the weighted average of the conclusions $w_i(x)$ where the weighting factor depends on the activity level of the rules or basis functions b_i due to the input x,

$$y(x) = \frac{\sum_i w_i(x)\, b_i(x)}{\sum_i b_i(x)} \quad \text{with } b_i(x) = \kappa_i \prod_j MF_{ij}(x_j). \tag{1}$$

Within this very general formulation we are free in specifying the form of a parameterized membership function MF. If we define the conclusions to be constants, $w_i(x) = w_i$, and the MFs to be Gaussians which are parameterized by their centers μ_{ij} and variances σ_{ij} we obtain a typical normalized radial basis function network (Moody and Darken, 1989),

$$b_i(x) = \kappa_i \prod_j MF_{ij}(x_j) = \kappa_i e^{\left(-0.5\left(\sum_j \frac{x_j - \mu_{ij}}{\sigma_{ij}}\right)^2\right)} \tag{2}$$

For monotonous fuzzy expressions a logistic MF with a weight and bias parameter may be more appropriate. After the network is initialized with a set of rules, a semantic-preserving backpropagation-based learning algorithm is used to ensure that the optimized rule base is more easily interpretable after training (see Neuneier and Zimmermann (1996) for details).

Since rules given by a human expert are generally low dimensional and each rule takes only a small number of input variables into account, the resulting architecture of our neuro-fuzzy system is very sparse. The complexity of the network is further reduced by the mentioned semantic-preserving learning algorithm which forces the parameters to meet some constraints. The resulting sparse network structure prevents the network from overfitting because the number of free parameters is small.

In our experiments, 99 very simple rules with 3 different membership functions for each input are used. A single rule describes the relationship between the last change of the DAX value and one other input derived from the past course of the DAX (see

Table 1). After initialization, the network is trained on the data until the error on the cross validation set starts to increase.

To test the surrogate-cumulant data selection method, in a second experiment we train the initialized net only on the selected data without any cross-validation data until convergence (see Table 3 for a description of the partitioning of the data).

The models are evaluated by comparing their P&L curves, which measure the return of a trading system by $r_t = \sum_{k=1}^{t} \left(dax_{k+1} - dax_k\right) sign\left(NN_k\right)$ where NN_k is the output of the network for time step k and $sign(NN_k)$ is the predicted direction of the DAX.

Table 1: Input variables

Input Variable	*Description*
1	relative difference of the DAX for the last 2 days
2	moving average for the last 5 days
3	moving average for the last 10 days
4	difference of the last 2 momentum for 5 days
5	difference of the last 2 momentum for 10 days
6	relative strength index for 5 days
7	relative strength index for 10 days
8	overbought / oversold indicator for the last 5 days
9	overbought / oversold indicator for the last 10 days
10	averaged overbought / oversold indicator for the last 5 days
11	averaged overbought / oversold indicator for the last 10 days
12	relative difference of the total volume of the transactions for the last 2 days

Obviously, the model trained with data selection shows superior profitability (see Figure 2, left). The model with data selection is also compared to the performance of the following heuristic trading systems:

- Buy&Hold: buy the DAX at the beginning of the test set and sell it at the end.
- naive prediction: buy or hold the DAX if the last difference is positive and sell otherwise.

The model with data selection clearly beats the Buy&Hold benchmark, but is only superior to the naive prediction on the more recent part of the test set. This observation is consistent with the results of Figure 1.b, where the significance test shows more structure at the end of the generalization set.

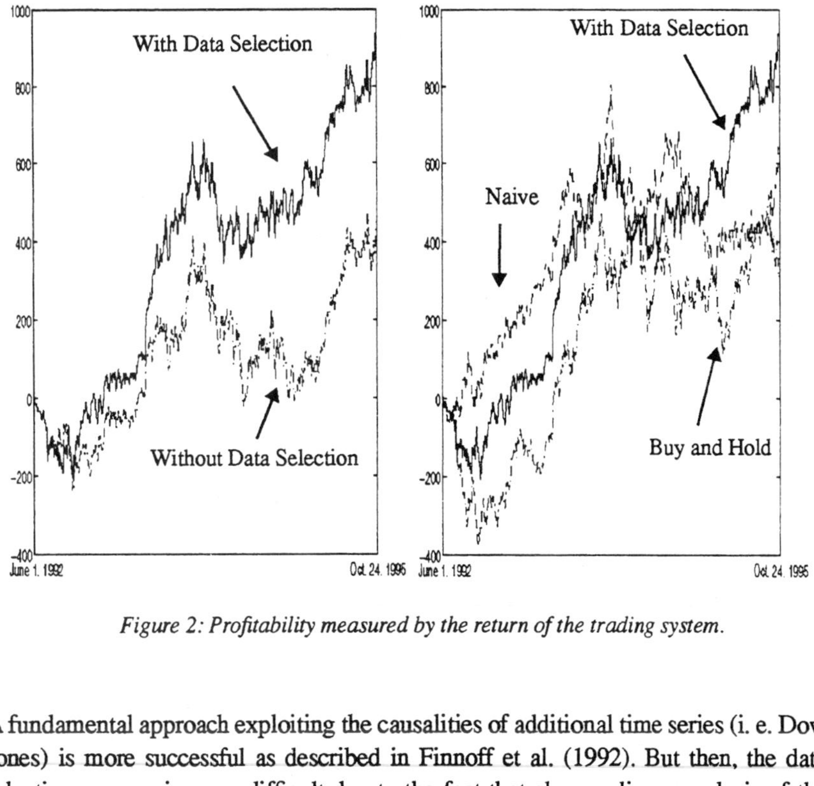

Figure 2: Profitability measured by the return of the trading system.

A fundamental approach exploiting the causalities of additional time series (i. e. Dow Jones) is more successful as described in Finnoff et al. (1992). But then, the data selection process is more difficult due to the fact that also nonlinear analysis of the cross correlation between different time series is required. This is the subject of further research.

Additionally, we plan to combine the cumulant-surrogate method with other modeling approaches like linear regression, multilayer perceptrons and RBF to achieve a empirically more founded judgement if and for which models the proposed data selection method can significantly improve the performance.

Table 2: Partitioning of the data

Set	*Start*	*End*	*Data number*
Training	Jan. 18. 1983	May 31. 1991	2184
Cross Validation	June 1. 1991	May 31. 1992	260
Training with data selection	Jan. 18. 1983	May 31. 1992	1161
Test	June 1. 1992	Oct. 24. 1995	887

4 References

G. Deco and B. Schürmann, "Learning Time Series Evolution by Unsupervised Extraction of Correlations", 1995, *Physical Review* **E 51**, 1780.

G. Deco and W. Brauer, "Nonlinear Higher Order Statistical Decorrelation by Volume-Conserving Neural Networks", 1995, *Neural Networks* **8**, 525.

G. Deco and D. Obradovic, "An Information-Theoretic Approach to Neural Computing", 1996, Springer Verlag, New York.

W. Finnoff, F. Hergert and H. G. Zimmermann, "Improving generalization by Nonconvergent Model Selection Methods", 1993, *Neural Networks* **6**, 771-83.

C.W. Gardiner, "Handbook of Stochastic Methods", 1990, Second Edition, Springer-Verlag.

P. Grassberger, "Finite Sample Corrections to Entropy and Dimension Estimates",1988, Physics Letters A, **128**, 369.

H. Herzel, A. Schmitt and W. Ebeling, "Finite Sample Effects in Sequence Analysis", 1994, Chaos, Solitons and Fractals, **4**, 97-113 .

J. Moody and C. Darken, "Fast Learning in Networks of locally-tuned Processing Units", 1989, Neural Computation, **1**, 281-94.

R. Neuneier and H. G. Zimmermann, "Neuro-Fuzzy Architectures and Learning Algorithms for Financial Analysis", 1996, Proc. of EUFIT'96, p. 2191-95.

M. Palus, V. Albrecht and I. Dvorák, "Information Theoretic Test for Nonlinearity in Time Series", 1993, Physics Letters A, **175**, 203-9.

M. Palus, "Testing for Nonlinearity Using Redundancies: Quantitative and Qualitative Aspects", 1995, Physica D, **80**, 186-205.

A. P. Refenes, "Neural Networks in the Capital Market", 1994, Wiley & Sons, New York.

T. Takagi and M. Sugeno, "Fuzzy identification of systems and its applications to modelling and control", 1985, *IEEE Trans. on Syst., Man and Cybernetics*, 1, **15**, 116-32.

J. Theiler, S. Eubank, A. Longtin, B. Galdrikian and J. Farmer, "Testing for Nonlinearity in Time Series: The Method of Surrogate Data", 1992, Physica D, **58**, 77-94.

V. Tresp, J. Hollatz and S. Ahmad, "Network Structuring and Training Using Rule-Based Knowledge", 1993, In S. J. Hanson, J.D. Cowan, C. L. Giles (editors), Advances in Neural Information Processing Systems 5, 871-78.

L. X. Wang and J. M. Mendel, "Generating Fuzzy Rules from Numerical Data, with Applications", 1991, Univ. of Southern Cal., tech. report USC-SIPI REPORT, 169.

NEURAL NETWORK COMPATIBLE MEMORY WITH CONTROLLED DEPTH AND RESOLUTION FOR FINANCIAL TEMPORAL FORECASTING DATA

JOHN M. MASON, ATTA BADII
School of Information Systems
Nene College, Park Campus
Northampton, U.K.
E-Mail: john.mason@nene.ac.uk
atta.badii@nene.ac.uk

ABSTRACT

Consideration is given to the development of architectures that support the functional decomposition of time series predictive analysis. The concept of a Long Term Memory (LTM) module is introduced which is used to store global profile / contextual trend information of the time series. A set of Profile Units are used to create a basic LTM module of a form that is compatible with published Short Term Memory (STM) and Predictor modules. A systematic investigation as to the manner in which architectural integration may be realised is described and implementation as an integrated Architecture for Financial time series analysis is investigated. Preliminary results suggest that the composite architecture enables useful performance improvements to be realised during the early learning phase of a network.

Keywords
Temporal Variability Encoding *Predictive Analysis* *Time Series* *Forecasting* *Financial*
Modular Neural Networks *Time Delay Networks* *Long Term Memory* *Short Term Memory*

1 Introduction

Application of neural networks to the task domain of financial time series forecasting has been the focus of a number of studies as reported, for example, in (Azoff 1993) and (Refenes et al 1996). Some of the architectures have shown promise in the complex function approximation of temporal data without requiring detailed causal insight into the underlying process model. This has meant that the approach has been viewed an attractive complementary technique to conventional statistical and technical analysis techniques (Hill et al 1994) .

Early studies in this area focused mainly on monolithic network architectures. The application of such networks posed a number of problems for example in accommodating the necessary efficient encoding of temporal variability in the pattern space (Haykin 1994). Techniques to address this problem included that based upon an.autoregressive model in which sequenced time slices were applied to the network (Lapedes 1987). Training of the network thus enabled a short-term correlation function to be established between fixed period time windows.

The use of a memory component allowed later models to incorporate historic data. Indeed, in this task domain of predictive analysis of time series, the use of a memory component has been a salient feature in providing enhanced performance (Elman 1990). Accordingly, the application of tapped delay line and recurrent architectures for this purpose have been extensively reported (for example Aussem 1995, Connor et al 1994, Day 1993).

Furthermore, it has been shown that monolithically mapped single architectures suffer from limitations in temporal analysis, for example arising from cross-talk degradations between non-orthogonal feature systems. A system-theoretic modularisation suggests that it is the network rather than the mapping that should be decomposed into components that essentially lead to create a composite network. Such a network will admit the mapping of features that are maximally linearly independent for both training and testing (Hrycej 1995).

It is therefore expected that the mapping and predictive analysis of complex temporal series can benefit from a multi-model approach which supports orthogonal functional processing during training and testing.

Mozer 94 presented an elegant generalisation of the short term memory and predictor requirement paradigms in which he also noted the problems attendant with ensuring compatibility between the above two functional requirements such that the predictor element was able to maximally exploit all the information stored in the memory component.

In the context of the memory component, references have been made to two properties, namely depth and resolution. In the context of the present study, depth is taken to refer to the retrospective time duration over which data is retained in the memory, whereas the resolution, in practice, refers to the number of sampled elements within that duration.

Thus the memory element is normally characterised in terms of depth and resolution (de Vries 1992). It is noted that tapped delay line architectures provide low depth with high resolution whilst recurrent architectures typically provide memory with high depth and low resolution. In particular, recurrent architectures have been found to be somewhat lacking in practical applications for processing of long duration complex functions and have been shown to suffer from problems in efficient implementation of appropriate control strategies (Mozer 1994).

2 Motivation

Given the established requirement of a modular viewpoint which separates the memory element and the predictor as the two necessary co-operative sub-systems (Mozer 1994), it is clear from the above observations that a predictor compatible memory architecture is required which would address the dimensions of both depth and resolution.

The architectures proposed so far have concerned themselves mainly with optimising prediction performance based on only one property of the memory element that of either depth, or, resolution.

In this paper we consider the representation of depth in terms of both Short Term Memory (STM) and Long Term Memory (LTM) consistent with the psychophysically significant classes of memory (Arbib 1989) which have been the focus of extensive study in other work relevant to pattern recognition and retrieval. Furthermore consideration of the functional decomposition that is achieved by the resulting architecture shows an interesting consistency with the principles motivating State Space Filtering approaches to pattern analysis (Young 1994).

In particular, in the context of financial time series data LTM can be seen to address attributes of longer periods (business cycles) whereas short term or seasonal trends would be handled by STM. This is realised in terms of a composite architecture comprising predictor compatible elements of STM and LTM memory (figure 1). LTM in the form of an architectural component has received little consideration in the financial application domain.

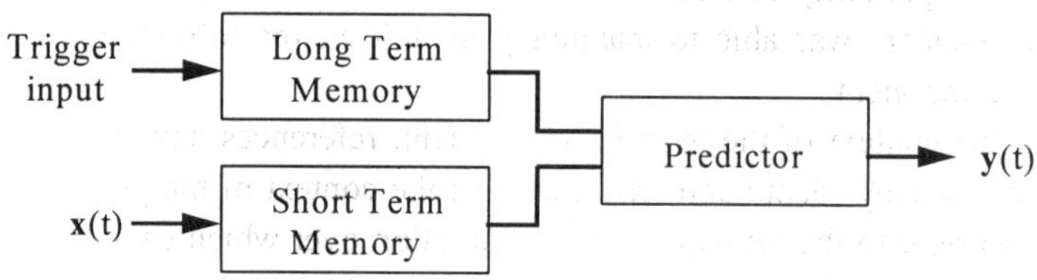

where **x**(t) is input vector at time t
y(t) is corresponding predicted output vector at time t

Figure 1: Composite architecture of memory and predictor elements.

This paper examines the hypothesis that analysis and prediction of temporal data can be better processed by an appropriate integrated grouping of neural network architectures - the components of which address separately the predictive, STM and LTM functions. Specifically, the scope of the presently reported work is restricted to a systematic consideration of the manner in which a LTM module might improve the performance of existing predictor and STM modules.

We demonstrate how it is possible to integrate a LTM module consisting of Profile Units with a prototypical predictor and STM module configuration.

3 Long Term Memory Architectures

Time series data storage in von Neumann based architectures enables a predefined depth and resolution to be specified and it supports integrity of retrieval. However, there is an overhead requirement of precise address encoding and decoding and the inherent sequential processing of each data item. Connectionist systems offer the alternative of content addressable memory that supports mass data retrieval from a single, not necessarily accurate, input pattern. Particular associative network architectures are known to provide associative/content addressable memory and their use is well established in the fields of image processing and pattern recognition.

In view of the extensive theoretical and empirical studies to which associative networks have been subjected (for example Abu-Mustafa et al 1985, McEliece et al 1987, Kang 1994, Francois 1996) they might reasonably be considered to fall within the candidate space of the above application, where they could be viewed as long term memories. In the study of such networks the integrity of stored data and its retrieval and the capacity of the network are prime considerations. It is found that there are difficulties in achieving robust retrieval and adequate capacity. Indeed when the capacity limitation and spurious state retrieval problem of certain architectures is examined it becomes apparent why their extensive use in image processing and pattern matching applications has not been replicated in the financial time series domain. In fact the requirement in this application area for retrieval accuracy and precision is, of course, not consistent with the approximation and generalisation characteristics exhibited by neural networks. In this case, memorisation and the consequential loss of generalisation can be considered as desirable features for a LTM function.

In searching for an appropriate and compatible architecture it is noted that the predictor module will be of a feedforward configuration (Mozer 1994). Since feedforward architectures can also be used as hetro-associative memories it would seem that these structures might offer some promise in support of the integration requirement. For this reason the current work has been restricted to an investigation of LTM in the form of a hetro-associative, feedforward, network as a means for the storage and retrieval of time series data and it suggests that such an approach could be applied beneficially to financial time series prediction.

A content addressable memory may be obtained by a simple two layer network in which a single input trigger pulse is mapped via a linear transform function to the required series of data values as represented in a linear array of neurons at the output layer. The temporal encoding achieved allows the dimensions of memory depth and resolution to be pre-defined and systematically investigated.

4 Profile Memory

Figure 2 shows the manner in which a single output neuron and its associated fixed weight connection can be used in order to represent a single element of a time series.

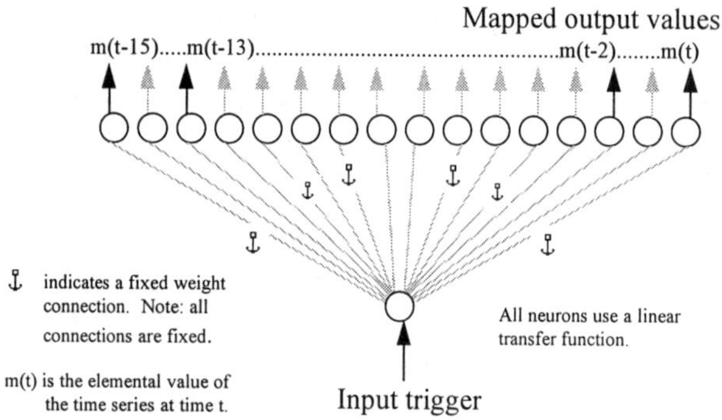

Figure 2: Single layer memory array.

With a practical limit on the size (*S*) of the output array, such a one-to-one representation produces a product relationship between the Memory Resolution Factor (*MRF*) and memory depth (*D*):

i.e. $S = MRF * D$

where *S* is the number of output neurons in LTM array
MRF is the ratio of the number of stored data elements to the number of elements in the original time series
D is the number of elements in the original presented time series

In the case of a LTM consisting of neurons that support variable encoding it is time that is the resolution variable rather than the value associated with the time increment. Hence low resolution would be characterised by a limited number of elemental values across a given time period. The individual values could well be stored to a high precision (e.g. single or double point precision). This consideration is analogous to the concept of sampling resolution and we find it helpful to define a Memory Resolution Factor (*MRF*). A *MRF* of unity is obtained when all of the elements in the original time series are stored in the LTM. i.e. there is one output neuron for each element in the series. A *MRF* of 0.1 is obtained when there is one output neuron for every 10 data items.

If it is assumed that LTM stores coarse, global rather than detailed, local information then it is implied that the depth of the time series should form the dominant variable. In this case it is possible to consider LTM as storing low resolution envelope or profile information. Detailed higher resolution data, covering a restricted duration, can be represented in the STM component of the integrated architecture.

For a linear array LTM of given original size in which depth and corresponding *MRF* have been selected, the depth variable may be consistently controlled by the simple truncation of those neurons in the output array that contain sequentially earlier data. Alternatively it follows that if the required depth and*MRF* are known then the necessary memory size can be pre-determined for a given number of data elements.

Clearly, such a memory architecture does not provide a compact form of storage and multiple pattern and compression techniques could be used to computational advantage. However, for the present preliminary investigation the described architecture was used as an appropriate experimental vehicle.

5 Integration of Architectures

A basic tapped delay line backpropagation configuration with five input neurons was chosen as the STM and predictor modules. The single hidden layer neurons used a tanh transfer function while a single output neuron was employed. Through layer connections were not used. In the spirit of earlier recurrent architectures in which context units were identified as the integrated memory module (Elman 1990) we refer to the LTM neurons that are used to store time series profile data as Profile Units. The manner in which these neurons were integrated to the tapped delay module was determined during subsequent work as described in the following sections.

In order to enable a systematic investigation into the feasibility of the proposed integrated architecture and to support comparison with other techniques, both the tapped delay and the LTM modules were of deliberately simple design. The literature contains a wealth of alternative and sophisticated forecasting architectures that would allow the development of the basic model.

6 Experimental Investigation

In order to systematically investigate the effects of pre-defined LTM depth and resolution on the predictive analysis of time series, a set of controlled training convergent profiles and testing regimes were applied to architectural combinations.

As is usual in such procedures, the inherent set of inter-relating variables means that it would be possible to generate a vast number of experimental runs. To address this combinatorial problem a planned sequence of tests was conducted that enabled the progressive filtering of dependent variables whereby observed best features of particular architectures were progressively selected during the experimental sequence.

In broad terms, the architecture was tested without LTM (taken as the base condition) and then with the LTM module connected in various integrated configurations. Memories of different depth and resolution with different connection architectures were investigated. Results for different STM delay durations and different 'step-ahead' predictions were also examined. In order to test the effect of stored coarse profile information the range of the ahead step was extended beyond that usually applied in such architectures. The effects arising from the use of curvilinear (i.e. tanh) and linear transfer output functions were investigated as was the impact of different numbers of hidden layer neurons.

Reported results are based upon an epoch size tuned for the particular input data set and the means obtained from 20 different initial random weight conditions.

7 Data

For consistency with the use of basic architectures, training and test data was selected to be of elemental form that was relevant to typical financial time series data. In particular, graphical components of known mathematical construct were used consisting of Line; Square; Cubic; and Sine-line.

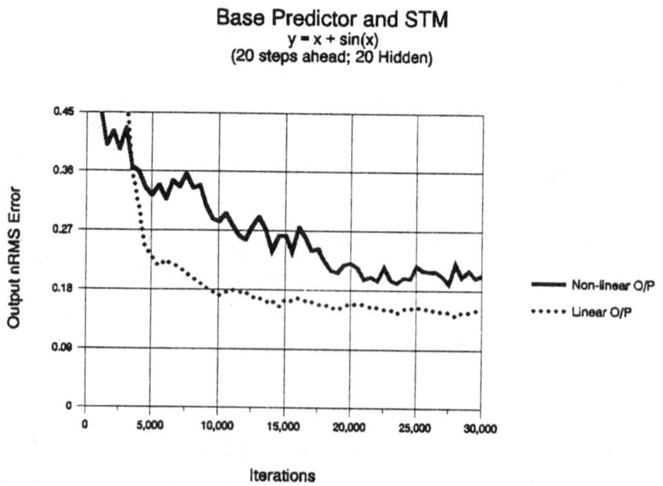

Figure 3: Example base condition (no LTM) convergence profile.

On completion of the initial set of experiments, subsequent analysis was conducted using published time series data (section 10).

Pre-processing consisted of normalising each data set to be compatible with the range of the tanh transfer function. Each set comprised 360 data items; a randomly selected 10 % of which was retained for validation. Both random and sequential order data presentation was applied and as expected for such simple input functions, no particular advantage arose from either presentational form.

Figure 2 shows a trigger neuron for the LTM and this was incorporated as a fan-out component in the STM and predictor input layer. A binary signal as the first element in each data record was used as the trigger pulse.

8 Results and Findings

Results obtained from each set of experiments were recorded as convergence profiles and comparison made to the base, without LTM, condition. An example arising from the evolved network is provided in figure 4.

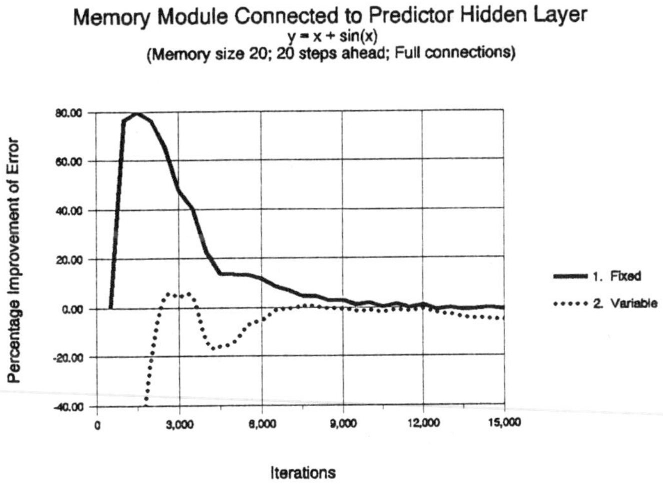

Figure 4: Results obtained from LTM integration.

Obtained results indicate:

8.1 The use of appropriately integrated LTM can provide convergence profiles with improvements that are particularly apparent during the early stages of training and testing.

8.2 STM and predictor architecture

a linear output function yields less dispersive, faster training;

the more complex input functions and further ahead predictions are associated with longer convergence times

a greater number of input delay neurons provide enhanced performance for the further step ahead predictions.

8.3 Connection architecture

Superior results are obtained with the LTM connected to the predictor hidden layer neurons using full fixed connections.

8.4 Predictor hidden units

A number towards the bottom of the investigated range provided the best results.

8.5 *MRF*

With the exception of the smallest memories, increased resolution with fixed depth (and hence increased LTM size) did not produce improved performance.

8.6 Matched LTM and hidden

Results do not indicate that a matched LTM and predictor hidden layer size yield enhanced convergence.

8.7 Depth

Increased depth with fixed resolution (and hence increased LTM size) provides marked improvements in performance.

9 Discussion

The results associated with the tapped delay module are in agreement with other widely published material and are thus taken as representing an acceptable baseline performance. Findings associated with the use of integrated LTM are, in some cases, not as might be expected and call for further discussion.

Early recurrent networks (Elman 1990) used a one-to-one or corresponding connection paradigm between the recurrent and hidden layer components with fixed input and trainable output. Fixed weight connections simplify the control strategy and support computational efficiency. We note that more recent work on financial prediction with recurrent structures (for example Bassi 1996) have used a similar full set connection configuration.

For a LTM of given size the variables of resolution and depth are not mutually exclusive (section 4). Indeed one interpretation of the obtained results could be that it is the memory size rather than resolution or depth that is significant in determination of convergence rate. It is submitted that the considerable difference between results obtained for the resolution and the depth tests based upon LTMs of identical size refutes such an interpretation. The sensitivity of the depth and resolution variables is shown in figure 5. It supports the intuitive view that for coarse profile information capture, it is the depth of memory rather than its resolution that forms the sensitive variable.

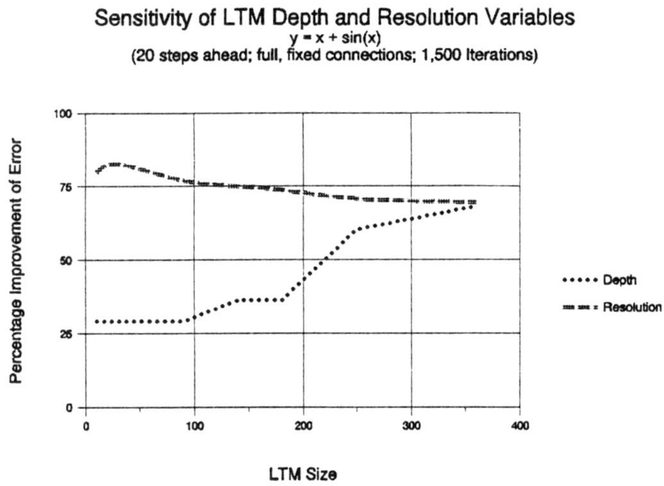

Figure 5: Memory depth and resolution sensitivity.

10 Performance with Financial Data

The architecture of LTM size 20, full fixed connected to a 20 hidden predictor module, that evolved from the described series of experiments was evaluated using published financial data as follows:

London FT All Share	Closing data 24 December, 1993 to 12 August, 1996)	Composite
S&P500	Closing data 21 July, 1989 to 3 March, 1993)	indices
Data Set C	Weigend et. al. 1994	Benchmark Exchange Rate

Typical results are summarised in figure 6. It is seen that significant improvement in early convergence profile performance is demonstrated for each of the selected data sets.

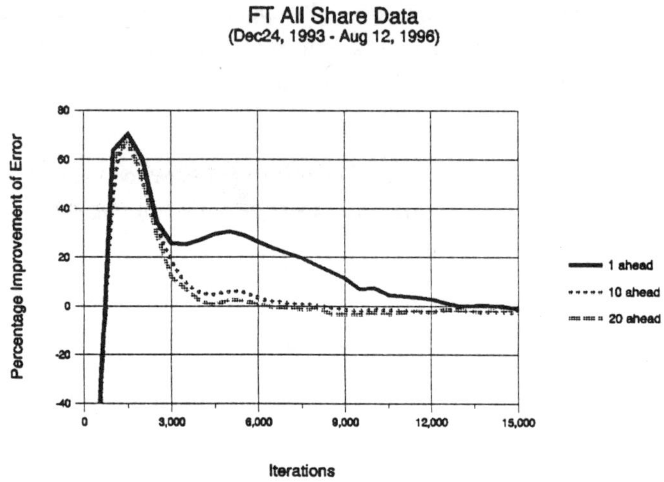

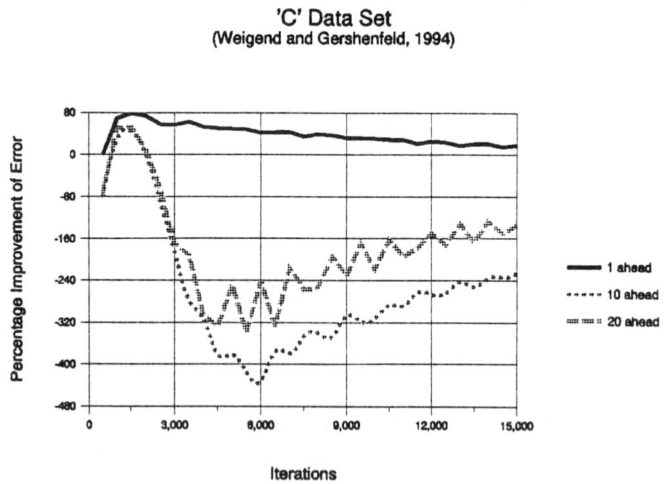

Figure 6: Application to financial data.

Where an inherent smoothing factor is associated with the time series (e.g. FT All Share), a maximum improvement of some 70% is recorded for the three investigated step-ahead predictions. In this case the sampled envelope data as held in LTM provides accessible global information that is representative of elemental data values.

Data set C, however, is acknowledged to hold difficulties for step-ahead prediction techniques that arise from the high frequency and variable interval nature of its data. Hence in this case pre-processed sampled profile data held in LTM may not provide an indication of particular elemental values. The results show that while convergent profile improvements are obtained for the one step-ahead condition, these are not maintained for further ahead conditions.

11 Conclusions

To date, the use of neural network Long Term Memory (LTM) architectural modules has received little attention in the financial application domain. The work described in this paper, has been based upon deliberately simple architectural components, that have enabled best feature determination through a series of progressive experiments.

The integration of LTM to a Tapped Delay-line neural network has been studied and the effect on network forecasting performance of the pre-defined memory variables of depth and resolution has been investigated. It has been shown how LTM storage of coarse envelope or profile data from a time series can enhance and extend conventional step-ahead prediction performance.

The work has demonstrated the feasibility of integrating an appropriate Long Term Memory module with existing Short Term Memory and Predictor architectures for application to the forecasting analysis of financial time series.

Within the limitations of the reported work, results indicate that such a composite architecture can provide mean performance improvements of some 50% during the early learning phases of a network. It is suggested that such improvements might find use in near real time applications.

12 References

Abu-Mustafa, Y S., St.Jacques J-M., Information capacity of the Hopfield model.*IEEE Trans on Information Theory,* Vol IT-31 No 4 pp 461-464, July, 1985.

Arbib, M A., *The metaphorical brain 2: Neural networks and beyond.* Wiley, 1989.

Aussem, A., Dynamical recurrent neural networks - towards environmental time series prediction. *Int Jnl of Neural Networks,* Vol 6 No 2 pp 145-170, 1995.

Azoff, E M., Reducing error in neural network time series forecasting. *Neural computing and applications,* Vol 1 No 1 pp 240-247, 1993.

Bassi, D F., Stock price predictions by recurrent multilayer neural network architectures.*Neural Networksin Financial Engineering: Proc 3rd Int Conf on Neural Networks in the Capital Markets,* pp 331-340. Edited by Refenes, A P., Abu-Mostafa, Y., Moody, J., Weigend, A. World Scientific 1996.

Connor, J., et al., Recurrent neural networks and robust time series prediction.*IEEE Transactions on neural networks,* Vol 5 pp 240-254, 1994.

Day, S P., Continuous-time temporal back-propagation with adaptive time delays. *IEEE Transactions on neural networks,* Vol 4 No2, 1993.

de Vries, B and Principe, J., The Gamma model - a new neural net model for temporal processing. *Neural Networks,* Vol 5 pp 565-576, 1992.

Elman, J L., Finding structure in time. *Cognitive Science,* Vol 14 pp 179-211, 1990.

Francois, O., New rigorous results for the Hopfield's neural network model.*Neural Networks,* Vol 9 No 3 pp 503-507 1996.

Haykin, S., *Neural networks - a comprehensive foundation.* Chapter 13, MacMillan, 1994.

Hill, T., Marquez, L., O'Connor, M., Remus, W., Artificial neural network models for forecasting and decision making. *International Journal of Forecasting,* Vol 10 pp 5-15, 1994.

Hrycej, T., *Modular learning in neural networks.* Wiley 1995

Kang, H., Multilayer associative neural networks (MANN's): Storage capacity versus perfect recall. *IEEE Trans on Neural Networks,* Vol 5 No 5 pp 812-822 September, 1994.

Lapedes, A., Farber, R., Non-linear signal processing using neural networks: Prediction and system modelling. *Tech Rep LA-UR-87-2662,* Los Alamos National Laboratory, 1987.

McEliece, R J., Posner, E C.,, Rodemich E R., Venkatesh, S S., The capacity of Hopfield associative memory. *IEEE Trans on Information Theory,* Vol IT-33 No 4 pp 461-482 July, 1987.

Mozer, M C., Neural network architectures for temporal processing.*In Time series prediction - forecasting the future and understanding the past,* Edited by Weigend, A., and Gershenfeld, N., Addison-Wesley, 1994.

Refenes, A P., Abu-Mostafa, Y., Moody, J.,, Weigend, A., (Editors) *Neural networks in financial engineering: Proc 3rd int conf on neural networks in the capital markets,* World Scientific, 1996.

Weigend, A S., Gershenfeld, N A., (Editors), *Time series prediction: forecasting the future and understanding the past.* Santa Fe Institute Studies in the Sciences of Complexity, Proc. Vol. XV, Addison-Wesley 1994.

Young, P C., Time-variable parameter and trend estimation in non-stationary economic time series *Journal of Forecasting,* Vol 13 No 2 pp 179-210, 1994.

Part 4
Foreign Exchange Trading and Analysis

SYMBOLIC CONVERSION, GRAMMATICAL INFERENCE AND RULE EXTRACTION FOR FOREIGN EXCHANGE RATE PREDICTION

STEVE LAWRENCE[a], C. LEE GILES[b]

NEC Research Institute, 4 Independence Way, Princeton, NJ 08540

AH CHUNG TSOI

Department of Informatics, University of Wollongong, NSW 2522 Australia

Financial forecasting is challenging due to small sample sizes, high noise, non-stationarity, and non-linearity. Statistical and probabilistic methods have difficulty with small sample size, high noise data due to correlations between input and output variables which are caused by noise and are random in nature. We present a noisy time series prediction method which is based on the notion that short term dynamical evolution predictability is possible but is obscured by observed correlations due to noise. The task considered is the prediction of daily foreign exchange rates, specifically, the prediction of whether the exchange rate will increase or decrease at the close of business for the next day. The high level of noise in the signal is addressed with conversion into a symbolic representation using a self-organizing map. The problem then becomes one of predicting the change given a sequence of symbols. A recurrent neural network is trained on the resulting grammatical inference problem in order to capture any predictability in the evolution of the series. With an extensive set of 4500 predictions covering 5 different foreign exchange rates significant predictability is found to exist with a 47.1% error rate in the prediction of the direction of change. The error rate reduces to around 40% when rejecting examples where the system has low confidence in its prediction. The system facilitates the inference of rules and rules related to well known behavior are extracted, often with exceptions which vary depending on the segment of data in question.

1 Noisy Time Series Prediction

Traditional models for noisy time series prediction are statistical in nature and essentially estimate the probability that a particular event will occur given a set of past information. Typical neural network models are closely related to statistical regression, and can be shown to estimate Bayesian *a posterior* probabilities when given an appropriately formulated problem (Ruck *et al.*, 1990). For high noise, small sample prediction, correlations between input and output variables which are due to noise present difficulty for these methods.

[a] `lawrence@research.nj.nec.com`, `http://www.neci.nj.nec.com/homepages/lawrence`

[b] Lee Giles is also with the Institute for Advanced Computer Studies, University of Maryland, College Park, MD 20742.

Neural networks have been very successful in a number of pattern recognition applications, and are considered by many to provide state-of-the-art solutions to noisy time series prediction problems such as financial prediction (Refenes, 1995). For noisy time series prediction, neural networks typically use a delay embedding (Farmer & Sidorowich, 1987) of previous temporal inputs [c] which is mapped into a prediction. The models can be loosely grouped into two classes: those which address the temporal relationship of their inputs by maintaining an internal state, and those which do not.

For models like the standard multi-layer perceptron (MLP) neural network, the traditional vector space input encoding gives the model no hint as to the temporal relationship of the inputs. A short temporal pattern can be difficult to distinguish from patterns caused by correlations between the input and output variables which are due to noise, although these noise induced patterns may not occur in temporal order.

Recurrent neural network models employ feedback connections and have the potential to represent certain computational structures in a more parsimonious fashion (Elman, 1991). Such models are suited to the detection of temporal patterns. However, for noisy time series prediction, correlations with the most recent data induced by noise can swamp any predictability based on earlier data. Even short temporal patterns can become difficult to distinguish.

The method introduced here is based on the notion that short term dynamical evolution predictability is possible but is obscured in traditional models by observed correlations between input and output variables which are due to noise and are random in nature. The time series is first converted into a sequence of symbols using a self-organizing map. The problem becomes one of grammatical inference – the prediction of a given class from a sequence of symbols. It is then possible to take advantage of the known abilities of recurrent neural networks to learn deterministic grammatical rules which capture predictability in the evolution of the series. Without the symbolic encoding it is harder to distinguish temporal patterns from correlations with the most recent inputs induced by noise. The use of a recurrent neural network is significant for two reasons: first, the model addresses the temporal relationship of the series by maintaining an internal state, and second, it is possible to extract rules from the trained recurrent networks which may be interpreted by humans. These rules are in the form of deterministic finite state automata and a regular language.

---

[c] For example, $x(t), x(t-1), x(t-2), \ldots, x(t-N+1)$ form the inputs for a delay embedding of the previous N values of the series (Takens, 1981).

2 Financial Prediction

2.1 Foreign Exchange

Foreign exchange rates exhibit very high noise, and significant non-stationarity. Here, the task considered is the prediction of the direction of change in the exchange rates for the next business day (many financial institutions that are trying to predict foreign exchange rates evaluate algorithms using the percentage of times that the algorithm predicts the right trend from today until some time in the future (Lequarré, 1993)).

A number of people have applied neural network technology to exchange rate prediction and trading, e.g. Weigend *et al.* (1992). In this work, application to exchange rate trading is secondary (the use of external variables or a trading policy is not considered, for example) and the focus is on our approach to noisy time series prediction and the creation of deterministic finite state automata which can be used to explain the evolution of the series. Such simple models of what is undoubtedly a complex system can be useful for a number of reasons, e.g. the models can reveal new insights to domain experts, and they can give ordinary people a comprehensible picture which helps to explain how the system works.

2.2 Data

The data used here is the same as the data used in Weigend *et al.* (1992). The data is from the Monetary Yearbook of the Chicago Mercantile Exchange and consists of daily closing bids for five currencies (German Mark (DM), Japanese Yen, Swiss Franc, British Pound, and Canadian Dollar) with respect to the US Dollar. The data covers the period September 3, 1973 to May 18, 1987 (there are 3645 data points). In contrast to Weigend et al., the prediction of all five exchange rates in the data set and prediction for all days instead of just Mondays is considered here. The data is available from http://www.cs.colorado.edu/~andreas/Time-Series/Data/Exchange.Rates.Daily.

3 Prediction System

It is common to use a delay embedding (Takens, 1981) of the previous k values of the series. However, creating an estimator which is a function of the last k raw values of the series can be problematic if the series contains a trend (e.g. the range of the values in the training set could have little overlap with the range of the values in the test set, resulting in poor generalization) as shown in figure 1. A common solution, which is used here, is to take the first difference of the series. Additionally, in order to compress the dynamic range of the series and reduce the effect of outliers, a log transformation of the data is used. We then use a delay embedding of the resulting series [d]. The delay embedding forms the input to a self-organizing map neural network (SOM) which performs the symbolic encoding. The output of the SOM is the topographical location of the winning node. Each node represents one symbol in the resulting grammatical inference problem. An Elman recurrent neural network (RNN) is then trained on the symbol sequence created by the SOM. A high-level block diagram of our system is shown in figure 2.

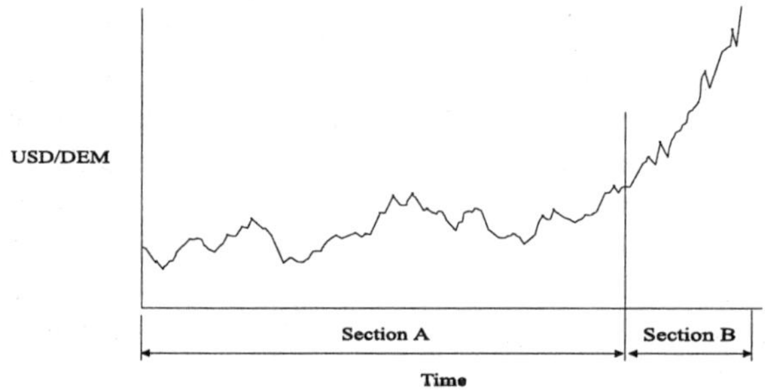

Figure 1: An example of the difficulty in using a model trained on a raw price series. Generalization to section B from the training data in section A is difficult as the model has not been trained with inputs in the range covered by section B.

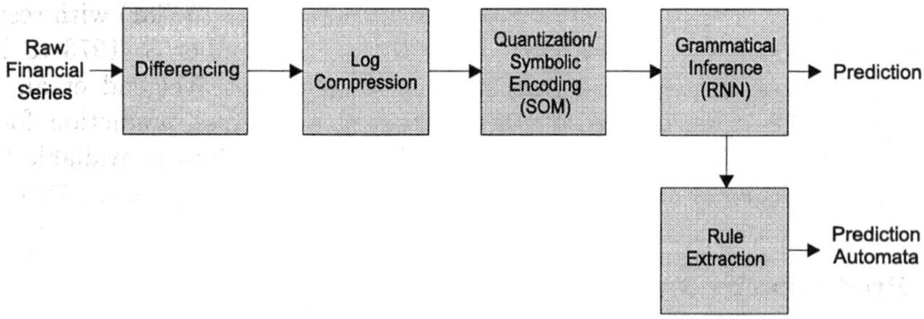

Figure 2: A high-level block diagram of the prediction system.

[d] Note that this embedding does not restrict the amount of past information that the system can employ because of the subsequent use of a recurrent neural network.

3.1 The Self-Organizing Map

The self-organizing map, or SOM (Kohonen, 1995) is an unsupervised learning process which learns the distribution of a set of patterns without any class information. A pattern is projected from a possibly high dimensional input space to a position in the map, a low dimensional display space. The display space is often divided into a grid and each intersection of the grid is represented in the network by a neuron. Information is encoded as the location of an activated neuron. The SOM is unlike most classification or clustering techniques in that it preserves the topological ordering of the classes in the input space in the resulting display space. Similarity as measured using a metric in the input space is preserved in the display space. The SOM can be considered a non-linear projection of the probability density of the input patterns (Kohonen, 1995). The SOM training process works by iteratively locating the closest node to each training pattern. A neighborhood function is used which causes topographically nearby nodes to be updated towards the training pattern along with the closest node at each step in the training process. The neighborhood function reduces in size as training proceeds, causing a smoothing effect which leads to a global ordering of the map. In our prediction system the SOMs used have only one dimension.

3.2 Recurrent Network Prediction

In the past few years several recurrent neural network architectures have emerged which have been used for grammatical inference (Kremer, 1996). There has been much discussion of the computational power of these networks and it has been shown that a particular class of recurrent networks are at least Turing equivalent (Siegelmann, 1995). The recurrent neural network used for grammatical inference here is the Elman neural network. The Elman network has fully connected feedback among the hidden layer neurons. For the examples here, the networks had three input neurons, one hidden layer with five neurons, and two output neurons – one each for prediction of the probability of positive and negative changes. The set of symbols from the output of the SOM are linearly encoded into a single input for the Elman network. The linear encoding is important and is justified by the topographical order of the symbols. If no order was defined over the symbols then a separate input should be used for each symbol, resulting in a system with more dimensions and increased difficulty due to the curse of dimensionality. Delayed inputs are used for the other two input neurons, aiding in the training process. The networks were trained with backpropagation through time (Haykin, 1994) for a total of 500 updates. Weights in the network were updated after all patterns were presented (batch update), as opposed to stochastic update where weights are updated after every pattern presentation (stochastic update typically performs poorly when the data is very noisy). All inputs were normalized to zero mean and unit variance. All nodes included a bias input which was part of the optimization process. Weights were initialized as shown in Haykin (1994). Target outputs were -0.8 and 0.8 using the *tanh* output activation function and the quadratic cost function was used. A search then converge learning rate schedule was used (Darken & Moody, 1992) with an initial learning rate of 0.5.

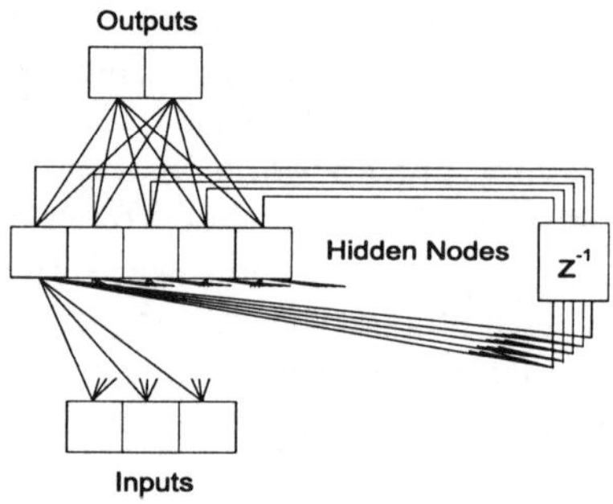

Figure 3: An Elman recurrent neural network.

3.3 Non-stationarity and Overfitting

The approach used to handle non-stationarity here is to build models based on short time periods only. There is a noise vs. non-stationarity tradeoff (Moody, 1995) as the size of the training set is varied. If the training set is too small, noise makes it harder to find true patterns in the data. If the training set is too large, the non-stationarity of the data means that more data with statistics that are less relevant for the task at hand is used when creating the estimator. Based on preliminary experiments (using a separate segment of data that was not part of the subsequent training and test datasets), models were trained using 100 days of data in order to balance the noise/non-stationarity tradeoff. After training, each model is tested on the next 30 days of data. The entire training/test set window is moved forward 30 days and the process is repeated, as depicted in figure 4. Test sets of 30 days are used instead of one day (i.e. a new model every day) in order to reduce the amount of computation by a factor of 30, and enable us to perform a much larger number of tests, thereby increasing the significance of our results.

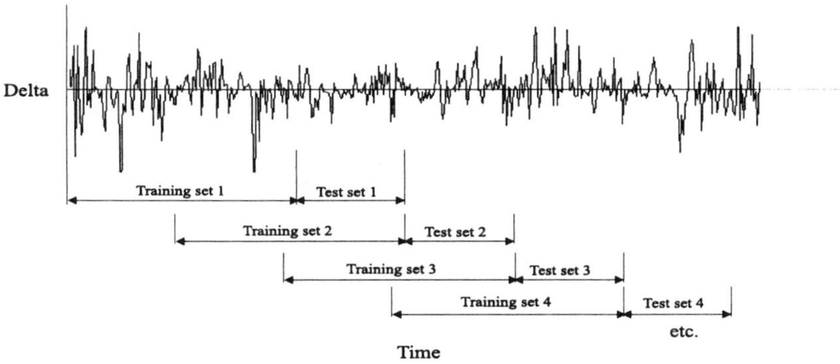

Figure 4: A depiction of the training and test sets used.

3.4 Generalization and Overfitting

Neural network practitioners often use a validation set in order to control the bias/variance tradeoff (Geman *et al.*, 1992) of the model. Tests showed that using a validation set for this problem seriously affected performance. This is not surprising because there is a dilemma when choosing the validation set. If the validation set is located before the training data (in terms of the temporal order of the series), then the non-stationarity of the series means the validation set may be of little use for predicting performance on the test set. If the validation set is located after the training data, we again have a problem with the non-stationarity – we would like to make the validation set as small as possible to alleviate this problem, however it cannot be made too small because it needs to be a certain size in order for the results to be statistically valid and therefore useful for controlling the bias/variance tradeoff. For the problem considered, a validation set would have to be large because of the high degree of noise [e]. With this in mind, overfitting is controlled by setting simulation parameters for an appropriate stopping point *a priori*. This stopping point was determined from experiments with a separate segment of data that was not part of the subsequent training and test datasets.

3.5 Data Bias

For some financial data sets, it is possible to obtain better than average results by simply predicting the most common change in the training data (e.g.

[e] Note that leave-one-out cross-validation, bootstrap, etc. cannot be used because of the temporal order of the data.

noticing that the change in prices is positive more often than it is negative in the training set and always predicting positive for the test set). Although predictability due to such data bias may be worthwhile, it is uninteresting in the present context because it can obscure any results due to the model learning short term predictability of the dynamic evolution of the series. Such bias can also present problems to model training algorithms because the lower mean squared error of the simple solution (predict always positive or always negative) can prevent gradient descent algorithms from finding any better minima. Figure 5 shows a simplified depiction of the problem – if the naive solution, A, has a better mean squared error than a random solution then it can be hard to find a better solution, e.g. B. In our system the models have been prevented from acting on any such bias by ensuring that the number of training examples for the positive and negative cases is equal. (The training set actually remains unchanged so that the temporal order is not disturbed but there is no training signal for a number of positive or negative examples near the beginning of the series).

Figure 5: A depiction of a simplified error surface if a naive solution, A, performs well. A better solution, e.g. B, can be difficult to find.

4 Results

Figure 6 and table 1 show the average error rate as the number of nodes in the SOM was increased from 2 to 7 for embedding dimensions of 1 and 2. The best performance was obtained with a SOM size of 7 nodes and an embedding dimension of 2 where the error rate was 47.1%. Experiments were also performed where the RNN was replaced with a standard MLP – performance in this case was very poor.

The prediction corresponding to the random walk model is equal to the current price, i.e. no change. We cannot obtain a percentage of times the model predicts the correct change for the random walk model. However, our models can be used with data that corresponds to a random walk and the results can be compared to those obtained with the real data. We performed these tests by randomizing the classifications in the test set. For each original test set we created five randomized versions. The randomized versions were created by

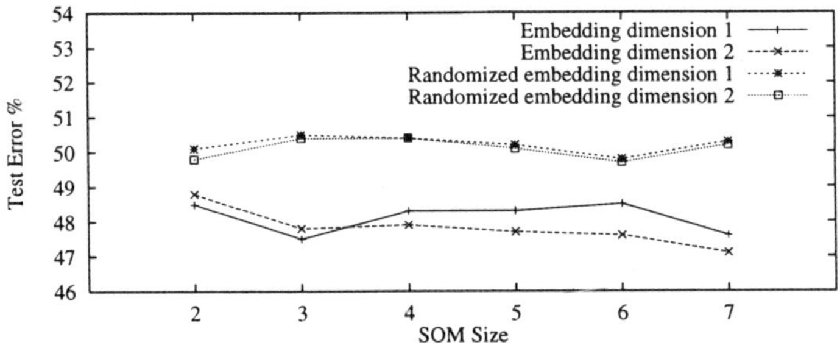

Figure 6: The error rate as the number of nodes in the SOM is increased for SOM embedding dimensions of 1 and 2. Each of the results represents the average over the 5 individual series and the 30 simulations per series, i.e. over 150 simulations which tested 30 points each, or 4500 individual classifications. The results for the randomized series are averaged over the same values with the 5 randomized series per simulation, for a total of 22500 classifications per result (all of the data available was not used due to limited computational resources).

repeatedly selecting two random positions in time and swapping the two classification values (the input values remain unchanged). An additional benefit of this technique is that if the model is showing predictability based on any data bias (as discussed in the previous section) then the results on the randomized test sets will also show this predictability (the original and randomized test sets contain identical numbers of positive and negative examples).

Table 1: Simulation results as in figure 6.

	SOM embedding dimension: 1					
SOM size	2	3	4	5	6	7
Error	48.5	47.5	48.3	48.3	48.5	47.6
Randomized error	50.1	50.5	50.4	50.2	49.8	50.3

	SOM embedding dimension: 2					
SOM size	2	3	4	5	6	7
Error	48.8	47.8	47.9	47.7	47.6	47.1
Randomized error	49.8	50.4	50.4	50.1	49.7	50.2

4.1 Reject Performance

A confidence measure was calculated for every prediction based on the magnitude of the winning output and the difference between the winning output and the other output (for outputs transformed using the *softmax* transformation (Haykin, 1994)). We assigned a confidence threshold which was used to reject predictions with confidence values below the threshold. Figure 7 shows the classification performance of the system (percentage of correct sign predictions) as the confidence threshold is increased for the normal test sets and for the randomized test sets. We can see that a significant increase in performance can be obtained by only considering the 10-20% of examples with the highest confidence. This benefit is not seen with the randomized test sets.

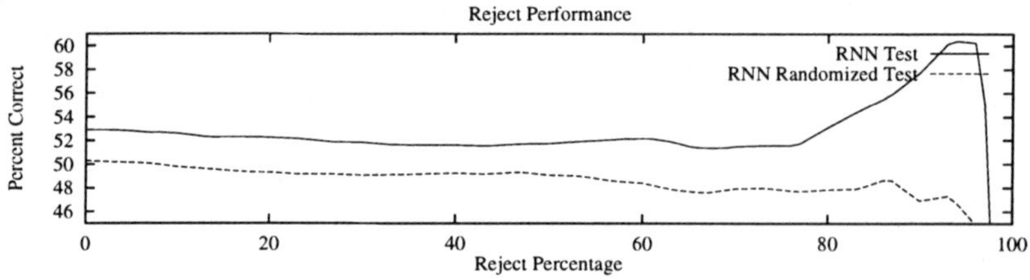

Figure 7: Classification performance as the confidence threshold is increased for both the normal and randomized test sets. The drop at the end is due to the granularity of the threshold tests (the rejection threshold was varied in equal steps rather than the rejection percentage) and the fact that the classifier cannot get anything correct when 100% of the examples are rejected.

5 Rule Extraction

The extraction of symbolic knowledge from a trained neural network can aid in the interpretability of the solution. Deterministic finite state automata (DFA) and the corresponding production rules can be extracted from RNNs with an algorithm based on clustering the activation values of the recurrent state neurons (Omlin & Giles, 1996a). This algorithm is based on the observation that the activations of the recurrent state neurons in a trained network tend to cluster. The output of each of the N state neurons is divided into q intervals of equal size, yielding q^N partitions in the space of outputs of the state neurons. Starting from an initial state, all input symbols are considered in order. If an input symbol causes a transition to a new partition in the activation space then a new DFA state is created with a corresponding transition on the appropriate symbol. In the event that different activation state vectors belong to the same partition, we choose the state vector which first reached the partition as the new initial state for subsequent symbols. The extraction would be computationally infeasible if all q^N partitions had to be visited, but the clusters corresponding to DFA states often cover a small percentage of the input space. Sample extracted automata can be seen in figure 8 for a SOM size of 2 and a SOM embedding dimension of 1. The DFAs have been minimized using standard minimization techniques (Hopcroft & Ullman, 1979). As expected, the DFAs extracted in this case are relatively simple. In all cases, the SOM symbols end up representing positive and negative changes in the series – transitions marked with a solid line correspond to positive changes and transitions marked with a dotted line correspond to negative changes. For all DFAs, state 1 is the starting state. Double circled states correspond to prediction of a positive change, and states without the double circle correspond to prediction of a negative change. DFA (a) can be seen as corresponding to mean-reverting behavior – i.e. if the last change in the series was negative then the DFA predicts that the next change will be positive and vice versa. (b) and (c) can be seen as variations on (a) where there are exceptions to the simple rules of (a), e.g. in (b) a negative change corresponds to a positive prediction, however after the input changes from negative to positive, the prediction alternates with successive positive changes. In contrast with (a)-(c), (d)-(f) exhibit behavior related to trend following algorithms, e.g. in (d) a positive change corresponds to a positive prediction, and a negative change corresponds to a negative prediction except for the first negative change after a positive change. More complex behavior can be seen when extracting automata corresponding to larger SOM sizes.

This work considers the acquisition of knowledge which requires hidden state information, and we note that recurrent neural networks can perform knowledge refinement when a partial domain theory is available (Omlin & Giles, 1996b). For the application domain considered here, financial experts may provide a partial domain theory by encoding rules (Omlin & Giles, 1996b) or using hints (Abu-Mostafa, 1993).

6 Summary

The method of noisy time series prediction presented here deals with a fundamental problem in the prediction of high noise data using relatively small sample sizes: the problem of finding correlations between input and output variables which are due to noise and are random in nature. The method has found significant predictability in foreign exchange rate data.

The method facilitates the inference of rules which explain the operation

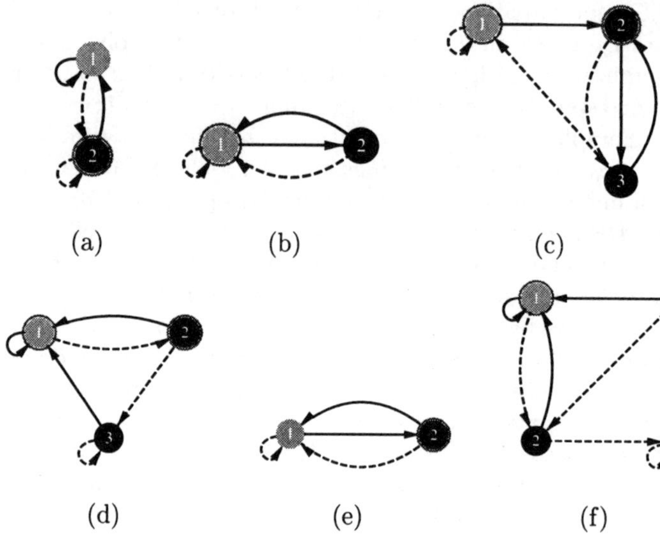

Figure 8: Sample deterministic finite state automata (DFA) extracted from trained financial prediction networks using a quantization level of 5.

of the system. Results for the extraction of rules in the problem considered here are positive and show that symbolic rules which have meaning to humans can be extracted from noisy time series data. Such information can be very useful and important to the user of the technique.

References

Abu-Mostafa, Y. 1993. Hints and the VC dimension. *Neural Computation* **5**(2), 278–288.

Darken, C. and J. Moody. 1992. Towards faster stochastic gradient search. In *Neural Information Processing Systems 4*, pp. 1009–1016. Morgan Kaufmann.

Elman, J. 1991. Distributed representations, simple recurrent networks, and grammatical structure. *Machine Learning* **7**(2/3), 195–226.

Farmer, D. and J. Sidorowich. 1987. Predicting chaotic time series. *Physical Review Letters* **59**, 845–848.

Geman, S., E. Bienenstock and R. Doursat. 1992. Neural networks and the bias/variance dilemma. *Neural Computation* **4**(1), 1–58.

Haykin, S. 1994. *Neural Networks, A Comprehensive Foundation.* Macmillan, New York, NY.

Hopcroft, J. and J. Ullman. 1979. *Introduction to Automata Theory, Languages, and Computation.* Addison-Wesley Publishing Company, Reading, MA.

Kohonen, T. 1995. *Self-Organizing Maps.* Springer-Verlag, Berlin, Germany.

Kremer, S. C. 1996. *A Theory of Grammatical Induction in the Connectionist Paradigm.* PhD thesis, Department of Computer Science, University of Alberta, Edmonton, Alberta.

Lequarré, J. Y. 1993. Foreign currency dealing: A brief introduction (data set C). In *Time Series Prediction: Forecasting the Future and Understanding the Past,* A. Weigend and N. Gershenfeld (eds). Addison-Wesley.

Moody, J. 1995. Economic forecasting: Challenges and neural network solutions. In *Proceedings of the International Symposium on Artificial Neural Networks.* Hsinchu, Taiwan.

Omlin, C. and C. Giles. 1996a. Extraction of rules from discrete-time recurrent neural networks. *Neural Networks* **9**(1), 41–52.

Omlin, C. and C. Giles. 1996b. Rule revision with recurrent neural networks. *IEEE Transactions on Knowledge and Data Engineering* **8**(1), 183–188.

Refenes, A. (ed). 1995. *Neural Networks in the Capital Markets.* John Wiley and Sons.

Ruck, D., S. Rogers, K. Kabrisky, M. Oxley and B. Suter. 1990. The multilayer perceptron as an approximation to an optimal Bayes estimator. *IEEE Transactions on Neural Networks* **1**(4), 296–298.

Siegelmann, H. 1995. Computation beyond the Turing limit. *Science* **268**, 545–548.

Takens, F. 1981. Detecting strange attractors in turbulence. In *Dynamical Systems and Turbulence,* D. Rand and L.-S. Young (eds), vol. 898 of *Lecture Notes in Mathematics,* pp. 366–381, Berlin. Springer-Verlag.

Weigend, A., B. Huberman and D. Rumelhart. 1992. Predicting sunspots and exchange rates with connectionist networks. In *Nonlinear Modeling and Forecasting, SFI Studies in the Sciences of Complexity, Proceedings Vol. XII,* M. Casdagli and S. Eubank (eds), pp. 395–432. Addison-Wesley.

WHAT IS THE "TRUE PRICE"? – STATE SPACE MODELS FOR HIGH FREQUENCY FX DATA

JOHN MOODY, LIZHONG WU
Oregon Graduate Institute, Computer Science Dept.,
Portland, OR 97291-1000
also at:
Nonlinear Prediction Systems
P.O. Box 681, University Station, Portland, OR 97207

In previous work, we have found statistically-significant structures in tick-by-tick interbank foreign exchange (FX) price series on various time scales. These structures include negative autocorrelations in successive tick-by-tick returns and positive autocorrelations (trends) on longer time scales. To account for the observed structures, we propose state space models for financial time series in which the observed price is a noisy version of an unobserved, less-noisy "true price" process. The "true prices" in our models are stochastic processes with short-term, long-term, or multi-scale memory structures. The processes we consider include random walks, random trends, and fractional Brownian motions. For fractional Brownian motion processes, we represent the multi-scale correlational structures using self-similar wavelet decompositions. We estimate the state space model parameters using the Kalman filter and EM algorithms. Since both the observational noise and the changes in the true price series have non-gaussian distributions, the Kalman filter and EM algorithms are not able to completely separate the observational noise from the true price components. To improve this separation, we perform a neural-network-based independent component analysis (ICA) using algorithms developed for the blind separation of signals. Statistical analysis of our true price models supports our assertion that the estimated true prices are significantly different from the observed prices, and that significant non-random structures may exist in the FX markets. Sonification of the observed price and "true price" series supports this finding by revealing obvious perceptual differences between the signals. We believe that our proposed "true price" models may enable us to discover new arbitrage opportunities and to construct better forecasting and trading models.

1 Introduction

The motivation of this study comes from our analysis of tick-by-tick, interbank foreign exchange rate data, (Moody & Wu, 1994; 1995a; 1995; 1996). This set of data consists of non-binding quotations from market makers. In this work, we have identified two properties of the correlational structure of tick-by-tick FX data: (1) Negative correlations in successive tick-by-tick price changes; see Figures 1 and 2. (2) Positive autocorrelations on longer time scales; see Figure 3. This second effect is not necessarily easy to measure, since the strong tick-by-tick anticorrelations can mask it.

The strong anticorrelation at lag 1 in the tick-by-tick returns as shown in Figures 1 and 2 is believed by financial economists to be caused by market microstructure effects, particularly the inventory effect (Lyons, 1993; O'Hara, 1995). Regardless of its cause, we will argue that it can be explained empirically as an effect due to additive observational noise in the indicative price quotes.

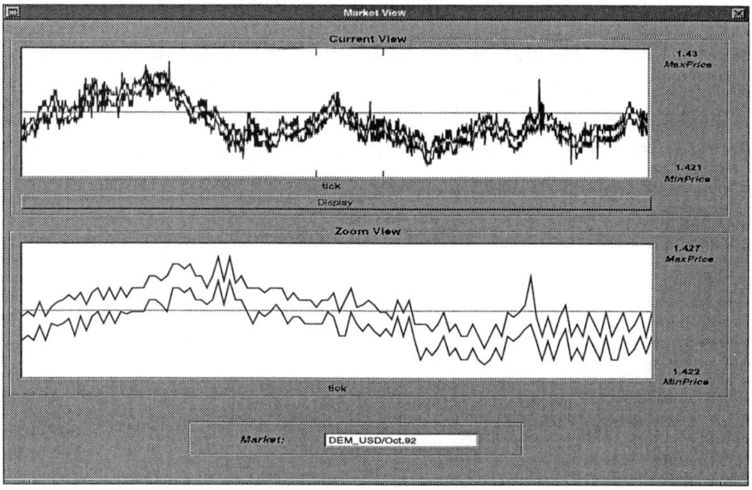

Figure 1: Bid and ask prices extracted from DEM/USD on October 1, 1992.

To reliably detect the presence of long term memory structures in financial time series when short term autocorrelations are present, we proposed a new unbiased rescaled range statistic R/S^* that eliminates the contaminating effects of autocorrelations on time scale q. Figure 3 shows our R/S^* analysis of FX prices (Moody & Wu, 1996). As explained in the figure caption, the apparent price behavior on time scales up to 100 ticks changes completely as the effects of tick-by-tick negative autocorrelations are removed. The apparent behavior of the tick-by-tick DEM/USD series shifts from mean-reverting to mean-averting. From this experiment, we can see that the spuriously observed mean reversion in the original price series is actually due to short-term negative autocorrelations, rather than to intrinsic dependencies in the price movements, and that the underlying behavior of the series on longer time scales is actually trending.

Our goal is to estimate unobservable underlying prices (assuming some price process) by removing the noise in the indicative quotations. The outline of this paper is as follows. Section 2 formalizes and defines models for the given problem. We describe three models which we will study and compare in this paper. These three models are: the steady model, the linear growth model, and the fractional Brownian motion model. The first two models assume that the underlying prices are independent or short-term dependent, while the fractional Brownian motion model assumes that the underlying prices may have long-term memory. We briefly describe model estimation for the first two models in Section 2 and focus on estimating fractional Brownian motion in Section 3. We first review several modeling techniques for fractional Brownian motions and then describe wavelet decomposition methods for estimating fractional Brownian motions. Empirical results are presented in Section 4, where we first compare the "true prices" obtained based on different models studied in this paper, and then show the long term correlation structure revealed by our "true price" models. We conclude in Section 5.

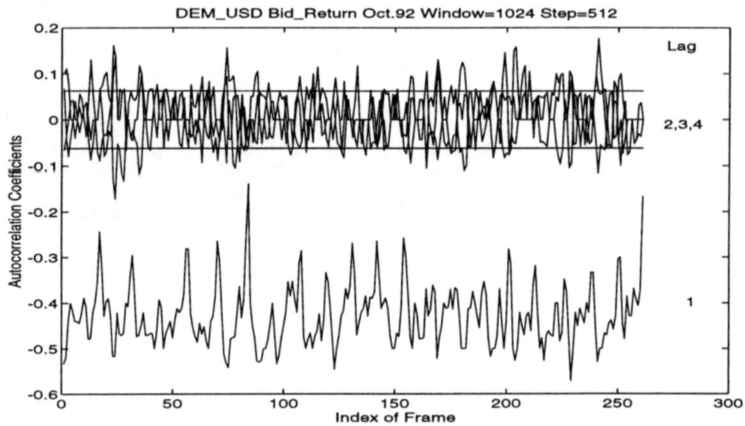

Figure 2: Autocorrelation coefficients {1,2,3,4} versus time frame for DEM/USD during October 1992. Each time frame contains 1024 ticks and successive frames overlap by 512 ticks. A strong negative autocorrelation at lag 1 is apparent, and its magnitude exhibits a daily volatility cycle. This cycle is clearly audible when the data is sonified (Section 4.3).

2 State Space Models

State space or "true price" models assume that the recorded price quotations can be described by

$$q(t) = p(t) + \varepsilon(t) , \tag{1}$$

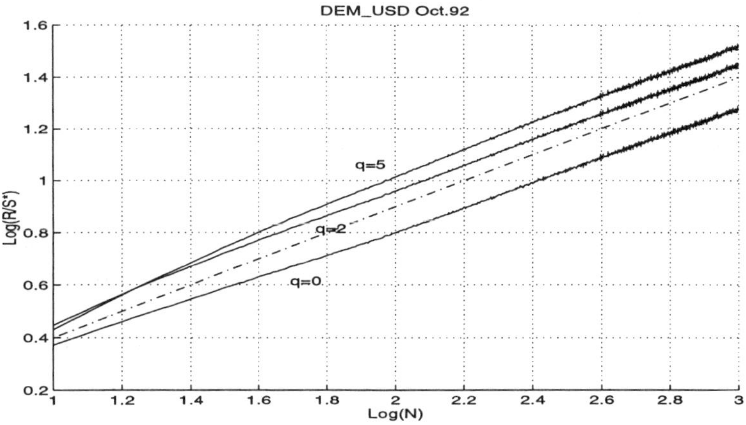

Figure 3: $[R/S^*](N)$ for the DEM/USD bid returns in October 1992 using lag parameters $q = \{0, 2, 5\}$. $[R/S^*](N)$ (Moody & Wu, 1996) is an unbiased rescaled range (R/S) analysis and considers the effect of the short-term covariances (with $q > 0$). When $q = 0$, $[R/S^*](N) = [R/S](N)$. The figure shows that while the raw price series suggest that FX prices are mean-reverting (R/S curve with $q = 0$), the underlying true prices in fact exhibit trending behavior. The dashed line corresponds to random-walks.

where $p(t)$ is the underlying "true price" and $\varepsilon(t)$ is zero mean random noise. Our task is thus to estimate $p(t)$ assuming some model, given the observed series $q(t)$. [a] In this paper, we study and compare the following three types of models for the underlying price $p(t)$:

1. Steady model (Random Walk + Noise): This model assumes that the underlying prices follow a random-walk process, i.e

$$p(t) = p(t-1) + \delta(t) \ , \tag{2}$$

where $\delta(t)$ is a process noise. Assuming that both the observation noise ($\varepsilon(t)$ in Eqn(1)) and the process noise are white, the autocovariances of the observed returns $r_q(t) = q(t) - q(t-1)$ are

$$E[r_q^2(t)] = 2\sigma_\varepsilon^2 + \sigma_\delta^2 \tag{3}$$

$$E[r_q(t)r_q(t-1)] = -\sigma_\varepsilon^2 \tag{4}$$

$$E[r_q(t)r_q(t-\tau)] = 0 \ , \ \text{for } \tau \geq 2 \ . \tag{5}$$

It is straightforward to estimate σ_ε^2 and σ_δ^2 from measurements of the autocovariances. The state $p(t)$ can be estimated via the Kalman filter.

[a] (Bolland & Connor, 1996) have used state space models to identify triangle arbitrage opportunities in groups of currencies.

The autocorrelation coefficients are $\rho_1 = -\sigma_\varepsilon^2/(2\sigma_\varepsilon^2 + \sigma_\delta^2)$, and $\rho_j = 0$ for $j > 1$. Theoretically, the value of ρ_1 for the steady model can range between -0.5 when $\sigma_\delta^2 = 0$ and 0 when $\sigma_\varepsilon^2 = 0$. For the DEM/USD returns in figure 2, $\widehat{\rho}_1 \approx -0.4$ and $\widehat{\rho}_2 \approx \widehat{\rho}_3 \approx \widehat{\rho}_4 \approx 0$ on average, suggesting that the returns on very short time scales are well described by the steady model, and that the returns are mostly observational noise.

The steady model is not completely satisfactory, however, since $\widehat{\rho}_1 < -0.5$ at some points, $\widehat{\rho}_j$ for $j > 1$ are significantly different from 0 too frequently, and weak, positive correlations on longer time scales are not explained.

Figure 4 plots the *Signal-to-Noise Ratio* of the model, defined as $SNR = \sigma_\delta^2/\sigma_\varepsilon^2$, for DEM/USD in September 1995. Its nonstationarity requires that our model should be adaptive through time. The observed SNR is remarkable for two reasons: (1) it is usually much less than one, and (2) it varies significantly in magnitude, suggesting that there are periods with significant price movements (high SNR) separated by periods of almost no price movement (low SNR).

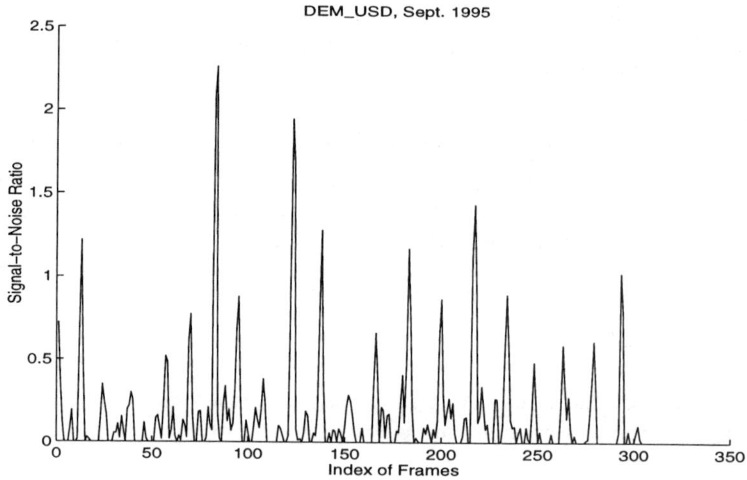

Figure 4: SNR in the steady model for DEM/USD in September 1995. Each frame consists of 1024 ticks; the frames overlap by 512 ticks. A daily volatility cycle is apparent.

2. <u>Linear growth model (Random Trend + Random Walk + Noise)</u>: This model assumes that the underlying prices follow:

$$p(t) = p(t-1) + \beta(t-1) + \delta_1(t) \tag{6}$$

$$\beta(t) = \beta(t-1) + \delta_2(t) \ . \tag{7}$$

With the assumption that the process and observation noises are white, we can solve this model using the Kalman filter.

3. Fractional Brownian Motion (FBM) model: Here, the underlying price series is assumed to follow fractional Brownian motion. Fractional Brownian motion is a generalization of the usual Brownian motion or random-walk. It was introduced to model processes that have long memory or $1/f$-type spectral behaviors (Beran, 1994), and have a statistical self-similarity property (Feder, 1988). Since Mandelbrot et al. first found the presence of long-memory components in asset returns, see for example Mandelbrot & Van Ness (1968), there have been many empirical reports to support this finding (Granger, 1980; Peters, 1989; Diebold & Rudebusch, 1989). For FBMs, the dependence between distant observations, though small, is by no means negligible. Compared to short memory series such as ARMA processes, the dependences of long-term persistent processes decay hyperbolically instead of exponentially. Conventional approaches like ARMA models are therefore inadequate to capture the correlational structures embedded in long memory series.

In the next section, we will study fractional Brownian motion modeling with wavelet representations.

3 Estimating Fractional Brownian Motion with Wavelet Decompositions

There have been many models developed for fractional Brownian motion processes. Some well-known and recently developed models include: filtered white noise (Mandelbrot & Van Ness, 1968; Feder, 1988), aggregation of short-memory models (Granger, 1980), fractional difference models (Granger & Joyeux, 1980; Hosking, 1981), driving white noise through an infinite cascade of pole-zero sections (Keshner, 1982) and orthonormal wavelet basis expansions with uncorrelated random coefficients (Mallet, 1989; Flandrin, 1992; Wornell & Oppenheim, 1992). To compare these approaches systematically is another topic of study. However, the latter approach, wavelets, has certain advantages for estimating state space models. Bjorn (1995) has also used wavelets for financial time series analysis, but not in a state space context.

3.1 Estimating Wavelet Decompositions via the EM Algorithm

The wavelet transform decomposes a signal into self-similar wavelets which are derived from one elementary waveform by means of shifts and dilations. Fractional Brownian motions also exhibit self-similarity, since any portion of a given process can be viewed, in a statistical sense, as a scaled version of a larger or smaller sample of the same process. The above correspondence sets up a bridge between the wavelet transform and fractional Brownian motions. In fact, the multi-resolution analysis with wavelet decompositions is particularly well suited to analyzing the underlying statistical property of fractional Brownian motions when observational noise is present.

Taking the wavelet transform of Eqn(1), see for example Daubechies (1988), Mallet (1989), we get

$$Q_n^m = P_n^m + \varepsilon_n^m \text{ , for } m \in \mathcal{M} \text{ and } n \in \mathcal{N}(m) \text{ ,} \tag{8}$$

with m representing the scale level and n for the time index of the components. Under the Gaussian assumption, P_n^m can be estimated by (Flandrin, 1992; Wornell & Oppenheim, 1992):

$$\hat{P}_n^m = \mathbf{E}[P_n^m | Q_n^m] = S(m, \theta) Q_n^m \text{ ,} \tag{9}$$

where

$$S(m, \theta) = \frac{\sigma^2 \beta^{-m}}{\sigma^2 \beta^{-m} + \sigma_\varepsilon^2} \tag{10}$$

is a wavelet analog of the Wiener filter that serves as a smoothing function. Denoting the wavelet basis functions as $\psi_n^m(t)$, this yields the following estimate of the "true price"

$$\hat{p}(t) = \sum_{m,n} \hat{P}_n^m \psi_n^m(t) = \sum_{m,n} S(m, \theta) Q_n^m \psi_n^m(t) \text{ .} \tag{11}$$

The model parameters $\theta = (\beta, \sigma^2, \sigma_\varepsilon^2)$ can be estimated using the EM algorithm. Note that the factor $S(m, \theta)$ has a thresholding or smoothing role: at coarser scales (small m) where the signal predominates, the coefficients Q_n^m are retained, while at finer scales (large m) where noise predominates, the coefficients Q_n^m are attenuated.

In Figure 5, we visualize Eqn(11) for a set of DEM/USD tick-by-tick prices. The smoothing factor $S(m, \theta)$ decays from 1 to 0 as the scale level m goes from coarse to fine. At coarser scales, the signals are mostly retained, while at finer scales, the signals are mostly removed.

3.2 Independent Component Analysis

Since both the observational noise and the changes in the true price series have non-gaussian distributions, the Kalman filter and EM algorithms are not able to completely separate the observational noise from the true price components. To improve this separation, we perform a neural-network-based independent

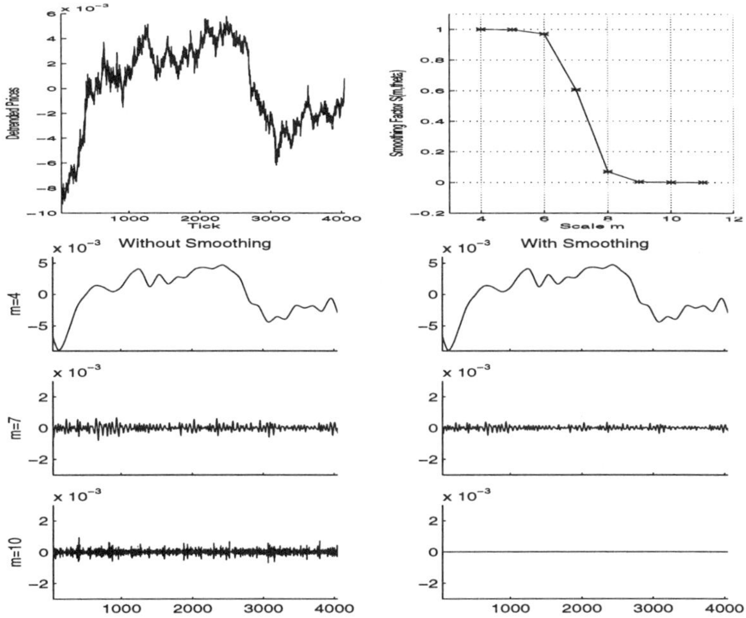

Figure 5: Visualizing Eqn(11) for a set of DEM/USD prices after being detrended as shown in the upper-left panel. The smoothing function $S(m, \theta)$ is plotted in the upper-right panel. Lower panels compare the original and smoothing reconstructed signals at scales of 4, 7 and 10. The signals are mostly retained at coarser scales (small m), while at finer scales (large m), the signals are mostly removed.

component analysis (ICA) using algorithms developed for the blind separation of signals (Bell & Sejnowski, 1995; Amari *et al.*, 1996).

ICA finds a separation of the signals with reduced statistical dependence at not only second order (cross-correlations), but at higher orders as well (eg. fourth order cross-cumulants). Our ICA is performed by using the true price and observational noise components estimated via the Kalman filter or EM algorithms as reference inputs to the blind separation algorithm.

4 Empirical Results and Discussions

Figure 6 compares a segment of "true prices" to the observed prices. We see that the "true prices" are much smoother and less noisy.

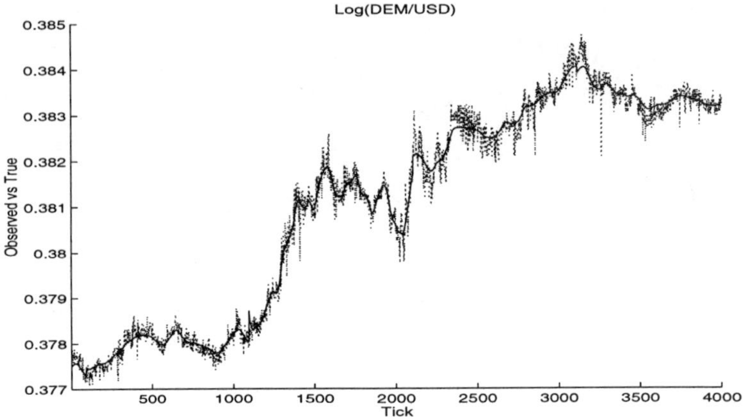

Figure 6: Observed DEM/USD (dotted curve) and the "true prices" estimate under the model of Fractional Brownian motion assumption (solid curve).

4.1 Comparisons between models

We have estimated three "true prices" based on different models. The question that arises is: how do these different estimated prices differ and relate? To answer this, we did pair-by-pair homogeneous χ^2 testings for the distributions of the estimated returns for the different models. As shown in Figure 7, our analysis accepts the hypothesis that the returns come from different populations. Thus, all "true price" return series are significantly different from the observed price return, and the choice of "true price" model among the three models studied yields significantly different results.

4.2 Autocorrelation Analysis

Figure 8 shows short-run autocorrelations during September 1995 for the original returns and compares them to autocorrelations for changes in the noise and "true price" components. The true price model is estimated under the FBM assumptions, and the autocorrelation analysis is performed after further separating the signals using ICA. Autocorrelations for lags up to 50 ticks (about 8 minutes on average) are computed in windows of length 1024 ticks.

From the figure, we can see that both the noise component returns and the original returns show very similar autocorrelation functions, which are dominated by significantly negative, first-order autocorrelations. The mean values for the other orders are basically equal to zero. The autocorrelations of

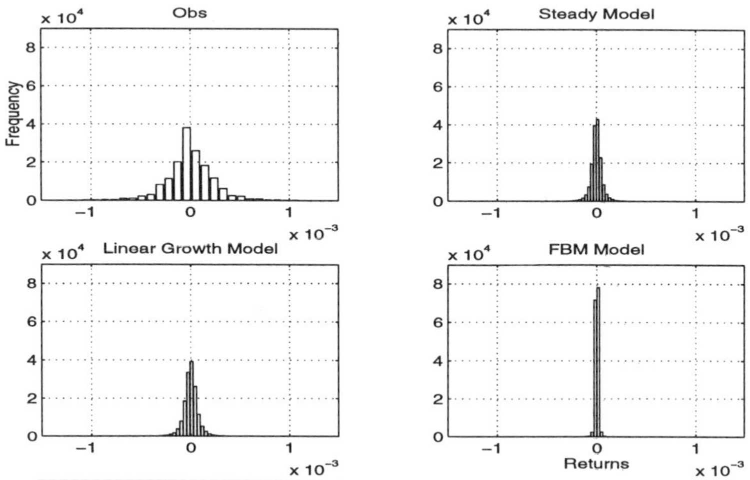

Returns	Obs.	Steady	Linear Growth	FBM
Obs.	-			
Steady	+	-		
Linear Growth	+	+	-	
FBM	+	+	+	-

Figure 7: Comparison of histograms and pair-by-pair homogeneous χ^2 testings for observed returns and denoised and smoothed "true price" returns for three state space models. "-" indicates that the hypothesis that the pairs of returns come from different populations is rejected, and "+" indicates that the hypothesis is accepted. The significance level is 99%. The data are DEM/USD price quotes for Sept. 1995.

the "true price" component show positive correlations except at first-order.

The above autocorrelation analysis suggests the following:

1. Changes in the "true prices" for the FBM model exhibit slight, but significant trends on tick-by-tick time-scales. Whether this is an artifact introduced by the wavelet smoothing must still be determined. However, these results are consistent with those indicated by R/S^* analysis in Figure 3.

2. The autocorrelation function of original returns reflects only the anticorrelation of price changes at lag 1 (believed by economists to be due to the inventory effect). This suggests that the existence of the strong, short-term anticorrelations will foil a standard autocorrelation analysis on longer time scales. These results may be model-dependent and should

be considered preliminary. However, they suggest that "true price" models may be effective in uncovering underlying structure that is obscured by additive noise.

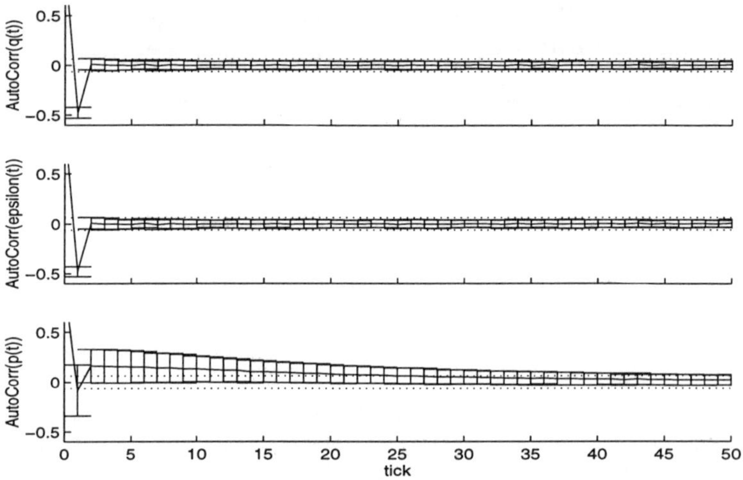

Figure 8: Comparison of autocorrelation functions of the returns for the original series (the upper panel), the observational noise component (the middle panel) and the "true price" component (the lower panel) for the FBM model. DEM/USD data for September 1995 is divided into 293 subsets of 1024 tick windows which overlap by 512 ticks. The autocorrelation results presented here are the means and standard deviations for the 293 windows. The horizontal dotted lines represent the 95% confidence band for a single 1024 tick window.

4.3 Sonification of True Prices

The statistical differences between the observed price series, estimated true price series, and white noise can be easily perceived by playing the price changes through a sound generator. The results are quite striking. In particular, the true prices for the FX markets exhibit periods of relative quiet, occasional waves of activity, and intermittent impulse noise (presumably due to news).

5 Concluding Remarks

We have proposed using state space models to analyze high frequency financial data. These models decompose the observed prices into unobserved, underlying "true prices" plus observational noise. We have presented three such true price models, including random walks, random trends, and fractional Brownian motions. The random walk and random trend models are estimated using Kalman filters, while wavelet decompositions and the EM algorithm are used to estimate the FBM models.

These models are able to explain observed correlational structures in the DEM/USD exchange rates. These include anticorrelations in successive price changes and positive correlations (trends) on longer time scales. Our statistical modeling of high frequency intra-day FX price series has demonstrated that trends may in fact exist in noisy FX data and that the conventional random-walk models of efficient market theory do not explain the correlational structures that are present in the high frequency data. Further studies are required.

We are hopeful that our proposed "true price" models will enable us to discover new arbitrage opportunities (Bolland & Connor, 1996) and to construct better forecasting and trading models.

Acknowledgements

We would like to thank Olsen & Associates, Chemical Bank, and Citibank for providing us with the data used in our analysis, and Michel Dacorogna and Yoni Cheifetz for useful discussions. We gratefully acknowledge support for this work from ARPA and ONR under grant N00014-92-J-4062, NSF under grant CDA-9309728, ARPA under contract DAAH01-96-C-R026, and Nonlinear Prediction Systems.

References

Amari, S., A. Cichocki and H. Yang. 1996. A new learning algorithm for blind signal separation. In *Advances in Neural Information Processing Systems 8*, D. Touretzky, M. Mozer and M. Hasselmo (eds). MIT Press: Cambridge, MA.

Bell, A. and T. Sejnowski. 1995. An information-maximization approach to blind separation and blind deconvolution. *Neural Computation* **7**(6), 1129–1159.

Beran, J. 1994. *Statistics for Long-Memory Processes.* New York: Chapman and Hall.

Bjorn, V. April 1995. Multiresolution methods for financial time series prediction. In *Conference on Computational Intelligence for Financial Engineering.* IEEE Press, Piscataway, NJ.

Bolland, P. and J. Connor. 1996. Identification of fx arbitrage opportunities with a non-linear multivariate kalman filter. In **Neural Networks in the Capital Markets**, *Proceedings of the Third International Conference (London, Oc-*

tober 1995), A. Refenes, Y. Abu-Mostafa, J. Moody and A. Weigend (eds). World Scientific, London.

Daubechies, I. Nov. 1988. Orthonormal bases of compactly supported wavelets. *Commun. Pure Appl. Math.* **41**, 909–996.

Diebold, F. X. and G. D. Rudebusch. 1989. Long memory and persistence in aggregate output. *Journal of Monetary Economics* **24**, 189–209.

Feder, J. 1988. *Fractals.* Plenum Press, New York.

Flandrin, P. March 1992. Wavelet analysis and synthesis of fractional brownian motions. *IEEE Transactions on Information Theory* **38**(2), 910–917.

Granger, C. and R. Joyeux. 1980. An introduction to long-memory time series models and fractional differencing. *Journal of Time Series Analysis* **1**, 15–29.

Granger, C. 1980. Long memory relationships and the aggregation of dynamic models. *Journal of Econometrics* **14**, 227–38.

Hosking, J. 1981. Fractional differencing. *Biometrika* **68**, 165–76.

Keshner, M. 1982. 1/f noise. *Proceedings IEEE* **70**, 212–218.

Lyons, R. 1993. Tests of microstructural hypotheses in the foreign exchange market. Working Paper Series 4471, National Bureau of Economic Research, INC.

Mallet, S. July 1989. A theory for multiresolution signal decomposition: The wavelet representation. *IEEE Transactions on Pattern Analysis and Machine Intelligence* **11**(7), 674–693.

Mandelbrot, B. and J. Van Ness. 1968. Fractional Brownian motion, fractional noise, and applications. *SIAM Review* **10**.

Moody, J. and L. Wu. November 1994. Statistical analysis and forecasting of high frequency foreign exchange rates. In *International workshop on Neural Networks in the Capital Markets*, Pasadena, California.

Moody, J. and L. Wu. April 1995. Price behavior and Hurst exponents of tick-by-tick interbank foreign exchange rates. In *Conference on Computational Intelligence for Financial Engineering*, New York city.

Moody, J. and L. Wu. March 1995. Statistical analysis and forecasting of high frequency foreign exchange rates. In *First international conference on High Frequency data in Finance*, Zurich, Switzerland.

Moody, J. and L. Wu. 1996. Improved estimates for the rescaled range and hurst exponents. In **Neural Networks in the Capital Markets**, *Proceedings of the Third International Conference (London, October 1995)*, A. Refenes, Y. Abu-Mostafa, J. Moody and A. Weigend (eds). World Scientific, London.

O'Hara, M. 1995. *Market Microstructure Theory.* Blackwell Business.

Peters, E. July-August 1989. Fractal structure in the capital markets. *Financial Analysts Journal* , 32–37.

Wornell, G. and A. Oppenheim. March 1992. Estimation of fractal signals from noisy measurements using wavelets. *IEEE Transactions on Signal Processing* **40**(3), 611–623.

PRINCIPAL COMPONENTS ANALYSIS FOR MODELING MULTI-CURRENCY PORTFOLIOS

J. UTANS, W.T. HOLT and A.N. REFENES
Decision Technology Centre, London Business School
Sussex Place, Regent's Park, London NW1 4SA, England

A model input selection procedure based on Principal Components Analysis is presented. The procedure is applied to hourly exchange rates from the five year period 1989- 1994 and daily rates over a 21 year period (1973-1994). We show i) it is possible to reduce the number of input series to a model without significant loss of information, ii) principal components reveal the main uncorrelated factors driving the market.

1 Introduction

Neural networks have established themselves as powerful tools for the prediction of time series such as foreign exchange rates. Of crucial importance to the model specification stage of the modeling process is the selection of relevant input variables. These typically consist of lagged values of the times series yielding a non-linear autoregressive model. For the prediction of foreign exchange rates, past values of related series are included as input variables. These input variables may include other exchange rates or, for example, interest rates in the respective countries. The design step of selecting appropriate variables entails both the selection of appropriate time series to include as well as deciding how much historical data to use for building the model. Because financial and economic time series typically are non-stationary, this last step is of particular importance for building models. Choosing too much data can in fact reduce the performance of the model because only broad characteristics of the series that are valid for a large time horizon are represented. On the other hand, choosing not enough data will result in a poor model with high variance. Alternatively, with not enough data available one is forced to reduce the model complexity to avoid over-fitting and give up potentially improved performance. The pre-processing of data usually includes normalisation and transformation steps that ease these problems. For example, for foreign exchange rates one calculates the return series as the series of logged first differences, removing any linear trend and the need for the neural network to extrapolate the series. However, the time series obtained after these basic transformations may still be non-stationary (i.e. their statistical properties are not time invariant) and therefore difficult to model. In this paper we focus on the use of Principal Component Analysis (PCA) as a pre-processing tool for the modeling of multivariate non-stationary time series. Given a portfolio of major currencies trading in a liquid market, one expects to see a large amount of correlation, co-movement and/or cointegration among the market prices. It may therefore be possible to reduce the number of input series to a model by excluding components that only explain a small percentage of the variance, or those which appear to be completely non-stationary and therefore inherently difficult to predict.

The outline of the paper is as follows. In Section 2 we briefly introduce the concept of Principal Components Analysis. Rescaled range and Hurst exponent techniques are described to measure the stationarity of a time series. Section 3 describes the daily and hourly foreign exchange data used to generate the principal component series. Section 4 describes the PCA analysis performed on the foreign exchange data. Properties of the time series are demonstrated with rescales range analysis. Section 5 concludes the paper with a discussion of potential applications of the work.

2 Structural Time Series Analysis

2.1 *Principal Component Analysis*

PCA (Manly, 1986) is a linear transformation on the original input variables $x_1, x_2, \ldots, x_n$ such that they become uncorrelated. The new indices $z_1, z_2, \ldots, z_n$ thus measure different 'dimensions' of the data and are referred to as the Principal Components(PCs) of the original data. The principal components are ordered by explained variance such that $var(z_1) \geq var(z_2) \geq \ldots \geq var(z_n)$. PC's may be calculated by obtaining the correlation matrix of the original data:

$$C = \begin{bmatrix} 1 & c_{12} & \ldots & c_{1n} \\ c_{21} & 1 & \ldots & c_{2n} \\ \ldots & \ldots & & \ldots \\ c_{n1} & c_{n2} & \ldots & 1 \end{bmatrix}$$

where $c_{ij} = c_{ji}$ is the correlation between x_i and x_j. The variance of the PCs are given by the eigenvalues of C and the coefficients of the PCs by the eigenvectors of C. The coefficients or *loadings* give the weights of the linear transform and quantify the contribution of the original data to each of the PCs. For foreign exchange rates this step identifies the main uncorrelated factors which drive the market's fluctuations.

2.2 *The Hurst Exponent*

A formal test of stationarity is given by the Hurst exponent (Hurst, 1951), a model independent test for the random walk which makes few underlying assumptions about the data. Specifically, no distributional assumptions are made about the data. If we consider a time series $\mathbf{X}$ with t observations, the cumulative deviation around the mean M over N periods is given by

$$X_{t,N} = \sum_{u=1}^{t} (e_u - M_N) \tag{1}$$

We may then define the range of this interval to be

$$R = max(X_{t,N}) - min(X_{t,N}) \tag{2}$$

It is clear that the amount of variation increases with the length of time considered. Hurst generated a standardised ratio by dividing the range by the standard deviation of the observations. The Hurst exponent (H) is then defined as

$$R/S = (a \times N)^H \tag{3}$$

where R/S is the rescaled range and a is a constant. The Hurst exponent has been used to classify time series into the following categories: $H = 0.5$: Random walk, $H \in (0, 0.5)$: Mean-reverting series, and $H \in (0.5, 1.0)$: Trending series.

3 The Data

We present the analysis of two data sets. The first consists of a portfolio of four currencies (British Pound, German Mark, Japanese Yen and Swiss Franc) relative to the US Dollar. The dataset consists of hourly prices for the five year period 1989-1994. As there is trading in these major currency pairs on exchanges around the world, price data is available for all 24 hours of each day. Figure 1 and Figure 2 show the price and returns data for 1994 respectively. These are four major currencies in a highly liquid market for which one observes a high degree of dependence.

The second dataset consists of a portfolio of nine currencies (British Pound, German Mark, Japanese Yen, Swiss Franc, Canadian Dollar, Spanish Pseta, French Franc, Italian Lira and Swedish Krona) relative to the US Dollar. The data consists of daily prices for the 25 year period 1971-1996. As a fixed exchange rate system was in place prior to 1973, no data before this period was used for the analysis. Figure 13 shows data for the period 1973-1996. As would be expected, there is a high degree of dependence for the European currencies with the Canadian Dollar and the Japanese Yen having different behavior.

4 Results

To illustrate the results of PCA we first present an analysis for the year 1994 for the price series and the return series. PCA on the price series enables us to visually analyse the characteristics of the original data that are picked out by the principal components.

The results confirm that in fact a large percentage of the variance of the portfolio is due to the first few principal components as shown in Figure 4 for prices and Figure 7 for returns respectively. For the price series, the first component explains more than 92% of the variance with the first two components explaining more than 97%. For the return series, the first component explains significantly less variance. Nevertheless, the first two components together account for more than 91%.

Figure 3 shows the evolution of the principal components through time (the "eigen-series") for the prices for the year 1994. The first component clearly captures the main downward trend of the data. The second component captures the divergence of the Japanese Yen against the European currencies. The first two components exhibit significant structure while the remaining components are approximately mean reverting. The factor loadings (the components of the eigen vector corresponding to the eigen series) are shown in Figure 5 and reveal the details of the composition of the eigen series. The first component consists of about equal contributions from all four currencies. The second component explains about 5% of the variance with contributions primarily from the Japanese Yen and the British Pound; in fact the component is dominated by the difference between the Pound and Yen prices. The third component has negative contributions from the Franc and Mark and positive contributions from the Yen and Pound, capturing the difference between these groups of currencies. The forth component which explains less than 1% of the variance is dominated by the difference between the Franc and the Marc. Note that calculating the series of differences of two time series is a pre-processing step taken in the presence of co-integration (i.e. when both series are non-stationary but their difference is stationary).

Figure 8 depicts the eigen series calculated for the returns. Again the first two components exhibit significant structure. Note that the factor loadings (Figure 9) are comparable to the factor loadings obtained for the price series and the same observations hold (however, the dominant interactions are contaminated to a larger extent by the presence of contributions from other currencies). Nevertheless, this demonstrates that even after removing the linear trend present in the price series the PCA is a useful tool for further pre-processing.

A visual inspection of the eigen series of the prices and returns reveals that the last principal components appear to be stationary, a characteristic that will lead to easier model specification. In order to show this property, Hurst exponents have been calculated for the currency data and the principal components. Figure 6 shows the Hurst exponents for the price series data. It is clear that the principal components show increasing mean reversion. Figure 10 shows Hurst exponents for the returns. While the characteristics of the series are less clear than for the prices, 3 of the 4 components have lower Hurst exponents than the original price series. The Hurst exponent results broadly agree with work by Moody(1995) who showed that foreign exchange tick data has Hurst exponents of around 0.47 and Peters(1989) who calculated Hurst exponents for daily prices giving Hurst exponents of around 0.6.

Next we show results of a PCA covering the 6 year period from 1989 to 1994 for the returns series. The PCA was calculated over a rolling, overlapping window of length 3 months. We are interested in observing the explained variance for each of the principal components as well as their loadings as a function of time. Variations in explained variance will have implications for the removal of some components from the set of input variables for our model. If the factor loading vary with time then the composition of the eigen series in terms of the original data changes. These variations are flagging significant changes in the dependencies between the series that must be taken into account when building a model.

Figure 11 shows the percentage of explained variance over time. The results confirm that the variance explained by the first two components is consistently larger than 80%. The failure of the first or first two components to account for the majority of the variance indicates dissimilar movements in the underlying currency returns.

Note that, as shown in Figure 12, large changes in the loadings can be observed, in particular for the second and third components. The contribution to the first component which accounts for more than 60% of the variance, while slightly varying with time, stays qualitatively similar (at about equal contribution from all currencies). On the other hand, for the second component for the period around 30 the contribution of the Yen decreases and the contribution of the Pound increases sharply, accompanied by a large increase of the Yen contribution to the third component (a similar change can be observed around period 5). But note that for the second component the contribution from the Franc and Mark series, while not constant, move very closely together. For the forth component, the contribution from the Yen and the Pound is consistently very small with the major contributions being due to the Franc and Mark.

Figures 13 through 16 show the PCA for nine currencies over a 23 year period. The components obtained represent the long run factors driving the prices of these currencies. As expected with such a large group of currencies, the first component explains only 63% of the variance, however the first two components still explain over 90% of the variance. The first two eigen series (Figure 15) display considerable structure while the remaining series are approximately mean reverting. The Hurst exponent analysis shown in Figure 17 displays a consistent downward trend for the principal components. Thus the principal components display more mean reversion than the original price series.

5 Conclusions

We have demonstrated that the PCA reveals useful structure in the returns series as well as the character of non-stationarity present even after removing a linear trend. Making

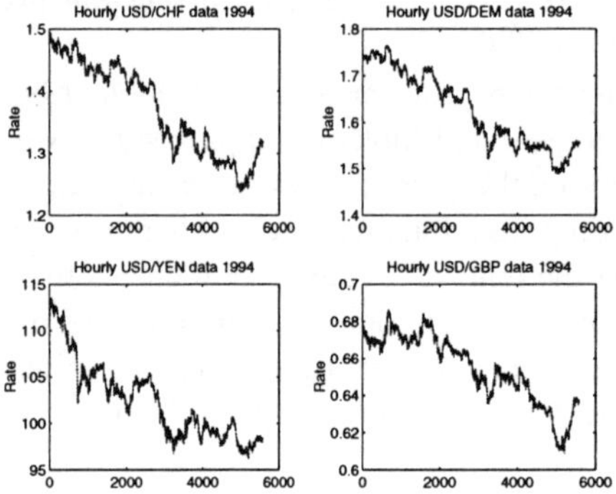

Figure 1: Hourly 1994 exchange rates against the US Dollar. Note the dominant downward trend common to all four series.

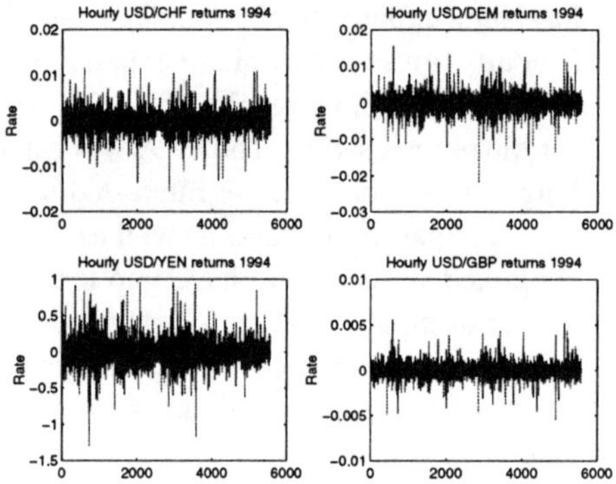

Figure 2: Returns series for 1994 hourly price data.

use of this analysis will lead to improved forecasting models as we are able to select input time series to our model which are more mean reverting than the original data series. Obvious applications of this work include trading, forecasting and hedging. A simple technical trading strategy may be implemented to directly trade a particular principal component series. The principal component series is more easily forecast than the price series. With the use of leveraging which is commonly available in foreign exchange trading it is possible to implement profitable trading strategies based on components that explain only a small amount of the variance of the original data. A simple hedging strategy against market moves in a group of currencies may be implemented by performing a PCA and using this information to hedge against the first few principal components.

References

1. H Hurst 1951 *Long Term Storage of Reservoirs* Transactions of the American Society of Civil Engineers **116**
2. B Manly 1986 *Multivariate Statistical Methods*, Second Edition, Chapman and Hall.
3. E Peters 1991 *Chaos and Order in the Capital Markets: A New View of Cycles, Prices and Market Volatility* John Wiley and Sons
4. J Moody and L Wu 1995 *Improved Estimates for the Rescaled Range and Hurst Exponents* Proceedings of the Third International Conference on Neural Networks in the Capital Markets World Scientific.

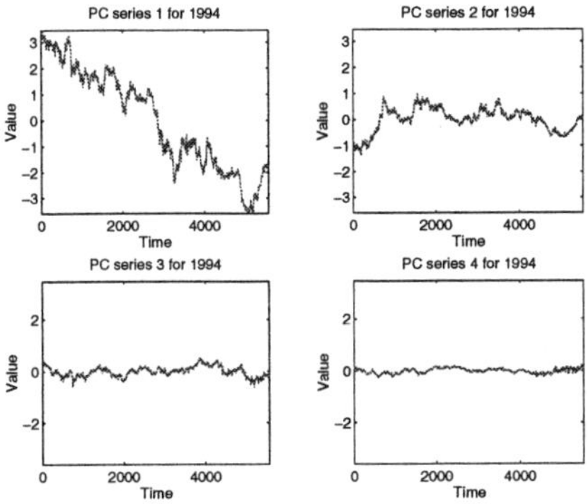

Figure 3: PCA of price series. The eigenseries of the original price series are shown. The first two components exhibit significant structure while the remaining are approximately mean reverting.

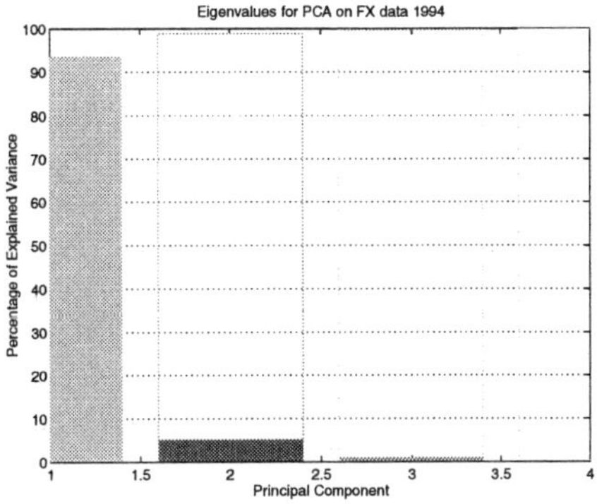

Figure 4: The relative magnitude of the eigenvalues corresponds to the variance explained by the principal components. For the price series the first two components together explain more than 97% of the variance.

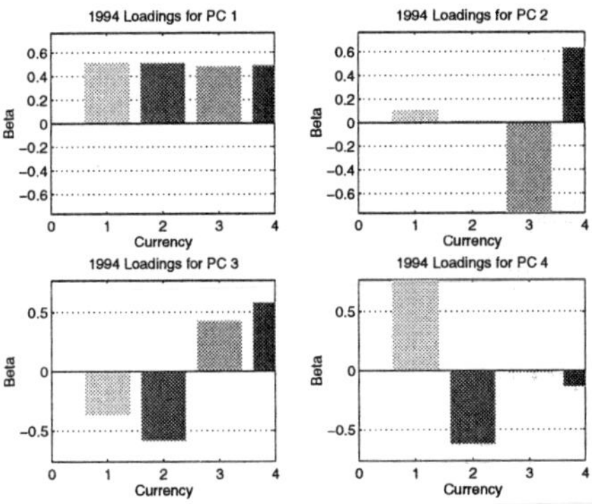

Figure 5: PCA of price series. The "factor loadings", i.e. the components of the respective eigenvectors reveal details of the composition of the eigen series.

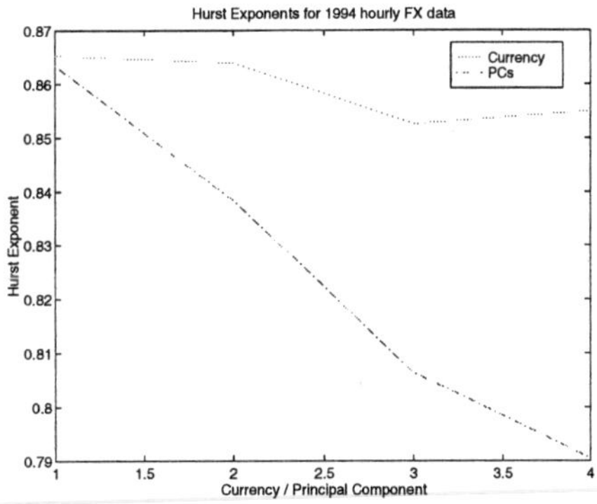

Figure 6: Hurst exponents for 1994 price series. Note the decreasing Hurst exponent for the PC's indicating increasing mean reversion. The Hurst exponents for the price series remain approximately constant.

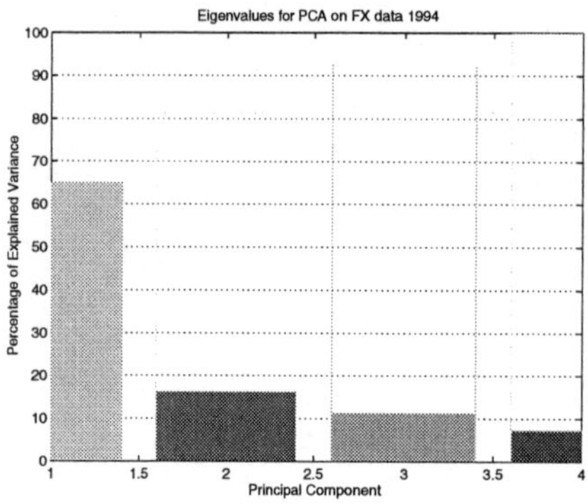

Figure 7: PCA of returns series. In contrast to the proce series, the first PCs explain a significantly smaller amount of the variance of the portfolio return (this is expected because by calculating the returns one effectively removes the linear trend component present in the price series). However, the first two components together explain more than 91% of the variance.

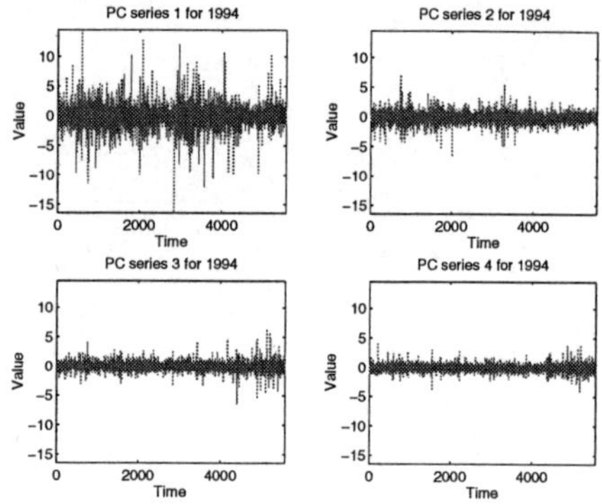

Figure 8: PCA of returns series. Here the eigen series obtained by transforming the original return series are shown. Again the first two components exhibit significant structure.

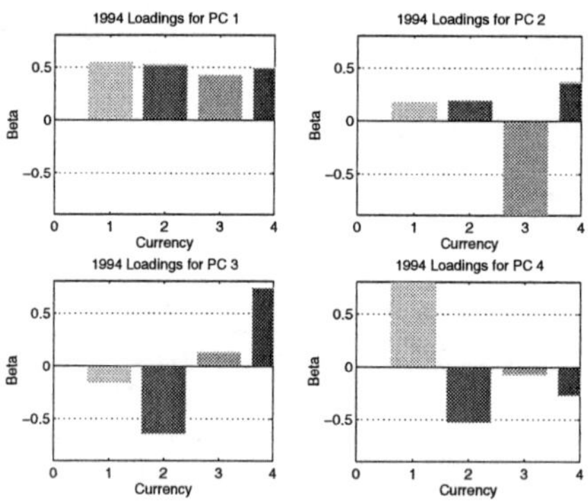

Figure 9: PCA of returns series. The factor loadings for the returns are very similar to the loadings for the price series, in particular with respect to the sign of the dominant factors.

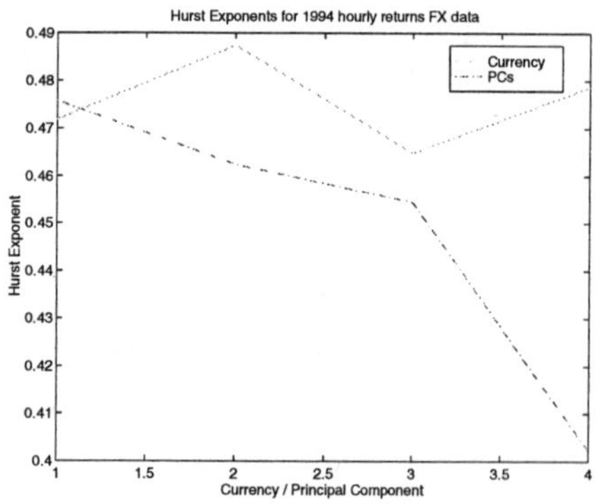

Figure 10: Hurst exponents for returns series. In contrast to the price series, the Hurst exponents of the PCs do not show a predominant increase in mean reversion. However, the Hurst exponent of the PCs is lower than that of the price series for all but one of the PCs.

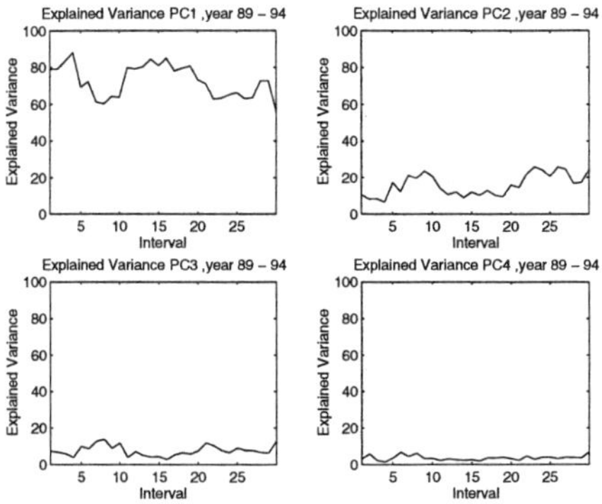

Figure 11: Explained variance over a 6 year period: The PCA was caclulated for overlapping windows of length 3 month periods covering hourly data from 1989 until 1994. The Figure shows the explained variance for each of the four principal component series. Note that the first two components consistently account for the dominant part of the variance.

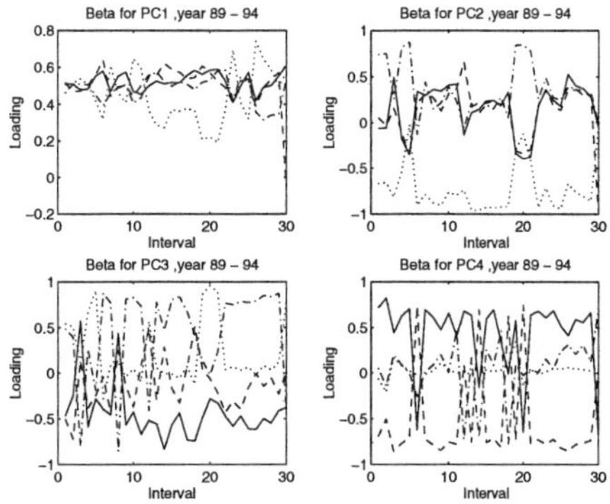

Figure 12: Factor loadings over a 6 year period: The PCA was calculated for overlapping windows of length 3 month covering hourly data from 1989 until 1994. The Figure shows the loadings for each of the four principal component series as a function of time.

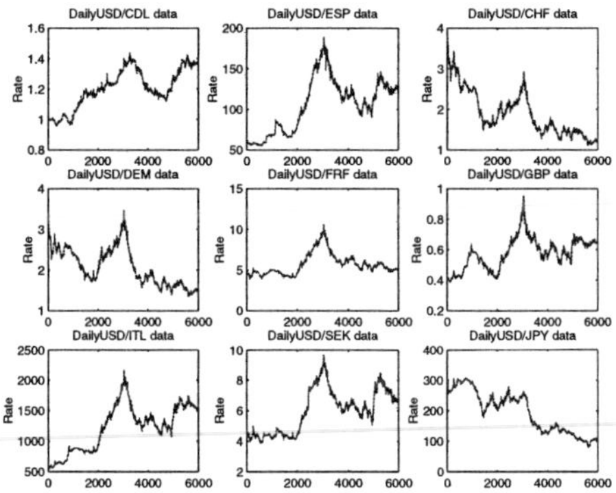

Figure 13: Exchange rates for nine major currencies against the US Dollar. Note the difference in behaviour of the Yen and Canadian Dollar to the European currencies.

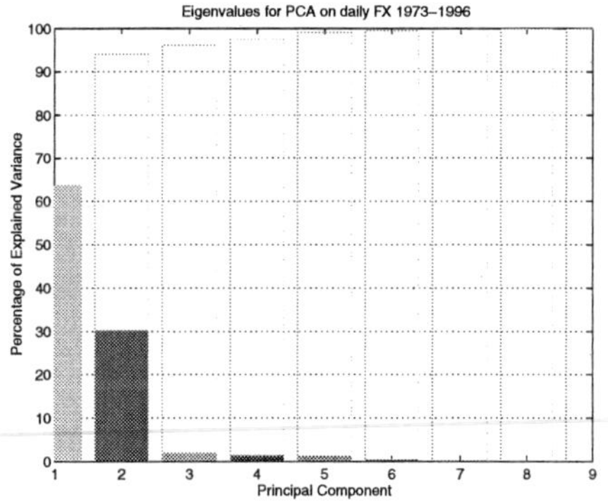

Figure 14: PCA of price series. The addition of more currencies to the PCA analysis reduces the explained variance of the first components. The first two PCs explain over 90% of the variance.

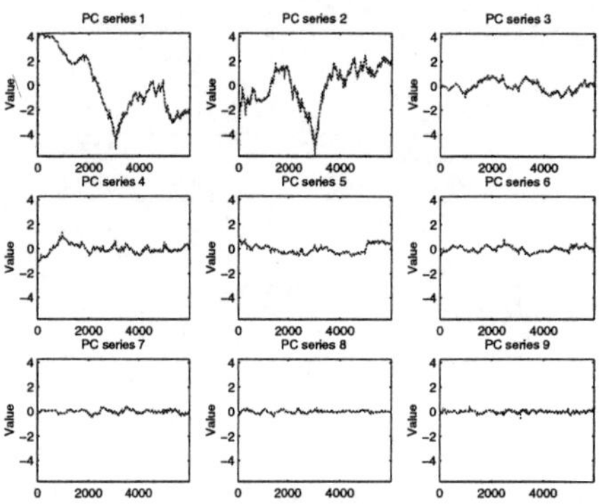

Figure 15: PCA of price series. The eigen-series of the transformed prices are shown. The first 4 components exhibit structure while the remaining are approximately mean reverting.

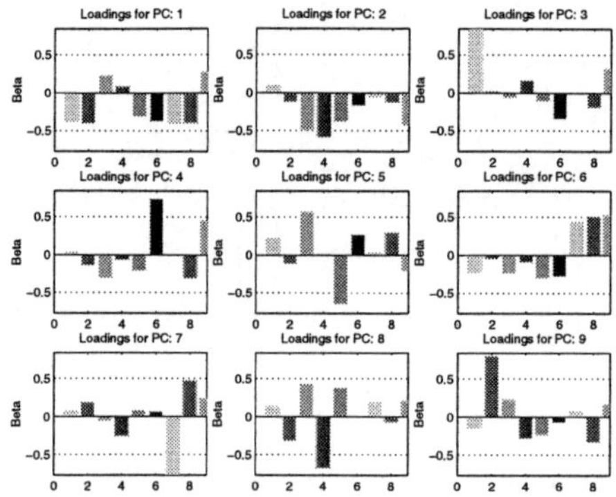

Figure 16: PCA of price series. The factor loadings for the price series giving details of the composition of the eigen series.

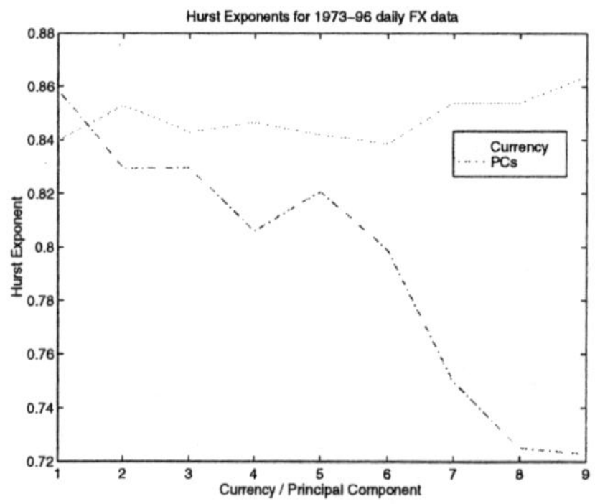

Figure 17: Hurst exponents for price series. Note the consistent downward trend of the PCs.

TESTING FOR NONLINEARITY WITH NEURAL NETWORKS
A Study for Daily USD/DEM Exchange Rates

U. ANDERS
ZEW — Center for European Economic Research
P.O.-Box 10 34 43, 68034 Mannheim, Germany

T.-H. HANN
University of Karlsruhe (TH)
76128 Karlsruhe, Germany

G. NAKAHEIZADEH
Daimler Benz AG, Research Center
P.O.-Box 23 60, 89013 Ulm, Germany

Most applications of neural networks to financial market data assume that capital markets behave in a strongly nonlinear way. Within the context of neural networks this assumption is seldomly questioned. In this paper we apply statistical inference techniques in order to find out whether neural networks can significantly improve on an exemplary linear \$/DEM exchange rate model. For this purpose we use LM–test procedures, called neural network tests, as developed by White (1989a) and Teräsvirta/Lin/Granger (1993). These procedures allow to test a given model by adding one or more additional hidden units to it. If the additional hidden units become accepted by the LM–test the nested model neglects some nonlinearity in mean and the use of a neural network is justified. In our application, the neural network tests indicate that there is no neglected nonlinearity in the chosen exemplary exchange rate model. We validate our results by comparing the out-of-sample performance of the linear models with that of nonlinear neural networks.

1 Introduction

Recently there is a growing interest in the modelling of nonlinear relationships. A variety of test procedures for detecting nonlinearities has been developed[a] and especially in capital markets nonlinearities are well documented. As neural networks are principally able to model such nonlinearities they are often used to forecast financial data. Here they most often serve as regression tools to predict future mean values of the target variables.[b]

However, in many applications the nonlinearity in mean is not so strong as to require very complex neural networks. Even more, some applications actually do not show any nonlinearity in mean at all. For this reason it is

[a]See Granger/Teräsvirta (1993) for an overview.
[b]E.g. Hsieh (1989) or Weigend/Huberman/Rumelhart (1991).

quite useful to test for the relevance of a neural network. Only if we find neglected nonlinearity in a linear model the use of a neural network could be justified.

In this paper, we model daily \$/DEM exchange rates. We apply a linear model to forecast one day ahead and test whether we can improve such forecasts by help of a neural network. The test procedures employed are LM–tests as developed by White (1989a) and Teräsvirta/Lin/Granger (1993). Such tests reveal whether we should extend an existing model by an additional hidden unit.

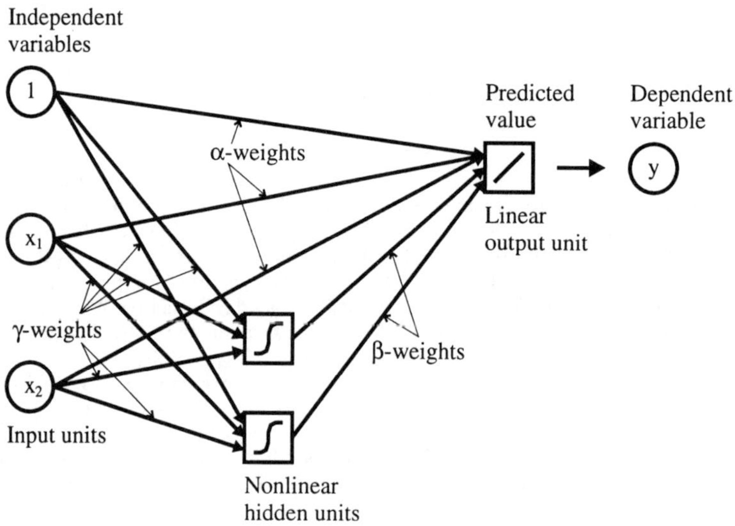

Figure 1: MLP–network with three layers.

The networks used in our study are single hidden layer feedforward neural nets with a linear output unit as shown in figure 1. Each neural network can be expressed as a function of the explaining variables $X = [x_0, x_1, \ldots, x_I]$ and the network weights $w = (\alpha', \beta', \gamma')'$. x_0 is constant and defined as $x_0 \equiv 1$ for all observations. I denotes the number of non-constant explaining variables and H the number of hidden units employed. The network shown in figure 1 has the following functional form $f(X, w)$:

$$f(X,w) = X\alpha + \sum_{h=1}^{H} \beta_h g\left(\sum_{i=0}^{I} \gamma_{hi} x_i\right) \tag{1}$$

The function $g(\cdot)$ is the so-called activation function of a neuron and is chosen to be the tangens hyperbolicus function.

2 LM–Tests in Neural Networks

Since multilayer perceptron neural networks are nonlinear regression models[c] the standard procedures for testing parameter significance like Wald–tests or LM–tests in principle apply. However, to perform these tests the (asymptotic) distribution of the network parameters is needed. This distribution was derived by White (1989c). If there exists a unique set of optimum parameters w^* that represent the best approximation of a true function by help of a certain network model, White shows that w^* can be consistently estimated through a set of parameters $\hat{w}$ obtained by maximum likelihood methods under quite general conditions.

Furthermore, $\hat{w}$ is asymptotically normal with mean w^* and covariance matrix $\frac{1}{T}C$, or alternatively

$$\sqrt{T} \cdot (\hat{w} - w^*) \sim N(0, C), \tag{2}$$

where T is the number of observations.

As it is the case with other approximation methods where the used function class may not contain the unknown regression function, neural networks are inherently misspecified models. The corresponding theory has been developed again by White (1982, 1994). He proved that the application of standard hypothesis tests, such as LM– and Wald–tests, is valid even for misspecified models, if the misspecification is taken account of in the computation of the covariance matrix $\frac{1}{T}C$ of the parameters.

If a neural network is estimated via the maximum likelihood method with log likelihood contribution $\mathcal{L}_t$, the covariance matrix of the parameters is given by $\frac{1}{T}C = \frac{1}{T}A^{-1}BA^{-1}$. The matrices A and B are defined as $A \equiv -E[\nabla^2 \mathcal{L}_t]$ and $B \equiv E[\nabla \mathcal{L}_t \nabla \mathcal{L}_t']$ where ∇ denotes the gradient and ∇^2 the hessian. As can be seen, the covariance matrix C is a generalization of the covariance formula in standard maximum likelihood theory. If the model is faithful, the asymptotic covariance matrix of the limiting distribution can be estimated by both, the inverse of the matrix A and the inverse of the matrix B. In this case A asymptotically equals B. Note, that the covariance matrix C accounts for misspecification in mean as well as in variance, i.e. a consistent estimate of C converges to the covariance matrix of the limiting distribution of $\hat{w}$ even if the

[c]White (1989c).

network does not encompass the true underlying function and the true error terms are heteroscedastic.

However, one severe problem remains. The optimum w^* is not unique for the network model given in (1), i.e. the model is not globally identified.[d] This problem is a rather hard one to deal with, and the question of identification will complicate the application of the hypothesis tests considerably. Two techniques have been proposed in the literature to circumvent the identification problem. One was developed by White (1989a) and its properties investigated by Lee/White/Granger (1993). The other was devised by Teräsvirta/Lin/Granger (1993) and compared to the former.

Both groups of authors start from the model $y = F(X) + \varepsilon$, where $F(\cdot)$ is the true function, ε an iid random noise with $E[\varepsilon\varepsilon'] = \sigma I$, $E[\varepsilon] = 0$ and $E[X'\varepsilon] = 0$. It is further assumed, that $F(X)$ has already been approximated by a parametric function $f(X, \hat{w})$.[e] The question which shall be answered by the neural network tests is now: can the approximation of $F(X)$ through $f(X, \hat{w})$ be improved by adding Q (one or more) hidden units in order to capture some neglected nonlinearities? If the answer is yes, the data can be explained more accurately by the following equation:

$$y = f(X, \hat{w}) + \sum_{q=H+1}^{H+Q} \hat{\beta}_q g(\sum_{i=0}^{I} \hat{\gamma}_{qi} x_i) + \hat{\eta} \tag{3}$$

The new residual is denoted by $\hat{\eta}$. The appropriate tests on the additional parameters β_q or γ_q are called 'tests against neglected nonlinearities'. If $f(X, \hat{w})$ in (3) is the linear function $f(X, \hat{w}) = X\hat{w}$, which implies $H = 0$, the test against neglected nonlinearities becomes a test of model linearity against model nonlinearity.

In order to circumvent the identification problem, White (1989a) suggests to draw the γ–weights of the additional hidden units from a random distribution. This amounts to a random choice of these parameters. The subsequent test on the significance of the corresponding β–weights is carried out conditional to the random values of the γ–weights. Alternatively, Teräsvirta/Lin/Granger (1993) propose the application of a third order taylor approximation to the additional hidden units which equally leads to an avoidance of the identification problem. The LM–procedure then tests on the

[d] See Anders/Korn (1996) for more details.

[e] The function $f(X, \hat{w})$ may be an arbitrary function (e.g. a linear function). It may but need not be a neural network.

significance of the coefficients in the taylor approximation.[f] The LM–tests are carried out as described by Davidson/McKinnon (1993).

As was shown by Lee/White/Granger (1993), the LM–Test due to White (1989a) shows good power against a variety of nonlinearities in mean as well as in variance. In the simulation study of Anders/Korn (1996) the power of the Teräsvirta/Lin/Granger (1993) test turns out to be even higher than the power of the White (1989a) LM–test procedure.

3 Data and Models

In this study we intended to perform a one day ahead forecast of the percentage changes in \$/DEM exchange rates. For this purpose we examined several daily financial data series with different lags between 1. January 1990 and 28. February 1996 by running rolling regressions. Each regression covered a time period of three years, where the time window was shifted by adding 20 new observations on the right and by dropping 20 observations on the left. In these regressions only the percentage changes in Dow-Jones, 10-years American bond yields, \$/Yen exchange rates, and the \$/DEM exchange rates itself, all with a lag of one day, showed in most of the times significant t-values on a 5% percent level. As this variable selection purely relies on linear measures, this investigation only considers a model in which the independent variables at least contribute linearily to the explanation of the dependent variable. However, in a more general case one could extend the linear model with variables that have a zero restriction and can as well test such extended models against neglected nonlinearities. As the study of this paper is more exemplary in nature, we refrain from the use of zero restrictions. Thus, we chose the following simple exchange rate model as our benchmark model:

$$\begin{aligned}\Delta \ln(\$/\mathrm{DEM})_t &= \alpha_1 \Delta \ln(\$/\mathrm{DEM})_{t-1} + \alpha_2 \Delta \ln(\mathrm{Bond10})_{t-1} \\ &+ \alpha_3 \Delta \ln(\$/\mathrm{Yen})_{t-1} + \alpha_4 \Delta \ln(\mathrm{DowJones})_{t-1}.\end{aligned}$$

4 Results and Interpretation

When running rolling regressions in the exchange rate model, the coefficients of the variables differed considerably. This suggested to us that the linear relationships between the variables are quite instable over time. Neural networks

[f] For a detailed explanation of the test procedures see Anders/Korn (1996).

will be able to improve on the forecasts in mean if some of the instabilities were caused by structured nonlinear processes, which were neglected in the linear model.

We investigated this by applying the LM–test procedures mentioned above.[g] We performed the tests on different subsamples, each containing a period of three years. In none of the four subsamples neither the White LM–test nor the Teräsvirta/Lin/Granger procedure accepted an additional hidden unit on a 5% significance level.

In order to validate these test results we compared the out-of-sample performances of the linear model with that of neural networks each containing the linear part and an additional hidden unit. As validation period we chose the month following the in-sample period. For the computations the data were standardized to a mean of zero and a variance of one.

For each subsample period we calculated the coefficient of determination R^2, the root mean squared error (RMSE), the mean error (ME) and the mean absolute error (MAE) in-sample as well as out-of-sample according to the following formulas. The tables 1 to 4 show the results for each subsample period.[h]

$$R^2 = 1 - \frac{\sum_{t=1}^{T}[y_t - \hat{y}_t]^2}{\sum_{t=1}^{T}[y_t - \bar{y}]^2}$$

$$\mathrm{RMSE} = \left(\frac{1}{T}\sum_{t=1}^{T}[y_t - \hat{y}_t]^2\right)^{\frac{1}{2}}$$

$$\mathrm{ME} = \frac{1}{T}\sum_{t=1}^{T}[y_t - \hat{y}_t]$$

$$\mathrm{MAE} = \frac{1}{T}\sum_{t=1}^{T}|y_t - \hat{y}_t|$$

[g] We adopted a modification of the Teräsvirta/Lin/Granger LM–test in order to make it applicable in larger networks (see Anders/Korn, 1996).

[h] In all four subsamples the variance of the dependent variable is smaller in the out-of-sample period than in the corresponding in-sample period. For this reason, the out-of-sample errors are smaller than the in-sample errors, although the R^2-measures show out-of-sample a worse correlation between the actual and the forecasted values than in-sample.

Table 1: Results for subsample 1.

Subsample 1	1.1.90 – 31.12.92	linear model	network
R^2	in-sample	0.1425	0.1698
	out-of-sample	0.1315	0.0299
RMSE	in-sample	0.9254	0.9106
	out-of-sample	0.7365	0.7784
ME	in-sample	0.0000	-0.0099
	out-of-sample	- 0.0194	-0.0361
MAE	in-sample	0.6954	0.6909
	out-of-sample	0.5398	0.5989

Table 2: Results for subsample 2.

Subsample 2	1.1.91 – 31.12.93	linear model	network
R^2	in-sample	0.1729	0.1939
	out-of-sample	0.4059	0.3642
RMSE	in-sample	0.9809	0.8972
	out-of-sample	0.4373	0.4530
ME	in-sample	0.0000	- 0.0046
	out-of-sample	0.0835	0.0896
MAE	in-sample	0.6810	0.6779
	out-of-sample	0.3624	0.3878

Table 3: Results for subsample 3.

Subsample 3	1.1.92 – 31.12.94	linear model	network
R^2	in-sample	0.1610	0.1867
	out-of-sample	0.1217	-0.0046
RMSE	in-sample	0.9154	0.9013
	out-of-sample	0.6391	0.6835
ME	in-sample	0.0000	-0.0063
	out-of-sample	-0.1880	-0.2203
MAE	in-sample	0.6825	0.6770
	out-of-sample	0.5462	0.5833

Table 4: Results for subsample 4.

Subsample 4	1.1.93 – 31.12.95	linear model	network
R^2	in-sample	0.1321	0.1379
	out-of-sample	-0.2365	-0.2720
RMSE	in-sample	0.9310	0.9279
	out-of-sample	0.7725	0.7834
ME	in-sample	0.0000	-0.0007
	out-of-sample	0.1790	0.1907
MAE	in-sample	0.7054	0.7024
	out-of-sample	0.6484	0.6543

The results in these table indicate that the LM–test procedures did well by rejecting the additional hidden units in all of the four subsample periods. The linear models outperform the neural networks on each out-of-sample period with respect to all performance measures. All the extra hidden unit does, is to improve the in-sample performance which goes on cost of the out-of-sample quality of the model.

However, we would like to emphasize that these results hold only for this particular exchange rate model against which the neural network tests were carried out. In a distinct context with other independent variables or different sample ranges the LM–tests may well accept one or more hidden units and thus indicate the existence of nonlinear dependencies.

5 Summary

This study shows, how hypothesis tests can be applied in order to justify the use of neural networks. We employed neural network tests due to White (1989a) and Teräsvirta/Lin/Granger (1993) in order to find out whether a certain linear exchange rate model neglects nonlinearity in mean. In our case, none of the tests gave evidence for neglected nonlinearity. Thus, the use of a neural network for daily exchange rate forecasting would not have been neccessary for the chosen independent variables.

In order to validate this result we compared the out-of-sample performances of the linear exchange rate model with that of the neural network. It shows that the linear model outperforms the neural network with respect to several performance measures.

The analogous results of the neural network tests and the out-of-sample comparisons suggest, that LM–test procedures applied in a neural network context are powerful tools to justify their use as well as to specify their complexity. Such tests can prevent users from applying neural nets in cases where there is no nonlinearity present in the data.

Acknowledgements

The authors would like to thank two anonymous referees for making some valuable comments.

References

Anders U., Korn O. 1996. Model Selection in Neural Networks. *ZEW Discussion Paper 96-21.*

Anders U., Korn O., Schmitt C. 1997. Improving the Pricing of Options — A Neural Network Approach. *Journal of Forecasting,* forthcoming.

Davidson R., MacKinnon R.G. 1993. *Estimation and Inference in Econometrics.* Oxford University Press.

Granger C.W.J., Teräsvirta T. 1993. *Modelling Nonlinear Economic Relationships. Oxford University Press.*

Hornik K., Stinchcombe M., White H. 1989. Multilayer Feedforward Networks are Universal Approximators. *Neural Networks* **2**, pp. 359–366.

Hsieh D.A. 1989. Testing for Nonlinear Dependence in Daily Foreign Exchange Rates. *Journal of Business* **62**, pp. 339–369.

Kräger H., Kugler P. 1993. Nonlineraties in foreign exchange markets: a different perspective. *Journal of International Money and Finance* **12**, pp. 195–208.

Lee T.-H., White H., Granger C.W.J. 1993. Testing for Neglected Nonlinearity in Time Series Models. *Journal of Econometrics.* **56**, pp. 269–290.

Teräsvirta T., Lin C.-F., Granger C.W. 1993. Power of the Neural Network Linearity Test. *Journal of Time Series Analysis* **14** (2), pp. 209–220.

Weigend A.S., Huberman B.A., Rumelhart D.E. 1991. Predicting Sunspots and Exchange Rates with Connectionist Networks. In *Nonlinear Modeling and Forecasting,* Casdagli M., Eubank S. pp. 395–432. Addison–Wesley.

White H. 1982. Maximum Likelihood Estimation of Misspecified Models. *Econometrica* **50** (1), pp. 1–25.

White H. 1989a. An Additional Hidden Unit Test for Neglected Nonlinearity in Multilayer Feedforward Networks. *Proceedings of the International Joint Conference on Neural Networks, Washington, DC.* SOS Printing, II, pp. 451–455.

White H. 1989b. Some Asymptotic Results for Learning in Single Hidden–Layer Feedforward Network Models. *American Statistical Association* **84** (404), pp. 1003–1013.

White H. 1989c. Learning in Neural Networks: A Statistical Perspective. *Neural Computation* **1**, pp. 425–464.

White H. 1994. *Estimation, Inference and Specification Analysis.* Cambridge University Press.

QUANTIZATION EFFECTS AND CLUSTER ANALYSIS ON FOREIGN EXCHANGE RATES

W. M. LEUNG, Y. M. CHEUNG AND L. XU
*Department of Computer Science and Engineering,
The Chinese University of Hong Kong*

This paper studies the features of some common foreign exchange rates which exhibit cluster distributions caused by the quantization property of the exchange rate data. We demonstrate the quantization effects of the returns in these series and investigate their properties by fitting the clusters into regression models.

1 Introduction

We examine some common foreign exchange rates, namely US Dollar vs. Deutsche Mark (DEM), British Pound (BRP), Swiss Franc (SWF), Japanese Yen (YEN), French Franc (FRN), Australian Dollar (AUD) and Canadian Dollar (CAD). We discover the clustering features of these series, which are caused by the quantization property of the exchange rate data. Analyses are performed on their characteristics - we artificially partition the exchange series and identify the regularity within each cluster.

This paper is organized as follows. Section 2 demonstrates the quantization effects of USD-DEM. Section 3 compares the features of the other six exchange series as mentioned above. We analyse their clustering properties in Section 4 and conclude the whole paper in Section 5.

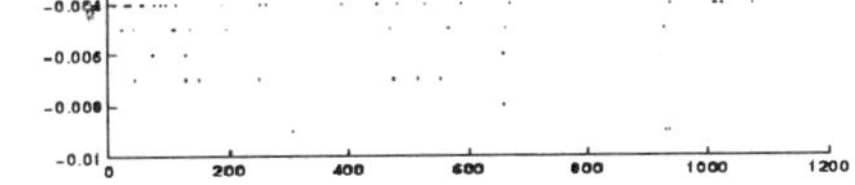

Fig. 1: USD-HKD increment.

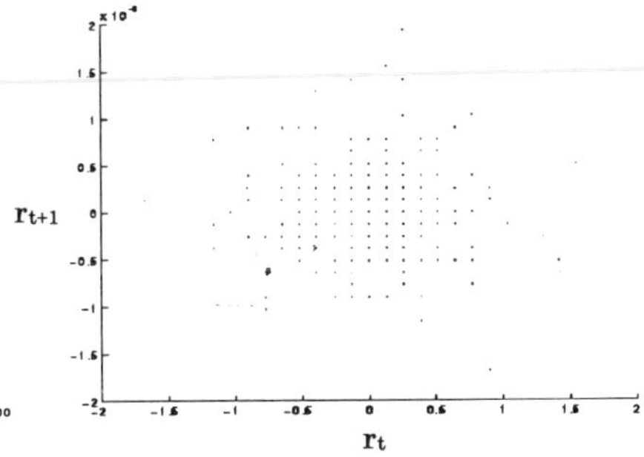

Fig. 2: 2D-plot of USD-HKD.

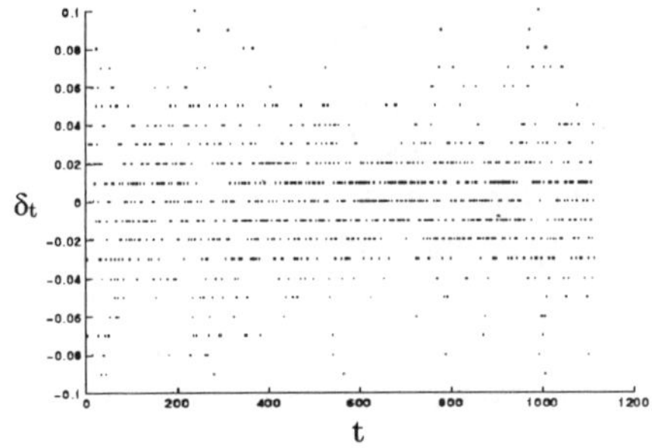

Fig. 3: DEM-HKD increment.

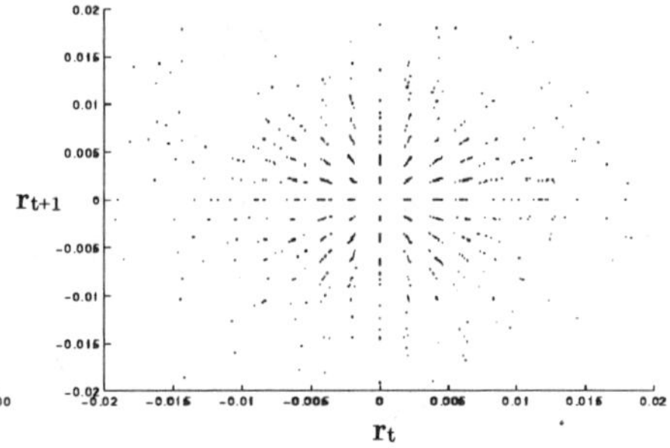

Fig. 4: 2D-plot of DEM-HKD.

2 Quantization effects of USD-DEM series

All nominal exchange rates are displayed in discrete format (i.e. values are recorded with finite digits). This gives raise to the quantization property of the exchange series. To illustrate the quantization effects, we define an exchange series $\mathbf{Z} \equiv [z_1, z_2, \ldots, z_N, z_{N+1}]^T$. The increment δ_t of the series is

$$\delta_t = z_{t+1} - z_t \tag{1}$$

We transform the series as

$$r_t = \ln(z_{t+1}/z_t) \tag{2}$$

where $\mathbf{R} \equiv [r_1, r_2, \ldots, r_N]^T$ is the return (in log scale) of the exchange series. The USD-HKD and DEM-HKD increments over time (δ_t vs. t) are shown respectively in Fig.1 and 3, where we can observe some finite and discrete 'trails' with fixed interval. The 2D-plot (r_{t+1} vs. r_t) of USD-HKD displays a very clear and regular distribution of clusters in Fig.2. The DEM-HKD series show a similar pattern (Fig.4), whereas in each cluster, points distribute with larger variety than USD-HKD.

We study the USD-DEM series and discover some interesting features. Our series includes 1112 points (26 Nov., 1991 - 30 Aug., 1995). Since we do not have the data, we calculate the USD-DEM series $\mathbf{Z}$ by

$$z_t = u_t/g_t \tag{3}$$

where $\mathbf{U} \equiv [u_1, u_2, \ldots, u_{N+1}]$ and $\mathbf{G} \equiv [g_1, g_2, \ldots, g_{N+1}]$ are USD-HKD and DEM-HKD series respectively. A very interesting feature of the return is that some 'trails', or simply called states, dominating the majority of points in the time-plots (r_t vs. t) as shown in Fig.5. From the plot we can obtain 11 states covering 91.45% of the total population.

The 2D-plot of USD-DEM series (Fig.6) presents a clear distribution of clusters. The small clusters distributes regularly along horizontal and vertical direction, while a few points scatter around. Following the 11 states of the time-plot, we divide the points into 121 partitions (by dotted line in Fig.6), covering 84.95% of the population.

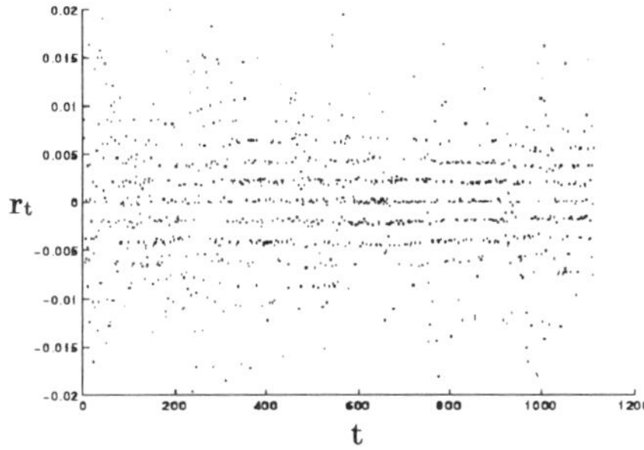

Fig. 5: Time-plot of USD-DEM.
(11 states: 91.45%)

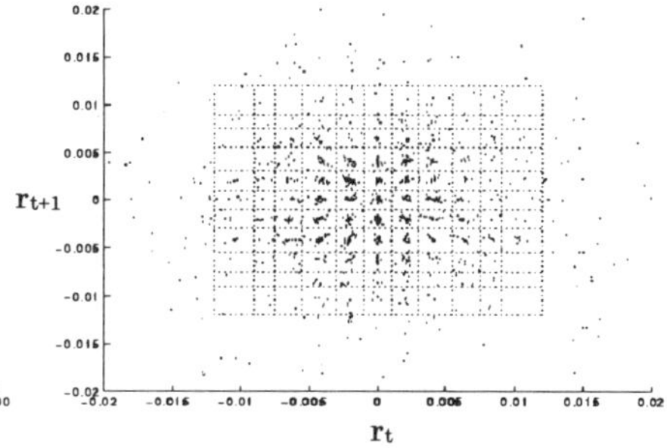

Fig. 6: 2D-plot of USD-DEM.
(121 clusters: 84.95%)

3 Comparison of exchange series

We study the series of USD-BRP, USD-SWF, USD-YEN, USD-FRN, USD-AUD and USD-CAD. These series are obtained in the similar way as USD-DEM. We use 1112 points (26 Nov., 1991 - 30 Aug., 1995) for illustration and the corresponding plots are presented from Fig.7 to 18. All series share similar patterns as USD-DEM's except USD-BRP (Fig.7 and 8), whose points scatter less regularly than its counterparts. However, USD-FRN exhibits very sharp clustering features with only 5 dominating states (Fig.13 and 14). The display of data points is restricted in the range of [-0.02, 0.02] for the ease of comparison and inspection.

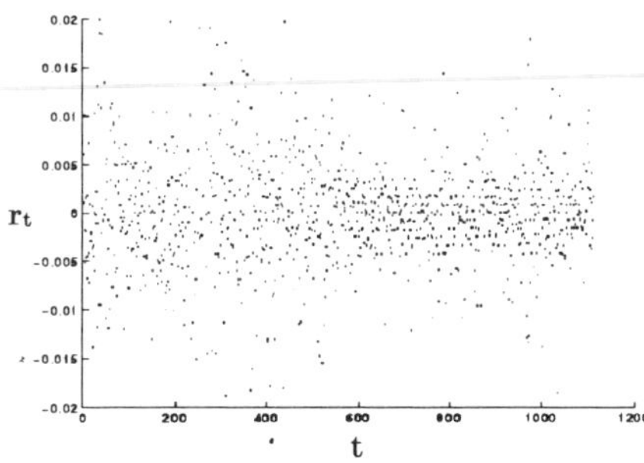

Fig. 7: Time-plot of USD-BRP.
(weak partition)

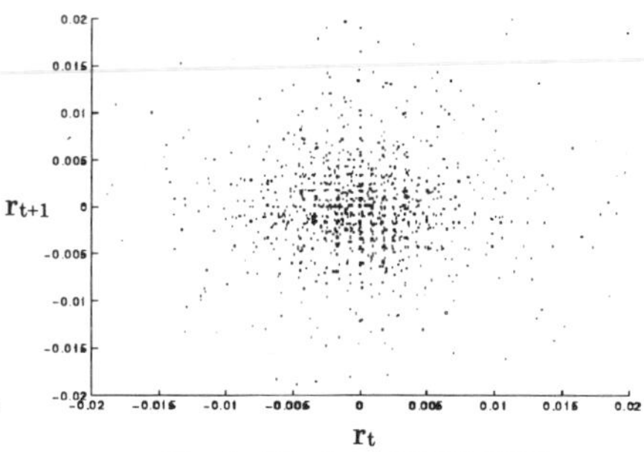

Fig. 8: 2D-plot of USD-BRP.
(weak partition)

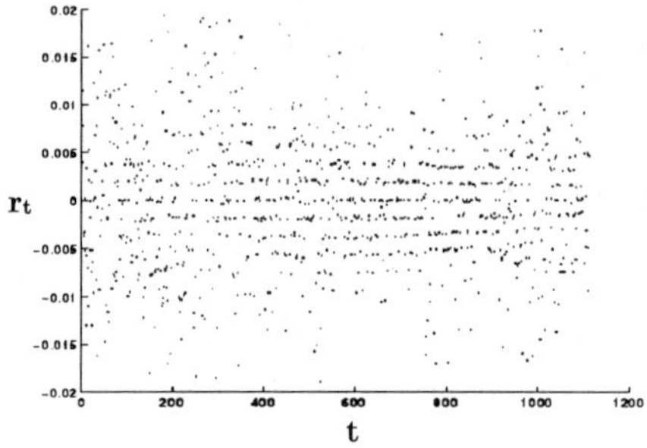

Fig. 9: Time-plot of USD-SWF.
(11 states: 86.41%)

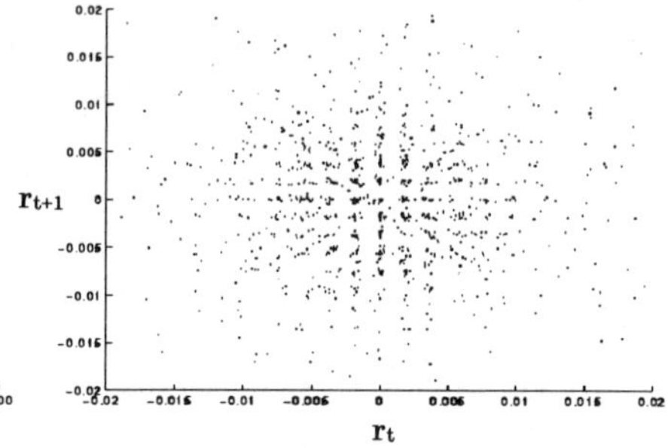

Fig. 10: 2D-plot of USD-SWF.
(121 clusters: 76.31%)

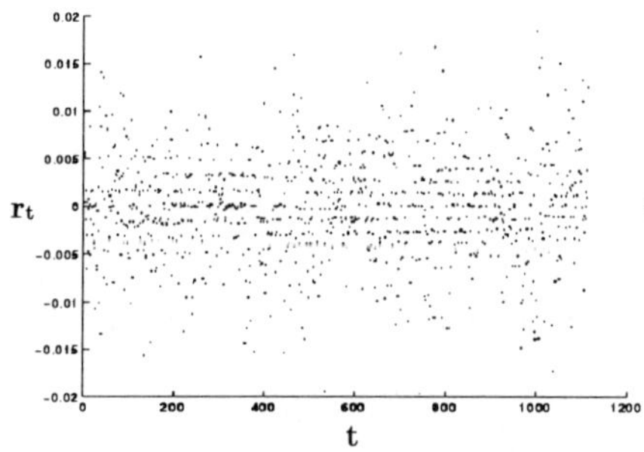

Fig. 11: Time-plot of USD-YEN.
(11 states: 87.58%)

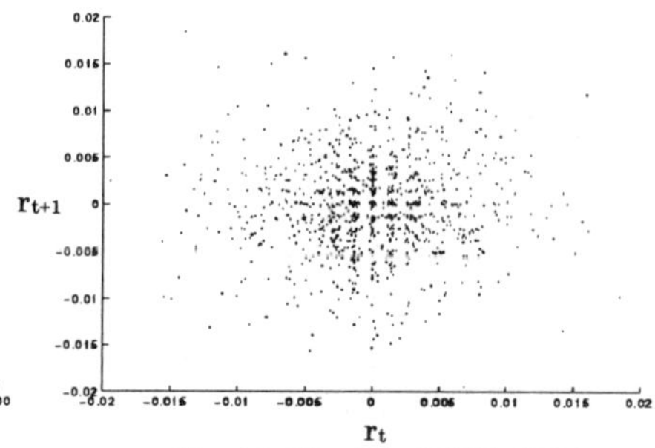

Fig. 12: 2D-plot of USD-YEN.
(121 clusters: 78.20%)

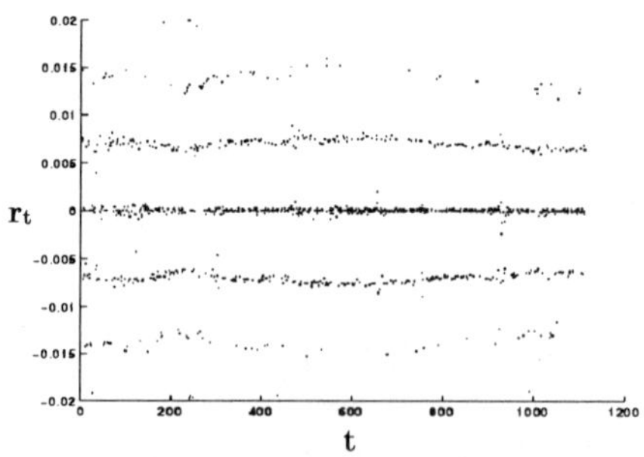

Fig. 13: Time-plot of USD-FRN.
(5 states: 96.31%)

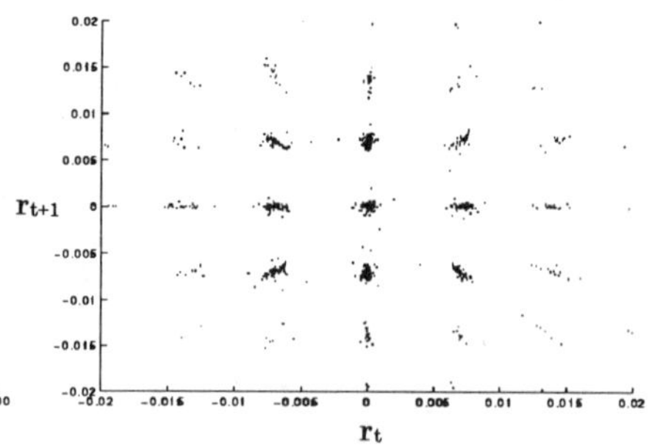

Fig. 14: 2D-plot of USD-FRN.
(25 clusters: 93.33%)

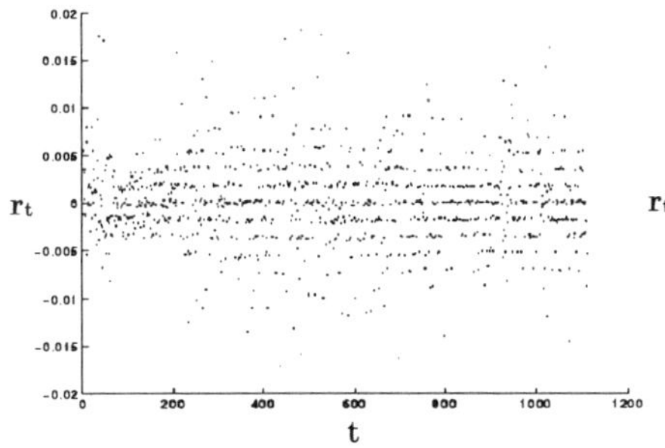

Fig. 15: Time-plot of USD-AUD.
(9 states: 93.16%)

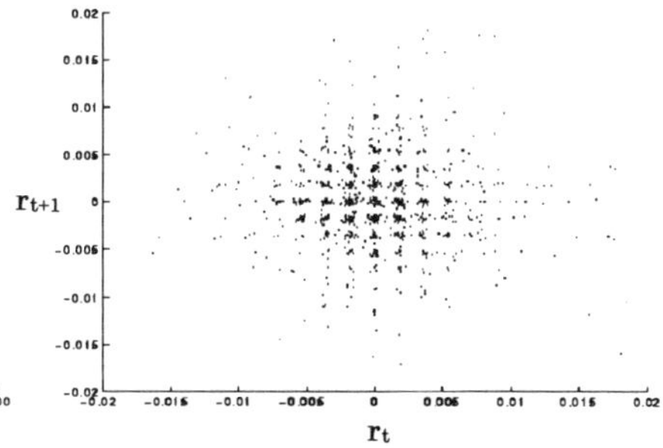

Fig. 16: 2D-plot of USD-AUD.
(81 clusters: 87.30%)

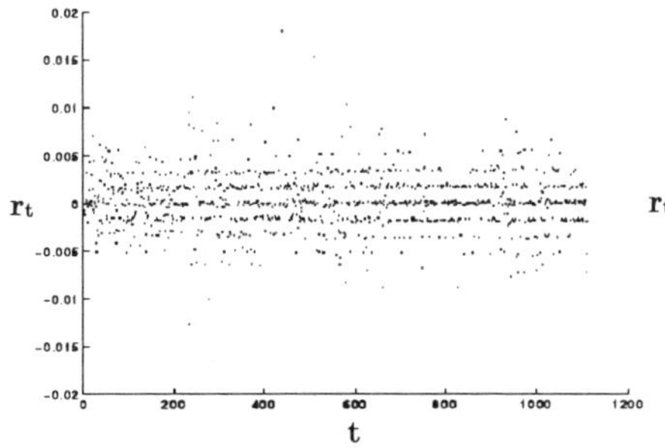

Fig. 17: Time-plot of USD-CAD.
(7 states: 94.15%)

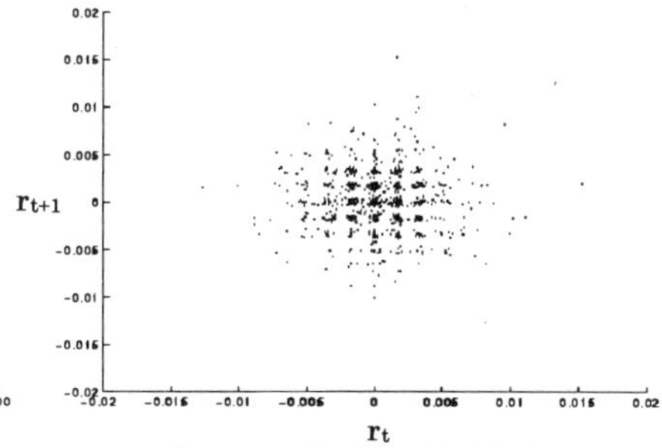

Fig. 18: 2D-plot of USD-CAD.
(49 clusters: 89.55%)

4 Cluster analysis

As shown in Fig.5, the USD-DEM series are dominated by 11 states. Consider a 3D-plot (not shown in this paper) of the series similar to Fig.6. We divide the set of triples $R(t) \equiv (r_t, r_{t+1}, r_{t+2})$, $t = 1, \ldots, N-2$, into $11^3 = 1331$ clusters. We denote C_j as the j-th cluster and $C^m = \{C_j \mid \#C_j = m, j = 1, 2, \ldots, M\}$, where M is the total number of clusters formed. For $R(t) \in C_j$ and $\#C = m$, we define $\mathbf{x_i} = (x_{i1}, x_{i2}, \ldots, x_{id}) \in \mathfrak{R}^\mathbf{d}$ where $x_{ij} = r_{t+j-1}$, $y_i = x_{i\,d+1}$ and $d = 2, 3$ in our analysis. We assume the linear model

$$y_i - \bar{y} = \mathrm{f}(\mathbf{x_i} - \bar{\mathbf{x}}_\mathbf{i}) \tag{4}$$

and regress on $(\mathbf{x_i}, y_i)$ for $\#C_j > d+1$:

$$\hat{y}_i = (x_i - \bar{x}_i)\mathbf{b} + \bar{y} \tag{5}$$

where $\mathbf{b} = (b_0, b_1, \ldots, b_d)$ is the regression coefficient. We define

$$\textit{Regression Sum of Squares (SSR)} = \sum_{i=1}^{m} (\hat{y}_i - \bar{y})^2 \,, \tag{6}$$

$$Total\ Sum\ of\ Squares\ (SST) = \sum_{i=1}^{m} (y_i - \bar{y})^2\ , \tag{7}$$

$$Error\ Sum\ of\ Squares\ (SSE)\ =\ SST - SSR. \tag{8}$$

Then the ***multiple correlation coefficient*** of C_j is

$$\gamma_j = \sqrt{\frac{SSR}{SST}} \tag{9}$$

$\gamma_j \in [0,1]$ indicates the fitness of the regression model. $\gamma_j = 1$ implies that the model can perfectly explain the linear relationship of $(\mathbf{x}_i, y_i)$. The higher the value of γ_j, the better the model is. We construct two regression models - *Model A (d = 2)* and *Model B (d = 3)* to verify the relationship of points in each partition. For m > d+1, the *average* γ of C^m and the *total average* γ are defined respectively by

$$\bar{\gamma} = \sum_{C_j \in C^m} \gamma_j / \#C^m\ , \qquad \bar{\gamma}_T = \sum_j \gamma_j / \sum_m \#C^m \tag{10}$$

For each individual cluster, we check the adequacy of the models with the test of hypothesis as

$H_0 : b_k = 0,\quad k = 1, \ldots, d$ *(insignificant regression)*

$H_1 :$ *Not all* $b_k = 0$.

We perform the F-test and reject H_0 at α-level of significance if $f > F\alpha$ $(d, m\text{-}d\text{-}1)$ where

$$f = \frac{SSR/d}{SSE/(m-d-1)} \tag{11}$$

and α is set to be 0.25 in our analysis. For $C_j \in C^m$ and m > d+1, the *passing percentage* of C^m and the *total passing percentage* are defined respectively by

$$p_m = \frac{\#(C_j \text{ passing the } F\text{-test})}{\#C^m} \times 100\%\ ,\ p_T = \frac{\sum_m (p_m \times \#C^m)}{\sum_m \#C^m}\ \% \tag{12}$$

The clustering statistics are listed in Table 1. The artificial clustering of USD-DEM series covers 79.3% (*Covering Percent*) of the total points. 484 non-empty clusters are formed, accounting for 36.4% (*Non-empty Percent*) of the cluster population (*Total Cluster*). For Eq. (11) to be meaningful, m must be greater than d+1. Therefore, we only regress the cluster C_j whose $\#C_j$ > d+1. Table 2 and 3 present the analysis results, in which we regress on $C_j \in C^m$ where m = 1, .. 4. The average γ for C^4 is 0.823, whereas the total average γ is 0.786 using Model A, etc. The *average f*, similarly defined as average γ, are listed in

Table 4 and 5. Totally 40.00% of the regressed clusters can pass the F-test (Table 6).

We repeat the analysis for the other series using 1112 points (26 Nov., 1991 - 30 Nov., 1993). As USD-BRP exhibits less regular patterns than the other series, we exclude it from our cluster analysis. In general, γ attain a higher value in m = 4 and 5 for Model A and B respectively (Table 2 and 3). However, it varies from clusters to clusters with a wide variety. The total average γ of the series using Model A are higher than that using Model B, except USD-DEM and USD-YEN. As shown in Table 6 and 7, the average passing percentages of Model A are much higher than that of Model B, except USD-YEN's. These demonstrate that the former model, in general, is more appropriate. Model A is the best to explain the regression relationship of USD-FRN (P_T = 55.56%, Table 6).

	DEM	SWF	YEN	FRN	AUD	CAD
Total Cluster	1331	1331	1331	125	729	343
Non-empty Cluster	484	520	514	102	365	227
Non-empty Percent	36.4	39.1	38.6	81.6	50.1	66.2
Covering Percent	79.3	67.9	70.2	90.5	82.2	85.3

Table 1: Cluster statistics of six common exchange series using Model A.

5 Conclusion

This paper studies some popular exchange series including USD-DEM, USD-BRP, USD-SWF, USD-YEN, USD-FRN, USD-AUD and USD-CAD in which obvious clustering distributions are observed except USD-BRP. This phenomenon arises from the quantization effects of the exchange rate data. Analysis demonstrates the linear relationship of data points in some of these clusters.

6 Acknowledgement

The clustering property of USD-DEM series (Fig.5) was first discovered by Mr. John P.F. Sum, a Ph.D. student in the Department of Computer Science and Engineering, The Chinese University of Hong Kong. The first author of this paper thanks Mr. Sum for helpful discussion.

	Model A (d = 2) : $\bar{\gamma}$					
m	**DEM**	**SWF**	**YEN**	**FRN**	**AUD**	**CAD**
4	0.823	0.828	0.699	0.871	0.834	0.875
5	0.773	0.606	0.784	0.777	0.677	0.770
6	0.700	0.731	0.348	0.600	0.772	0.814
7	0.754	-	0.417	0.905	0.653	0.623
8	-	-	-	0.830	0.799	0.613
9	-	-	-	0.616	0.515	0.528
10	-	-	-	0.566	0.689	0.484
11	-	-	-	0.451	0.407	0.140
12	-	-	-	0.633	0.389	0.480
13	-	-	-	-	-	0.808
14	-	-	-	0.549	0.141	0.352
15	-	-	-	-	-	0.460
>15	-	-	-	0.418	0.536	0.431
$\bar{\gamma}_T$	0.786	0.773	0.697	0.598	0.706	0.636

Table 2: Analysis results (average γ) of six common exchange series (Model A).

	Model B (d = 3) : $\bar{\gamma}$					
m	**DEM**	**SWF**	**YEN**	**FRN**	**AUD**	**CAD**
4	-	-	-	-	-	-
5	0.880	0.505	0.938	0.681	0.835	0.851
6	0.753	0.812	0.873	0.866	0.626	0.865
7	0.645	-	0.448	0.804	0.600	0.553
8	-	-	-	0.366	0.758	0.583
9	-	-	-	0.526	0.710	0.704
10	-	-	-	0.561	0.540	0.503
11	-	-	-	0.655	0.851	0.385
12	-	-	-	0.732	0.414	0.838
13	-	-	-	-	-	0.577
14	-	-	-	0.414	0.086	0.368
15	-	-	-	-	-	0.438
>15	-	-	-	0.291	0.230	0.415
$\bar{\gamma}_T$	0.800	0.581	0.877	0.466	0.647	0.635

Table 3: Analysis results (average γ) of six common exchange series (Model B).

	Model A (d = 2) : $\bar{f}$					
m	DEM	SWF	YEN	FRN	AUD	CAD
4	**64.54**	**17.50**	**3.234**	***Large***	***Large***	***Large***
5	**5.238**	**7.193**	**5.292**	**19.54**	**5.351**	**10.75**
6	**4.678**	1.723	0.207	2.242	**5.400**	**4.304**
7	**2.704**	-	0.421	**9.074**	**3.993**	**3.866**
8	-	-	-	**5.606**	**4.936**	**3.620**
9	-	-	-	**2.519**	1.543	**2.538**
10	-	-	-	**5.771**	**5.113**	**2.408**
11	-	-	-	1.025	0.793	0.090
12	-	-	-	**4.832**	1.156	**3.026**
13	-	-	-	-	-	**9.419**
14	-	-	-	**3.298**	0.111	0.821
15	-	-	-	-	-	**2.031**
>15	-	-	-	**5.294**	**2.615**	**2.697**

Table 4: Analysis results (average f) of six common exchange series (Model A, α = 0.25, *Large* = f $\geq$ 300; cluster's $\bar{f}$ passing the F-test appears bold).

	Model B (d = 3) : $\bar{f}$					
m	DEM	SWF	YEN	FRN	AUD	CAD
4	-	-	-	-	-	-
5	4.278	0.126	***Large***	1.151	**64.16**	**47.85**
6	2.692	1.291	2.139	**10.21**	1.272	2.905
7	1.877	-	0.252	1.834	0.807	1.440
8	-	-	-	0.249	**2.216**	1.952
9	-	-	-	1.036	**2.242**	**3.949**
10	-	-	-	1.096	1.041	0.790
11	-	-	-	**1.757**	**6.145**	0.411
12	-	-	-	**3.489**	0.770	**6.922**
13	-	-	-	-	-	1.495
14	-	-	-	1.473	0.025	0.530
15	-	-	-	-	-	1.248
>15	-	-	-	0.988	0.224	**1.901**

Table 5: Analysis results (average f) of six common exchange series (Model B, α = 0.25, *Large* = f $\geq$ 300; cluster's $\bar{f}$ passing the F-test appears bold).

	Model A (d = 2) : p (%)					
m	DEM	SWF	YEN	FRN	AUD	CAD
4	34.48	30.00	7.69	42.86	45.00	38.46
5	30.77	33.33	28.57	33.33	23.08	38.46
6	55.56	0.00	0.00	66.67	45.45	71.43
7	75.00	-	0.00	100.0	55.56	40.00
8	-	-	-	100.0	100.0	33.33
9	-	-	-	33.33	50.00	60.00
10	-	-	-	50.00	80.00	50.00
11	-	-	-	0.00	0.00	0.00
12	-	-	-	50.00	25.00	66.67
13	-	-	-	-	-	100.0
14	-	-	-	60.00	0.00	0.00
15	-	-	-	-	-	66.67
>15	-	-	-	62.50	100.0	50.00
p_T	40.00	28.57	13.64	55.56	45.71	46.05

Table 6: Passing percentage for F-test of six common exchange series. (Model A)

	Model B (d = 3) : p (%)					
m	DEM	SWF	YEN	FRN	AUD	CAD
4	-	-	-	-	-	-
5	7.69	0.00	42.86	0.00	38.46	38.46
6	22.22	0.00	0.00	66.67	9.09	42.86
7	50.00	-	0.00	0.00	0.00	20.00
8	-	-	-	0.00	66.67	33.33
9	-	-	-	33.33	50.00	40.00
10	-	-	-	0.00	20.00	0.00
11	-	-	-	100.0	100.0	0.00
12	-	-	-	100.0	25.00	100.0
13	-	-	-	-	-	0.00
14	-	-	-	20.00	0.00	0.00
15	-	-	-	-	-	33.33
>15	-	-	-	18.75	0.00	50.00
p_T	19.23	0.00	33.33	26.32	24.00	34.92

Table 7: Passing percentage for F-test of six common exchange series (Model B).

A COMPUTER SIMULATION OF CURRENCY MARKET PARTICIPANTS

MICHAEL DE LA MAZA
Artificial Intelligence Laboratory
Massachusetts Institute of Technology
Room NE43-815
545 Technology Square
Cambridge, MA 02139

Redfire Capital Management Group
950 Massachusetts Ave., Suite 209
Cambridge, MA 02139-3174

This paper defines a computer simulation of a currency market that is designed to mimic the system put in place by the European Rate Mechanism. Five market participants – small speculators, large speculators, hedgers, central banks, and bid/ask traders – are defined along five dimensions – information set, model set, algorithm set, constraint set, utility function – and each calibrates a neural network using real market data. The price behavior in the simulated currency market is compared to the price behavior of the real currency market and is shown to be qualitively similar.

1 Introduction

In this paper, I describe a computer simulation of market participants in a currency market that is designed to mimic the currency system that was put in place by the European Exchange Rate Mechanism (ERM). This research is part of a broad research program which has as its goal to achieve a top to bottom understanding of financial markets. One of the short-term goals of this research is to provide a clear-cut test of the efficient market hypothesis. Since its inception, this research program has made extensive use of computer simulations to study questions that are of interest to both academics and practitioners.

Computer simulations provide the ability to perform "prosthetically controlled thought experiments of infinite complexity"(Dennett, 1994), thus permitting the careful examination of previously all but unexplorable questions. In recent years, researchers (Sargent, 1993; LeBaron, 1994; delaMaza & Yuret, 1994) have begun to embrace computer simulations as an important tool in finance.

This paper is divided into three main sections:

- History of the European Monetary Union. This section describes the precursors of the EMU and its development.
- Model. This section communicates the essentials of the model that is implemented in the computer simulation.
- Results. This section summarizes the key results that were obtained when the price behavior of the simulated currency market was compared to the price behavior of the real currency market.

2 History of the European Monetary Union

The European Monetary Union (EMU) is one in a long line of monetary and, more broadly, economic unions in Europe. The Zollverein of 1834 brought together several German-speaking countries and led, in 1871, to the creation of modern Germany in 1871. In 1861, Belgium, France, Greece, Italy, and Switzerland combined to form the Latin Monetary Union which created a common currency that could be used in all five of those countries. This Latin Monetary Union was dissolved in the 1920s when World War I found some member countries supporting armed aggression against other member nations.

The immediate precursors of the EMU came into existence shortly after World War II. In 1957, the European Economic Community was formed by France, Germany, Italy, and the Benelux countries. Further structure was added to this international organization ten years later, in 1967, with the formation of the European Community (EC). Denmark, Ireland, and the United Kingdom were to join the EC in 1973 followed by Greece in 1981 and Spain and Portugal in 1986.

The establishment of the EC came shortly before the collapse of the gold standard and, when currencies became free-floating, a currency "snake" was established in 1972. The "snake" system, which features adjustable (and, as happened to be the case, often adjusted) currency bands, is so-called because the movements of the currency bands, when shown as a standard financial time series, resemble a snake. The European Monetary System (EMS) was established in 1979 and with it came the introduction of 2.25% currency bands (6% for the lira). Between 1979 and 1987, when the "Single European Act" codified the goal of a single European market and set Europe on course to achieving monetary union, these currency bands were re-aligned eleven times.

The EMU began stage one in 1990 with the elimination of capital movement among member countries. In February, 1992, the Maastricht treaty, the most important of the EMU documents, was signed and it laid out a timetable for achieving monetary union. The Maastricht treaty immediately created turmoil in the currency markets. Between 1987 and 1991 not a single re-alignment took place among member nations, but in 1992 both the United Kingdom and Italy were forced to leave the EMS when they suffered from enormous devaluations. Immediately following these events, the bands were widened to 15%.

Despite these difficulties, European nations continued to work towards monetary union and in 1994 the European Monetary Institute was established. In 1995, Austria, Finland, and Sweden joined the EU, an impressive vote of confidence.

Monetary union is scheduled to take place in 1999 when exchange rates will be fixed; however, as of the beginning of 1997, only Luxembourg met the Maastricht Treaty conditions for entering the union.

The creation of the EU and the EMU certainly ranks as one of the outstanding economic developments of our time and has broad implications for international trade, currency movements, and government policy. Because of this importance and the enormous difficulty of modeling the unification process with traditional methods, the EMU is a prime candidate for computer simulation.

3 Model

The computer simulation contains five participants, each of which are defined along five dimensions. The five market participants are:

- Small speculators. Small speculators do not trade professionally. They typically have small accounts and are over-leveraged

- Large speculators. Large speculators trade professionally and have access to large pools of capital and to information that is unavailable to other traders.

- Hedgers. Hedgers attempt to eliminate gains and losses due to currency fluctuations.

- Central banks. Central banks attempt to maintain currencies within their respective bands.

- Bid/ask traders. The bid/ask traders, or market makers, are extremely short-term traders who provide liquidity to the market.

The descriptions of each market participant shown above are given only to develop intuitions about the types of trading that each market participant performs. They are not part of the model. Each market participant is defined along five dimensions:

- Information set: the set of information that the market participant has access to (e.g., price and volume, macroeconomic data).
- Algorithm set: the set of algorithms that the market participant can use to optimize its utility function (e.g., linear programming, backpropagation, dynamic hill climbing, simulated annealing).
- Model set: the set of models that the market participant can use to express its understanding of the regularities in market behavior (e.g., differential equations, sums of sigmoids).
- Constraint set: the set of constraints that define the scope of the participant's allowable behavior (e.g., margin requirements, transaction costs).
- Utility function: the function that the market participant seeks to optimize (e.g., Sharpe ratio, profit).

The first four of these are identical to the ones described by Yuret and de la Maza (delaMaza & Yuret, 1994). These five variables were set by examining descriptions of what market participants say they do and what others say they do. I am aware of the limitations of such an approach: market participants (and observers) may not have access to hidden state in the market participant. In addition, most of the studies suffer from a paucity of data. Nevertheless, they are the best available empirical sources of the actual behavior of market participants.

In addition to characterizing the market participants, I implemented a simplified currency market. Five currencies (the Italian lira, the British pound, the French franc, the Swiss franc, and the Deutsche mark) are traded in this market. Market participants may have positions in these markets (to the extent allowed by their constraint set) or in a risk-free asset, but may not have positions in any other market. Market participants incur transaction costs when trading.

In all of the simulations that I ran, the following hold:

- The only action that a market participant can take is to buy or sell a currency. Market participants cannot, as central banks often do, issue policy statements or warnings.
- For all five market participants, the algorithm set is always backpropagation and the model set is always a standard neural network with one hidden layer.

- Large speculators dominate small speculators. The information set for the large speculator is always a strict superset of the information set for small traders. The constraint set is always less limiting for large speculators than it is for small speculators. For example, large speculators have lower transaction costs and lower margin requirements.

- The utility function of the central banks is unimodal, with the minimum at the middle of the currency band. Intuitively, each central bank is heavily penalized when its currency strays out of the currency band and rewarded when the currency is in the center of the band.

- Hedgers attempt to eliminate currency-based fluctuations in their portfolios.

- Bid/ask traders are required to always have a price at which they are willing to buy and a price at which they are willing to sell. In contrast, the other four types of market participants may choose not to trade no matter what the price is.

All of the market participants use actual market data, both technical and fundamental, to train a neural network to optimize their utility functions, subject to the limitations of the constraint set. The inputs to a participant's neural network are the financial time series in the participant's information set and the neural network's objective function is the participant's utility function.

4 Results

Over the period 1979 to 1996, the European currency system can be divided into three distinct periods:

1. 1979-1987. Currencies are in narrow 2.25% bands (6% for lira). Eleven realignments take place.

2. 1987-1992. Currencies remain in narrow bands and no realignments take place.

3. 1992-1996. Currencies are highly volatile and, as a result, the narrow bands are replaced by 15% bands.

My experiments with this currency market simulation fall into two distinct categories. The first set of experiments sought to verify that the simulation was accurate by testing whether or not the behavior of market participants in the simulation was similar to that observed in the actual currency markets during the period under study. The second set of experiments was designed to answer questions about scenarios that differed slightly from that of the ERM.

In the first set of experiments, the model was calibrated and tested during each of these three periods. The calibration involves training the neural network and trying various combinations of information sets and constraint sets for each market participant with a view towards duplicating the price behavior. The testing set, which is kept separate from the calibration set, is used to determine whether or not the modeling has been successful by checking the price behavior of the actual currency market against the price behavior generated by the simulation.

The first set of experiments can best be illustrated by example. During the narrow band phase the business media widely reported that some speculators, and in particular the Central Bank of Malaysia, consistently profited by selling when a currency reached the top of its band and buying when a currency reached the bottom of its band. In the computer simulation, similar behavior was observed in large speculators after they had verified that the bands were credible. This result suggests that highly credible currency bands provide opportunities for some market participants, namely large speculators, to consistently make above average returns. After the simulation suggested this possibility and provided a description of the mechanism by which this price behavior might be attained, I learned that Svensson(Svensson, 1991) had explicitly tested whether or not ERM currencies exhibited random walk behavior, as opposed to mean-reversion behavior, and had concluded that, with the possible exception of the Italian lira/Deutsche mark cross, all of the original ERM currencies exhibited mean-reversion behavior.

Importantly, there is considerable evidence that large speculators did in fact make considerable profits during the period when narrow bands were in place. Presumably, most of these profits came from small speculators and central banks.

Quantitatively, the results are very poor for the first set of experiments. In the testing set, the prices of the currencies in the simulation quickly diverge from the prices generated by the actual currency market. Qualitatively, however, the simulation and the real market track closely. When there is a currency realignment in the real market a realignment often occurs in the simulated market. Typically, the timing of the realignment differs slightly while the magnitude of the realignment differs significantly.

In the second set of experiments, the behavior of the market participants was observed under conditions which differed from those which exist under the ERM. In one of the most interesting experiments, central banks were allowed to communicate their intentions to large speculators. Under certain conditions, large speculators found it in their interest to cooperate with the central banks.

5 Final comments

These results have practical implications both for students of the markets and for market participants. For academics, the simulation provides a low-level, micro-level explanation for price behavior. By observing price behavior researchers can and have characterized the distribution of returns in the currency markets. However, explanations of why these distributions obtain have been conspicuously few and far between. This computer simulation, by modeling each market participant, provides one mechanism by which the price behavior of the actual market could be generated.

For market participants, this computer simulation serves as an intuition pump that can be used to generate ideas that lead to profitable trading strategies. At Redfire Capital Management Group we have employed a very similar approach to trade the U.S. stock market and have produced portfolios with Sharpe ratios in excess of 3.00. These trading strategies have been used to manage trading capital since mid-1996 and, as of the beginning of 1997, the real-time results were on par with the results on historical data. More broadly, this simulation can be used by speculators, central bankers, and regulators to test the outcomes of investment policies and regulatory schemes.

This computer simulation differs from standard modeling attempts in several respects. First, market participants have limited information sets and realistic constraint sets. Unlike many models, the actors are not assumed to have instantaneous access to all available information and the market is not assumed to be frictionless. Second, market participants learn a strategy for optimizing their utility functions. These utility functions differ from market participant to market participant. Third, and most importantly, the market model has many parameters, orders of magnitudes more than in standard economic models. Because markets are made up of many local pockets of regularity, standard models with few parameters fail utterly in predicting the direction of market movements. Only models with many parameters have the potential to adequately characterize the phenomena by capturing the many local regularities.

More broadly speaking, this model provides a testbed for answering a host of questions, including:

- How should Eastern European countries be incorporated into the EMU?
- Would currency unions benefit other groups of countries, such as Latin America, the Pacific Rim, and the Middle East?

- What can be done to prevent destabilizing devaluations, like those that occurred in 1992?
- How can appropriate incentive structures be created to discourage attacks by currency speculators?

By building on results such as the ones described in this paper, computer simulations have the potential to become one of the cornerstone techniques in the rapidly growing field of computational finance.

References

de la Maza, M. and D. Yuret. 1994. A futures market simulation with non-rational participants. In *Proceedings of the Fourth International Workshop on the Synthesis and Simulation of Living Systems*, R. Brooks and P. Maes (eds), pp. 325–330.

Dennett, D. 1994. Artificial life as philosophy. *Artificial Life* **1**(3), 291–292.

LeBaron, B. 1994. An artificial stock market. MIT AI vision seminar colloquium.

Sargent, T. J. 1993. *Bounded Rationality in Macroeconomics.* Clarendon Press, Oxford.

Svensson, L. E. 1991. Assessing target zone credibility: Mean reversion and devaluation expectations in the EMS. *National Bureau of Economic Research, Inc. Working Paper Series* **3795**.

Appendix

DATA MINING IN FINANCE: REPORT FROM THE POST-NNCM-96 WORKSHOP ON TEACHING COMPUTER INTENSIVE METHODS FOR FINANCIAL MODELING AND DATA ANALYSIS

ANDREAS S. WEIGEND
Department of Information Systems
Leonard N. Stern School of Business, New York University
44 West Fourth Street, MEC 9-74, New York, NY 10012
aweigend@stern.nyu.edu
www.stern.nyu.edu/~aweigend

The conference *Neural Networks in the Capital Markets* was followed by a workshop at Caltech on November 23, 1996. The purpose of the workshop was to bring people together to share their experiences and ideas on designing and teaching new courses in financial engineering, bridging the gap between computationally advanced methods for learning from data, and real world problems in finance. This report highlights some of these ideas, and describes in detail one specific course taught at the Leonard N. Stern School of Business at New York University. That course, *Data Mining in Finance*, focuses on computer intensive data analysis methods that are relevant to financial problems. The methods originate in fields such as statistics and probability, artificial intelligence and machine learning, computational science, applied mathematics, and engineering. They include neural nets, genetic algorithms, bootstrap methods, Bayes nets, Hidden Markov models, and clustering techniques. These methods are applied to problems that include building and evaluating technical trading strategies, and computing and managing market and credit risk. Beside the theory and the lectures, that course has two hands-on components. For each method, a computer assignment on a real world data set is placed between two lectures. The first lecture introduces the problem, discusses the essentials of the method to solve this problem, and demonstrates a software implementation. After students have gained some experience with the method and software in the lab, the second lecture summarizes strengths and weaknesses, and discusses further applications in the capital markets. The second hands-on component is a group project. It explores one of the approaches presented during the semester on a problem and data set selected by each individual group, usually in collaboration with a Wall Street firm. The course concludes with several Wall Street traders giving their perspectives on the practice and promise on data mining in finance.

In recent years the application of data mining–statistical artificial intelligence, machine learning, information extraction, knowledge discovery–to technical trading and finance has seen exciting results, as witnessed by several conferences, including NNCM (Neural Networks in the Capital Markets) in 1993 and 1995 (Refenes *et al.*, 1996) in London, in 1994 and 1996 (Weigend *et al.*,

1997) in Pasadena, and CIFEr (Computational Intelligence in Financial Engineering) in New York City since 1995 (CIFEr, 1997). In addition to ideas originating in academia, Wall Street firms have also contributed methods that are emerging as industry benchmarks for risk transparency and management (RiskMetrics, 1997; CreditMetrics, 1997)

The successful application of these new methods in the financial services industries require analytical maturity, mathematical skills, and statistical sophistication. The organizers of NNCM-96 felt that the course offerings in areas of financial data mining, computational finance, and financial engineering were lagging behind academic research and Wall Street practice. To provide a forum for ideas on how the teaching in this area can be improved, I organized a post-NNCM-96 workshop at Caltech on November 23, 1996. The participants, most of them teaching at universities, came from Europe and the United States.

It is impossible to list all the rich and complex ideas, experiences and questions that were brought up. To give some flavor to what is possible in a business school environment, this report describes one specific realization of such a course that I have developed at New York University's business school.

The course focuses on data mining techniques that are relevant for finance and business. It introduces state-of-the-art approaches and results from the fields of financial engineering and computational finance, and provides the relevant background from other disciplines such as statistics, machine learning, and traditional finance.

The **objectives of the course** include:

- relate and integrate often disparately experienced pieces of knowledge that the students have been exposed to in earlier courses;

- show the strengths and weaknesses of each of the methods on financial data;

- provide a hands-on exploration for every method, and demonstrate industrial-strength software packages when available;

- deepen the knowledge and understanding of one of the techniques through a group project in conjunction with one major financial firm;[a]

[a]Ideally, these group projects form around a problem and data set one of the members of the group, typically a part-time MBA's, brings from his or her workplace. Group projects also emerge from consulting and interactions with affiliate firms to the program. In all cases, a tight coupling is important between the group of students and the firm providing problem definition and data.

- compare the promise of the new methods with the practice on Wall Street through some lectures and in-class discussions with several traders from key financial institutions.

The **teaching strategy** is based on the fact that hands-on experiences greatly facilitate the mastering of theoretical concepts and also help the student retain significantly more than from lectures alone. Therefore, the course goes every week through the following lecture–lab–lecture sequence:

- the instructor introduces the problem to be solved, explains the key aspects of the new method in sufficient detail, and briefly demonstrates the implementation in the classroom;

- the students apply the method to a real world problem in the computer lab;

- the lab experiences are reviewed and the general principles extracted, and further examples of successes and failures of this method on financial problems are presented, again in the classroom.

The **target audience** consists of several student populations, reflecting the diversity and interest in this emerging field:

- *Master of Science in Statistics with Specialization in Financial Engineering* from the Stern School (NYU's business school),

- *Financial Engineering Track for MBAs*, also from Stern,

- *Masters of Science in Mathematics in Finance* from the Courant Institute (NYU's mathematics and computer science departments).

These programs are two-year programs taken by full time students. Both MS programs require a total of 12 courses. The course described here is usually taken by students in their last semester when they have a solid foundation not only in finance, but also in applied probability and statistics, including courses on time series and on multivariate regression. It is an elective for the other two programs. It can also be taken by any Ph.D. student at Stern.

Apart from selecting from the full spectrum of more traditional finance courses at Stern,[b] there are several other courses that also include some hands-on experience and complement this data mining course. They include *Financial Information Systems* (taught by Bruce Weber, Information Systems Department) that uses derivatives analysis software, and *Statistical Computing with*

[b]In its latest survey of MBA programs (October 21, 1996), *Business Week* ranked Stern's Finance Department fourth in the nation.

Application to Finance (developed by Sean Chen, Statistics and Operations Research Department) that focuses on sampling methods for finance and includes a module on iterative sampling methods (Markov Chain Monte Carlos), and a module on Bayesian inference and decision making. Furthermore, the course *Knowledge Systems in Organizations* (developed by Vasant Dhar, Information Systems Department) gives an overview of knowledge discovery and data mining techniques as they are important for organizations, focusing on their impact on business and issues regarding their deployment.

The **high-level outline** of this course on data mining in finance is divided into four parts:

1. Introduction (3 weeks);
2. Building and Evaluating Trading Models (5 weeks);
3. Managing Risk (3 weeks);
4. Projects, Practice, and Promise (3 weeks).

Wk	*Topic*
1	Introduction: *i)* Computer environment, *ii)* Statistics background
2	Explorative data analysis (Visualization, Sonification, Wavelets)
3	Model evaluation and testing (Bootstrap, Simulation)
4	Time series prediction using nonlinear neural networks
5	Trading strategy development using neuro-fuzzy modeling
6	Trading rule discovery using genetic algorithms
7	Nonlinear regime switching models (Hidden Markov models)
8	GARCH and stochastic volatility (State space models)
9	Market risk (Value-at-Risk, *RiskMetrics*)
10	Credit risk (Nonlinear logistic regression, *CreditMetrics*)
11	Transaction risk (Bayes nets and graphical models)
12	Student projects (groups of five in collaboration with firms), and
13	Presentations by Wall Street traders and discussion, and
14	Special topics (pairs trading, execution, ICA, new products, ...)

Table 1: Week-by-week schedule for *Data Mining in Finance*. The schedule for the group projects is given in Part 4 the main text.

The table lists the contents on a week-by-week basis, and each week is described in detail througout the remainder of this document.

1 Part 1: Introduction—Understanding through Visualization and Simulation

1.1 Tutorials: Managing Backgrounds and Expectations

The first class (of tutorial nature) takes place in the lab and goes through the mechanics of computer use, ranging from the specific setup in the computer labs and the access of the data sets for the assignments, to simple examples of the two main packages used in this course, S-Plus and Matlab.[c] In the first week, the students fill out a questionnaire about their expectations, technical backgrounds, and interests. Answers will help the instructor identify problems early and optimally adjust the level of the course. For the group project, students are asked whether they have any specific problems in mind that they would be interested working on. Furthermore, part-time MBA students, usually working in related fields, often have access to specific data sets from their workplace. The learning experience of the group project draws on these real questions and real data from some of their members. Integrating these real world projects and presenting the final results both at Stern and in the firms is an important ingredient in the last part of this course.

The second class (also of tutorial nature) reviews some concepts from probability and statistics that the students are expected to be familiar with.[d] This class also makes the expected background knowledge explicit and points to the pertinent literature that can help refresh some potentially rusty knowledge. At the end of the second class, groups of five students are formed. Care is taken to have in each group at least one student strong in theory, and one student strong in practical computer issues. Furthermore, students who already have a specific problem they want to model are distributed evenly across the groups.

The next two weeks continue with introductory character. Each week is dedicated to one of the two main software packages used in the course. The general approaches and specific commands that will be useful throughout the course are explained in conjunction with some interesting real world data.

---

[c] An argument can be made that the education should be streamlined into one single software package that the students have encountered in prior classes, such as Minitab. However, in a course covering such a wide terrain such as this one, it is important to draw on the advantages of different packages. Furthermore, familiarity with several modeling languages is an important asset.

[d] These concepts include random variables, distributions, the correlation coefficient and its meaning, linear regression and the error on parameters, the maximum likelihood framework, conditional probabilities, conditional expectations, conditional variances, the Expectation Maximization algorithm.

1.2 Exploring Data Through Visualization and Sonification

The second week uses a cross-sectional data set of equity returns, firm size, and book-to-market value.[e] Fama & French (1992) argued that size and book-to-market play a dominant role in explaining cross-sectional differences in expected returns. Re-analyzing their data with Trellis graphics (a method of conditional histograms) uncovers some striking features, including the complete disappearance of the risk premium on size (Knez & Ready, 1997). The background reading is an introduction to S-Plus , and the lab consists of reproducing the Trellis plots and further exploring the data that could lead to an understanding of the economic forces underlying the size effect. Besides gaining some initial familiarity with S-Plus, the students learn to appreciate the power and importance of exploratory data analysis and visualization. If time remains, there will also be a demonstration of various ways of revealing structure and information through rendering time series data in the auditory domain (sonification), as well as examples of multi-scale analysis with wavelets, two examples of modern exploratory data analysis.

1.3 Understanding Results Through Simulation (Monte Carlo and Bootstrap)

The third week introduces bootstrapping, a computer intensive method to generate distribution of variables of interest, such as the profit of a certain trading strategy. The lab uses both computer generated examples and real world data to gain an appreciation of the inherent uncertainty of results in noisy environments. The synthetic data is generated to show just how easy it is to fool oneself about the profitability of a trading strategy. The reading includes chapters on model evaluation and testing procedures of a forthcoming book by Blake LeBaron (Economics Department, University of Wisconsin, Madison). The students obtain a deeper understanding of the stochastic nature of financial markets and experience the central importance of absolutely clean methodologies for model testing, in particular the use of true out-of-sample data in any performance evaluation. This assignment is carried out in Matlab.

2 Part 2: Building and Evaluating Prediction and Trading Models

Making predictions and building trading models are central goals for financial institutions. They were the earliest areas of the application of modern machine

[e] The data include all NYSE, AMEX and Nasdaq non-financial firms in the monthly CRSP tapes for the period July 1963 through December 1990.

learning techniques to real world problems. In this course, we now turn to estimating the parameters of a model. In contrast, the methods in the first part assumed that a model already existed, and that the sole task was their evaluation.

Consisting of five weeks, this second part of the course is the longest individual part. The readings are taken from several sources, including *Neural Networks in Financial Engineering* (Refenes *et al.*, 1996), *Decision Technologies for Financial Engineering* (Weigend *et al.*, 1997), and the Proceedings of *Computational Intelligence for Financial Engineering* (CIFEr, 1997).

One important ingredient throughout this part is the methodology of turning predictions (e.g., the expected value of a future return and its variance) into actions (e.g., taking a position of a certain size). For students not familiar with statistical decision theory and the utility function framework, the concepts needed for this part of the course will be presented in an extra lecture of tutorial character at the beginning of this part.

Most of the hands-on components use either Matlab or S-Plus. When appropriate, comparisons to Excel are presented since most students are familiar with spreadsheets. Presenting two conceptually different approaches to one problem clarifies the advantages and disadvantages of the different computational paradigms.

The five weeks of this part range from neural networks and neuro-fuzzy models, over trading rule discovery using genetic algorithms, to nonlinear time series models with hidden states. The details of week 4 through week 8 are given below.

2.1 Nonlinear time series prediction

This week begins reviewing–from the perspective of data mining–the concepts the students had been exposed to in the prerequisite time series course, as well as presenting some implementations of linear time series models in S-Plus and Matlab. The central part of this week introduces "classical" neural networks for regression, corresponding to a nonlinear autoregressive model if the inputs consist of past values of the time series (tapped delay line). This framework is easily extended to incorporate inputs that are of various quantities which are derived from the time series itself (e.g., exponential moving averages, curvatures, volatility estimates), as well as additional exogenous time series (e.g., interest rates, indices, other markets, news). In the lab, the students use both linear methods and nonlinear neural networks on the same data sets, in order to understand the strengths and problems of the more flexible neural network approach. One example shows that nonlinear methods can indeed outperform linear methods on financial forecasts, and also that the problem of overfitting can be very serious.

2.2 Neuro-fuzzy trading model

The second week on neural networks extends the framework to incorporate rules and relationships some traders believe in. The learning algorithm moves their parameters and adjust their weights. In addition to this neuro-fuzzy framework, the class presents various methods to combat overfitting, including pruning (removing parameters that model the noise rather than the signal), clearning (the combination of cleaning the data and learning the model), and adding adaptive noise to the inputs (to prevent the weights from learning more than there is). During this week, as an exception, the lab is replaced by a one-day workshop where a practitioner shows the entire process of building a successful trading model, using SENN (Simulation Environment for Neural Networks). The data set of daily data compiled from multiple sources is provided by Georg Zimmermann (Siemens AG, München). The students are to gain an appreciation of the different phases and iterative nature of the modeling process; however, they are not expected to reproduce the model in detail. Students who cannot attend the full-day workshop (held on a Saturday), complete an assignment on predicting conditional variances and conditional percentiles in addition to the usual conditional mean (in Matlab), serving as a preparation for risk management.

2.3 Trading rule discovery using genetic algorithms

This week introduces genetic algorithms as a search technique and shows how it can be used to solve problems such as volatility prediction, portfolio optimization, and stock picking. Often, in very complicated search spaces, the genetic algorithm can find interesting niches or relationships among variables. We show how genetic algorithms can be used to create rule-like models for prediction and classification. While these resulting models are less flexible than general neural networks, they are more amenable to interpretation. More importantly, genetic algorithms can produce many alternate models of the phenomenon which are similar in performance. The derived rules can be discussed with experts, and modified or discarded when they seem not to make any sense. The assignment uses futures data from an equity index to build models that forecast volatilities. The subsequent discussion shows how techniques influence the formulation of a problem and the representations chosen for the data and the model.

2.4 *Time series with discrete hidden states*

The time series and trading problems so far have all been framed as regression problems. While this has made the computation relatively easy, time specific information is ignored: reshuffling all the input-output pairs of training would not have changed the resulting model. In contrast, this and the following week exploit time series specific information by introducing hidden states that are non-local in time. This week's framework of hidden Markov models uses several discrete states with nonlinear neural networks as sub-models (also called experts or agents). We assume that we know the number of sub-models and their structure; the algorithm estimates the parameters of the sub-models, the probabilities of transition between them, and, for each time step, the probabilities to be in each state. The assignment first analyzes a toy problem where the hidden state is known from the way the data was generated. However, it is not used in building the model, but afterwards, in order to verify that the model indeed discovered the hidden states. On the real world data, the students discover that the regimes form according to market volatility, rather than according to other possible dynamic criteria they might have expected (such as trending vs. mean reverting). The assignment is based on an implementation in Matlab by Shanming Shi (J.P.Morgan, New York).

2.5 *Time series with a continuous hidden state*

State space models, the focus of this week, keep the assumption that the dynamics is hidden, but–in contrast to having several discrete hidden states with individual dynamics–they assume that the dynamics is captured by a continuous hidden state. State space models apply to time series processes with observational noise, i.e., noise that is not fed back into the systems but added during the observation.

The assignment uses the state space approach to model volatility,[f] showing the striking advantage of this model class in the presence of observational noise over a standard autoregressive approach. The state space model is compared to stochastic volatility models and to generalized autoregressive heteroskedastic models, as implemented as S+GARCH. The data consists of eight years of

[f] The source for "observational noise" for volatility time series is not a mistake in recording the observation, as the term might imply, but the following: The model describes, as always, the evolution of the expected value. We, however, do not observe the expected value, but a realization drawn from a distribution with that expected value. For example, if the returns were Gaussian, their squares would be χ^2-distributed with one degree of freedom. Such realizations are very noisy; their standard deviation is of the same size as the value itself! This is the source for the "observational noise" in volatilities.

high-frequency foreign exchange data (in ϑ-time), kindly provided by Michel Dacorogna (Olsen and Associates, Zürich).

3 Part 3: Statistical Modeling in Risk Management

Risk is the degree of uncertainty of future returns. Risk management has become a central concern for financial institutions, since derivatives have become a major component of the markets. The approaches to risk management are becoming increasingly sophisticated in their computational and statistical methodology.

Risk stems from a variety of sources and exposures. The first of the three weeks addresses *market risk,* the uncertainty of future earnings resulting from changes in market conditions. The second week addresses *credit risk,* the possible inability of a counterparty to meet its obligations. Both of these weeks draw heavily on methodology developed by J.P.Morgan, released in 1994 and 1997, respectively. The third week discusses *transaction risk,* using the example of identifying credit card fraud, one of the success stories of data mining techniques for financial problems.

During these three weeks, the students are also carrying out exploratory studies in preparation for their final group projects. This implies that the hands-on homework assignments require slightly less individual work than those in the first half of the semester.

3.1 Market risk

Market risk is the uncertainty of future earnings due to changes in market conditions, such as prices of the assets, exchange rates, interest rates, volatility, and market liquidity. The students are introduced to FourFifteen, a state-of-the-art tool, named after J.P.Morgan's internal market risk report, which was originally produced daily at 4:15 p.m. FourFifteen is a risk engine and a set of reporting tools. It is based on J.P.Morgan's RiskMetrics framework (RiskMetrics, 1997). Version 2 of FourFifteen is the result of J.P.Morgan teaming up with a software and interface company (The MathWorks Inc., the company that produces Matlab), and with a data company (Reuters).[g] FourFifteen is an excellent didactic tool, allowing the students to compare the original RiskMetrics variance-covariance approach with historical value-at-risk and Monte Carlo value-at-risk computations. They learn to break down the

[g] Up-to-date data will be obtained from `www.riskmetrics.reuters.com`.

different contributions to market risk, and gain a deeper understanding of the implications of the choices that have to be made in modeling market risk.

3.2 Credit risk

The booming global economy in recent years has created a business environment which enticed many institutions to take more credit risk. The proliferation of complex financial instruments has created uncertain and market-sensitive exposures that are more difficult to manage than traditional instruments. Active credit risk management, that includes the generation of consistent risk-based credit limits and rational risk-based capital allocations, is currently among the hardest challenges in the risk area.

The course uses J.P.Morgan's CreditMetrics, a portfolio approach to credit risk analysis that treats all elements of the portfolio on an equal basis (CreditMetrics, 1997). This approach also considers the correlations of the changes in credit quality. It gives not only expected losses, but also their uncertainty (i.e., variance), expressed in the same value-at-risk framework as market risk.

In the assignment, students use CreditManager, J.P.Morgan's software implementation of CreditMetrics, to evaluate investment decisions, credit extension and risk-mitigating actions. They learn to identify concentrations of risk within a single portfolio, and to explore various scenarios by investigating marginal risk statistics.[h] They also compare different risk measures (value-at-risk, standard deviation, percentiles), to gain an appreciation of the decisions that need to be made in modeling credit risk, and how these decisions affect the outcome. The data set includes historic probabilities of default and migration (upgrade and downgrade), correlations, recovery rates, and credit spreads.

3.3 Transaction risk

With the widespread use of credit cards and rise of more complex transactions in electronic commerce, detecting fraudulent transactions automatically has become a major area for the use of data mining techniques. While credit risk is essentially a static problem (or made static by incorporating migration), transaction risk is fundamentally dynamic: whether a transaction is likely to be fraudulent depends on both the usage pattern in the past and recent history. Bayes nets naturally incorporate prior knowledge in the structure by exploiting conditional independence and modeling as much as possible locally. They are a powerful method for discovering patterns and hidden causes in problems

[h] Marginal risk refers to the difference between the total portfolio risk before the marginal transaction in comparison to it after that transaction.

with categorical variables (e.g., merchant type). After introducing Bayes nets, we apply them to predict the probability that a transaction is fraudulent, and we show how to select one of the possible actions in this setting of a asymmetric payoff matrix. In the lab, the students can choose between three hands-on approaches to the problem of detecting fraudulent transactions on credit cards; their choice tends to be influenced by the method they decided to use in their group project. The first approach uses a Bayes net to reinforce the concepts they had just encountered in class. The second approach uses a genetic algorithm to find relationships likely to indicate fraudulent behavior (see week 6, Section 2.3 above). The third approach uses nonlinear logistic regression expressed as a neural network (see week 4, Section 2.1 above). All approaches will be compared to ordinary logistic regression.

This part concludes with the discussion of a business case featuring First Union National Bank (Charlotte, NC). This bank, the nation's sixth largest banking company, uses a neural network in their non-linear transaction processing. This case study, written by Vasant Dhar at Stern (Dhar, 1997), serves as the transition from risk management to the final part of the course that focuses on the role data mining methods are playing (and are going to be playing) in business and finance.

4 Part 4: Projects and Contact with Wall Street Traders

The physical and intellectual proximity between Stern and Wall Street gives us access to world-class traders who are willing to share some of their insights on applying the methods discussed in the course. One of the elements of the last three weeks are *presentations by guest speakers* to the class with sufficient time for discussion. One of the talks is complemented by a case study from a firm where the students are asked to critique the process and the results and suggest and justify alternative methods. Besides allowing students to obtain further information, these interactions allow the trader to get to know some of the students. Such informal interactions often yield to valuable contacts including internships and jobs for the students after obtaining their degrees. Most of these presentations are scheduled in the last three weeks of the semester.[i] One or two classes are reserved to present special topics, ranging from execution issues (that the students already encountered in *Financial Information Systems*) to modern techniques such as independent component analysis (ICA)

[i]A viable alternative is to lighten the load in the second part by eliminating the topic of either week 5 or week 7. This makes space for one external presentation on trading models at the end of the second part.

applied to pairs trading.

In the last three weeks, besides attending the lectures and discussions, the students are expected to primarily focus on their group projects.[j] These *group projects* are an important part of the course: they deepen the understanding of the specific method for each group, and they are true real world introductions to some of the unforeseen and unforseeable problems that are an integral part of working with new data.

The time line of the project is the following. Based on students' interests, groups of five students were formed at the end of the second class. In the third week, one specific project from the past was discussed in detail, highlighting the ingredients that contributed to its success. It is important to give a good example of the scope of the project and to clarify its role in the learning process. By week 4, each group will submit two one-page proposals that includes a description of the data sets. Several iterations with feedback from the instructor and the teaching assistant, as well as learning about new techniques during the course, tends to change the proposal significantly. By week 8 (before spring break), each group is required to converge on one of their two proposals. The selected proposal is finalized in week 9 to a well-focused and sufficiently narrow contract between the group members and the instructor. It is important that the expectations and evaluation criteria are made clear. Weeks 10 and 11 explore the data and obtain simple benchmarks for the subsequent evaluation of the proposed method. In the remaining three weeks, the entire lab time is focused on obtaining results and writing up the project. During the week of final exams, half a day is set aside for the presentation of the course projects. These case presentations give students the gratification to show off what they have learned and applied to a problem they were genuinely interested in. This event is also open to first-year students as a preview of what they could learn in their next year, and to the sponsoring companies as a glance of this exciting field of data mining and financial engineering at Stern.

This report describes one "realization" of a course that grew out of the post-NNCM-96 workshop. I would like to thank the participants for this open and fruitful discussion. This document by no means pretends to do any justice to the full complex exchange at the workshop, but I hope it may serve as a specific example for what can be done in a single-semester course at a business school. I thank Sean Chen, Vasant Dhar, Steve Figlewski, Joel Hasbrouck, Ed Melnick, Sridhar Seshadri, Bruce Weber and Norm White for their valuable feedback

[j] No readings, prepared lab sessions, or individual home works are assigned in the last three weeks.

and help with coordination with their courses at Stern. I thank Fei Chen and Balaji Padmanabhan for sharing the students' perspective, and last but certainly not least Caroline Kim for all her help with proofreading, logistics, and everything else. I thank Sean Curry of The MathWorks Inc. for his truly enthusiastic support with MATLAB, and Doug Martin of the University of Washington (Seattle) and Mathsoft, Inc. for data, code, and support with S-Plus. I genuinely welcome any comments, related experiences and suggestions.

References

CIFEr. 1997. *Proceedings of the IEEE/IAFE 1997 Conference on Computational Intelligence for Financial Engineering.* IEEE Service Center, Piscataway, NJ.

CreditMetrics. 1997. *CreditMetrics–Technical Document.* J.P.Morgan, New York, first edition.

Dhar, V. 1997. Managing credit risk through embedded intelligence in on-line transactions processing: First Union National Bank, Charlotte, NC. Technical report, Department of Information Systems, Leonard N. Stern School of Business, New York University.

Fama, E. F. and K. R. French. 1992. The cross–section of expected stock returns. *Journal of Finance* **47**, 427–465.

Knez, P. J. and M. J. Ready. 1997. On the robustness of size and book-to-market in cross-sectional regressions. *Journal of Finance* **52**, 1355–1382.

Matlab. 1997. *Getting Started with MATLAB; Using MATLAB (Version 5.1).* The MathWorks Inc., Data Analysis Products Divsion, Natick, MA.

Refenes, A.-P. N., Y. Abu-Mostafa, J. Moody and A. Weigend (eds). 1996. *Neural Networks in Financial Engineering (Proceedings of NNCM-95, London).* World Scientific, Singapore.

RiskMetrics. 1997. *RiskMetrics–Technical Document.* J.P.Morgan / Reuters, New York, fifth edition.

S-Plus. 1997. *User's Guide (Version 4.0).* Mathsoft Inc., Data Analysis Products Divsion, Seattle, WA.

Weigend, A. S., Y. S. Abu-Mostafa and A.-P. N. Refenes (eds). 1997. *Decision Technologies for Financial Engineering (Proceedings of NNCM-96, Pasadena).* World Scientific, Singapore.

AUTHOR INDEX & CONTACT INFORMATION

KEYWORD INDEX